THE DIVINE ECONOMY

THE DIVINE ECONOMY

How Religions Compete for
Wealth, Power, and People

PAUL SEABRIGHT

PRINCETON UNIVERSITY PRESS
PRINCETON & OXFORD

Requests for permission to reproduce material from this work should be sent to permissions@press.princeton.edu

Published by Princeton University Press
41 William Street, Princeton, New Jersey 08540
99 Banbury Road, Oxford OX2 6JX

press.princeton.edu

ISBN 978-0-691-13300-3
ISBN (e-book) 978-0-691-25878-2

British Library Cataloging-in-Publication Data is available

Editorial: Hannah Paul and Josh Drake
Production Editorial: Jenny Wolkowicki
Jacket design: Chris Ferrante
Production: Erin Suydam
Publicity: James Schneider and Kathryn Stevens
Copyeditor: Maia Vaswani

Jacket images: Marzufello / sreewing / Shutterstock

This book has been composed in Arno Pro and The Future

Printed in the United States of America

10 9 8 7 6 5 4 3 2 1

In memory of Diana, 1932–2023

CONTENTS

ACKNOWLEDGMENTS

I have been immensely fortunate in the many friends, family, and colleagues who have given generously of their time, expertise, and judgment to help improve this book. For comments on all or part of the manuscript I am grateful to Bina Agarwal, Ingela Alger, Richard Andrews, Terri Apter, David Austen-Smith, Margaret Bent, Jeanet Sinding Bentzen, Corinne Bonnet, Robin Briggs, Wendy Carlin, Eric Chaney, Tyler Cowen, Jacques Crémer, Etienne Danchin, Isabelle Daudy, John Drury, Jeremy Edwards, Rosalind English, Cécile Fabre, Roy Flechner, Guido Friebel, David Gellner, Peter Ghosh, Karen Gold, Tim Gowers, Carrie Gracie, Ashok Guha, Markus Haller, Thomas Hegghammer, Cecilia Heyes, Peregrine Horden, Sriya Iyer, Nicola Lacey, Jibirila Leinyuy, Hartmut Leppin, Debin Ma, Stephen Maurer, Rachel McCleary, Pepita Miquel-Florensa, Patricia Morison, Fitzroy Morrissey, Avner Offer, Sheilagh Ogilvie, David Parkin, Brett Parris, Alice Seabright, Edmond Seabright, Luke Seabright, Richard Sheahan, Kim Sterelny, Alan Strathern, David Vines, Chris Von Rueden, Charlotte Wang, Harvey Whitehouse, Andrew Wilson, and Michael Wilson. The book has been much changed and improved by their contributions, but they should not be presumed to agree that it has improved enough.

In addition to the above, Alain Alcouffe, Jean-Paul Azam, Jerrilyn Dodds, Stephen Greenblatt, Claire Hall, Sara Lipton, and Alberto Simpser gave me valuable advice on data sources, quotations, and illustrations.

A conversation two decades ago with Giuseppe Bertola convinced me that it was worth devoting serious time to studying the economics of religion. A much more recent conversation with John Fingleton opened my eyes to the importance of organizational characteristics in understanding the Catholic Church. Talking on many occasions to Brian Boyd was a formative experience in thinking about narratives. Kim Sterelny has repeatedly challenged my lazy thinking about religion and its origins. Conversations with Gani Aldashev, Coren Apicella, Robert Barro, Samuel Bowles, Gloria Carnevali, Jean-Paul Carvalho, Eric Crubézy, Richard Dawkins, Daniel Dennett, Mireille Gealageas, Andrew Goreing, Susan Greenfield, Pauline Grosjean, David Hart, César Hidalgo, Angela Hobbs, Antoine Jacquet, Hillard Kaplan, Agnès Klarsfeld, Alain Klarsfeld, Nathalie Luca, Mary Morgan, David Newbery, Rory O'Connor, Jean-Philippe Platteau, Nicholas Rawlins, Rupert Shortt, David Soskice, Susie Symes, Benoit Vermander, Frans de Waal, and Se Yan have all left their mark on this book.

Over the more than ten years that I have been working on this project, my colleagues in Toulouse, at both the Toulouse School of Economics and the Institute for Advanced Study in Toulouse (IAST), have been a constant source of inspiration and delight. Delphine Pouts was an outstanding administrative support to me during the nine years I was director of IAST. As well as those I've already thanked, I'd like to mention Jean-François Bonnefon, Margot Dazey, Maxime Derex, Ray Duch, Mohamed Saleh, Manvir Singh, Jennifer Stephenson, Jonathan Stieglitz, Jean Tirole, and Karine Van Der Straeten, with all of whom I've had fruitful discussions of these issues.

Much of the book was written while I was a Two-Year Fellow at All Souls College, Oxford, from 2021 to 2023, for the first year of which I was fortunate to have sabbatical leave from the University of Toulouse. I'm extremely grateful to John Vickers, warden of All Souls, as well as to the Fellows for allowing me this privileged time of quiet and reflection. David Addison, Katherine Backler, Ruth Harris, James Malcolmson, Miriam Meyerhoff, Catherine Morgan, Stephen Smith, and Amia Srinivasan gave me many valuable ideas and suggestions.

My coauthors on topics related to this project include Emmanuelle Auriol, Diego Delissaint, Maleke Fourati, Selin Goksel, Julia Hoefer, César Mantilla, Emanuela Migliaccio, Josepa Miquel-Florensa, Amma Panin, Eva Raiber, Weiwei Ren, Suping Shen, Charlotte Wang, Donghui Yang, and Ling Zhou. It has been a privilege to work with you.

For outstanding research assistance I'm grateful to Amandine Belard, Julia Hoefer, and Sunny Wang. In particular, Sunny Wang prepared most of the figures in the statistical appendix, and Julia Hoefer read the whole manuscript to check the coherence of the citations and the completeness of the bibliography. The accuracy of the citations remains my responsibility.

I have been associated with Princeton University Press for over twenty years. Richard Baggaley and Peter Dougherty were excellent colleagues from early on. I'm grateful to my editor Hannah Paul for her judgment, enthusiasm, and patience; to Jenny Wolkowicki for steering the book through production; to Maia Vaswani for copy-editing, and Virginia Ling for preparing the index; and to Josh Drake and Dimitri Karetnikov for managing the figures and illustrations. My agent Catherine Clarke has for more than two decades been an unfailing source of advice and encouragement (and, where appropriate, tactful discouragement of my more harebrained ideas). A word at the right time with her can provide inspiration, unlock a disagreement, or avoid months of fruitless effort.

Finally, Alice, Edmond, Luke, Isabelle, Charlotte, Jack, and Diana all supported me in other ways too numerous to list.

Introduction

This participation of all men in suffering weighs heavily on the mind of the Beloved of the Gods.

—from an edict of Indian emperor Ashoka,
third century BCE

The Generosity of the Poor

Why do some very poor people give money to some very rich people? The question was at the forefront of my mind as I talked to a young woman I will call Grace, in Accra, the capital of Ghana, in February 2015. She had come to a room at the Central University College to take part in an economic experiment with my team of researchers. Grace was twenty-four years old, simply but neatly dressed, with a quiet but alert composure. I guessed her to have a reasonable education and to be working as a clerk in a small business or a government office.

I could not have been more wrong. Six days a week Grace walks up and down between the lines of cars that queue at the traffic lights on one of the main roads into Accra. She sells iced water in little plastic sachets stored in a basket above her head. From this she earns the equivalent of a little over a dollar and a half a day. After twelve hours of this debilitating work, inhaling exhaust fumes on a hot and dusty highway six days a week, she goes home to a tiny house she has built in a slum neighborhood with her aunt, with whom she came to the city a few years ago.

MR JOHN CALAS *a French* Protestant *Merchant* BROKE *on the* WHEEL *by order of the* Parliament *of* Thoulouse.

The public torture and execution in 1762 of Jean Calas, a French Protestant convicted on trumped-up charges of killing his son to prevent him from converting to Catholicism. The memory of this was still very fresh in Toulouse when Adam Smith began his visit to the city in 1764, a visit during which he began writing *The Wealth of Nations*.
Credit: Chronicle / Alamy stock photo.

On Sundays, she goes to church. She's an usher, greeting people as they come into the church and directing them to their seats in the pews. She then sings in the choir, and is an assistant in a Sunday school group. She gives money to the church, by paying tithes—the traditional 10 percent of her tiny income—as well as by giving to the collection during services, which brings the total she gives up to around 12 percent. She is aware that the money she gives to the church can't be used for other purposes, like paying for medical treatment for her aunt, who is often sick.

The main beneficiary of her donations and the leader of her church, whom I will call Pastor William, is an energetic, smiling, and charming man who is very rich, and wants everyone to know it. He drives a large Mercedes, and wears a belt with a big round buckle decorated with a dollar sign. He no more needs Grace's money than he needs another impeccably pressed suit. Yet Grace gives him her money, willingly. Why?

The one answer you can't give is that Grace is stupid, or deceived. She knows exactly what she's doing; she's more lucid about her finances than I am about mine. She knows that she could choose to go to another church, or remain in this one and avoid paying her tithes or putting money in the collection box. Yet she stays in this church, and she pays regularly, and always on time.

A more promising answer would be that there's nothing surprising about Grace's generosity because poor and not-so-poor people give money to rich people all the time—indeed, that's the main reason rich people are rich. The people who pay don't usually describe what they are doing as making a donation, though. They're usually aware that when they buy food from Walmart, or renew their Netflix subscription, or buy a Louis Vuitton handbag, or charge their credit card for an Amazon delivery, they're contributing to making a few very rich people even richer than they were before. But whether or not this bothers them (and it might even please them, if the person they're paying is a certain kind of celebrity), it's a by-product of paying for a product or a service. Maybe we should think of what Grace is doing in the same way. Suppose that, instead of giving money to Pastor William because she thinks he needs it or deserves it, she's giving him money because she believes she's getting something in return. What kind of product or service might she be paying for?

Without visualizing in detail the exhausting awfulness of Grace's everyday labor, it may be hard to understand why going to church on Sunday means so much to her. She can wear a clean dress; she can greet people and be greeted respectfully as she shows worshippers to their seats. In Sunday school she can take some responsibility for younger and even more vulnerable people than herself. She can sing with other singers; she can chat to different people from the street hawkers with whom she spends her working days. She has some chance of finding friends— and who knows, maybe one day even a husband, one who is less likely to drink or to beat her than alternative suitors she might find at random in this scary city. She can do all this as part of a community that recognizes and respects her. If going to church costs her an eighth of her income, it may even seem cheap at the price. We, the observers, might wonder by what right the very rich Pastor William asks this very poor woman to pay her tithes. But for Grace that's not the question: if the tithes are what she needs to pay to belong, she will pay.

There's a further twist. If you don't pay your Netflix subscription you will no longer be able to stream; if you don't pay at the checkout in Walmart you can't take your groceries out the door. But even if Grace no longer pays her tithes, she will still be welcome at the church. Only perhaps she may not feel quite so welcome as she did before—the pastor's smile may be replaced by a concerned frown; one of the assistant pastors may ask her whether she's all right. She may wonder whether her trusted position as a Sunday school assistant is secure. The esteem she feels in her community, in such sharp contrast to the aggression and contempt she receives every day in her working environment, depends not only on her coming to church but on her coming there willingly, prepared to make a donation that's big enough to hurt. Both Grace and Pastor William understand this. He, and the community he manages, can make her feel special. They do this all the more effectively because Grace believes that Pastor William stands in a special relationship to God.

Billions of people around the world in the twenty-first century respond to the call of religious leaders by giving time, energy, and money to the movements they lead. Like Grace, they mostly do so lucidly and reflectively, and as a result religious movements have accumulated tremendous power. Sometimes religious leaders go even further: they may ask, literally and not metaphorically, for people's lives.

Icons into Battle

At four o'clock in the morning of February 24, 2022, nearly three thousand Russian battle tanks, accompanied by many thousands more troops in trucks and lightly armored vehicles, began a journey across the border between Russia and Ukraine. Inside the tanks were thousands of young men, many barely more than schoolboys, who had been ordered into battle to defend an idea. It was fundamentally a nationalist rather than a religious idea, but it had been supported by some heavy religious artillery the previous day, in a fiery sermon by Patriarch Kirill of the Russian Orthodox Church.[1] Over the following weeks and months, Patriarch Kirill would redouble his rhetoric in support of the war. He urged soldiers to fight as their patriotic duty, and promised them that "sacrifice in the course of carrying out your military duty washes away all sins."[2] He also offered them the protection of religious equipment, such as a gilded icon of the Virgin Mary, which he donated in March 2022 to General Viktor Zolotov, director of the Russian National Guard, and of which Zolotov in his acceptance speech said "this icon will protect the Russian army and accelerate our victory."[3]

The young men in the Russian tanks certainly needed protection. They had been told they would be met with welcome smiles and posies of flowers, but in fact they were met with antitank missiles, fired by men of their own age. In the days and weeks to follow, priests of the Ukrainian Orthodox and Catholic Churches would use prayer and biblical exhortation to stiffen their countrymen's will to resist. And among the outpouring of support and offers of military and humanitarian supplies, many thousands of rosaries have been manufactured and delivered to Ukraine, to raise the morale of both civilian refugees and frontline troops.[4]

Icons and rosaries are just two of an immense variety of religious technologies that have been deployed throughout the ages to stiffen the resolve of young men ordered by their elders into combat: a recent study in the violent eastern part of the Democratic Republic of Congo reported forty-six different objects, potions, and rituals used by armed groups.[5] Religions also deal centrally with the aftermath of war—the edict of Emperor Ashoka that I quoted at the beginning was carved on several rock surfaces in India to express his remorse at the brutal slaughter he had inflicted during the conquest of Kalinga, remorse that would lead him later to become a major patron of Buddhism. The text is in some ways shocking in its narcissism, giving as much prominence to the troubled emotions of the emperor as to the violence he had unleashed. But it also illustrates one of the most poignant features of the great world religions. Their ambition, and an important part of their appeal, lies precisely in their seeking to find some meaning in the vast suffering in the world, and some call to account even of the powerful, though religious leaders have so often contributed to the suffering by their calls to violent sacrifice.

Warfare is only one of the many theaters of religious persuasion. From battlefield to ballot box, from boardroom to bedroom, religious movements enjoy immense power in the world today. This power arises mainly because the leaders of these movements have persuaded their members to grant it to them—most religious people, including Grace in Accra and many millions like her, are enthusiasts, not prisoners. Their relationship with their religious leaders is mostly voluntary (often much more so than their relationship with their political and military leaders). There's a real problem in some Muslim-majority countries where the fact that the law prescribes the death penalty for apostasy or blasphemy creates a climate of fear for those who wish to renounce Islam publicly or even to leave it quietly.[6] But there are many nominal Muslims who are only minimally observant if at all, and the enthusiasm of the majority cannot be attributed to coercion. Still, the bad news is that, since most of the world's religious people are not prisoners, it's difficult to hold a reasoned discussion about how to make the leaders of their movements accountable, to ensure this power is not abused—as it has certainly been abused on the battlefields of Eastern Europe, and in many other places too.

This book is about how the world's religions have gained such power, what they do with it, and how abuses of this power can be constrained.

When we see politicians instrumentalize religion as they so often do, it's easy to conclude that the most important source of religious power is political influence. It's true that political leaders have often granted vast powers to religious movements—by establishing them as official religions, by granting them subsidies and tax breaks, or by giving them legal power to punish people who don't accept their authority. But this doesn't explain why political leaders—who as a rule don't like giving power to anybody—should want to grant it to the leaders of religion. The truth is that they do so because religious movements have gained their power independently, through persuading people like Grace to join them. Political leaders are envious of the legitimacy that comes with it. The question that will occupy us here is how religious movements gain that power.

A natural way of thinking about this is that religions flourish because they preach a particularly moving spiritual message, a narrative that speaks to important human needs. While convincing as far as it goes, this doesn't explain *why* some messages succeed in moving their hearers more than others do. After all, most of the spiritual movements that were ever founded have disappeared without trace. What makes the best religious messages so moving, then—so enchanting, in the best sense of that multifaceted word, whose several meanings we'll return to unpack later in the book? There's a surprising answer to this question: it's economics. What exactly does that mean?

Religious movements may preach in poetry, but for their work to be effective they must minister in prose. They must be the fruit of system, not just of serendipity—and the more modern the movement, the more important is the system. The messages religious movements send to their members and potential members may be practical or uplifting, informative or transfiguring. But it's not their content alone that gives them their power. The organizations themselves that make up these movements—churches, mosques, madrassas, synagogues, temples, prayer groups, ashrams, monasteries, meeting houses—must engage in what the nineteenth-century economist Alfred Marshall called "the ordinary business of life."[7] They recruit, raise funds, disburse budgets, manage premises, organize transport, motivate employees and volunteers, and get their message out. They do this while being keenly aware that they compete—for funds, loyalty, energy, and attention—with other religious organizations, potentially no less inspiring than they are, as well as with secular rivals and the pull of lassitude, indifference, skepticism, or outright hostility. Without economic resources behind them, the most beautifully crafted messages will struggle to gain a hearing in the cacophony of life. The velvet glove of enchantment clothes an iron fist of organization.

Saying that religions compete does not imply they are motivated by greed or profit (though they might be), any more than a restaurant owner, winemaker, theater director, or manager of a biotech or software start-up must be motivated by greed or profit. They may be driven by passion or pragmatism, but competing is what they must do to command the necessary economic and human resources to survive and flourish.

Religions, in short, are businesses. Like most businesses, they are many other things as well—they're communities, objects of inspiration or anxiety to observers from outside, cradles of ambition and frustration to their recruits, theaters of fulfilment or despair to those who invest their lives or their savings within them. But they are legitimate businesses—a fact that should give pause to some of their detractors, but also empower those (their supporters as well as their critics) who believe they should be accountable to society as other businesses are. And they need to be understood in terms of their organization as well as in terms of the mission they inherit from their founders. A convincing account of the success of businesses like Microsoft or Apple can't stop with charming stories of their teenage founders coding obsessively in their parents' garages. It needs to understand the current structure of these businesses, their logistics, and their corporate culture. A convincing account of the success of religious movements requires no less comprehensive an investigation.

The history of religious movements has focused overwhelmingly, and for good reason, on the personalities of their founders and the poetry in the messages they communicate. This book is about the underlying prose, which shapes what it is possible for others to hear. It has made all the difference between a message that may move a few hearers before fading into oblivion and one that continues to thunder down the centuries. Pastor William is an intriguing man, but we're going to see much more of Grace and her friends, as well as their counterparts in Islam, Hinduism, Buddhism, and the world's other religions, than we see of him in the pages to come.

Religion and Economics—an Age-Old Partnership

It may seem strange that the power of an other-worldly message to move multitudes could be shaped by such a worldly constraint as economic competition, but to Scottish philosopher and economist Adam Smith in the eighteenth century it was only common sense. Theologians in the Church of England were much preoccupied with the growth in popularity of the so-called New Dissenters, and particularly the Methodists led by John Wesley. In terms reminiscent of the way some populist politicians are discussed in broadsheet newspapers and on digital media today, Methodist preachers were accused of "bewitching" their listeners, making "people go mad," and persuading them that the parsons of the established Church were "blind guides and false prophets."[8] But an Irish minister may have revealed more than he meant to when he set about the Methodist preacher John Smythe with a club, exclaiming "how dare you go about preaching, setting the whole neighborhood out of their senses, and thinning my congregation."[9]

For Adam Smith this was the whole point: what was going on was competition to attract an audience. He thought the reason the Methodists were good at it was that they had stronger incentives. As Smith wrote in book 5 of *The Wealth of Nations*, Methodists faced a different set of economic rewards than the parsons of the Church of England. Parsons typically enjoyed a comfortable salary independently of how well they preached. But a Methodist minister who could not summon an enthusiastic congregation would not earn a living. As Smith put it with gentle sarcasm: "The clergy of an established and well-endowed religion frequently become men of learning and elegance, who possess all the virtues of gentlemen." But they were much less interested in, and therefore much less good at, filling the pews.[10]

Smith was interested in how economic incentives might shape not just the quality but also the content of the message delivered by churches. This was literally a matter of life and death. Europe in Smith's time still bore the scars of the violent wars of religion that had convulsed the continent for over a century leading up to the end of the Thirty Years' War. There were still periodic outbursts of religiously fueled violence, as well as persistent repression of religious minorities such as the Protestant Huguenots in France.[11] Smith began writing *The Wealth of Nations* in 1764, during a long visit to my home city of Toulouse, in southwest France. Toulouse had been wracked during the previous two years by recriminations over the torture and execution of Jean Calas, a Protestant, on the false charge of killing his son. The son had committed suicide, but it was alleged that Calas had murdered him to stop him from converting to Catholicism. The case had been taken up by the philosopher Voltaire, who made it a centerpiece of his attacks on the intolerance of the Catholic Church.[12] Amid the swirling controversies about religion, violence, and persecution, Smith must have reflected very hard about why he was living in such religiously turbulent times.[13]

Voltaire often wrote as though he thought religion was essentially intolerant, and many partisans of one religion would argue that the intolerance they perceived in rival religions was part of their intrinsic nature. Smith strongly disagreed. Whether religions preached a tolerant or an intolerant message, he wrote, was not the result of some quality inherent in religion, but the result of the incentives religious leaders faced. Just as in other fields of life competition was good and monopoly was bad for ordinary people, he argued that when many religions competed with one another on an equal basis, they would be obliged to preach a more benevolent message.[14] It's clear Smith meant rivalry between any movements that had the freedom to shape their own message, including rival Protestant churches in the same town. Only if the number of religions in a society were limited to a very few, he claimed, would their leaders be able to preach violence and discord. And this in turn was likely to happen only if *political* leaders granted protection to some religious movements over others.

So why would political leaders want to do this? What benefit could they gain from granting power to religious movements? Smith thought they might, for example, offer the protection of the state to one or a small number of privileged faiths, sheltering them from competition in return for legitimation of the state's political leaders by the religion's ideological leaders.[15] He developed this idea into a theory of the natural life cycle of religious movements: new movements would be energetic and dynamic, and the successful ones would attract the envy of political leaders, who would offer them privileges and protection in return for their ideological support. Politicians like nothing better than to have priests, pastors, rabbis, or imams preaching to attentive congregations on their behalf. But Smith warned that protection would weaken religious leaders' incentives to listen to their members, so they would eventually become unable to compete effectively against even newer religious movements that challenged them in turn.

Smith's point was not that the content of the message preached by religious leaders didn't matter—far from it. Nor was he suggesting that religious leaders were interested only in economic gain. His point was rather that their teachings responded to the economic and political circumstances in which the leaders of the various movements found themselves. There was no point in urging the churches to change their message if that was the one it was in their interest to deliver. And, as poor Jean Calas discovered to his cost, a church that was entitled by law to break him and kill him if he disagreed with its teachings had no incentive to do the hard work necessary to make those teachings more persuasive.

In the two and a half centuries since Smith wrote, we have learned much more than he knew about both economics and religion, and of course our societies have changed almost beyond recognition, so we are no longer studying the same world. Almost . . . but not entirely. We'll see that Smith's conclusions are often inaccurate to describe today's world, but his way of thinking about the problems of his time remains astonishingly relevant even in the twenty-first century.

Religion today is big business—a study published in 2016 estimated that faith-based organizations in the United States received revenues equal to 378 billion US dollars. That's an enormous inflow of resources, greater than the revenues in the same year of Apple and Microsoft combined, and greater than 2 percent of total personal income in the United States.[16] It's 60 percent of the revenues of the media and entertainment industries—film, gaming, books, music, the lot.[17] It's half of what all the restaurants in America earned together.[18] That doesn't even count the time, energy, and contributions in kind made by members of faith-based organizations. It's impossible to get comparable international figures, so we can only conjecture what may be happening elsewhere. But there are quite a few countries, particularly in Africa (Ghana, Nigeria, Kenya, Zimbabwe, and South Africa, for instance) and Latin America (Brazil, Guatemala, El Salvador, and Honduras, for instance), where there is a strong Pentecostal presence and where it's reasonable to think that at least one adult in ten is paying tithes (10 percent of their income). If another two adults in ten are paying 5 percent of their income, then even if no one else is paying anything, this would yield total revenues of faith-based organizations of similar importance relative to the size of their economies.

Religion and Politics

Religion is also big politics, just as Smith predicted. Political leaders around the world, in countries from Azerbaijan and Brazil to Yemen and Zimbabwe, have sought legitimacy for their regimes from religious authorities.[19] The more theocratic among them justify their repression of dissent by claiming that political opposition is tantamount to rebellion against the Almighty, as in the case of the Iranian rapper executed in December 2022 for "waging war against God," which raises the question why the Almighty should be so much in need of human defense.[20] The government of Israel that took office in December 2022 has a finance minister who has called for the restoration of the Torah justice system as "in the days of King David."[21] Russian president Vladimir Putin has extolled the virtues of the Russian Orthodox Church, and even referred to the destiny of Russian Orthodoxy in support of his 2022 invasion of Ukraine. As we saw earlier, the leadership of the Russian Orthodox Church continued to support the invasion enthusiastically even as the human costs of that invasion became more visible.[22] President Recep Tayyip

Erdogan has made his personal religiosity a key component of his political strategy for Turkey since his time as mayor of Istanbul in the 1990s, turning initiatives like the reinstatement of the Hagia Sophia as a mosque into major political statements.[23] And the initiative does not come only or even mainly from leaders with a previous track record of religious conviction. Whether it's Donald Trump discovering the attractions of praying with evangelical pastors, Narendra Modi worshiping at Hindu temples, Xi JinPing sponsoring the reconstruction of Buddhist temples, or Binyamin Netanyahu presiding over a religious transformation of educational curricula in Israel, leaders who were never known for their piety have shown growing enthusiasm for cultivating their inner devotee.[24] Perhaps the weight of office provokes greater humility before the mysteries of the spiritual life. Then again, perhaps not.

As we'll see in later chapters, there are many reasons why politicians turn to religion. Sometimes it's as simple as the fact that many citizens listen to religious leaders in deciding whether and how to cast their vote—there's convincing evidence, for instance, that church attendance has a positive causal impact on political turnout.[25] Sometimes it's a way for political leaders to claim to be more honest or more morally righteous than they would otherwise appear. It can be more subtle: religious leaders often have a talent for articulating narratives that make sense of sacrifice and loss, predicaments that politicians usually struggle to explain to their citizens, but which they may hope to legitimate by expressing them in religious language.

Whatever the motivation for the transaction, when religion and politics are entwined, the stakes are high. In return for their explicit or implicit support, religious organizations favored by politicians can be granted great privileges. The Christian Church, for example, acquired enormous material resources after its political establishment in Europe in the Middle Ages; it's estimated that by the year 750 CE the Church owned around one-third of all the agricultural land in western Europe.[26] Much of this accumulation came in the form of donations and bequests from wealthy patrons who believed that their fate after death might be influenced by the piety to which these donations bore witness. Similar processes have been documented over the same centuries for Hindu and Buddhist temples across Asia and for mosques throughout the Islamic world.

The Catholic Church lost most of those resources again, massively, after the Protestant Reformation. This happened not only through the Dissolution of the Monasteries in England, spearheaded by Henry VIII's minister Thomas Cromwell, but throughout Europe where the Reformation spread, as recent research has shown.[27] But even churches that are not established often enjoy great material privileges even today. Though they take money from members of the public, they typically pay no tax. In many countries they publish no accounts (unlike secular charities), and are partly exempt from the laws that govern the employment and other practices of firms.[28] They are often enabled (and sometimes encouraged) to use the law against members of the public who oppose them, whether these are members of rival religions or simply ordinary citizens who wish to live their lives in ways of which other people disapprove. When this happens, it's tempting to think that religious organizations are powerful because they enjoy these privileges; there is some truth in that. More importantly, though, they enjoy these privileges because they are independently powerful. And they are powerful, by and large, because they have persuaded their members to make them so.

It follows that privileges cannot make religious organizations durably powerful unless they've already won this power through gaining committed followers. We see this in the repeated failure of political leaders to undercut the legitimacy of some religious organizations by granting privileges to rivals that the political leaders prefer, but that have not passed the basic test of developing a following of their own. As I write, the French government is seeking to combat Islamic radicalism by launching a "moderate" Islamic Council, having apparently learned nothing from the failure of a previous attempt to do the same nearly two decades earlier.[29] The Chinese government has for years supported an "official" Chinese Catholic Church, as well as official Protestant and Muslim organizations, but none of these appear to enjoy as much popular support as the unofficial organizations in these traditions. For similar reasons, there are signs that the increasing political influence of evangelical Christian organizations over the Republican Party in the United States is leading many Americans to turn away from evangelical churches, attending church less often even if they may still identify as evangelical.[30] As Adam Smith had already warned, political power may be a poisoned chalice that churches come to regret.

Power can also be damaging to religion in another way. In recent years, thanks to investigations by many individual reporters and media outlets, and brave decisions to break silence on the part of victims, we have come to understand the massive scale of physical, psychological, and sexual abuse perpetrated by many people elevated to positions of trust within religious movements. This abuse is continuing to come to light, and in organizations of all religious traditions and denominations. Abuse can occur in all social environments, secular as well as religious, but it's most common in those that grant leaders unchecked authority over vulnerable people. The veneration accorded to charismatic religious leaders makes it particularly hard for their victims to protect themselves, or even sometimes fully to believe what is happening to them, to call abuse by its proper name. They fear, often rightly, that even if they can believe their own senses they may not be believed by others. When the truth eventually emerges it can discredit not only the individual abusers but the whole culture that enabled and protected them. Though it may be painful to admit it, religious organizations have everything to gain from avoiding the accumulation of too much unchecked power over their members.

The Questions This Book Will Answer

What this book will show is both simple and novel. Religious movements are a special kind of business—they are *platforms*. Platforms are organizations that facilitate relationships that could not form, or could not function as effectively, in the platforms' absence. Platforms reward those who create and manage them by appropriating some of the benefits those relationships make possible.

In the twenty-first century the word "platforms" conjures up the digital universe of search engines, social media, and smartphone applications for everything from dining to dating to decorating. Their ubiquity

online blinds us to the fact that platforms using predigital technology—
the voice; the handshake; the song; the dance; the drinking cup; the
knife, the fork, and the spoon—have been around since the dawn of
history. They have included the matchmaker who introduced couples;
the interpreter who united linguistic strangers; the market trader who
helped farmers and artisans find buyers; the merchant adventurer whose
wanderings brought silks, spices, and the plague to people who had
never traveled away from their birthplace; as well as the temple, the
church, the mosque, and the synagogue that built communities. But
community building is not magic—it's the fruit of hard work and
organization as well as inspiration, and religious movements have found
ways to marry hard work with thoughtful strategy to create enchantment.
This book will recount how it has been done, from prehistory to the
twenty-first century. It will show that as religious movements have mod-
ernized, they have moved the platform component of their operations
to center stage. In the process we shall see how to bring accountability to
the exercise of the immense power these religious movements have built.

The book will address difficult questions that many standard accounts of religion struggle to answer. These questions are of three main
kinds. First, there are the intimately personal questions: What are the
needs in individual human beings to which religious movements speak?
Is religiosity a distinct psychological trait, or is it a bundle of diverse
traits that have little in common? How can religion claim to bring order
to the unweeded garden of human perceptions and desires? How can it
give so many people a sense of purpose in their lives that secular institutions often struggle to articulate? If religion really does speak to universal human needs and longings, why has it been claimed that women are
on average more religious than men? And why is religion booming in
many parts of the world when observers in Europe and North America
are convinced it's in terminal decline?

The second type of question the book will address is organizational.
Why do religious movements take so many different forms, from tiny
cults to vast international organizations? What are the most important
differences between religious platforms and secular ones? How does technological innovation, from cave painting to printing to artificial

intelligence, affect the intensity of rivalry between religious movements? When is such rivalry peaceful and when does it become angry, even violent? Why do religious movements so often clash over abstruse points of theology or ritual that are hard for most of their members to understand, let alone decide? When do religious movements flourish and grow, when do they splinter, when do they die? Can a large, centralized movement like the Catholic Church survive in the modern world, or is it destined to break up? How do movements as different as Islam, Hinduism, Buddhism, and Protestant Christianity maintain fidelity to their practices and rituals in the absence of centralized authorities to enforce orthodoxy?

The third type of question is political, in the broadest sense of the word: these are questions about power, its use and its abuse. Why have movements that affirm moral values seen an epidemic of sexual abuse? Why do political leaders so often claim religious support for war and repression? When are religious hostility and religious violence directed at perceived heretics within religious movements, and when are they directed at members of different movements? And, finally, can authoritarian religious messages survive in a world of increasing education, falling fertility, and female emancipation? Or will religion provide the secret sauce for a successful authoritarian backlash against the hard-won gains of the last two centuries in equality, democracy, and freedom for minorities?

The platform model of religious movements casts new light on all these questions and more. These features of religion are the fruit of countless commitments made by individuals to the religious platforms that invite them to join. They owe their form to competition between those platforms to attract members and resources, competition that will shape what is possible for religious movements and their political backers in the coming century.

Outline of the Book

Part I will begin by defining what religion is and describing what religion looks like in the world today. It will show that, despite what many have claimed, religion is not in decline; it is in many ways more powerful than it has ever been.

Part II will then look at what religious power consists in, and where it comes from. The most successful religious organizations have developed their competitive strategies over thousands of years, and have continued refining them in recent decades. They're successful because they speak more convincingly than many of their secular rivals to needs shared by most, though not necessarily all, human beings. These include both material and spiritual needs, including the need for a sense of community and for a compelling shared narrative of our lives and our place in the universe. The secular institutions of twenty-first-century democratic industrial capitalism have furnished our lives abundantly with appliances and activities, but citizens of the modern world are still often in search of ways to furnish them with meaning. Some find that meaning without any help from religion, but many find it more fully in religion than anywhere else. The genius of religious movements has been to provide meaning through the creation of platforms—communities that create shared meaning not as an abstract idea, as in a philosophy class, but as the natural product of shared experiences. These may be lived in a group or lived alone, but they are interpreted through a language and a symbolism that make sense only in the light of the group. It is through the group that discipline can paradoxically create and nourish enchantment. The most successful religious movements today are those that have been developing and adapting the platform model for the demands of the twenty-first century.

Part III will look at how religious organizations use their power—politically, socially, economically, psychologically, sometimes to good ends and sometimes to bad ones. Mostly we shall try simply to understand how they do so, without judgment. However, in part IV we'll look to the future, and see whether our understanding of the sources and uses of religious power can suggest ways to manage that power for the good of everyone, the religious and the nonreligious alike.

Anyone who cares about how power is exercised in the modern world should care about why religions have so much of that power. So should anyone who cares about the beauty and poetry of religious messages. Those messages have reached us only because of the hard work and strategic thinking of the entrepreneurs and their successors who found ways to convey them. We may all, to varying degrees, have within us the potential to be moved by the mysteries of existence, whatever explanations of those mysteries we may choose to believe. And we should be endlessly curious about the processes by which religious leadership, like the poet's pen in the words of Shakespeare, "turns to shapes the forms of things unknown, and gives to airy nothing a local habitation and a name."[31]

What Does Religion Look Like in the World Today?

Part I of this book sets out some features of ancient and modern religion that the rest of the book will try to explain. What do we mean here by religion, and what are the main features of religion that matter in the modern world? In chapter 1, I suggest thinking of religion as a set of activities that turn around people's interaction with spirits who are not visible to the ordinary senses, but are believed to be capable of influencing human life for good and ill, and of hearing our call. These activities have taken many forms over the centuries and across the world. In the last three millennia the predominance of local "immanent" religions, with whom human interactions are typically frequent and often transactional, has been challenged by the growth of more global "transcendental" religions. These have kept many traditional features but also offer narratives of individual salvation, which speak to the suffering and hardship of individual lives (immanent religions also acknowledge hardship, but typically claim to offer cures in the here and now, not philosophical explanations of why suffering happens). Transcendental religion has not eclipsed immanent religion, but it has taken much of the place it previously occupied. And since transcendental religion consists of a diverse set of activities, it follows that religiosity—the psychological propensity to be drawn to religion—is not a single psychological trait but a bundle of diverse traits. What it means to be religious—which parts of our brains and our personalities are engaged by religion—differs enormously across societies and across historical time periods. The religiosity of a medieval crusader is not the same kind of mental or behavioral attribute as the religiosity of a Sufi mystic, a Pentecostal congregant, or a Buddhist nun.

Chapter 2 tries to paint a picture of what is happening to religion in the world in recent decades, using two alternative sources of information—namely, surveys and censuses. Surveys interview relatively few people and ask them many detailed questions, while censuses interview far more people and ask them far fewer questions. Using surveys over the last three or four decades, I suggest that, contrary to a widely held view, individual religiosity is not declining in the world as a whole, though it is declining in some countries and in some circumstances. Using census data over a longer period of about seven decades, I link this to the growth in the share of the world population that professes membership of global transcendental religions, especially the two fastest growing religions, which are Islam and Christianity. These religions have become increasingly corporatized and globalized. They have developed forms of organization, and ways of interacting with their members, that will make them a strong presence in the world for the foreseeable future. This sets the stage for part II, which will ask how the world's religious organizations have managed to achieve this degree of dynamism and energy. It will find the answer in the idea that religious organizations function as special kinds of platform. They construct communities that share many forms of practical reciprocity and are united above all by shared narratives and practices of private and collective prayer and ritual.

It's worth making two disclaimers. The first is that I shall not try to survey the many fascinating debates about what religious experience intrinsically involves, nor the many forms it takes across time and space. To do so would require a vast book and more expertise than mine. In particular, though I mention debates about "secularization," the hypothesis that religion is intrinsically threatened by the conditions of modernity, I don't claim to do them justice. I confine myself instead to the question of whether religious organizations are declining in importance in recent decades, and if so why. On several aspects of religion more generally, there are many researchers whose work I would have loved to share with my readers, but can't find a way to fit into the story I have to tell.

The second disclaimer is that this book neither criticizes nor defends the decisions of individual religious members and religious leaders. Though an important minority of cults and religions in some societies can threaten to use force against members who leave, most decisions to join and to stay with religious movements are voluntary in the modern world. While I spend much time trying to understand why individuals act as they do, I leave to others the question of whether such decisions are ones they wish to endorse, emulate, or decry. Where they lead to suffering or exploitation of the vulnerable, I have tried to understand why. Sometimes I suggest ways in which such consequences might be avoided, but I'm not interested (in this book) in judging anyone for acting as they do.

I have no personal religious belief or affiliation, but that's not relevant to any of the arguments here—though only others can tell whether I resemble those "objective observers" writing about Zen Buddhism of whom Alan Watts once wrote that "they invariably miss the point and eat the menu instead of the dinner."[1] Where I look (as I often do) at examples of incompatibility between rival theologies, or between theological claims and the claims of atheists or secular scientists, it's not to decide who is right, or who is being most reasonable. Nor, when such disputes occur within a religious movement, is it to decide which doctrines represent most faithfully the authentic spirit of that movement. In short, this book does not engage in theology, a discipline for which I am neither trained nor temperamentally suited. Instead, I want to understand how people deal with such incompatibilities. When do they argue over them, when do they fight over them, when do they simply ignore them? I draw on many scientific arguments and studies, and do not endorse claims of miracles. That's because, in a social scientific study of anything (religious or political or business or secular humanitarian movements, for example) we don't accept the unsubstantiated assertions of anybody unless we have independent corroboration. If a political leader claims they have some way to reduce unemployment or make their citizens happy, but there's no reliable independent evidence that they do, it would not be good practice to report the claim as if it were true. Religious claims demand a similarly sober treatment.

From time to time, I report what I have personally seen happen in religious movements across the world, sometimes as part of my academic research, and sometimes in the course of everyday life. My curiosity goes back a long way: nearly forty-five years separate the earliest episode I report, in chapter 12, from the most recent, in the introduction. Occasionally these episodes have provoked my spontaneous human responses of puzzlement, amusement, wonder, or distress. I report such reactions not to persuade anyone to share them, merely to be as lucid as possible about what I am reporting at first hand. Almost always I rely instead on the work of other researchers, a vast community of people dead and living, engaged in an enterprise of collective understanding that is sometimes rivalrous but mostly collaborative, and of which it's a privilege to be a member.

CHAPTER 1

What Is Religion?

When the last red man shall have perished from the earth, and his memory among the white men shall have become a myth . . . these shores will swarm with the invisible dead of my tribe; and when your children's children shall think themselves alone in the fields, the store, the shop upon the highway, or in the silence of the pathless woods, they will not be alone. In all the earth there is no place dedicated to solitude.

—attributed to Chief Seattle, 1854[1]

Invisible Spirits

Nowhere in the inhabited world is the night air completely silent.[2] On the Mediterranean hillside where I am writing, the ambient sound is an orchestra of crickets, broken by the occasional whirr of a bat, the snoring of a neighbor, and once in a while the growl of a truck making its way uphill several miles away across the valley. On the South Indian plain where I once lived, frogs were the rhythm section, with solos from underfed dogs and from time to time the complaining bass line of an uncomfortable cow.

As a healthy and well-nourished citizen of the twenty-first century, living in a country at peace, I find it easy to interpret these sounds, and to tell myself they are made by processes in nature that mean me no harm. Twenty thousand years ago my ancestors, less educated people

"Immanent" religion in everyday life. A Greek marble relief of *c.* 300 BCE depicts a pious family offering a ram to two deities dining at a table in a temple. The male deity is presumed to be a deified hero, as the head of the horse in the background was a symbol of heroization.
Credit: ChrisO, Wikimedia Commons.

The first glimmerings of "transcendent" religion? The Egyptian god Osiris (*right*, accompanied by Isis and Nephthys) supervises the weighing of the heart of Hunefer from *The Book of the Dead*. Anubis brings Hunefer (*left*) into the judgment area and supervises the scales. Hunefer's heart is in a pot in the left scale, and the feather, representing Maat (order or righteousness), in the right. The "devourer," a creature part crocodile, part lion, and part hippopotamus, lies in wait.
Credit: British Museum, Wikimedia Commons.

but no less mentally and far more physically agile than I am, would have listened to the night sky in a much more alert and cautious state. It paid them to do so, for mistakes could be fatal. They were skilled at detecting predators, both animals and other human beings. But the minds whose presence they inferred in the world around them, whether hostile or friendly, were not confined to those of living corporeal beings. Although they have left no written records that state this explicitly, we have a mass of evidence suggesting that their world was also peopled by spirits who were not visible to the everyday senses. These included dead members of their own communities, the spirits of the game they hunted, and the local deities of rivers and forests as well as the grander denizens of the skies. They shared many of the qualities of the natural world—they were angry when it thundered, and they were mournful when it rained. They were not merely decorative accompaniments to these people's lives—they were busy, active, interventionist spirits, with an ambitious agenda and impressive if capricious powers, and my ancestors spent both time and material resources anticipating and placating them. My ancestors also conceived the possibility of their own transformation into spirits after death. They were willing to place luxuries in the graves of their own departed relatives in the hope that their surviving kin would later do the same for them.

Why did our ancestors believe this? These were people used to pitting their wits against nature and one another. Their senses had been honed for accuracy by millions of years of evolution to identify real threats and opportunities in their environment, and not to waste energy negotiating imaginary ones. So why did they populate their universe with so many creatures who, if they were there, left no traces that modern science can see? As far as we can tell, our chimpanzee cousins make no such inferences, though they lead a complex social life and face evolutionary challenges that are every bit as daunting as our own. The dog asleep at the fireside may be startled by an imagined intruder, but once it has checked that all is well it does not trouble itself again with the supposition that the intruder is nevertheless invisibly there. Only *Homo sapiens* has such a crowded imagination. Only we live in an enchanted universe—which is surprising since only we of all living species have developed a systematic form of reasoning that directs a fierce searchlight into the physical world, in whose glare such enchantment seems to have no place.

In the last two thousand years or so the spirit world inhabited by humanity has been downsized but certainly not dismantled. Nearly two-thirds of the world's population professes allegiance to religions that acknowledge a single god—the true spirit that, according to believers, underlies the many different manifestations that our ancestors perceived. Of the rest, a majority still accepts polytheism in one form or another. Still, as we shall see later, the distinction between monotheism and polytheism is far from clear. Many believers inhabit a heavily populated spiritual universe, in which it is not always transparent who are gods and who are ancestors, prophets, saints, or other intermediaries. Nor is it always clear when rivals to a supreme deity are considered to have been defeated, as opposed to being proven not to exist.[3]

As we'll see in chapter 2, although scholars once argued that prosperous modern societies were fated to become purely secular, this now seems to have been a false extrapolation from the nineteenth- and twentieth-century development of some European countries whose dominant Churches had previously occupied a privileged and sometimes a monopoly position in national life. It was a privilege that some thought majestic, others thought suffocating; its erosion has seen religion decline in importance in those countries, but certainly not disappear. In much of Asia, Africa, and Latin America, religion is awake and on the march. In China, though it's difficult to get reliable statistics, there are now probably at least as many active Christians and Muslims as there are members of the Communist Party, perhaps more.[4] Even in the United States, the world's richest and most scientifically advanced society, there is a decline in reported membership of churches, but few citizens (and even fewer politicians) are willing to declare themselves to be atheist or agnostic. Although the character of religion has changed a great deal over recent centuries, and will certainly continue changing during the twenty-first century, there's not the slightest evidence that religion in the world is in decline.

Yet the distance between the world views underpinned by scientific enquiry and those envisaged by religion has grown even wider in the modern world than it was in classical or medieval times. Phenomena that were once thought to bear the fingerprints of spirit life have gradually been revealed to have more mundane physical causes. Dreams that were once scrutinized for messages from the gods are now described in terms of electric activity in the brain. Although modern physics abounds in hidden forces, none of these have intentions toward us or any concern for us. While deep puzzles remain about the origins and nature of the universe, credible solutions to these scientific puzzles might envisage at best the existence of an austere and distant kind of spirit, hardly the kind that would care much for, let alone intervene in, the fate of some quarrelsome apes on a piece of rock circling round an otherwise unexceptional star. They seem more compatible with belief in a god who is indifferent to us than in one whose interventions in the affairs of his chosen species have so persistently failed to prevent its suffering. And the more we know about how events in the brain shape our awareness and our character, the less evidence remains for the possibility that the disintegration of our brains at death could leave intact anything in our personality worth preserving. Think how disorder in the neurons translates into disorder in the awareness and behavior of dementia patients—then extrapolate to the complete disintegration of the brain.

In the eyes of most believers, these arguments are no matter for concern. For some, they show the unreliability of the scientific world view. For many others, less hostile, they show that science and religion can cohabit without difficulty because they occupy different spheres of knowledge. Most citizens of the modern world live comfortably with the knowledge that they can visit a doctor when they fall sick and can also seek religious inspiration and consolation for the many conditions of life that their doctor has no idea how to treat.

Believers and skeptics alike should be curious to know how this cohabitation has happened. Whether we consider our sense of the world's enchantment as a wonderful faculty that allows us a glimpse of deep spiritual truths, or as a form of encephalitis that clouds our understanding of our true place in the universe, it should fascinate us that it has evolved in the same brains that play host to the skeptical, empirical reasoning that has enabled us to analyze and dominate our physical world.[5]

This is fascinating not just because our brains are large enough to encompass both patterns of thought. More practically, our sense of enchantment also leads us to make large material sacrifices that offend against the prudence our rational minds evolved to defend. And rival conceptions of enchantment can lead their adherents to engage in serious, even deadly struggle over status and resources in the material world. People kill one another every day because of disagreements about what invisible spirits have done and said.

Immanent and Transcendental Religion

In writing as I just did of human beings' natural fear of processes in nature that might do us harm, unless we have learned to understand their physical causes, I was missing out something important. It's easy to understand why we might believe in an angry god of thunder when we are shivering before a storm—but most of the gods who have crowded our universe have not been just personifications of natural forces. They are social beings, and if we believe in their existence, it's because others have told us about them.

Anthropologist Marshall Sahlins describes in detail the several gods who attended the process of repairing the canoe of a chief of the Tikopia people, who live on one of the Solomon Islands and whose culture was described by another anthropologist, Raymond Firth.[6] There were gods who inhabited the canoe, who guided its path on fishing expeditions and were responsible for their success. This meant that sacrificing part of the catch was not a way of offering to the gods something that belonged to the people, but rather of showing deference and gratitude to the gods for something they had offered to the people. But these gods had to be induced to leave the canoe so that a different eel god, residing in the repair tool, could be allowed in to do its work, after which the gods of the canoe would return. There was a congestion problem, in short, because the supernatural world of the Tikopia people was crowded, and it was crowded because Tikopia storytellers had made it so.

There are vast differences between the religious life of the Tikopia people and that of the members of a Pentecostal church in Atlanta, of a synagogue in Jerusalem, of a Hindu temple in Uttar Pradesh, of a Quaker meeting house in London, of a mosque in Lagos. Marshall Sahlins was much preoccupied with the difference between what have been called "immanent" and "transcendental" forms of religiosity, following a distinction that historian Alan Strathern has used to illuminate how different religions in the world have interacted with one another in the course of history.[7] Immanent religion is focused on multiple interactions with invisible spirits, who may, if approached in the right way, offer help to human beings in the here and now, but may also be threatening to them if not suitably placated. Transcendental religion is based around the hope of salvation from the human condition, and typically involves interaction with a more distant spiritual world, which is thought of as leaving human beings, most of the time, to govern their own affairs. The philosopher Karl Jaspers (following earlier work on the idea of a "moral revolution" by several scholars, including John Stuart-Glennie and Max Weber)[8] located the development of transcendental religion to the beginning of what he called the Axial Age, from around 800 to 200 BCE. In this period, he claimed, the civilizations of China, India, the Near East, and Greece began a cultural revolution that challenged immanent religion with a vision of religious observance that was doctrinal, abstract, and, to an extent that varied across regions, universal in its ambitions—that is, both moralizing and somewhat egalitarian, proposing that the powerful no less than the powerless were responsible to higher laws, and offering a compensation for the sorrows of this world in some vision of salvation.[9] This cultural revolution was never total, as is obvious to anyone who sees pilgrims praying for miracle cures in the Catholic shrine of Saint Bernadette of Lourdes, or worshippers performing *puja* at a temple to Lakshmi, the Hindu goddess of prosperity. Historian Peter Brown has written of the way in which, for Christians in the late Roman period:

> The highest powers inhabited the shining upper reaches of . . . a vast universe. To human beings . . . they communicated their benevolence through hosts of lower spirits, who brushed the earth with their ministrations, ever open to human requests for aid and comfort, and

redoubtable when slighted. . . . In the words of Augustine: "There are those who say 'God is good, He is great, supreme, eternal and inviolable. . . . But these things of the physical world and of our present times—*ista vero saecularia et temporalia*—belong to *daemones* and to the invisible Powers.' . . . They leave aside God, as if these things did not belong to Him; and by sacrifices, by all kinds of healing devices, and by the persuasive advice of their fellows, they seek out ways to cope with what concerns this present life."[10]

The accuracy of Jaspers's historical account has been challenged, particularly by studies that use comparative cross-cultural data.[11] It now seems likely that different characteristics of transcendental religion arose at different times in a wide range of societies, including some that Jaspers did not consider—such as Egypt, where features of transcendental religion became apparent as early as 1200 BCE (or even earlier if one counts the unusual figure of Akhenaten, who introduced the cult of Aten, the disc of the sun—or the cult of Osiris, who held out the possibility of an afterlife dependent on how the individual had behaved in life).[12] But that there was a qualitative transformation of many religious people's world view over the course of the centuries is a conclusion shared by many researchers who in other respects differ radically about the details. The authors of a large comparative historical study published in 2019 argue that the rise of transcendental religion—the arrival of Axial Age religion, in other words—"is a consequence of passing a certain threshold in the scale and structure of human societies. . . . [O]nce this threshold is passed, societies must adopt more prosocial and egalitarian moral principles if they are to survive the twin specters of external conquest and internal collapse."[13]

We shall return to this transformation later, and ask whether it really changed the everyday life of religious believers (as opposed to that of a small elite) as much as some have claimed. We know very little about what ordinary illiterate people may have believed in any society at any time. We do know that religious authorities have regularly expostulated against their lax habits of religious observance, which suggests that the high-minded doctrines of the Axial Age may have had more difficulty making headway than later scholars typically admit.[14] Either way, we should not let this distinction between immanent and transcendental religions obscure something they all have in common. They all appeal to the presence of spirits who are not visible in an everyday way, who are aware of what human beings do, who can act in ways that make a difference to human lives, and who are open to at least some prayers and entreaties. These shared features are remarkable, given that these spirits are not present to us through the senses that let us perceive the world's other inhabitants. Nor are they perceptible to the instruments of science—as are subatomic particles, for instance. Some religions have a much larger cast of spirits in their pantheon, some have only one. In some varieties of Buddhism and Hinduism the spirits may be so austere and abstract that we may wonder whether they should be called spirits at all. And some secular political leaders have been known to speak of "destiny" or "the nation" as if they were spirits with a will of their own.[15] But arguments about definition are not important here: whether you call them religion or not, this book is about those activities that turn around the interaction of human beings with invisible spirits.[16]

Religious organizations do much, much more than interact with invisible spirits. They may perform rituals; create and nurture a community for their members; provide them with social, moral, financial, educational, and medical support; and weave for them a narrative that helps them make sense of their place in the world. Some of these activities are more important to religion than others: only some religious institutions provide financial or educational support for their members, but almost all have at least some kind of ritual (though so do many political, sporting, and cultural associations that have no religious affiliation at all). But the invisible spirits are central to the notion of religion in the way that none of the other elements are.[17]

Of course, some individual members of religious organizations may take part in their activities without ever giving invisible spirits much thought—religious traditions differ in how much they insist that their members share supernatural beliefs, with evangelical Christianity insisting quite a lot, liberal Judaism insisting very little, and some religious communities, like the Druze of Lebanon, putting much emphasis on dress and ritual with apparently very little in the way of shared belief. Even among small-scale forager communities there is a wide range of degrees of religiosity, with some, like the Hadza of Tanzania, for whom the presence of spirits is at most a shared background assumption but rarely a topic of conversation.[18] But even if a synagogue may contain many members who participate enthusiastically in its activities while having little in the way of conventional religious belief, the activities of the synagogue would be meaningless without the shared tradition of belief in the god who made the Jews his chosen people. Similarly, the various dimensions of support (education, finance, health, and so on) that religious organizations provide for their members are not just fringe benefits. They have a different meaning for members than would apparently similar services they might obtain from secular providers elsewhere. Coming together to interact with invisible spirits is the hook on which all the other activities of religious organizations hang.

This perspective also helps us to make sense of a distinction that is often made but rarely understood—the distinction between religion and magic. The respective roles of religion and science in "the decline of magic" at the end of the Middle Ages in Europe have spawned a rich historical literature, in which it is hard to avoid the suspicion that "magic" is often used to designate religious activities of which the author disapproves or considers ridiculous. In any case its usefulness for historical research is subject to a vigorous debate.[19] It is equally controversial in the history of religion in the United States—where, for example, the question whether (in the words of historian Michael Quinn) "magic and treasure-seeking were an integral part of the . . . religious quest" of the family of Joseph Smith, the founder of the Mormon religion, has been instrumentalized by opponents and defenders of Mormonism.[20] We don't have to take sides between religion and magic to understand that the two activities differ in an important dimension (though, as Keith Thomas continually reminds his readers throughout his great work *Religion and the Decline of Magic*, the two were often found together, and were practiced by the most educated in the land as well as by the illiterate).[21] Magic is essentially a form of *technology*—it's about trying to manipulate the world through an understanding of its internal workings. If you've grasped those workings, it's a matter of following the formula—though finding the formula may be a life's work, as astrologers and alchemists knew only too well. Religion, by contrast, is a form of *diplomacy*—it's about thinking, speaking, and acting in such a way as to communicate with the spirit or spirits that animate the universe—either by actively directing your thoughts toward them or by allowing them to see into your soul. If you are to use religion to make your life better, it must be by persuading the spirits, not by manipulating them. Magic and religion use very different human skills— magic deploys our talents for manipulating the physical world, while religion evokes our interpersonal communicative skills. Even if many or even most religious ceremonies have also involved magical elements, from the dawn of history down to our own day, what makes them religious is the presence of spirits with whom the human beings believe themselves to be in some form of communication.[22]

In a similar vein, anthropologists (among others) have been much preoccupied with the distinction between magic and witchcraft (or sorcery), a distinction I will ignore in most of this book. Witchcraft has come to mean the use of supernatural methods for causing harm (sometimes unconsciously). It is a subbranch of magic that's used mainly for malevolent purposes—though, as use of the term "white witch" suggests, there's no unanimous agreement on that either. It has been estimated that well over a billion people in the world would say if asked that they believe in the reality of witchcraft; they're much more likely to do so if they also say that religion plays an important part in their lives.[23] Belief in witchcraft seems to be much less prevalent than belief in God, particularly in industrial societies, but some of the apparent difference may be due to greater reluctance to admit to it among the people who respond to surveys. Witchcraft is itself a very diverse phenomenon— the white witchcraft practiced as a minority interest in prosperous, urbanized societies, as by the London covens described in the 1980s by the anthropologist Tanya Luhrmann,[24] is obviously different in many respects from the practice in societies where belief in magic processes is more mainstream.[25] There's a large literature analyzing witchcraft, which I won't try to cover here, except where it happens to cast light on the broader phenomenon of religion.[26]

To summarize, then, religion is the very large and diverse set of human activities that directly or indirectly involve interaction with invisible spirits who intervene causally in the world, and who can be influenced by appropriate appeals from human subjects. In the rest of this book, I shall use the term "enchantment" to describe the sense that the world contains such spirits, whether many or only one, whether close or distant. This isn't the way the term "enchantment" has always been used—Max Weber, for example, talked about the "disenchantment" of the world to describe several distinct phenomena, including the decline of magic.[27] Still, no one has a monopoly on uses of the term, and using "enchantment" to describe the sense of spirit presence will be readily understood. I shall look at why religion has such a central place in human life, and what are the consequences of this.

Weber's work has come to be widely associated with the idea that secularization (a set of changes intrinsically tied up with the nature of modern life) would gradually diminish the importance of religion in the modern world. This was also a repeated theme in the work of other writers such as Karl Marx, Friedrich Nietzsche, James Frazer, Emile Durkheim, and Sigmund Freud.[28] It has also been greatly refined by modern scholars (whose work is considered in more detail in the appendix). But his arguments have been much misunderstood.[29] He clearly thought that modernity posed a challenge to which religious movements would have to adapt. More and more of us go to doctors rather than shamans to treat our physical ailments, and we are nowadays more likely to ask someone with an engineering degree to repair a boat than someone who claims to be able to summon the eel god. Nobody could seriously dispute the phenomenon of secularization in this sense. But Weber nowhere suggested that religious movements would be unable to adapt to this challenge. He might have been surprised by the evidence of the ingenuity with which they have done so, but the idea that secularization in Weber's sense would lead to the terminal decline of religion is not one that Weber himself ever held. We might even summarize the change he envisaged as a move away from religion-as-technology in the direction of religion-as-diplomacy. As we'll see, that move has fundamentally strengthened rather than weakened the place of religious movements in the modern world.

So, having defined what we are studying, let's begin by taking a snapshot of the state of religion in the world today. What does it look like, and how has it changed in recent years? It's much harder than you might think to answer this question, for many reasons. The most immediate reason is that what people call their religious identity often tells us little about what that leads them to think, feel, and do. What they call their religious identity can even vary according to whether they're talking to official census enumerators, to survey administrators, or to social anthropologists, as well as according to what precise questions they are being asked.[30] Still, in chapter 2 we'll look at what people have been telling census and survey enumerators over the last century or so. Even that information, partial though it is, reveals some surprising patterns in the way in which religion is developing in the modern world.

CHAPTER 2

What Is Happening to Religion in the Modern World?

The twentieth century was the century in which extensive religious plurality first became an inescapable feature of the urban social and cultural environment in almost every continent.

—Brian Stanley, *Christianity in the Twentieth Century*

Globalization Comes to Kumbo

It is mid-December 2005, time for Friday prayers at the central mosque in Kumbo, a bustling town of some eighty thousand inhabitants in northwestern Cameroon. Men are filing in through the back door while the women climb the stairs to the gallery. In the pile of shoes outside I notice how many of the traditional sandals have now given way to Nike sneakers, probably fakes but convincing ones if so. I slip in alongside the other men, grateful that the imam has invited me to observe the prayers and to hear him preach. I try to stand discreetly at the back, but many eyes turn in my direction. On the way to the mosque with me, the imam's son stopped to greet an old schoolfriend, now in his early thirties and grown a little portly, wearing a full black beard that is clearly more than a fashion statement. "He recently came back from studying in Saudi Arabia," the imam's son tells me afterward. "He's become very critical of our way of life here, which he says doesn't live up to what the

38

View of a Bamum mosque in Cameroon, 1910. Arabic writings are painted above the door. Postcard of the Société des missions évangéliques de Paris (Paris evangelical missionary society).
Credit: Anna Wuhrmann, Wikimedia Commons.

Religious competition: the new Mohamed al Amin Mosque (*right*, completed in 2002) next to the Maronite Cathedral of Saint Georges, in downtown Beirut, finished in 1894.
Credit: Lebnen 18, Wikimedia Commons.

Quran demands. I'm worried about him. And I'm sure he's worried about me."

Friday prayers begin, and after the initial orations the imam launches into his sermon. Less than five minutes in, everyone's attention is distracted by the ringtone of a cell phone that someone has forgotten to switch to silent mode. The imam stops speaking. Eyes turn to glare at the phone's embarrassed owner, who fumbles for a few seconds in the pocket of his djellaba before managing to turn it off. The tune is familiar to me, but in this unfamiliar setting I have trouble placing it. At last, I recognize one of Antonin Dvorak's Slavonic Dances. It brings an incongruous whiff of Bohemia into the heat of this African mosque. I reflect that globalization is heading for Kumbo, fast.[1]

Nine years after my 2005 visit, globalization makes an even more visible mark here: it is announced that the *fon*, the traditional ruler of the Nso people, whose palace is on the southern outskirts of Kumbo, has converted to Islam. He is reported to be constructing a mosque. Since he was nominally a Catholic before this, with a royal seat in the Kumbo cathedral (albeit one he rarely occupied), the local press describes this as heralding "a bleak future for Christianity."[2] But the most significant changes had already happened long before, first under German then under British colonial rule. The fon was traditionally the source of religious as well as political authority, in charge of "keeping the ancestors happy"; he was regarded as a deity whose actions should not be questioned.[3] Most of his subjects would have been recorded in the census not as Christians but as followers of traditional religion. His acknowledgment of the authority of first one, and now a second world religion might seem like a setback to the traditional order. But it's more accurate to see them as judicious compromises—and the latest compromise may be even more favorable to him than the first. It runs in both directions: the fon will not challenge Islam, but neither will the local imams challenge the fon. Unlike the cathedral, the mosque will be built in the grounds of his palace. Statistically speaking, it's one more step in the march of global Islam across the African continent. In terms of what will change for his people, it's much harder to know what it means. What is really going on?

It's one thing to spot signs of religious globalization here and there, but it's quite another to document and track it in a systematic way. Many readers might be surprised to realize how hard it is to find reliable statistics about religion in the modern world. As a rule, when you go to church, or to the mosque, or to the temple or the synagogue, nobody is recording your presence, or what you do there. Nobody, that is, who might make the results available to the public or to interested researchers. Of course, your smartphone is transmitting a lot of data about you to the manufacturer, and to the makers of various apps. The local security services may be taking an interest in your behavior, especially if you belong to one of that country's minority religions. But good luck trying to get hold of such information if all you want to use it for is research.

Religious organizations in many countries (including the United States) are under no obligation to report information about their revenues or membership, as firms are required to do. If you work or shop at Walmart, that fact will be recorded, and used in the compilation of the official statistics that Walmart is obliged to report and that researchers can consult. But if you volunteer at your church or put money in the collection box, no public record of your actions need ever be created.

To understand the changing shape of religion today, we must therefore rely on two kinds of source, census data and surveys—neither of which fully captures the complexity of religious activity. Census data track shifts in shares of population across broad categories of religious affiliation. They have the advantage that they cover all, or almost all, of the population of each country. They have the disadvantage that censuses happen only once a decade or so, and rarely ask any questions about religion except what broad religious category people belong to. Surveys, in contrast, can track complex changes in the types of religious activity people are willing to admit to engaging in. But they ask many fewer people, and it's often hard to know whether those who are willing to take part are representative of the population, let alone whether they're prepared to answer truthfully the much more intrusive questions surveys usually ask.*

---

* "One in three internet users fail to question misinformation," announces a UK government report (Ofcom 2022). The report doesn't tell us what proportion of authors of government reports fails to question the information reported in surveys.

Still, it's surprising how much we can do with these two sources of data. Let's start by investigating the widespread belief that religion today is in terminal decline.

Is Religion in Decline?

When I type into a Google search box the words "Is Christianity," the first suggestion that comes up to complete my search is the word "declining." Even more dramatically, if I type in the words "Is religion," the first suggestion I receive is "dying."[4] Google is not alone: the phrase "Decline of Christianity in the Western World" has its own *Wikipedia* page. Presumably anything that has its own *Wikipedia* page must be a real thing, no? But then, Santa Claus has his own page, and so does Donald Trump's hair.[5]

Still, the view that Christianity in the modern world is on the retreat has a lot of takers, and it comes in many flavors. One is that Christianity is the loser in a "clash of civilizations," to take the title of a widely cited article and book by Samuel Huntington in the mid-1990s.[6] Populists in Europe and North America particularly like to claim that Christianity is declining against a resurgent and aggressive Islam. A variant in vogue with far-right movements in Europe is the "great replacement" theory, popularized in a book of the same name by the French writer Renaud Camus.[7] It claims that the white, Christian population of Europe is being replaced by Arabs, Berbers, Turks, and Muslims from sub-Saharan Africa.[8] But it isn't only populists who talk about a Christian retreat: a headline in the *Financial Times* in 2019 read "Pope Francis Fights a Losing Battle in the Middle East: The Mass Flight of Christians from the Region Continues Unchecked."[9]

Even observers who do not want to single out Islam as a rival often conclude that Christianity is on the decline. In a *Foreign Affairs* article in 2020 headlined "Giving Up on God: The Global Decline of Religion," and then in a book entitled *Religion's Sudden Decline* published the following year, sociologist Ronald Inglehart claimed that "from 1981 to 2007, most countries became more religious—but from 2007 to 2020, the overwhelming majority became less religious."[10] His book has been widely cited—for example, in the *New York Times*—as an authoritative demonstration that "the decline in religiosity is a global phenomenon."[11] Other sources have concentrated on Western countries in general or the United States in particular. Political scientist Dominic Johnson refers to "the current decline in religious belief (at least in many western countries)" as an established fact, and sociologist Kevin McCaffree begins his book *The Secular Landscape: The Decline of Religion in America* with the stark claim: "Traditional religion is dissipating in the West. Like a slowly moving glacier, secularization continues nearly unimpeded, save for the occasional bouts of religious revival or religious apathy."[12] Press reports and academic studies are no less categorical about trends in the United States: in March 2021, Gallup reported "U.S. Church Membership Falls Below Majority for First Time," while in December that year the Pew Research Center reported that "about three-in-ten U.S. adults are now religiously unaffiliated."[13] A poll conducted by the National Opinion Research Center in March 2023 for the *Wall Street Journal* reported that 39 percent of Americans thought religion was "very important," although in 1998 62 percent had thought so.[14] It has even been suggested that "the quest for secular redemption through politics" is displacing God in the minds and lives of Americans.[15] And it's not just church members: the polling organization Barna Group reported in November 2021 that 38 percent of US pastors had seriously considered leaving the ministry within the previous year (though the stress of the Covid-19 pandemic was partly to blame).[16] The United States is not alone: census data released in November 2022 showed that the proportion of the population in England and Wales who identified as Christian had dropped to 46 percent in 2021, from 59 percent in 2011—prompting press articles with headlines such as "Christianity now a minority religion" and "Britain's crisis of unbelief" (the latter followed by the alarmist subheadline: "In a nation that binds spiritual and temporal power, will the end of the old metaphysical order threaten the state itself?").[17]

How seriously should we take such claims? One reason to be at least mildly skeptical is that it would be hard to find any period in history when the older and more conservative members of society have not been convinced that religion was on the decline among the irreverent youth and the less educated of all ages. The Hellenistic philosopher Plutarch, a priest at the temple in Delphi during the latter part of the first century CE, devoted a whole long essay to the subject, entitled *On the Decline of the Oracles.*[18] The American Puritan Cotton Mather (already known to many for his part in the prosecution of several victims of the Salem witch trials) bemoaned what appeared to him in 1702 the uncontestable fact that after the first European settlers had colonized New England, "religion brought forth prosperity, and the daughter destroyed the mother."[19] A century and a half later, across the Atlantic, the Anglican clergyman Samuel Earnshaw wrote that "the Christian religion has almost entirely lost its hold on the artisans of this country."[20] A study from Kent in southeast England by historian Clive Field shows that religious authorities have bemoaned the lax churchgoing habits of ordinary people since the first evidence he collected, in the early sixteenth century.[21] In 2019 Pope Francis warned the Vatican's hierarchy that "the faith in Europe and in much of the West is no longer an obvious presumption but is often denied, derided, marginalized and ridiculed."[22] He might have been surprised if his attention had been drawn to echoes in what he said of the writings of an anonymous Egyptian of the third century CE, who had attributed the decline in religion he perceived in his own day to the fulfilment of a prophecy by the temple priest Hermes Trismegistos that:

> The entire divinity will cease in Egypt, and it will flee up to heaven, and Egypt will be widowed, it will be abandoned by the gods. . . . [T]he country that is more devout than all countries will become irreverent. No longer will it be full of temples, but it will be full of tombs; nor will it be full of gods, but of corpses. O Egypt! Egypt, your cults will become like the fables, and your divinities will no longer be believed in.[23]

Whether it's actual decline or merely perceived decline that is found in so many diverse societies and historical periods is impossible to know—these laments, though numerous, are entirely anecdotal. If we want to use more systematic evidence, we must decide what we want that evidence to measure. What exactly is this thing, religion, that is supposedly declining? Religion is about belief and about belonging, about ritual and reflection, about ethics and aesthetics, about prayer and performance, about inner contemplation and outward display. It's about the external identity you acknowledge and about the private identity that shapes you. It can be about fighting boldly for your beliefs or about suffering quietly for them. It's hard to distinguish concerns that religion is declining from disagreements between religious people about the aspects of religion they think are most important; what looks like decline to some may be seen by others as a welcome rebalancing of priorities. And what people feel comfortable telling census and survey enumerators about their religious practices may vary greatly from one society to another and from one generation to another.

In short, religiosity is such a complex phenomenon that to understand it fully we would need a much wider range of statistical measures— ones that distinguished, for example, between belief and attendance at religious ceremonies, or between private and collective spirituality. Many such measures exist, but usually only for some countries and for some time periods.

In the appendix I set out in detail what we can conclude from the statistical evidence that does exist for a large range of countries; here I'll just summarize the main messages. We can draw on census returns over more than a century about what religion people state they belong to, and on survey evidence over about forty years about how important they say religion is in their lives. There's much that remains unknowable, but there are eight things we can say, some of them quite surprising.

1. The common belief that Christianity commands the loyalty of a declining share of the world's population, squeezed between a Godless secularism on one side and a resurgent Islam on the other, is a pure statistical illusion.* Both Christianity and Islam are alive and well, and are both increasing their share of the population in most regions of the world.
2. Christianity appears to have declined only because it has been concentrated in parts of the world whose populations are

---

* It's a version of an illusion known as Simpson's paradox; the appendix provides more details.

growing relatively slowly. But population growth rates are converging fast across the world; Christianity's demographic deficit
will soon be a thing of the past.

3. The share of Christianity in Europe and North America has
indeed been declining—but it's a very different story, with
different causes, from what's happening in the rest of the world.

4. Throughout much of the world, there has been a sharp decline in
the share of Christians belonging to the mainstream churches,
but a rapid increase in the share belonging to evangelical and
Pentecostal churches. This partly explains why Christians from
the mainstream traditions are so convinced that Christianity is
in overall decline. Their concern for their own kind of Christianity is entirely legitimate, but it's not representative of the world.

5. The reported importance of religion in people's lives *has* been
declining in the United States and Canada, and in some other
countries such as Spain, Ireland, and Chile. But in almost all other
countries, it's not declining. It's either fairly low but holding steady,
as in the United Kingdom and Western Europe, or in Japan. Or it's
high and stable or even increasing, in the Muslim world but also in
a wide range of predominantly Orthodox or Pentecostal Christian,
Hindu, and Buddhist countries across Eastern Europe, Asia,
Africa, and Latin America. The average change in the importance
of religion, for the seventy-eight countries for which we have
comparable data, is −0.39 percentage points from the early 1990s
to the late 2010s, which is statistically indistinguishable from zero.

6. Other indicators of religiosity show a divergence between
measures of belief and measures of religious participation. The
average percentage of people reporting belief in God has increased by 1.1 percentage points over the same period, which is
also statistically indistinguishable from zero. The average percentage of people reporting that they attend religious services at
least once per month has fallen by 3.6 percentage points, which
is a large and statistically very significant change.

7. The secularization hypothesis, well known from the work of
Max Weber as well as that of other thinkers of the nineteenth

and early twentieth centuries, captures something of the changing nature of religion over the last century—religion is adapting,
just as the rest of our behaviors and institutions are adapting, to
the challenges of modern life. But secularization can mean
many things, and none of them implies that religion is declining,
or likely to decline further, in the twenty-first century. It's likely
instead that societies will settle into one of two patterns, in
which religion (in whatever form it takes) is important either for
most people in a society, or for somewhat less than half of them.
Which pattern prevails will depend on whether religion comes
to be seen as politically neutral or politically polarizing.

8. Finally, where religion has declined in importance recently, it is
usually because of events that discredited religious leaders in the
eyes of their followers, turning religion from a politically neutral
phenomenon into a polarizing one.

To get a flavor of what has been happening, let's look at those first two
conclusions in more detail. They're based mainly on census data. Unlike
most surveys, censuses have been asking the same or similar questions
over many decades. A large comparative project based at Boston University, called the World Religion Database, has been gathering census
data on religious affiliation across the entire world since the beginning
of the twentieth century. Where the census data are incomplete the
project has supplemented them with best guesses based on surveys. Yes,
the claim that Christianity has been declining, in the face of competition
from secularism and from Islam, looks true on the surface. Over the last
century or so, the share of self-professed Christians in the world population has indeed declined, from 35 percent in 1900 to 32 percent in 2020.
And yes, the share of atheists and agnostics has risen, from zero in 1900
to 12 percent in 2020, while the share of Muslims has roughly doubled,
from 12 percent in 1900 to 24 percent in 2020. But the share of Christians
has declined because, in 1900, Christianity was concentrated in parts of
the world (notably Europe and the Americas), whose population would
grow relatively slowly over the next century. Islam, on the other hand,
was concentrated in parts of the world (particularly in Asia) that were

going to grow very fast. Christianity has attracted 6 percentage points *more* adherents since 1900 than would have been predicted from the divergences in countries' demographic growth alone. Islam has attracted around 5 percentage points more than would have been predicted. And the reason why the share of atheists and agnostics in 1900 was recorded as zero is that no census thought to ask about them. Once they did begin asking, the recorded share of agnostics and atheists in the world began to grow until it peaked at 19 percent in 1970 (a development that owed more to Stalin and Mao Zedong than to Voltaire). Since then, it has been in continuous *decline*, reaching its estimated share of 12 percent in 2020.

Overall, both Christianity and Islam have proved extremely dynamic and successful at attracting adherents during the last century. In the next century, the previous divergences between the population growth rates of the world's Christian-majority countries and its Muslim-majority countries will start to disappear. A case in point is Iran, where the number of children per woman fell dramatically during the 1980s and 1990s, largely because of the rapid increase in the education of girls. It fell faster, in fact, than it had in one-child China in the previous decade. More generally, you can't project past differences in population growth rates between countries into the decades to come. They may diverge for a while, but afterward they tend to converge. In fact, the world is converging demographically in the twenty-first century, and fast.*

That doesn't mean things are rosy for all the Christian denominations. It's difficult to find reliable figures for the share of Roman Catholics in the overall Christian population going back more than a couple of decades.[24] But Catholics now make up around 50 percent of the world's Christians, including around 5 percent who report an affiliation to non-Catholic denominations as well. That is almost certainly a lower proportion than ever. Catholics compose between around 30 and a little over 40 percent in all major regions of the world except Latin America, where they make up around 80 percent (including the doubly

---

* In November 2021 it was announced that India's fertility rate had dropped below replacement level (Kaul and Dutt 2021). That is a truly momentous development.

affiliated). And throughout the world, among the non-Catholic Christians, there has been a striking fall in the share belonging to the mainstream denominations, in favor of the evangelical and Pentecostal churches, whose share has been rising very fast. This is harder to document systematically, as censuses typically don't ask such detailed information. But a recent survey in Kenya reported that the share of Christian respondents belonging to traditional Christian churches had fallen from 72 to 43 percent from 1998 to 2021, while the share belonging to Pentecostal churches had risen from 22 to 50 percent.[25] Similar trends, if not always so rapid, have been observed in many countries in Asia, Africa, and Latin America.

If Islam and Christianity were both increasing their share of the world population, whose share was declining? To get a sense of the answer, let's look at Africa. In 1900, Muslims represented 33 percent of Africa's population, a share that had risen by 2020 to 42 percent. Christians represented a mere 9 percent of the population in 1900, but by 2020 this had risen by an astonishing 40 percentage points, to 49 percent. So which religions were losing out?

The answer is many different practices that are recorded in the data as "ethno-religions." These local and folk cultures encompass everything from spiritual healing to rites of passage, fortune-telling, and preparations for love, death, and war. They may recognize gods of the village, the river, the forest, and the mountain.[26] They have many points in common across the continent, but they also reflect local particularities and traditions. And while they commanded the allegiance of 58 percent of Africa's population in 1900, this share had dropped to a mere 8 percent by 2020.

Africa is not alone. Asia has also experienced a sharp fall (from 45% to 14%) in the share of the population professing adherence to local and folk religions, notably those that continued to command the allegiance of many Chinese through the centuries, resisting the efforts of centralizers from Confucius to Mao Zedong. In Latin America, where the Roman Catholic Church made inroads much earlier, most ethno-religions disappeared (from the census data, at least) in the nineteenth century.

What explains the remarkable spread of these two global religions, Christianity and Islam, during the last century? The answer is that religious movements create communities, and communities function best when they operate as platforms. The platforms that Christian and Muslim communities have been able to construct help their members to navigate the challenges of the modern world, with its increased migration from the country to the city, its loosening of family ties, and its hazards of sickness, unemployment, and loneliness against which the traditional institutions of family, village, and folk religion can no longer help to protect them.

It would be wrong to think that folk religions represent an entirely local outlook. This was not true two millennia ago and it is not true today. Historians Peregrine Horden and Nicholas Purcell have argued that "the cults which brought large numbers of travelers across the ancient Mediterranean, especially the healing cults, functioned as places at which acculturation could take place relatively painlessly. They provided an 'interface' between the diverse ethnicities of the ancient world."[27] Pilgrimages to religious festivals contributed to a form of "competition for religious prestige" between localities.[28] Historians Thomas Galoppin and Corinne Bonnet have documented how "ancient polytheisms" provided a way for local cults to be connected into wider trans-Mediterranean networks, with the names of global gods such as Zeus, Yahweh, or Aphrodite being appropriated in local contexts for very diverse purposes.[29] The same is surely true of local and folk religions in Africa and Asia today. They differ from the major world religions in their greater variety of ritual and practice, and in the strength of their attachment to a local place. But their practitioners are often highly aware of their links to a network of related religious practice in a wider world. Still, the change is undeniable. The world is coming to be dominated by a handful of global religions to an extent that has never been seen before. Folk religions have not been displaced but absorbed into a global religious culture. The religious movements that have spread fastest across the world, while benefiting from global visibility, have also creatively adapted themselves to the local culture—whether it's the imams of Kumbo welcoming a mosque in the grounds of the fon's palace, or a Pentecostalist preacher deploying traditional African music as part of the liturgy.

In the countries where the global religions have been advancing most rapidly in terms of the religious affiliation of the population, there is also the most robust tendency to report that religion is important in people's lives. To see this, we need to look at evidence from surveys.

The Importance of Religion in Individual Lives

The survey data that cover the world over the longest period in a reasonably representative way come from the World Values Survey (WVS), a large international project that has conducted repeated surveys of public opinion about values and beliefs across nearly one hundred countries, beginning in 1981. As the appendix reports, they show that for most countries in the world in the last forty years, the importance of religion in individual lives has remained steady or increased, albeit at very different levels. A steady 40 percent or so of the population in the United Kingdom and Western Europe (and a lower but still steady proportion in Japan) report that religion is very important or somewhat important in their lives. That number is much higher—80 or even 90 percent—for many countries in Eastern Europe, Asia, Africa, and Latin America.

Still, there are some countries where the importance of religion has clearly declined, and it's important to understand where it has done so, and (if possible) why. The country for which we know most is the United States, where the WVS reports a rapid decline in the proportion of people answering that religion is very important or rather important in their lives, from 83 percent at the beginning of the 2000s to only 56 percent at the end of the 2010s. Organizations such as Gallup, the Pew Research Center, and the National Opinion Research Center have also been documenting American religious attitudes and behavior over several decades, and they also show declining levels of religiosity in the last two decades or so. In 2020, according to Gallup, the share of American adults reporting that they are members of a church, synagogue, or mosque (for some reason they forgot to mention temples!) fell to 47 percent, down from 70 percent in the late 1990s. That's partly due to more Americans reporting no religious affiliation at all (up from 8% to 21%). It's also partly due to those who do have a religious affiliation saying they don't belong to any particular church, synagogue, or mosque (up from 27% to 53% over the same period). There's a clear difference by generation—millennials are significantly more likely than baby boomers to report having no religious affiliation, and both cohorts have become more likely to do so over time. But apart from generation, what's striking is that declining religiosity is reported across all main demographic categories and to broadly similar degrees—men and women; whites, African Americans, and Hispanics; liberals and conservatives; married and unmarried; more and less educated.[30] It's not just Gallup— evidence from the Pew Research Center tells the same story.[31] The General Social Survey, a nationally representative survey conducted by the National Opinion Research Center that has been running since 1972 with around two thousand observations per wave, reports that the proportion of "nones" in America—those who declare no religious affiliation, though some believe in God and may even attend religious services—rose from 6.8 percent in 1974 to 23 percent in 2018.[32]

Furthermore, there's evidence that these trends have major social consequences. A study circulated in early 2023 showed that the startling increase in deaths from drug poisoning, suicide, and cirrhosis of the liver, which was particularly concentrated among lower-educated, middle-aged white Americans, was preceded by declines in religious participation (though not necessarily in religious belief) that were also concentrated among these groups. In US states where the declines were the strongest, the increase in these "deaths of despair" was also the largest relative to previous trends.[33]

So there *is* a story to tell here—but it's a story about the United States of America, not about the rest of the world. The United States has some interesting and exceptional characteristics, compared not just with the rest of the world but even with other rich countries. For one thing, it has consistently displayed far greater levels of religiosity in the past than almost all other countries with similar levels of prosperity. Its religiosity as reported by the WVS remains around twice as high as that in Scandinavia and the Netherlands, and around 50 percent higher than in France and Germany. The United States also has a recent political and social history that is very different from that of other countries. And its increase in deaths from opiate poisonings has no real counterpart in other comparable countries.[34] If there's a decline in religion taking place in the United States, it's not clear what the message is for those other countries. We'll return to this in more detail in chapter 10.

Still, the United States is not alone in experiencing a decline in religiosity from previously high levels. Let's look at two Western European countries where this has happened, Ireland and Spain. Ireland was unusual among Western European countries in having extremely high levels of religiosity as late as 1990: the WVS records over 83 percent of people saying that religion was very important or rather important in their lives. That figure fell steadily over the next two decades, to just under 75 percent in the late 1990s and 66 percent in the mid-2000s. You might think this fits the secularization thesis nicely—Ireland was enjoying very impressive economic growth throughout that period. Yet the secularization thesis has a problem: Ireland's level of GDP (gross domestic product) per person had already grown level with Spain's by the early 1980s.[35] In Spain in 1990, only 53 percent of people said religion was very important or rather important in their lives, more than 30 percentage points below Ireland.[36] The WVS has no religiosity data for Spain going back earlier than 1990, but it's a safe bet that they would have reported high levels of religiosity in, say, the late 1960s. Spain evidently had a steep fall in religiosity much earlier than Ireland did. It would fall still further in the decade after 1990, to 45 percent. For the whole of the twenty-first century so far, Spain has reported levels of religiosity comparable to those of France, Germany, and the United Kingdom—between 35 and 40 percent. But the bulk of that fall occurred when Spain was much less economically developed than Ireland would be in its comparable period of religious decline. So, if it isn't economic prosperity that explains the difference in the timing of the trajectories of Spain and Ireland, what is it?

An Alternative to Secularization:
Adam Smith's Political Life Cycle Story

The death of Franco in 1975 ended a period in which the Catholic Church had been strongly sustained by a political regime to which it had in turn given legitimating support. Not all elements in the Catholic Church had supported Franco—indeed, significant numbers of priests had spoken out bravely against the regime, particularly in Catalonia and the Basque country, and many were imprisoned for their actions.[37] The Church also played a largely constructive role in the transition to democracy that followed Franco's death. Still, the relationship between the religious and the political authorities under Franco had conformed closely to the model that Adam Smith foresaw in chapter 5 of *The Wealth of Nations*. As we saw in the introduction, Smith had written that successful religious movements attracted the attention of political leaders, who envied their popular legitimacy. In return for the support of religious leaders, political leaders would offer them protection from competitors as well as financial support. Roman Catholicism was the only religious activity authorized in Spain under Franco; Catholic instruction was compulsory even in public schools; the state paid the costs of the Church in priestly salaries and even in the restoration of many ecclesiastical buildings. In return Franco had reserved the right to name bishops, as well as to veto other appointments, even down to the level of the parish priest.[38] The identification of the Church with the regime had also been entrenched by the savage persecution of priests in Republican-controlled areas during the Civil War, with the loss of some 20 percent of clergy and the execution of twelve out of twenty-eight bishops.[39]

Smith would therefore have predicted that the zeal of the church in fashioning an appealing message would be much diminished by this comfortable enjoyment of monopoly power. Protection by the state could delay a reckoning with its members, but not put it off forever, particularly if the political regime's intrinsic legitimacy began to falter. It would not have surprised him that once the lid of repression was lifted, the hold of the Catholic Church over its flock would begin a steep decline. The situation remains complex: many Spaniards remain culturally Catholic, taking part, for example, in religious festivals and continuing to hold religious weddings and baptisms, and religiosity as reported in the WVS has not declined further since the year 2005.[40] A third of Spanish taxpayers were reported in 2021 as still donating 0.7 percent of their income tax to the Church (though since this does not increase their total tax bill it's not a costly gesture).[41] But even practicing Catholics are much less willing to accept the legitimacy of the Church to dictate practice in matters of personal morality than they once did. And younger Spaniards show less religiosity than older ones, so the extent to which cultural Catholicism will persist into the longer term remains very unclear.

The Catholic Church in Ireland was almost as strongly implicated in the state as it had been in Spain. But Ireland never went through a comparable period of dictatorship, and the events that led to the loosening of the Church's political power there were quite different. After the Irish famine of 1845, the folk Catholicism that predominated in rural areas "came to be replaced by centralized control, Roman devotions, regular practice, sexual abstinence, and intense clerical supervision." This was the project of Paul Cullen, archbishop of Dublin, Ireland's first cardinal, and "the principal architect of the dogma of papal infallibility."[42] The foundation of the Irish Free State (later the Republic of Ireland) in 1922, and particularly the constitution of 1937, gave formal political expression to the powerful influence the Church had already accumulated over many aspects of Irish life. The Constitution of 1937 stated that "the State recognizes the special position of the Holy Catholic Apostolic and Roman Church as the guardian of the Faith professed by the great majority of the citizens." Divorce and remarriage were outlawed under the 1937 Constitution and remained illegal until 1995. Contraception was illegal in Ireland until 1980 and not freely for sale until 1992, while homosexuality was illegal until 1993, and abortion until 2018. The Church owned and controlled many hospitals and most schools (not least because the newly independent state had no resources with which to undertake the capital expenditure to create the necessary infrastructure). Censorship of publications deemed unacceptable to the Church was enforced long after they had become available in other European countries (the International Family Planning Association's 1971 manual *Family Planning* was banned until a decision of the Supreme Court in 1976 ruled that it was neither indecent nor obscene, the first challenge brought to the legislation in fifty years).[43] Senior churchmen regularly brought informal pressure on leading politicians to follow their opinions on controversial issues including legislation.[44]

There was no dictator in Ireland whose convenient death would bring a stark realization of how ineffective the Church had become in meeting the needs of its members. Instead, there was a slowly gathering storm formed in the 1970s and 1980s as public pressure for reform met condescension and dismissal from the Church, leading to the gradual distillation of impatience into anger. The anger found its outlet with sudden effectiveness at certain triggering events, such as the outrage across the political spectrum in 1990 against a government minister's sneering criticism of Mary Robinson, candidate for the presidency, on the grounds that she neglected her duties as a wife and mother. Having been trailing up to then in the opinion polls she went on to win, becoming the first woman president of Ireland. Other triggering events followed, notably scandals involving secret families of Catholic priests, including bishops; rapes of children by other priests, which had been covered up by Church officials; and the revelation of startling levels of sexual and physical abuse of children and unmarried mothers in Catholic institutions as well as by individual priests.[45] These events, horrific as many of them were, would hardly have had the tidal impact they did on public opinion had the Church not previously enjoyed such a comfortable relationship with the political authorities, one that gave it power over the Irish population and shielded it from criticism. As Smith predicted, trading legitimacy for power meant that the Church in the long run would lose both power and legitimacy. Irish citizens have responded to these developments in a complex range of ways (recently described by anthropologist Hugh Turpin),[46] so there is no single typical response. But the hold of the Church over Irish public and private life has weakened irreversibly.

Smith's theory of the political life cycle of religious movements makes no predictions about how religiosity will rise or decline with overall levels of prosperity. It also leaves open how to interpret situations, like those of many Muslim countries today, where there is political support of a religion (Islam) but vigorous competition among organizations within that religion. So it's not incompatible with the secularization hypothesis: perhaps both have a part to play in explaining events in Spain and Ireland. There may be a tendency for religiosity to decline with higher levels of prosperity, even if that tendency can be offset, and its timing influenced, by the relation between political and religious leaders in any given country. Economic prosperity may also contribute to undermining the political regimes that support some religions—by improving education and communications, and by making it easier for citizens to travel to other countries. But changes in religiosity over years or even decades can be triggered by events that have nothing to do with changing prosperity, even if economic growth is occurring at the same time.

The case of Poland illustrates these points well. At the beginning of the 1990s, as in Ireland, the Catholic Church in Poland enjoyed extremely high levels of popular support. In diametrical opposition to Ireland, it had achieved such popularity precisely because it was repressed by the Communist state. It had served as a beacon for citizens suffering under the repression of the state—helped, of course, by the election of the Polish Pope John Paul II in 1978. So once that state collapsed, the Church's legitimacy was enhanced. The World Values Survey reports that 56 percent of the population at that point reported religion as very important or rather important in their lives, a number that rose to 82 percent by the late 1990s and was still nearly 80 percent at the end of the 2010s. At the same time, Poland was enjoying historically unprecedented economic growth. In 1984, when Ireland overtook Spain's GDP per capita, Poland had little over half that level, but by 1998 it reached the point where those two countries had been in 1984. By 2017 Poland's GDP per person had reached where Spain's had been as recently as 2004—and Spain itself was growing fast. But while Spain's religiosity was collapsing—by the 2005–9 wave of the WVS survey, religion was very important or rather important for less than 40 percent of Spaniards—Poland's was holding firm. The secularization hypothesis has nothing to say about this.

As Smith predicted, the Catholic Church's enviable degree of legitimacy nevertheless attracted political emulation. Much more recently, the Church has become increasingly implicated in the political actions of the Law and Justice Party, which has enjoyed both the presidency of the country and a parliamentary majority since 2015. There is a growing mutual dependency, in which political leaders claim the support of the Church for their actions, and in return support political measures demanded by the Church's leaders. This has resulted in developments such as the complete outlawing of abortion (since January 2021), except where the pregnancy results from rape or incest, or its continuation poses a threat to the mother's life or health. It would be a mistake to see the Law and Justice Party's popularity as deriving only or even mainly from Church support (it has also adopted shrewd redistributive measures such as the "500 plus" child subsidy program).[47] But Smith's theory gives us a clear prediction for the future of the popularity of the Church. Resorting to political dealmaking rather than persuasion to achieve its aims will sooner or later cost it dear.

Is there a way in which we can reconcile these developments in Poland, Ireland, Spain, and the United States with the fact that, in most countries, religiosity does not seem to be changing much over time, despite big differences between countries? There is—but it requires us to move beyond Adam Smith's political life cycle theory. Smith proposed that when a religious movement is co-opted by political leaders, its religious leaders lose the incentive to make their teachings attractive. The examples of Ireland and Spain suggest a different explanation. Political co-option of a movement does not diminish the general attractiveness of religious teachings. Instead, it taints the movement as partisan (while also making it hard for rival movements to operate). The movement can thereafter appeal at best to a subset of members of society—namely, those who are disposed to support the political regime. While the regime maintains broad support the movement may do so too. But when events discredit either the regime (as in Spain) or the movement directly (as in Ireland), religiosity may decline among the public rather than be transferred to the movement's rivals. A country like Poland saw a large increase in religiosity as its authoritarian regime crumbled, because the Church had courageously defended a broad cross-section of society. It may later see a corresponding decline as the Church abandons neutrality to lend its support to the successor regime.

This perspective underlines the flexibility of religious platforms, which allows them to adapt their appeal as their members' needs evolve over time. In a society where religion is perceived as politically neutral (as it was for most of US history from the founding of the Republic until the late twentieth century), religious movements can hope to appeal to a majority of the population. Secularization is no threat to them (though it obliges them to adapt). But where religion comes to be perceived as politically partisan, the best it can hope is to appeal to a majority of partisan voters. It's probably too early to tell whether this is the explanation for the reported decline in religiosity in the United States in the twenty-first century—a question we'll return to in later chapters. But if politicians in the United States succeed in co-opting religious movements so that religion itself is widely seen as partisan, we can confidently expect American religiosity to continue its decline. It will not stabilize until it reaches a level more like that of Western European countries such as France, Germany, or the United Kingdom. In those countries, the long-standing association of the Christian Churches with political conservatism gradually reduced the natural catchment area of religious movements during much of the twentieth century.

The Corporate Transformation of Religion

As both the census and the survey data suggest, the big story of religion in the last century is not one of ideological struggle between Christianity and Islam, with Islam winning. It's a story of growing *corporatization*, with local and folk religions everywhere being gradually but inexorably absorbed into a culture dominated by churches and mosques affiliated with two of the world's main religious brands. Hinduism and Buddhism, the two other main brands, have been much slower to respond, but they are starting to change, and the growing religious assertiveness of India's ruling Bharatiya Janata Party is just a foretaste of much bigger things to come.

   On this interpretation, the changes in the shares of major religions have something important in common with the displacement by Walmart and Target of local grocery stores across the United States (or Tesco, Carrefour, and Lidl across the United Kingdom and Europe). You may regret that or welcome it, but it has so far proved unstoppable. To be sure, there's a fair bit more uniformity among supermarkets than among religious denominations across countries. And we should be careful before rushing to conclusions from data on affiliation. We don't know exactly what is going on underneath these responses that people give to census enumerators; we'll dig deeper in later chapters. Researchers who look in detail at the process of recording religion in censuses, like anthropologists Sondra Hausner and David Gellner, emphasize that all kinds of pressures to record the population under certain (often politically salient) headings can distort the reality of people's actual religious behavior.[48] And as philosopher Rachel McCleary has documented for Guatemala,[49] the neat classifications of census data often fail to capture the sheer variety of religious movements in many societies.

It seems likely that people in many religious traditions maintain multiple loyalties. Attendance at churches, mosques, and temples in cities and towns can co-exist with observance of local cults and festivals when people return to their families in rural areas, or when dates believed to be auspicious are celebrated in their neighborhoods. That's no different in principle from people who have changed their shopping habits to buy most of what they need at Walmart while still buying occasional groceries from the corner store. It may represent a massive change in people's behavior, even if it doesn't involve them completely abandoning their former habits. But without more detailed evidence on that behavior, we can't say much from statistical evidence alone about whether and how folk religion continues to survive.

Still, even with these caveats, a very clear message does come out of this analysis of census and survey data over time. Historically, religions have competed in three main ways: war and conquest, demographic rivalry, and persuasion (in the marketplace, we might say). Of these, war and conquest were the most important vehicle of religious competition through most of history until the nineteenth century.[50] Most people belonged to whatever religion their political leaders told them to belong to, whether those leaders had adopted the faith of their parents or had converted to a new one.[51] But by the twentieth century, demographic competition had taken over from war and conquest as the most important form of religious competition. People have children, and they tend to transmit their religious affiliation to them. For the first time in human history, as far as religious rivalry was concerned, the twentieth century had made the penis mightier than the sword—and the womb mightier than either of them.

Yet demographic competition will fade in turn as the world's female children gradually have fewer of their own. It's competition through persuasion that will be the dominant feature of the coming century. Competing through persuasion is something that both Christianity and Islam have proved very good at doing.

On a world scale—whatever populists may say—Christianity is not struggling; it is in more vigorous shape than ever. The marketplace is where most of the religious action is going to take place in the coming century. As in other marketplaces, the outcomes will be shaped not just by the choices of ordinary citizens but also by the forces of technology. In particular, there may be large returns to operating at scale, for those who can work out how to exploit them. That is why corporate religion is here to stay—and why we should expect it to consolidate its dominance. We'll explore in detail what corporate religion means in part II of this book.

Many writers have noted that the transformation underway in world religion has the potential to be invigorating even for those religious movements that it appears to threaten. American theologian Harvey Cox, for example, noted in 2011 that "today, Christianity is living through a reformation that will prove to be even more basic and more sweeping than the one that shook Europe during the sixteenth century. That earlier reformation . . . was confined to one small corner of the globe. . . . The current reformation, however, is an earth-circling one. [It] is shaking foundations more dramatically than its sixteenth-century predecessor, and its results will be more far-reaching and radical."[52] The transformation is as much about organizations, incentives, and business models as it is about doctrine—though doctrine itself responds to the incentives in a sophisticated two-way interaction.

If this corporate transformation does indeed represent a response of the world's religions to the pressures of the marketplace—pressures that have intensified through migration, urbanization, and rapid improvements in communication technologies—it's time to ask what the world's religious believers are looking for in pursuit of their devotion. What is this demand that religions are seeking to supply? This will be the subject of part II, beginning with chapter 3.

How Do Religions
Gain Their Power?

Part II of this book looks at how the world's religious organizations recruit, keep, and motivate their members. It begins in chapter 3 by asking what people seek that religious organizations can provide. In the language of economists, this amounts to understanding the "demand side" of religion. The variety of different potential needs is vast: many people have little or no need for religion, but the demands of those who do range from ordinary material needs such as education, health, or financial services to more directly spiritual needs such as participation in prayers and rituals, to the sharing of narratives about the origin and purpose of our lives. Providing for this variety is at the heart of religious communities: what religious individuals seek is not the private enjoyment of this or that good or service, but rather participation in an activity that makes sense only as part of a community.

Chapter 4 therefore tackles the "supply side" of religion, introducing the notion of religious communities as platforms. Platforms are organizations that facilitate relationships between the communities' different members. It explains how platforms work, and how religious platforms differ from their secular counterparts. Among other things, individuals use religious communities to network, to find social, business, and romantic partners—but that doesn't mean these communities function just like secular social or professional or dating networks. On the contrary, it's central to the way they function that their value as networks consists in bringing together individuals who share a spiritual vision.

Chapters 5 through 7 therefore look at three main components of that spiritual vision—namely, ritual, belief (or doctrine), and narrative. In each case I not only review the scientific evidence about what individuals want in each of these dimensions, I also ask how much these wants have been shaped by the effect of natural selection on our psychology. Chapter 8 takes a more holistic approach to the question how our religious needs are compatible with natural selection. It looks at what we know, or can reasonably infer, about how religious behavior and religious institutions evolved throughout prehistory.

Finally in part II, chapter 9 draws the threads together by asking what kinds of platforms can flourish in the religious ecosystem. It draws on the large literature on the business models of different secular firms to ask how a religious movement's mission, structure, strategies, and message are shaped by its environment and by the vision of its leaders. This helps to understand why religious movements take the variety of forms they do, and how this has helped religion to remain such a dynamic and successful presence in the world in the twenty-first century.

CHAPTER 3

The Demand for Religion

It is frequently at the edges of things that we learn most about the middle: ice and steam can reveal more about the nature of water than water alone ever could.

—Walter Murch, *In the Blink of an Eye*

When I lived for several months in two villages while doing research in rural South India as a graduate student in the 1980s, I was intrigued and delighted by the intricate geometric diagrams laid out early every morning in slender white lines of rice flour in front of their houses by the senior woman in each household. Called *kolangal* (sing. *kolam*) in Tamil, these diagrams could be stunningly elaborate on feast days. But even on ordinary days, even the poorest and the most harried working women would pause for a few moments to trace out a simple kolam in the dust. I once said to the woman in whose house I was staying: "I've read that anthropologists say you all draw these kolangal as a homage to the goddess Lakshmi, in the hope she will bring you prosperity. Can you tell me a bit more about it?" She looked at me with a faint half-smile on her lips and replied, "Oh, they told you that, did they? Well, I do it because I think they look beautiful."

For many years I interpreted this story as a rebuke to those of us who habitually overthink the behavior of others and underestimate the contribution of sheer serendipity to the choices that shape our daily lives. Still, as a researcher you don't get very far on hymns to serendipity, and

A simple everyday *kolam* (geometric design in rice flour) in front of a house in Tamil Nadu, India. Credit: Andrea Moed, Wikimedia Commons.

A more elaborate *kolam* drawn for the Pongal harvest festival, Tamil Nadu, India. Credit: Chenthil, Wikimedia Commons.

in any case some of the most earth-changing social transformations arise from the aggregation of many billions of human decisions, each one of which seems entirely mysterious, like the decisions to have fewer children that collectively make up what is known as the demographic transition. So I now interpret the story of the kolangal somewhat differently, as a reminder that the boundary between aesthetic, ethical, and spiritual decisions is at best wafer-thin, and sometimes impossible even to define. Thinking back to Grace, whom we met in the introduction, who is to say to what extent her relationship to her church is a matter of private benefit, of ethical obligation, or of aesthetic completion, the sense that it gives her life a proper and a necessary shape? Still, if we want to understand the world-changing transformation that is going on in religion today, this is territory on which we must tread, however carefully. Working out how religious movements can command the loyalty, and the financial contributions, of so many of the world's people requires us to see what these movements can do to make their members feel very special.

The Autonomy of the Vulnerable

Feeling special also makes you vulnerable. Abuse of the vulnerable in the world's churches, mosques, temples, and synagogues can take many forms, from physical and sexual abuse through fraud and extortion of unpaid labor to steering people away from sensible medical advice in the direction of quackery. But most pastors are not abusers—far from it. And we cannot understand why abusers can do what they do without understanding what gives all religious leaders their hold over the vulnerable in the first place. The main reason why poor people give money to religious leaders is that the leaders, and the communities they lead, have found ways to make their donors feel special.

Feeling special may even be enhanced by an awareness of your own vulnerability. Many Pentecostal churches regularly pause in the middle of their other activities to hold a ceremony known as the "healing ministry." Members are exhorted to pray for the sick among them, and specifically to imagine anything in their own bodies and minds that may be keeping them from full health. They can visualize tumors, or think about their diabetes, or focus on their feelings of anxiety. By praying with others, they are told, they can ask God to cure them. They will then be told of cases in their own community that have been cured after just such episodes of prayer (in a large church, the workings of chance will usually supply some witnesses who will happily corroborate these claims from their own experience).

When I asked the general secretary of the Ghanaian Council of Churches what he thought about the ethics of telling people that prayer alone might cure diabetes or cancer, he looked a bit uncomfortable, but then said, "You're right that praying will not necessarily lead to a cure. But you must remember that most such people could not afford any other treatment. And if prayer gives them hope, where is the harm in that?" There's no evidence the healing ministry does any better than a placebo in curing disease—indeed, it *is* a placebo, literally since it involves no medical intervention, and for some kinds of condition placebos have an impressive track record. But it's a very good way of making its participants feel special.

I've expressed these points in terms of what church members like Grace may be thinking, but of course I could not possibly presume to speak in her name. So what's the evidence that members of churches and other religious organizations do think like this? There are now quite a few recent studies that ask exactly this question. You might think it's surprising that there aren't more. After all, if religions provide services much as businesses do, why haven't economists and marketing experts studied them in the same exhaustive detail with which they've studied the reasons why people buy breakfast cereal, television subscriptions, life insurance, beer, cars, washing machines, or gardening tools?

Part of the answer seems to be that almost all economists have *not* thought of religions as businesses—or not until recently. Though Adam Smith was convinced that ordinary members of religious organizations put as much thought and care into making their religious choices as they did into making the other choices in their lives, his view was not widely shared during the two centuries that followed the publication of *The Wealth of Nations* in 1776. Economists mostly thought that religion lay outside the subject matter of economics—there's virtually no reference to it in Alfred Marshall's *Principles of Economics*, published in 1890, nor in Paul Samuelson's *Economics*, published in 1948. Some were openly dismissive of the idea that religious members might be exercising reflective choice: Karl Marx's famous dictum that religion is "the opium of the people," though open to multiple interpretations, has often been cited to disparage the rationality of religious belief.[1] It's true that scholars writing in the traditions of anthropology, history, and sociology, such as Frazer, Weber, Tawney, and Durkheim, were fascinated by the interaction of economics with religious life. But they mostly thought of religious cultures as an emergent property of individual actions, and were less interested in the ways in which they might reflect conscious choice.

That's particularly surprising, given how much historical evidence has accumulated to show that ordinary people *did* think of religion as something that brought them worldly benefits like those they might find in other places.[2] Historian Jeffrey Knapp has written of the way in which, in the England of the late sixteenth century,

> To many a godly Elizabethan, the new public theaters and the newly purified church were enemies in a war that the theaters appeared to be winning. Such pious antagonism toward the English stage marked a revolutionary change from the time of Miracle and Morality plays, when the Catholic church had welcomed the services of players; and it even marked a change from earlier days in the Reformation, when Protestant clergymen had embraced the English stage so wholeheartedly as to appear its "driving force."[3]

What made the theaters a threat to the church was not (or not mainly) "the opportunities for idleness, debauchery, and sedition that such mass audiences generated," nor even any false doctrines, or criticisms of official doctrines, that might be insinuated into the text of plays they performed. It was simply that going to the theater was more fun than going to church. As Knapp puts it:

> the most oft-cited evidence in Elizabethan England that the players had set out to undermine the church was the sheer popularity of the

players in comparison to the church. "Woe is me!" one scandalized observer among many exclaims, "The play houses are pestered, when churches are naked; at the one it is not possible to get a place, at the other void seats are plenty.[4]

So it was clear as early as 1587, when this comment was penned, that churches had to compete not only against other churches but also against notionally secular purveyors of entertainment. This was a subversive idea, for few churchmen would have been comfortable thinking of themselves as entertainers (though some movements, like the Jesuit order, explored enthusiastically the potential of the theater for communicating spiritual messages as well as drawing in the crowds).[5] Historians have cited many similar examples of competition between religious and secular entertainment: Michael Burleigh reports that in Italy in the 1920s, "both the Church and Balilla [Italian Fascist youth organization] aggressively competed for new members, with the Church often winning because of the superiority of its recreational facilities."[6] Yet it was an idea that took a long time to influence the way economists thought about religion—with the singular exception, as we've seen, of Adam Smith.

Only in the last few decades have researchers started to look in detail at how religious believers choose among the alternatives available to them, using the same research tools with which they analyze other choices people make in their lives. As in Walter Murch's remark about film editing I quoted above, these researchers have all used the edges of religious movements—the points where they compete with various rivals—to understand their otherwise mysterious middle. From the 1960s onward, sociologists including Peter Berger, Andrew Greeley, William Bainbridge, Roger Finke, and Rodney Stark, joined by economists such as Corry Azzi, Ronald Ehrenberg, Laurence Iannacone, and Eli Berman, began to analyze religious decisions using the approaches and insights of economics.[7] They emphasized that religious organizations are in a continual state of competition for members, for revenues, and for other resources such as members' time and energy. Even when this competition does not take place between religions, it takes place *within* religions—between churches, between mosques, between temples, between synagogues. It is competition not only to attract members but also to induce existing members to increase their investments of time, energy, and money. To be sure, Adam Smith observed that religious organizations that face no competition to attract away their members may also become lethargic about trying to inspire their existing members (in the words of economist John Hicks, "the best of all monopoly profits is a quiet life").[8] They may also choose to take advantage of their monopoly position to exercise coercive power over their members.

But even under severe coercion, members face alternative options. One of them is active engagement versus "inner emigration," a term coined in Germany after 1933 to describe one of the options for people who were opposed to Nazism but chose not to leave the country, and subsequently used for the actions of many opponents of Soviet communism.[9] We can learn a lot from the choices of religious members, however competitive or otherwise is the religious landscape in which they find themselves. This doesn't imply that people make their religious decisions in the same way as they decide whether to buy groceries or washing machines. One way to describe it is that they have "agency," meaning that they are reflective and balance up costs and benefits of alternative actions. They have no less agency in the religious side of their lives than in the rest. It also implies that religious leaders are strategic—they make decisions about how to run their organizations with a coherent long-term vision of how their members and potential members will respond.[10]

It's important to understand what this view of religious agency does and doesn't imply. It certainly doesn't rule out a place for passion, commitment, and even some degree of blind faith within the religious experience. One Ghanaian man with whom I discussed the phenomenon of giving to the church complained bitterly to me that his wife and her girlfriends "go crazy during the collection—if the sermon has been inspiring, they just open up their purses and empty them completely. However much money they have there, they just give it all to the church! They're not even thinking about the cost." I then asked him if he thought his wife, knowing what would happen during the collection, might be careful about how much money she put into her purse before leaving for church. "Oh yes, I certainly hope she is!" he replied. It's quite possible to know you're going to be unable to take prudent decisions when you're under the influence of passionate enthusiasm, but also to take prudent steps to limit the costs this susceptibility imposes on you. Most people behave similarly when they go shopping for Christmas presents. They're also quite capable of realizing that if they get drunk, or take drugs, they will do things they may later regret—and then take these risks into account in deciding how much alcohol or drugs to consume. Not everyone avoids regret—but most people know enough about it to avoid being surprised.

This doesn't mean, either, that everyone takes only those risks that a prudent counsellor who has their interests at heart would recommend. We know that in many areas of life, such as saving for retirement or looking after their health, people commonly take decisions that make little sense. An intriguing experiment in Malawi gave subjects tests in their homes for HIV and other sexually transmitted diseases. They were then told they might receive a small cash payment if they came to collect their results in a nearby clinic, where they would also receive counselling and treatment if necessary. The amount of the cash payment was determined by drawing a random token out of a bag, whose value might be zero or a one of a range of amounts up to two dollars (this last being equal to two days' wages at the time of the experiment). Of those who drew a zero, only one-third of subjects came to collect their results. But it was enough to offer a payment of ten or twenty cents (about the cost of a sandwich) for the take-up rate to jump to around three-quarters of all subjects.[11] You can tell a story that makes sense of people not wanting the test despite the enormous medical benefits (fear of the social consequences if they test positive, for example). But it's extremely hard to tell a convincing story that also explains why an inducement as small as the value of a sandwich is enough to make people's misgivings disappear. So when we say that we should consider people's religious decisions to be as lucid as the decisions they take in the rest of their lives, we're not setting an impossibly high bar. Many economic decisions are hard to justify as fully prudent or rational (Americans and Europeans don't do any better on average by this yardstick than Malawians do). But it does change our perspective. It makes a difference whether we think Grace knows what she's doing when she gives some 12 percent of her very meager earnings to her church.

There are good reasons to think religious decision-making feels subjectively different from, say, buying clothes or groceries or a washing machine. Religious decisions typically respond differently to prices. They're more like deciding whether to take up a job offer, or invest in a career, than making a short-term choice of food or clothing or household appliances. It's partly because they involve making a commitment, or a potential commitment, over the medium or long term. It's also partly because the choice affirms something about your identity to an extent that choices of food, clothing, or household appliances rarely do.

Imagine that you're faced with a choice between two job offers—one, with a large commercial firm, includes a high salary and little opportunity to interact with other people except when you're trying aggressively to sell them something. What you're selling may be bringing some happiness into these people's lives, but you can't be sure of that, and in any case you'll never see it directly. The second job offer, with a medium-sized charity, includes a much lower salary but the opportunity to interact with some of the people the charity is helping, so you can see at first hand some of the benefits you're making possible. Maybe you don't know which of these two offers would tempt you the most—the details matter, after all—but you might feel that the lower salary in the second job isn't just a disadvantage. In some ways you might even like the idea—that you're voluntarily giving up some of what you could be earning elsewhere as a symbol of your commitment to helping others. It's both a symbol and a signal, to yourself and others, of the kind of person you want to be. You might even feel better, in a charity job, about a low salary than a high one. Not all economic decisions are like choosing between brands of breakfast cereal.

The fact that some options involve a commitment to identity might seem to preclude reflective economic reasoning—after all, our identity is usually something we would not give up for "mere" economic inducements. But this underestimates the way that signaling our identity is something we can choose to do quite strategically. Many orthodox religious movements prescribe styles of dress and patterns of behavior that mark out believers from outsiders, and this may be a conscious choice both by the community's leaders and by its members: it makes it harder for believers to mix freely in the wider community. An exclusive view of identity has often been emphasized by political movements—for example, in South Asia, where an assertive Hinduism has been ascendant in both India and Nepal in recent years, in contrast with earlier times when political leaders were often happy to accept that Hindus could adopt practices of Buddhist traditions, as anthropologist David Gellner has shown.[12] But as economist Jean-Paul Carvalho has persuasively argued, we shouldn't underestimate how some identity markers can paradoxically help believers integrate in certain dimensions of the wider community—the labor market, for example.[13] Muslim women in many countries have taken to wearing the veil in greater numbers in recent years, a fact that is sometimes interpreted as evidence of increasing repression of women, with the implication being that these women would not wear the veil if they could avoid it, or were not brainwashed into doing so. This ignores the fact that in many countries it is educated Muslim women who are more likely to be veiled than less-educated ones, as recent research by economist Naila Shofia has shown, using ingenious analysis of more than a quarter of a million photographs of students in Indonesian high-school photographs over more than two decades.[14] Carvalho argues that many educated women use the veil as a strategic mechanism to help them take an active role in the labor markets—they can go to work while assuaging the anxiety of their families about the dangers of mixing with non-Muslims, since the veil signals their commitment to Islam. They may not be choosing between Islam and a rival religion, but they are taking conscious choices involving trade-offs in which identity is one of the important dimensions at stake.

Religious Choice and Agency

With these considerations in mind, let's look at what economic studies have shown about people's decisions on whether to undertake various kinds of religious commitment. The most comprehensive studies have taken place where religious organizations provide benefits that are also available from secular competitors. Some of these contexts have existed for a long time. Buddhist, Christian, Hindu, Jewish, and Muslim organizations have provided education and health services (sometimes at an explicit price and sometimes free) for hundreds and even thousands of years. Modern studies have shown that parents often choose religious schooling for their children not because they are indoctrinated to do so, and not just because it will help to transmit religious belief to their children, but also because they judge the religious alternatives as better, by objective standards. Economist Sriya Iyer has shown that parents in India who send their children to Islamic schools—madrassas—are often motivated to do so because their teachers have a better attendance record than teachers in state schools.[15] She has shown that many Hindu, Muslim, and Christian organizations in India provide not just education but food distribution, health care, childcare, employment, and a wide range of other services including blood drives, old-age homes, distribution of books and saris, and microfinance. The numbers that do so have been increasing over time, and many such organizations are precisely aware of who else in their neighborhood has been doing so as well—conscious of the competition, in other words.[16]

What about other kinds of secular competition? A careful study in the United States by the economists Jonathan Gruber and Daniel Hungerman showed that, in states that relaxed laws restricting retail activity on Sundays, church attendance and donations declined.[17] This suggests that church attendance and secular shopping are substituting for each other in some way, though it doesn't tell us exactly how. It's likely that, since both activities take time, anything that makes it easier to spend time shopping on Sundays raises the time cost of church attendance. Does this mean that church attendance provides benefits that are in any way like the benefits of secular shopping? Not necessarily. To answer that question, we need to look at a different kind of evidence, and the field of insurance provides plenty.

Religion and secular institutions compete on the same turf here too. People everywhere are vulnerable to unforeseen shocks—everything from sickness to earthquakes and flooding, from unemployment to burglary, from lightning strikes to warfare. Their ability to survive these shocks depends not just on their personal resilience but also on the reactions of others who support them in their loss. Many communities rely on implicit understandings that when some of their members are in difficulty others will help them. Modern institutions formalize these understandings in contracts to provide insurance. In exchange for a payment in advance, you can call on a payment to cover the cost of house repair, hospitalization, or hotel expenses if you're forced to leave your home. Some of these institutions are firms, operating in markets and selling insurance. Others are governments, offering an explicit promise to pay benefits (such as unemployment, sickness, or disability benefits) to those who have suffered shocks. Others again are charities, cooperatives, or other organizations that are neither completely private nor completely public.

Several studies have shown that religious organizations offer implicit insurance in a way that is a partial substitute for the explicit contracts proposed by these other, secular institutions. We must be careful how to interpret this evidence, though. Economist Daniel Chen, for example, showed that after the financial crisis of 1998 in Indonesia, people increased the intensity of their participation in local mosques, and those who had been particularly severely affected increased their participation most.[18] Philipp Ager and Antonio Ciccone have shown that religious participation was highest in American communities that were most exposed to agricultural risk through facing the most unpredictable rainfall.[19] Jeanet Bentzen has shown, using evidence from across the world, that experiencing an earthquake makes people more likely to pray and to tell survey enumerators that they believe in God. In historical research with Eric Force, she has shown that "the major religions of the modern world emerged in a remarkably tight band along seismically active plate-tectonic boundaries."[20] In separate work she also showed that Google searches for prayer rose by 30 percent in the early months of the Covid-19 pandemic, and remained 10 percent higher thereafter.[21] Rajeev Dehejia, Thomas Deleire, and Erzo Luttmer showed that members of religious organizations suffered smaller losses after natural disasters than people who were not members—presumably because they were being supported by those organizations.[22] Finally, when other social institutions provide a more reliable safety net for those who suffer shocks, the role of religious organizations tends to decline. Jonathan Gruber and Daniel Hungerman showed that the expansion of social spending in America in the 1930s after the launch of the New Deal led to a substantial decline in church charitable spending.[23] Kenneth Scheve and David Stasavage have shown a relationship through preferences in the opposite direction: more-religious individuals have lower preferences for social insurance offered by the state.[24]

These studies indicate that people are turning to religion after suffering losses, that those who have previously turned to religion are likely to suffer smaller losses, and that the availability of other sources of insurance reduces the demand for religion. But do they show that people are consciously aware of religion as a form of insurance? That's not so clear—maybe suffering losses just makes people more emotionally open to religion without their thinking of this in terms of costs and benefits; indeed, the two studies by Jeanet Bentzen just cited appear to suggest this.[25] How can we compare otherwise similar people who have different levels of vulnerability to losses, to see whether they express different levels of religious demand? One way to find out is through doing experiments.

That's what I and my colleagues (economists Emmanuelle Auriol, Julie Lassébie, Amma Panin, and Eva Raiber) decided to do in Ghana. We worked with a group of parishioners at various churches in the Assemblies of God network in Accra, offering them money, which they could choose (anonymously) to keep, or to donate to various charitable beneficiaries including their own churches. Most of the participants in our experiment were very generous, giving between a third and a half of the money we offered them to their church or another charity. We had previously decided to enroll a random subset of these participants in a private insurance program. This program provides people who face a death in the family with a substantial payout to cover the cost of funeral expenses, which is one of the biggest economic shocks that urban Ghanaians commonly face. The people we enrolled gave about 10 percent less to their church than did comparable people whom we did not enroll. This strongly suggests that the church, for them, is seen partly as a source of protection from life's shocks. When they have alternative protection available, they have slightly less need of the church. Incidentally, they believe in the protection of the church not necessarily because they expect it to support its members financially (though the evidence is strong that it often does). They also think that giving to the church will be seen as meritorious in the eyes of God. Our participants clearly believe that God is more likely to look after members who are meritorious than those who are not (and therefore that being less exposed to shocks slightly eases the pressure on them to be meritorious).[26] Our interpretation is supported by a more recent study by other researchers in Brazil. They find that church members are more likely to invest resources in the community if they share beliefs in the afterlife, and not merely in the willingness of the community to support them in distress.[27]

Studies like these are tiny in number compared to the innumerable investigations by firms and marketing researchers of the more mundane economic decisions of consumers. Yet religious leaders don't need to read marketing studies to be aware that members choose their religious commitments carefully. The strategies of those religious leaders reflect this awareness. Evangelical leader Jerry Falwell, for example, is quoted as saying in the 1990s:

> Business is usually on the cutting edge of innovation and change because of its quest for finances. . . . Therefore the church would be wise to look at business for a prediction of future innovation. The greatest innovation in the last twenty years is the development of the giant shopping centers. Here is the synergetic principle of placing at least two or more services at one location to attract the customers. A combination of services of two large companies with small supporting stores has been the secret of the success of shopping centers.[28]

Not all religious leaders would be as comfortable as Falwell with the idea of talking of religious members as though they were "customers." Language aside, what's important in Falwell's statement is the awareness that religious organizations need healthy finances to operate, and that strategies that have proved successful in restoring the finances of secular businesses might also be applicable to religious organizations.

Falwell's perspective also highlights something that is central to many people's experience of modern religion, and that would have surprised the citizens of classical Greece or Rome. An evangelical church that implements the Falwell formula offers its members a total, unitary experience, a one-stop shop in both literal and metaphorical senses. The same organization—the building plus its team of pastors—offers members an array of spiritual and secular services: ritual, choral music, childcare, advice on physical and mental health, community activities, spectacle, sports, companionship, an interpretation of events in the world and in individual lives, ecstatic experiences, accompanied Bible study, advice on family issues, help with finding employment. Anyone who wonders about how all of this fits together is welcome to take their concerns to any of the pastors. Compare this with the world of Roman religion as described by historian Andrew Wilson:

> Religion pervaded ancient life: people consulted oracles, soothsayers, and made sacrifices before embarking on undertakings both large and small, whether setting out for war or simply laying a mosaic floor. Temples and shrines abounded in ancient cities and rural sanctuaries; a polytheistic religious landscape populated all niches of the world with deities major and minor. Even the sewers at Rome had their own goddess, Venus Cloacina. No aspect of ancient life was untouched by the divine.[29]

Even though religion was present throughout daily life in ancient Rome (to a degree that many evangelical leaders like Jerry Falwell would surely envy), no single part of the religious ecosystem could claim to offer the whole package. Different components had different specialties. Wilson continues:

> Roman religion was transactional, as exemplified by the idea *do ut des*, "I give so that you may give". You sacrificed to a god and promised to dedicate an altar if the god ensured that some matter turned out favourably for you—a harvest; a business venture; success in love; etc. The innumerable votive altars set up across the Roman world testify to this, the practice being so common that the key formula *votum solvit libens merito* ("discharged his vow willingly to [the god who] deserved it") was often simply abbreviated to *VSLM*."[30]

The transactional spirit of religion in the ancient world did not, of course, mean that all petitioners got what they wanted. There is a much-commented-on scene in the *Iliad* in which Hecuba and the aged women of Troy go to the temple of Athena to plead with her to save their city. The "fair-cheeked Theano, daughter of Cisseus, the wife of Antenor, tamer of horses; [whom] the Trojans made priestess of Athene," pleaded with the goddess on their behalf. But Athena simply refused, without explanation.[31] Prayer and sacrifice in Greece and Rome were sometimes like that, unanswerably so.

The same transactional panorama could be seen in towns and cities in the Hellenic world, until Christianity became the official religion of the Roman Empire under Constantine in the early fourth century CE. There was an energetic plurality of entrepreneurs selling services of all kinds, from the blessing of harvests or commercial undertakings to the manumission (freeing) of slaves, from the organization of processions and festivals to— the last recourse of the powerless—the sale of curse tablets.[32]

These entrepreneurs were consulted by private individuals, and by the civic authorities. Historian Catherine Morgan writes that oracles were often used by the authorities "to achieve a consensus of opinion over difficult, often unprecedented, and potentially divisive decisions, [dealing] with exceptional problems outside the collective wisdom of the community elite." Even then, they were specific to the problem in hand: "oracles do not bestow overall divine authority upon particular rulers, nor do they predict the future."[33] Some temples claimed to offer a broad range of services, but none came close to offering the unified vision of individual life and its place in the cosmos that would be characteristic of the great world religions—Judaism, Zoroastrianism, Hinduism, Buddhism, Taoism, Confucianism, Christianity, Islam. If you wanted a solution to a particular problem, ancient Greek and Roman religion offered you a heady menu of possibilities; if you wanted help understanding the meaning of life, you had to turn to one of the philosophers. Philosophers could be priests too (like Plutarch) or could seek inspiration from religious oracles (as the Neoplatonist school did from the Chaldean Oracles). But religion had usually no pretensions to understanding the big picture, and in the absence of a single, all-powerful

God and a promise of individual salvation, rather than a pantheon of gods who might or might not respond to one's prayers, there was no reason to expect it to.

Historian Claire Hall has described how the early Christian theologian Origen of Alexandria, who lived in the early third century CE, developed a novel notion of prophecy as encompassing no less than "knowledge through reason of the cosmos and of the functioning of the elements and of time," knowledge inherent in the scriptures. This was a massively ambitious conception, involving a unification of the spheres of philosophy and religion, that was quite alien to the classical world's abundance of astrology, oracles, and soothsaying.[34] By the early fifth century, though, the idea that Christianity embodied a unification of these different viewpoints was sufficiently well anchored that Augustine of Hippo could write: "Indeed we laugh when we see them [the pagan gods] distributed by the fancies of human opinions to particular works, like contractors for tiny portions of the public revenue, or like workmen in the street of the silversmiths, where one vessel, so that it may go out perfect, passes through many craftsmen, when it might have been finished by one perfect craftsman."[35]

Judaism had already developed the crucial innovations some centuries earlier, as historian Diarmaid MacCulloch describes when writing of Judea under the Hasmonean dynasty in the late second and first centuries BCE:

> Synagogues were remarkable institutions, with little other parallel in the ancient world. They were not temples, because with the exception of a few insignificant rival institutions Jewish sacrifice now took place only in the Jerusalem Temple. . . . [S]ynagogues were the setting for prayer and the reading of sacred scripture, but they also provided a focus for the general activities of the community— especially education . . . not just education for an elite [but] for everyone in the Jewish community. . . . Judaism could make claim to providing a philosophy of life as well as a series of observances and customs for approaching the divine, an unusual feature in ancient religion.[36]

Though a pioneer, Judaism was not unique in this respect. The notion of religious organizations as broader communities than merely sites of ritual acts such as sacrifice, of which some glimmerings can be seen in classical Athens, began to take off in the Hellenistic period, with the formation of many associations dedicated to gods such as Apollo, Poseidon, and Hermes, consisting not just of leisured aristocrats but also of professional and artisanal occupations. This was a period during which long-distance trade was growing in importance, and membership of a religious community was increasingly taken as a signal of trustworthiness.[37]

The Distinctive Character of Religious Choice

Of course, the modern world still has its religious ecosystems, made up of individual entrepreneurs—fortune tellers, healers, sellers of icons or holy water, managers of saintly cults—of varying degrees of personal religiosity, some of them working in tacit collaboration with the leaders of churches, but many of them operating solo. You'll see more such individual entrepreneurs in places like Lourdes in southwest France, in Mecca or Jerusalem, or in the great temple at Madurai in southern India than in, say, Stockholm. But all the different traditions share the idea that religion involves a multitude of activities—whether these are all mediated by a single religious authority or composed by the individual believer from the many opportunities available. And that raises the question whether there's anything we can say about what all these activities have in common. What are the things we seek in religion that are distinct from what we seek in the rest of our modern lives?

At any moment, throughout the world, individuals are facing religious choices that involve balancing important advantages and costs. Consider all these:

- A parishioner deciding how much money to put in the church collection tray
- The imam of a village mosque weighing up how much time to devote to preaching at the expense of looking after his livestock

- An orthodox Jew deciding whether to take advantage of one of the available religious exemptions from service in the Israeli Defense Forces
- A Muslim in China thinking about what she can reveal about herself in a post on WeChat
- A tech entrepreneur in America wondering whether her colleagues will think her weird if she takes two evenings off every week for Bible study
- A young Muslim man calculating the risks of traveling to a war zone to undertake jihad
- A teenager deciding whether to take part in an all-night Easter vigil
- A Chinese civil servant with a PhD in astrophysics offering money and incense at a festival to celebrate the equinox
- A Mormon deciding whether to undertake the two-year service abroad
- A migrant from the Tanzanian countryside to Dar-es-Salaam hesitating between visiting a mosque or entering a church
- A Pakistani mother unsure whether to enroll her son in a madrassa or a government school
- A young Christian the morning after giving himself to Jesus, wondering whether he will ever again feel bliss as transcendent as that of being born again
- A woman in Cape Town fearful of vaccination and wondering whether the Lord will really protect her against Covid-19 as her friends have told her
- A member of the Church of Scientology digesting the shock of being told that he must sever ties with his parents
- A Japanese Buddhist monk preparing himself for a predawn meditation
- A Hindu making an offering to the goddess Lakshmi in the hope of bringing success to a business venture
- A gay Ugandan wondering how to reconcile his sexuality with the disgust it provokes among fellow worshippers at his church
- A Quaker wondering whether the violent state of the world makes the Society of Friends useless, or more needed than ever

- A young Catholic woman asking herself whether it's normal that her confessor has suggested they have dinner together
- A Chinese Protestant wondering whether to attend a house church despite knowing that it is under government surveillance
- A Hindu woman anxious about the consequences of spending time with a Muslim fellow student
- A Frenchwoman deciding whether to wear a veil to her workplace
- A Korean church member signing a covenant to pay her tithes
- A Muslim father wondering whether to go to Friday prayers in a mosque where he is regularly reproached by the imam for his lack of zeal
- A liberal Jewish American hesitating between two profiles on a dating website, one conservative Jewish and the other not Jewish at all

Every one of these is in a deliberation with a religious dimension, yet they are so different from one another that we might well wonder whether there is anything they could possibly have in common.

Diverse as they are, these deliberations share two important characteristics. They are not undertaken alone, in the way that a choice among ordinary consumer products might be performed alone. Each religious person is conscious of a community of fellow believers for whom their deliberation makes sense, and by whom the ensuing choice may be judged. They may also be conscious of someone—of a god, or gods, or a spirit, or an unnameable presence—with whom they are in a kind of dialogue, even if it doesn't exactly resemble a dialogue with a human friend. This dialogue doesn't stop the deliberation from being lucid, doesn't remove the human person's agency. But to understand how this capacity for lucid deliberation about religious matters gives rise to the whole range of religious activities, we need to think about how religious organizations respond to the needs their members articulate.

People's religious needs come from somewhere, of course—they're not just a physiological requirement like the need for food and water. They also vary between individuals to a remarkable extent. A significant minority of the world's population feels no need for the benefits of religion at all, and those who do have widely divergent ideas about which benefits matter most to them. The most obvious places these needs come from are our families, and our other geographical and social communities. So part of the answer to why people have the religious preferences they do is that they inherited these from their families and communities. But this makes the process seem far more passive than it is, as though culture were like bathwater and the human brain were like a sponge. One exciting aspect of the growing field of research in the economics of religion is that it emphasizes the conscious choices of those who transmit religious culture as well as those who receive it. Individuals invest in their own future religious sensibilities when they pray, follow a course of instruction, or decide to undertake spiritual exercises.[38] They invest in the religious sensibility of their children when they talk to them, or decide to send them to one school rather than another.[39] And those children in turn will respond reflectively to the options that the culture makes available to them. Some options will seem more natural and intuitive than others, and some will be given more critical reflection than others, but people don't always copy their parents unthinkingly. Nor do parents always decide unreflectively to pass on their own religious traditions, without thinking about what aspects of those religious traditions matter most to them.

This research on the religious choices people make also highlights just how wide is the range of activities that can come under the umbrella of religion, and therefore how unhelpful it is to think of religiosity as a special type of psychological trait. An influential tradition beginning with the work of the late nineteenth-century German theologian Rudolf Otto identified religiosity as the capacity to perceive and respond to a sense of the "numinous," which Otto characterized as a "mystery" that is at once "terrifying" and "fascinating."[40] This notion, which was taken up enthusiastically by writers such as Carl Jung and C. S. Lewis, has come to dominate thinking about religion in the Christian West. It's one thing to acknowledge that an experience of the numinous may be a powerful and valuable component of religious experience, but quite another to make the ability to experience the numinous a defining characteristic of religiosity. As anthropologist Robin Horton has put it:

> The sentiments of awe and reverence which we tend to regard as very closely associated with religious situations in our own culture are

replaced by some very different sentiments in the religions of other parts of the world such as West Africa. . . . A complex of sentiments and emotions common to all religions everywhere is as much of a chimera as an epistemological category which will contain all religious objects.[41]

Horton points out that William James had insisted long ago (in his pertinently titled *Varieties of Religious Experience*) that:

> There is religious fear, religious love, religious joy and so forth. But religious love is only man's natural emotion of love directed to a religious object; religious fear is only the ordinary fear of commerce, so to speak, the common quaking of the human breast in so far as the notion of divine retribution may arouse it; religious awe is the same organic thrill we feel in a forest at twilight or in a mountain gorge; only this time it comes over us at the thought of our supernatural relations.[42]

So: religious choice is reflective and takes place in a huge variety of settings, and there's not necessarily any single psychological state that accompanies it. I've emphasized the reflective aspect of religious choice because so much study of religion in the past has taken it to be passively absorbed—at least until some individuals rebel, if they ever do. But sometimes it takes vision for religious movements to articulate needs for their members; religious believers may not know what they need until someone else has expressed it for them. Let's return to Grace, the young woman from Accra whom we met in the introduction. One of the best things that could happen to her, given her very precarious economic and social condition, would be to get married to a man she meets in church. I'd even conjecture that finding such a man is an important part of the reasons why Grace goes to church. The church she attends no doubt has its share of scoundrels and sociopaths, but compared to any other way of looking for a husband in Accra, it surely represents the most reliable way of finding someone who will treat her well. Church also represents a good way to induce her future husband to turn up to service sober, in a clean suit, on a Sunday morning, knowing that many eyes will be watching to see whether he is treating his wife well. And when they have children, the church will help to provide a moral and social framework to help her and her husband bring them up.

Yet if I were to ask Grace whether looking for a husband is one of the reasons she goes to church, I am pretty sure she would say no. As a matter of fact, I *have* asked her, but it was part of our anonymous survey, so I do not know her reply. My guess that she would say no reflects the fact that nineteen out of every twenty people we asked about their reasons for choosing their church failed to list this one among the many possible options we suggested to them.

So why do I think finding a husband is an important motive for Grace (and many other people) to attend church? As well as asking people about their reasons for attending their current church, we also asked married participants in our study to tell us where they had met their spouses, and we asked unmarried participants to tell us where they expected to meet a future spouse. Over a quarter (28 percent) of our married participants had met their spouse through church, and a remarkable 60 percent of the unmarried participants expected to meet a future spouse through church. Another telling detail is that of the single men in our sample, of those who expected to meet a future wife in church, over half had paid their tithes that month, while of those who did not expect to meet a future wife in church, only a quarter had done so.[43] Those keen young men may not express it exactly this way, but it certainly looks as though the prospect of meeting a spouse is sharpening their enthusiasm. They probably also think that paying your tithes on time can't harm your marriage prospects.

It's hard to look at answers like these and not admit that Grace may be exercising some shrewd judgment in attending her church and in paying her tithes, even if we may be troubled by the vast disparity in wealth between her and the pastor of her church. This doesn't mean that she's choosing her church as she might choose a washing machine, if ever she could afford one. The important thing to realize is that she's choosing a community, and in doing so she's also expressing an important component of her identity. The economics of choosing communities is something that we've come to understand much better in recent years. This will be the subject of chapter 4.

Choosing Communities

The Platform Model of Religion

For thirty years I have kept safe the gold of foreigners and citizens, always with exemplary honesty.

> —second-century CE epigram on a banker's tombstone from Rhodes,
> which adds that this banker's "exemplary honesty" was due to his
> possession of a "divinely sanctioned sense of justice"

Priests and Mediators

Sometimes, what look like simple bilateral transactions turn out to make more sense when you see them as embedded in the relationships within a community. It's a hot afternoon in early June 2012 in rural Haiti, and I've come to see a Vodou priest. If your exposure to Vodou comes mainly from books or films from the United States or Europe, you might imagine someone in robes and a brightly painted mask, in a darkened room, preparing a sacrifice designed to inflict terror on the participants and discomfort or worse on some absent and unwitting victim. In fact, the priest is dressed in shirt and slacks, and we're standing outside, at the edge of his smallholding, discussing his career plans. "Vodou's been pretty good to me," he says. "It's been a useful sideline when my other activities haven't gone so well, and more and more people seem to value my services since we had the earthquake. But I'm

The Synagogue, print by Rembrandt van Rijn, Metropolitan Museum of Art.
Credit: Metropolitan Museum of Art.

Another form of religious community: worship service at the Word of Life Bible Church, Warri, Delta, Nigeria.
Credit: WLBC Media Team, Wikimedia Commons.

getting on, and I'd like to retire, so I can go back to the Church and die a good Catholic."

The people who come to consult the priest do so for all sorts of reasons. Many adopt as pragmatic an approach to their religious choices as the priest does to his choice of occupation. They juggle a portfolio of religious loyalties that often sees them switching attendance between churches according to which ones best meet their perceived needs. They also often participate in Vodou ceremonies to help them mark important moments in their lives, such as births, marriages, and deaths, or to help them cope with sickness, bereavement, or economic misfortune. This can be a delicate subject. Although Vodou was recognized as a religion by Haiti's President Aristide in 2003, this was not enough to overturn the suspicion with which it had been regarded by both political authorities and the Catholic Church, and the Church still tends to view it with disfavor. Sensitivity also persists about the lurid, patronizing, and often racist depictions of Vodou in foreign media, making people cautious about acknowledging their Vodou sympathies to outsiders. But an old joke, often repeated, has it that Haiti is 85 percent Catholic, 15 percent Protestant, and 100 percent Vodou. Vodou seems particularly appealing to people in times of stress.

A surprisingly important number of consultations, though, are about social problems rather than individual sufferings. Here, in rural Haiti, there are few of the institutions that might help regulate disputes between neighbors in other countries. The police are rarely seen, and even more rarely trusted. Rows could easily escalate into violence, and Vodou can provide a convenient de-escalation technology. If I suspect a neighbor of stealing my goat, rather than going round to beat him up I might consult the priest. He might remind me that Vodou taps into powerful magic that must be used with care, offer me a starter spell that promises to give my neighbor severe indigestion, gradually talk me out of my high dudgeon, and in the following days enquire discreetly of my neighbor whether he might possibly see his way to giving me my goat back. There are clear parallels with the curse tablets we saw in chapter 3, which were common in classical antiquity, and which allow angry sentiments to be vented without threatening the social order. The priest may also be playing a mediation role that's otherwise sorely absent from this fractured society. To the extent that he does, he offers a real community service.[1] Such mediation services are a long-standing feature of religious people and places across the globe: a settlement of *marabouts* (Muslim holy men) "keeps neutral a vital pass in the Moroccan Atlas through which two groups of transhumant shepherds must travel and in which they would otherwise regularly come to blows," just as a temple of Hercules in southern Italy mediated in disputes about the movement of flocks, and "in classical Greece, the sensitive border zone between Megara and Athens [was] sacred to Demeter [and] cultivation was rigorously prohibited."[2]

Talking to the Vodou priest recalled for me the descriptions by sociologist Sudhir Alladi Venkatesh of Maquis Park, a predominantly African American neighborhood on Chicago's South Side. There are long stretches of his vivid, almost novelistic descriptions of the dealing and hustling in Maquis Park that make you think Venkatesh is weaving an urban idyll, a hymn to cooperation in adversity and plucky ingenuity and solidarity and all the qualities that the poor are supposed to have more plentifully than the rich. And then, from time to time, along comes a remark so casual that you might easily overlook it entirely, but that lends the whole account a more somber tone: "a local pastor helps Marlene and other domestic workers find families to work for, but he charges 10 per cent for each successful placement."[3] Pastors are portrayed with a good deal of affection in this study, but they're as rapacious as anyone else, even if they're higher up the food chain and therefore able to afford some generous gestures from time to time. Some of their fellow citizens (like the prostitute who has slept with "most of the preachers in this community") become more cynical in consequence, while others yearn more fervently for a higher power who "has me a home waiting that no man can build."[4] Even if a pastor "just wants his money," to quote another woman, "so he likes to stay in control,"[5] that control can also bring the ability to do some community favors, like negotiating a peaceful compromise between rival gangs, or keeping playgrounds free of drug dealing during the daylight hours. You realize after reading Venkatesh for a while that this ecosystem is neither idyllic nor exemplary. It just exists—and those seeking to navigate it, whether as residents, visitors, or public officials, must do so at their own risk. What makes the difference between predators and prey is often just circumstance, the sheer luck of which side of the risky transaction they find themselves on. Some people see the pastors as predators, others see them as ministering to the victims of a corrupt and fallen society. It takes a perceptive outsider like Venkatesh just to see them as part of the ecosystem, one without which it could not function in the same way. Whether it's a good thing they play this role depends largely on what you take to be a realistic alternative.

Providing a service to an existing community is one thing; creating whole new communities is quite another. Protestant churches in Haiti now attract far more than the 15 percent of the population credited to them by the old joke. By some estimates they may even draw an overall majority—their numbers were given a powerful boost by the trauma of the 2010 earthquake, which left many people grieving, anxious, and afraid for their future.[6] When lawlessness in the country is growing, as it has done in recent years,[7] they also provide an emotional and even a physical refuge. They offer not just individual benefits but an enveloping group experience. In this they are like many other churches and other religious organizations all over the world, but it's something the new Protestant churches have shown themselves particularly skilled at doing.[8]

Community, Clubs, and Platforms

"Community" has a warm, fuzzy feel to it, and when applied to the group of users of a church, synagogue, temple, or mosque, it makes you think of the building, the crowd inside, and perhaps the way in which singing or chanting in unison makes the psychological boundaries between individuals begin to melt. But most people attending a service in one of these places are not just thinking about community in this way. We can imagine a gossamer network of intentional threads linking each person to a potentially large number of individual others—not just to the congregation, but also to some of its specific members. Peter hopes to meet Steve, who had mentioned he might know something about a job—though

Peter wants it to seem casual, so he doesn't look too desperate. He also would quite like to be noticed by Jill, especially since he's wearing a new suit this week. And then there are the friends who were going to organize an outing to go bowling—have they forgotten? Plus there are his cousins, whom he likes seeing and sees mainly in church. Martha wants to be noticed by Pastor George since he so nicely came to visit her when she missed last week's service. Also she really has managed to pay her tithes this month, and would love to give him a chance to ask. She wants to see Daisy again, because it's been a couple of weeks, and Daisy seemed so worried about her teenage sons. But the sons are here—they don't always make it—and maybe that shows things are getting better. Then there's that nice man who sings in the choir and has been smiling so nicely at her for the last few weeks—maybe she'll get a chance to ask his name.

The fact that what many people get out of their membership of a religious community is the opportunity to meet one another implies in turn that the members are not just the "customers" of a religious organization, those who benefit by its activities. They're also a part of what that organization is offering. The cliché that "if you aren't paying for the product, you are the product" has been attributed to many people, of whom the earliest is probably the American sculptor and video artist Richard Serra, who is recorded saying it in 1973.[9] It has been very often cited to describe the underlying business model of what are now known as *platforms*—businesses whose core activity consists in bringing together various groups of users. But the underlying insight, which can be expressed in a slightly less sinister form as "you can make your customers work for you," goes back much, much further than 1973.

In his first letter to the Christian community at Corinth, probably written in the year 54 or 53 CE, Saint Paul developed an analogy between members of a religious community and parts of the body. He wrote: "For by one Spirit are we all baptized into one body, whether we be Jews or Gentiles, whether we be bond or free; and have been all made to drink into one Spirit. For the body is not one member, but many. . . . But now are they many members, yet but one body."[10] You might think this is meant just to reassure members of the community that diversity is welcome, that they can all be members even if they don't fit into the same mold. After all, the early Christian Church was particularly good at appealing to the poor, to women, and to slaves, whose rights to equal respect it defended against the condescension and disdain with which Roman society treated them.[11] That might be an anachronistic reading: it's more likely to have meant that members should be conscious of their different stations in life. But in any case, if you read on carefully, you can see that Paul is doing more than this. He writes: "And the eye cannot say unto the hand, I have no need of thee: nor again the head to the feet, I have no need of you. Nay, much more those members of the body, which seem to be more feeble, are necessary." The "despised and neglected" of society are not just welcome, says Paul—they are actively needed.

In Paul's preaching to a different community, the one at Ephesus, we read (in the Acts of the Apostles) the now famous insight that "it is more blessed to give than to receive."[12] This is often interpreted as an exhortation, an encouragement to us to do something that does not come naturally to us. But it's better understood as a profound insight into the nature of human fulfilment—we are more truly ourselves when we give to others than when we are the passive recipients of their benevolence. There's a wealth of evidence, going back at least to the work of anthropologist Marcel Mauss and others on gift exchange, and visible even in the writings of the first-century philosopher Seneca, that human beings in a wide range of societies—from small-scale forest foragers to large-scale industrialized city dwellers—are embedded in webs of cooperative exchange.[13] An important consequence of this is that they can be more gravely hurt by being prevented from contributing than by being denied the contributions of others.

Anthropologists have noted that the two things that most accurately predict depression and anxiety among the Tsimane forager-farmers of the Bolivian Amazon are physical sickness and the inability to give food to other families.[14] Not the inability to receive—the inability to give. Behavioral economists studying the impact of unemployment on psychological well-being in industrialized societies have noticed that losing your job produces psychological turmoil far greater than can possibly be explained by the associated loss of income.[15] It's caused, they believe, by the sudden inability to provide for others. Churches that look after their unemployed members often understand that what they need is not to compensate for their lost income; what they need is to be needed again. The churches both help them and are helped by them in turn; their members are both their customers and their greatest productive asset. Many religious traditions emphasize "leading by example" as a way in which all the faithful can make of their personal witness a contribution to building the communities to which they belong, so that leadership becomes a feature of the whole community and not just of its most visible members.

So: a religious community is a web of interlocking relationships, united by need, including the need to be needed by others. This was as true for Christians in the fourth century CE as it is for Christians in the twenty-first century,[16] and as true today for Muslims in Indonesia as for Muslims in the United States.[17] It's about as far away as you can imagine from the picture of modern consumers choosing their washing machines or their takeout pizza. But members of the religious community still have agency, are still choosing their destiny, and the leaders who build and manage that community understand this.[18] A web of interlocking relationships might sometimes be heavy to wear, but it's like a suit of clothes that expresses you, not like a set of prison walls that confines you. More precisely, the religious community is a platform, to which members choose to belong in the light of what other members on the platform are doing.

Digital platforms such as Google, Twitter, and Instagram have become an ever-present feature of our online lives in recent years, to the point where we can exaggerate their novelty and overlook how important non-digital platforms have been for us in the past. A rough definition of a platform is that it is an institution that facilitates relationships.[19] It recovers the cost of its activities by appropriating part of the value of the relationships it helps to create. These may be commercial relationships, but they don't have to be—they can be sporting, musical, professional, sexual, or a multitude of other kinds of relationships. The embodiment of that platform may be a physical space, such as a stage in a theater, or a marketplace in the center of a city, or the dance floor of a nightclub where strangers meet to lose themselves together in music and movement. It may be a real person, such as the matchmaker in many rural communities around the world, or one of the fixers who introduces lobbyists to politicians and takes a cut for doing so. Or it may be an abstract entity defined by law and custom, such as the membership structure of an ancient Greek temple, a modern corporation, or a political, sporting, cultural, or religious community. Some platforms are markets, in the sense that individual members engage in explicit trade with each other. Not all markets are platforms—for instance, we can talk about "the labor market" just to indicate the millions of ways in which employers and employees interact—but many physical and online markets are set up to allow transactions to take place in a way that could not easily happen otherwise. The art and science of managing platforms have often been difficult to understand, codify, and transmit to others. But great advances have been made in recent years, and the face of religion is being transformed as a result.

The most important insight in the theory of platforms is this: because platforms facilitate relationships that could not form so easily without them, the terms under which the platform allows its members to participate have an impact on the types of relationships that form. Think, for example, of a nightclub whose main business consists in allowing heterosexual men and women to meet—with alcohol and dancing as aphrodisiacs. Many such nightclubs make most of their money by charging high prices to men, while charging much lower prices, and even offering inducements like free drinks, to women. You might wonder why they do this—wouldn't it be fairer to charge everyone the same? The answer is not just that women are more likely than men to be put off by high prices. It's also that the presence of more women in the nightclub is likely to increase the willingness of the men to pay for entry, while the presence of more men in the nightclub is not so likely to make the place more attractive to women. The women, in other words, are not just the nightclub's customers—they're also its assets, to a greater extent than the men (and for reasons that reflect complex currents in the feelings of men and women about the risks and attractions of meeting strangers in public places, as well as the value attached by women to the price the men have paid to enter). The low price charged to women reflects this important fact. A nightclub that tried charging men and women the same would probably end up with fewer women *and* fewer men.

Platforms everywhere charge different prices to different types of users. Search engines like Google, and social media like Facebook or Instagram, charge their advertisers a lot while charging the consumers that use them nothing at all. Makers of computer operating systems and application distributors for smartphones charge very different prices to the app users and the app developers. Broadcasters who sell advertising can charge little or nothing to their viewers and everything to their advertisers, while those who want to avoid advertising pay streaming subscriptions.

You might think this model of differentiated pricing can't really apply to the world of religious organizations, since many of these charge apparently similar prices to all their members. Think, for example, of the widespread "tithing system"—the practice of requiring all members to pay one-tenth of their income to their church. In fact, the tithing system is much less uniform than it sounds. It's not even a uniform price to begin with, because it requires richer members to pay more than poorer members. But even as a proportional price, it isn't applied uniformly, since there's an informal understanding that the pressure placed by church leaders on members will be sensitive to their individual circumstances—whether they have sick or elderly dependents, whether they are having employment difficulties or health problems, or business fluctuations. Members who are having difficulties can usually negotiate with the church to overlook their tithing obligations. But, in the process, they reveal a lot about themselves and their circumstances. This is information that enables the church to ratchet up the pressure again once things start going better for them.

Above all, the tithe is just the start of the expectations on church members. As well as tithing, members are typically expected to pay into the collection at each service. They're also expected to make special contributions. These may be to meet contingencies like the cost of church repairs, or to reflect their own special circumstances, such as a promotion or some other stroke of fortune (which the church leaders are usually quick to remind them is due to the grace of God). Such a system also sets in motion a form of competitive emulation among members. If my neighbor gave something when she was promoted, I will want to give as much as she did, if only to show my fellow members that my promotion was as important as hers. This is a major source of revenues for some religious organizations, though it's not one from which all are equally equipped to benefit. I recall the response of a Buddhist monk in a fine but dilapidated temple in Yunnan Province in Southwest China to my discreet question about whether it was difficult to raise funds for repairs. He shook his head sadly, and beckoned to me to come out onto the terrace, from where there was a magnificent view over the surrounding countryside. He pointed to a very large modern temple over a mile away, before which stood a massive statue of Buddha, perhaps thirty feet tall, painted in bright orange-yellow. "Nobody wants to give money to a temple like ours when they can give money to one like that!"

Competition for revenues between temples clearly takes place along multiple dimensions. The signal sent by the large orange-yellow Buddha is intended to reverberate throughout the region; many other donors have a more modest audience in mind. And we shouldn't forget that monetary contributions, important though they are, are just the start of members' obligations—they're also expected to contribute time and energy. The result of all this is that the actual amounts paid, as well as the contributions in kind, vary a great deal among church members. This not only helps to match contributions to individuals' ability to pay, it also accepts lower monetary contributions from those who contribute best to the community in other ways—exactly as the platform model would predict.[20]

When the economic theory of religious organizations began to be developed systematically in the last few decades of the twentieth century, an important innovation, due to economist Laurence Iannacone, was to think of religions as clubs.[21] The club's members would enjoy some collective benefit—such as a certain quality of worship and ritual—and they would pay a price that was the "entry fee"; higher entry fees typically signaled a higher quality of the collective benefit. The price might be in cash or in kind—say, in the form of restrictions on what you could eat or drink or how you could behave. Later work by many researchers developed an increasingly sophisticated understanding of clubs, with different categories of members, different dimensions of the benefits they receive, and different dimensions of commitment by the members.[22] The platform model takes the idea a step further. Members of platforms are more than consumers of the benefits that are provided for them—they are assets of the platform, and active in the delivery of such benefits to each other. And what they are paying for is not just a generalized good, available to everyone, but specifically access to other members of the quality that the church can credibly promise to give them.

At the end of chapter 3 I suggested some reasons why a young woman like Grace might find her church a hopeful place in which to look for a husband. It's not just spouses that church members are looking for. Around 40 percent of the 536 church members whom we surveyed told us that they preferred to interact with other church members as friends, as coworkers, and as business partners. A further 10 percent said they would choose coworkers or business partners exclusively among other church members, and 20 percent would choose their close friends exclusively within the church.[23]

There's nothing particularly unusual about our Ghanaian church members. All over the world, and in many different religions, there's evidence that people's religious communities shape their personal relationships, even in the wider secular sphere. That doesn't mean that everyone has in mind a clear view of religion as a sphere apart, using it to guide their behavior in the rest of life. Would such a distinction even make sense to a Hindu taxi driver whose statue of Ganesh hangs bobbing from his rearview mirror and is in his mind the most important thing protecting him from death on the lethal streets of Mumbai? What we can observe is that a religious community's network of loyalties spreads outward from the place where its strictly religious activities are conducted, to include other, secular activities. Though the community's members could interact with outsiders in the secular sphere, they may choose not to do so, in order to keep their interactions within the community. It doesn't have to be something the community insists on—it may happen naturally, as a by-product of the affinities created by the religious activities themselves.

This tendency for religious communities to form strong links among their members has been demonstrated to hold across the US population, in a remarkable study released in 2022 by economists Raj Chetty,

Matthew Jackson, Theresa Kuchler, and Johannes Stroebel. They examined the social network ties of over seventy million American Facebook users between the ages of twenty-five and forty-four. The data were anonymized, but the socioeconomic characteristics of the users (their income and education levels) were recorded, as were those of their friends. The authors were interested in what made relatively poor people more likely to be friends (well, Facebook friends . . .) with relatively well-off people. The reason this was important to the researchers is that having links to well-off people is a good predictor of upward social mobility across generations. If you're poor but you know more well-off people, your kids are less likely to be poor.

The study divided the factors that matter for enabling poor people to get to know better-off people into two kinds. The first is the factors that determine what kinds of organizations—school, workplace, social club, neighborhood, or religious community—they belong to. The second is the factors determining how likely they are to become friends with the better-off people in that organization. The authors discovered that religious organizations are much better than all other kinds of organization on the second measure. Poor people are much more likely to become friends with the better-off people they meet in their religious groups than with the better-off people they might meet in their schools, workplaces, or neighborhoods. So religious communities do really help their members reach out across the social divide. But there's a downside to that, which is that religious communities are even more likely than the other organizations to be highly segregated by income. It's as if a lot of rich people are thinking, not always explicitly: "Whichever church we go to, we're going to feel obliged to be friendly with everyone there. So let's make sure we pick a church that seems likely to have a lot of other members who are just like us."[24]

That's not to say that religious members conceive the benefits of community in solely economic terms. Far from it. Some may perceive their community as what Geoffrey Brennan and Philip Pettit have called an "economy of esteem," in which approval and disapproval are distributed among individuals in a way that no market system could achieve even in principle.[25] You can't buy the esteem of others, but part of what you value about your community may be that it esteems the kinds of quality you have, or hope to develop. Alternatively, some members may emphasize the help their community can give them in developing a personal relationship with God, as anthropologist Tanya Luhrmann has vividly described in her fieldwork among American evangelicals.[26] The benefits may include perceptible improvements in mental health, though of course you can't think yourself into an improvement in mental health just by willing it to happen. Interesting evidence about this comes from Sriya Iyer (whose work on religion in India we saw in chapter 3). She teamed up with economists Jane Cooley Fruehwirth and Anwen Zhang to study whether personal religiosity made any difference to the risk of depression in adolescence.

This is a hard problem to study statistically. In addition to a possible effect of religiosity on depression, being depressed might affect religiosity, either by persuading people to become more religious or by persuading them that it's pointless. Or religiosity and a susceptibility to depression might both be effects of some unknown third cause, which is generating a spurious correlation. The authors used data from the United States to provide one of the most convincing studies to date that people who are more religious are—on average—at a slightly but significantly *lower* risk of being depressed. The researchers avoided the spurious correlations I mentioned above by looking at random variations in the religiosity of different cohorts within a school. These induce random differences in the religiosity of otherwise similar individuals belonging to different cohorts, meaning we can study the impact of such differences without having to worry about the other reasons why religiosity can vary. Importantly for our understanding of community, their results strongly suggest that the way religiosity has this effect is not by creating a generally positive outlook on life. Instead, it provides adolescents with the emotional resources to deal with unexpected life shocks like sickness or bereavement, in a way that school activities and other friendships do not.[27] These are contexts in which the communitarian benefits of religiosity come strongly to the fore.

Religious organizations that successfully build community can become spectacularly profitable as a result. Their leaders include some of the richest people in their societies. It's hard to document this rigorously, because unlike other entrepreneurs they usually don't have to pay tax on the profits of the organizations they manage, and don't have to publish audited accounts. But some of the most expensive real estate in gated communities across the world, from Accra to Zanzibar, belongs to religious leaders. Which is surprising on the face of it, because religious platforms don't seem to be scalable in the way that, say, social-media networks are scalable. A successful megachurch may have several thousand members, not several million, and the members need bricks-and-mortar infrastructure for their meetings.

Two things explain the profitability of religious movements even though they're not naturally as scalable as digital platforms. First of all, successful preaching can, indeed, reach an audience of millions through broadcasting and social-media networks, which many religious leaders develop on the back of their physical networks. Secondly, though the costs of building religious communities are important, the services they provide can be priced very highly. The money that Grace gives to her church is more than she spends on any other item in her budget except food. And it's far greater than the minimal cost to the church of her membership (which might even be negative, given everything else she contributes to the community). But that doesn't mean Grace could find another church that could supply all this to her for a lower price. If she switched to another church, she could not take all these social ties with her. Any reduction in the cost to her of membership would see an even greater reduction in the benefits she receives. Community is a blessing, but it can also lock you in.[28]

It follows from this that the large revenues and profits of successful evangelical megachurches in the United States or in Africa are not threatened by competitors who set up churches nearby and try to draw away members from existing churches. This relative freedom from competition—due to the lock-in effect of community—also means that religious leaders enjoy a lot of freedom to do other things than strive for profit. They may engage in philanthropy and charitable outreach, or they may (like some media entrepreneurs) try to preach a particular theological or political message that's not necessarily the one their members would choose to hear. They may enjoy increased opportunities for sexual favors

from their members, or simply bask in greater fame or esteem. Or they
may, once they have an assured community, simply coast along, not ex-
erting themselves to do what their members most want, exactly as Adam
Smith predicted of the established churches of his own day. Freedom
from competitive pressure may come from political protection, or it may
come from the legacy of successful community building in the past, but
in either case we should expect to see a wide variety of motivations
among successful religious leaders.[29] Even fierce competition will not
lead to bland uniformity in the religious marketplace.

It's important to understand that what makes people choose their
business, friendship, and romantic relationships through their religious
communities is not just convenience. Nor even is it really about obligations, though the longer you belong to a community the deeper the web
of obligations you may create. It's also about confidence, and trust. The
reason why Grace is likely to find a husband through church is not that
she can't afford a subscription to an online dating site, or that she's too
shy to go to a singles bar. The church simply isn't competing in that space.
Paradoxically, she's more likely to find a husband at the church because
the people she meets there are not the kind of person who goes to church
just to meet a spouse. Church demands much, much more than just a
smart suit and a charming smile. Any potential husbands Grace meets will
have had to turn up sober before 9 a.m. every Sunday for a long, long
time; to sit through three-hour sermons; to show themselves keen to take
part in the church's other liturgical and social activities; to pay their tithes
regularly and to be willing to contribute a lot more; and to make sure
their activities as good citizens in the community attract the attention of
the pastors. Not that the pastors would betray any confidences—but
when Grace's aunt hears a pastor mention casually that so-and-so is an
"excellent" young man, from a "very good family," there's code in that
utterance, and the aunt, Grace, and the young man all know it. A man
who can do all that isn't just going to church to flirt.

Thinking of religious organizations as platforms helps us to understand how they function, how they attract members, and how they can
sometimes be so very profitable economically. But it's important to remember that they can do all this only because they're not just doing

what secular platforms do. A church can be a successful dating platform because it attracts people who don't think of it just as a dating platform. A synagogue or a mosque can be a successful way for businessmen to network (and it often is business*men*) because it's not just another chamber of commerce or a Rotary Club.

What *is* it, then, that makes religious platforms so distinctive? To find an answer we must look much more closely into two areas of religious life that seem, on the face of it, to have very little to do with economic competition—the domain of ritual and the domain of doctrine and belief. How is economic rivalry between religious organizations affected by what rituals members take part in, and by what they believe about the causal efficacy and the wider metaphysical significance of what they're doing? We begin by looking at ritual.

CHAPTER 5

Ritual and Social Bonding

Rabbi Israel Ba'al Shem, peace be upon him, said: When a man is
drowning in a river and gesticulates while in the water that people
should save him from the waters which threaten to sweep him away,
the observers will certainly not laugh at him and his gestures. So, too,
one should not pour scorn on a man who makes gestures while he
prays, for he is trying to save himself from the waters of wickedness.

—eighteenth-century Hasidic text

The Rapture

When a doctoral student from Cambridge called Harvey Whitehouse
arrived in October 1987 in the village of Dadul, in northwestern Papua
New Guinea, he was taken for a reincarnated ancestor, herald of the
long-awaited ushering-in of eternal bliss promised by the Pomio Kivung
millenarian movement established a quarter of a century earlier. Events
were to put some strain on the villagers' interpretation, including the
birth of his son a year and a half later (which had not been factored into
expectations of the ancestor's behavior). Nevertheless, once welcomed
into the movement, Whitehouse was able to provide a detailed and
gripping account of its everyday rules and rituals—but not only those.
He also recorded the extreme passions stirred by a breakaway splinter
movement, whose two leaders induced almost the entire populations
of Dadul and a neighboring village to stop their farming, slaughter their

Ritual publicly honored: a procession of sacrificial bulls, from the Parthenon South Frieze in Athens, Greece.
Credit: Capillon, Wikimedia Commons.

Ritual feared and repressed: a sketch (author unknown) of the eight Haitian Vodou devotees found guilty in 1864 in the affaire de Bizoton. Published in James Redpath's "The Civil War in Hayti" (*Harper's Weekly*, September 2, 1865, p. 545) and captioned: "Votaries of the God Vaudoux (Snake-Worshipers), Executed for the Crim of Cannibalism at Hayti."
Credit: Wikimedia Commons.

livestock, and crowd into a large roundhouse to chant, listen to intense orations, and await the arrival of the promised rapture. The rapture did not come. In the face of exhaustion, sickness, threats of legal action from public officials and relatives of members, and above all impending starvation, the members of the splinter movement eventually returned to their landholdings.

It would be natural to suppose these members were disgruntled and disillusioned, and to think that the criticism and ridicule they faced from inhabitants of other villages reflected widespread skepticism about the movement's core beliefs and efficacy of its rituals. Far from it. Though skepticism may have featured among some people's reactions, explanations for the failure of the ritual on that occasion were easy to come by—everyone had a theory. More importantly, there was a different thread to the criticism, and it wasn't that the rituals were no good. It's a theme found almost everywhere when competing religious movements challenge each other's rituals. As Whitehouse puts it, when a ritual is criticized it is "not on the grounds that it cannot work, but on the grounds that it is immoral."[1]

Throughout history this has led to vituperative disputes between devotees of competing rituals that, to many outsiders, are hard to tell apart. Writing in 1793, Antoine Dalmas, a French plantation surgeon living in Saint-Domingue (now Haiti), described in horrified tones the secret Vodou ceremony that was believed to have launched the slave rebellion two years earlier. The slaves had gathered "in the middle of an uncultivated wood" and slaughtered a black pig "as a sacrifice to the all-powerful spirit of the black race." As historian Laurent Dubois describes it, "for Dalmas, the offering of the animal, 'surrounded by objects they believe have magical power', was proof of the barbarity of the enslaved. . . . '[T]he greed with which they drank its blood . . . reveal[s] the characteristics of the Africans. . . . [I]t is natural that a caste this ignorant and stupid would begin the most horrible attacks with the superstitious rites of an absurd and bloodthirsty religion.'"[2] It does not seem to have occurred to this doubtless pious Catholic, whose religion asserted that its central sacrament involved drinking the real and not metaphorical blood of its founder, that there could ever be any comparability in bloodthirstiness between the Vodou religion and his own.

There's a reason why rituals of competing religions, whose differences are so clear to their practitioners, are often hard for outsiders to tell apart. It's that they're not designed to be legible by the ordinary standards of causal explanation. That's why they can do what they *are* supposed to do, which is to serve as markers of group membership—it's only insiders who can see the point. But this raises a serious challenge for the platform model of religious competition—how can rituals whose very point is opaque to outsiders ever be an attractive way of winning or keeping recruits? To understand the answer, we need to dig deeper into the many features of ritual that psychologists, anthropologists, and historians of religion have been able to document. Only by understanding what rituals, religious and secular, have in common across cultures and historical periods can we begin to understand why they vary from one time, one place, and one setting to another.[3]

The range of rituals in our everyday lives is enormous—from purely individual ones like praying with rosaries or trying not to step on the cracks as we navigate the sidewalk to rites of passage like weddings and funerals performed in the presence of family and friends, to mass group rituals like chanting at a sports game or Friday prayers in a large mosque, or the vast sacrifices of up to a hundred oxen (called a "hecatomb") in which the ancient Greeks would periodically engage, as recorded in Homer. Some people engage in rituals all the time, others less often, but it's rare to find anyone, however scientifically minded, who never does. As Harvey Whitehouse, who was inspired by his experiences in New Guinea to develop a general theory of rituals, has expressed it, "much of the psychology responsible for this is uniquely human. We are truly the ritual animal."[4] Other researchers have confirmed that other primate species do not engage in anything like ritual as it's known in human beings. As I mentioned, and as Whitehouse emphasizes, rituals are causally opaque. If they achieve something, it's mysterious how they do so. That doesn't mean they can't be used instrumentally—rituals have accompanied prayers for rain, medical interventions, laying the foundation stones of houses, exorcisms, launching ships, and a host of other activities whose practitioners thought they were bringing about important results in the world. But no one would ever claim to understand why the particular details of the rituals are necessary for achieving the effects. The ritual doesn't prescribe them because they're necessary; they're necessary because that's what the ritual prescribes. Seeing the point of the ritual doesn't require you to understand exactly why the ritual is like this rather than like that.

The result is that rituals are often especially puzzling to outsiders who happen to come across them, precisely because they have developed that way to give insiders a sense of distinctive identity. As we can see in the words attributed above to the Hasidic leader Rabbi Israel Ba'al Shem, the fact that outsiders might be tempted to mock the elaborate actions of the ritual can even be used to emphasize to insiders just how important it is for them to see the point of the actions ("don't be like one of those mocking outsiders!"). This general understanding of ritual, which stresses the way rituals create a sense of identity through moments of "collective effervescence," was developed by the sociologist Emile Durkheim in the early years of the twentieth century, and has inspired much theoretical and empirical research since then.[5] Roger Finke and Rodney Stark report how emigration to the United States in the nineteenth century gave many Catholics the opportunity to observe traditions they had not previously realized were approved by their church:

> The Catholic Church may have presented itself as the guardian of the "one true and holy, Roman apostolic faith", but the character of that faith differed greatly across the nations of Europe and therefore across the parishes of America. Members of a German parish might have been shocked to observe "tongue dragging" by women in Italian parishes, a feast day practice in which especially pious women dragged their tongues on the floor as they crawled or were carried down the aisle to the statue of the Madonna. Italians, in turn, might have been puzzled as to the religious significance of the huge, quasi-military pageants and processions held in German parishes to mark each of the major holy days.[6]

So, rituals are always causally opaque, but lots of things that aren't rituals are causally opaque too. I have no idea how my smartphone works, but it does (until it doesn't . . .). I have no idea how the mechanic who services my car makes it run more smoothly than it did when I brought it in, but it does (usually . . .). Whitehouse argues that the difference lies in a hypothetical—my confidence in both the smartphone and the car service procedure depends on my belief that there *is* a causal mechanism that someone understands, that doesn't involve supernatural intervention, and that could be explained to me by someone patient enough. In the case of most rituals, there's no such mechanism. No one even claims there's a mechanism, except occasionally in some occult sense. And this absence of mechanism is reflected in the way practitioners are trained. If I were told that the reason I should be confident my car will be competently serviced is that the mechanic learned through seven years' apprenticeship to bang on the hood with a wooden hammer in a rhythm set out in an ancient scripture, I would know this was a ritual and not a causal procedure.

The absence of a natural causal mechanism certainly doesn't mean that rituals don't matter to their participants. They can matter very much indeed. In February 2022 Father Andres Arango, a Catholic priest at Saint Gregory's parish church in Phoenix, Arizona, resigned "after diocese leaders discovered he had mistakenly used the phrase 'we baptize you' instead of 'I baptize you' for years."[7] Not only did Father Arango resign, but the Diocese of Phoenix informed all those who had ever been baptized by Father Arango that they needed to have their baptisms performed again. Why the urgency? In a website established to answer questions from the faithful, the diocese noted that baptism "is a requirement for salvation." And not just any baptism will do: "the words that are spoken (the sacramental *form*), along with the actions that are performed and the materials used (the sacramental *matter*) are a crucial aspect of every sacrament." You can't just dispense with the ritual if it's inconvenient or embarrassing, such as because it hasn't been performed correctly. The website continued: "sacraments are *efficacious* signs of grace, instituted by Christ and entrusted to the Church, by which divine life is dispensed to us."[8] On the face of it, this sounds very like a claim that a causal mechanism is involved (the failure of the ritual has had important causal consequences for Father Arango and incalculable numbers of his parishioners). But a closer reading of the diocese's statement makes it clear that the explanations for the importance of the correct performance of the ritual are couched in terms of spiritual authority, not in terms of describing what exactly goes wrong when the wrong words are used. Indeed, the text tries hard to avoid the implication that those whose baptisms are invalid will necessarily be denied salvation if they have the misfortune to die before the error is rectified.[9]

The importance of correct and repeated performance of ritual has encouraged believers of many faiths to seek mechanical assistance, which has greater stamina and is less likely to make mistakes than ordinary human agency. Tibetan prayer wheels probably date back as far as the fourth century CE, and are thought by some historians to have been the inspiration for the horizontal windmills that powered grain milling in Persia and China in the Middle Ages and later in Europe from the seventeenth century onward.[10] Though usually turned manually, as an alternative to the recitation of texts, they could also be powered by wind, or sometimes by water; nowadays electric prayer wheels can be bought online in a wide range of designs (and prices). Digital applications proliferate: anthropologists Hannah Gould and Holly Walters report that "the Taiwanese company *Acer* has developed Smart Prayer Beads that digitally count the user's *mantra* recitations, so that they don't lose track of their place or number, and tally them for 'merit' which can be shared on social media." They also note rapid growth in the use of robots for Hindu and Buddhist ritual, including the "robotic *puja* arm . . . developed by IBM Watson and Patil Automation Pvt Ltd (PAPL) performing the Ganapati Chaturthi *aarti* (lamp offering) in New Delhi in 2017."[11] Not surprisingly, the use of mechanical ritual aids has been more popular in those religious traditions that emphasize correct practice (orthopraxy) over correct belief (orthodoxy). It is particularly congenial to those traditions (such as Taoism and Zen Buddhism) that admire the virtue of *te*—what Alan Watts called "the unthinkable ingenuity and creative power of man's spontaneous and natural functioning—a power which is blocked when one tries to master it in terms of formal methods and techniques."[12] As Zen pupils know, the graceful and unconscious mastery of any skill is extremely difficult, and the more difficult the more we try—so what better way to achieve the task than to delegate it to a machine that is unconscious by design?

Ritual and Religious Platforms

There exists a vast literature on religious and other rituals and the functions they serve, which would be impossible to summarize in the space available here (citing all the relevant literature is something of a ritual for researchers like me, but it's a ritual we're allowed to forgo if we have a good reason).[13] In this case it isn't necessary, because what we need to understand is something more specific: How do rituals fit into the platform model of religious competition? What part do rituals play in the package of services that religious platforms offer? To answer this, we need to note two things: first, the existence of universal elements in our human response to ritual, and secondly, the fact that, in practice, different people respond to ritual in different ways. The first of these observations leads us to investigate what aspects of human cognition underlie our response to ritual behavior, and thus to see what general human needs are met by ritual. The second helps us to see how members of religious organizations recognize kindred spirits among fellow members, and therefore to understand how the platform has done them a service by putting them in touch with one another. Paradoxically, rituals are divisive, so they may unite. What do I mean by that?

Let me summarize some general features of our response to ritual. Everything starts with the way human beings learn. One way to learn is by observing our natural environment and adjusting our behavior to match it. There's a low ceiling beam in my house, on which I used to hit my head regularly after I first moved in, till my brain learned to make me duck when I pass by. But it took a while, and my IQ dropped an unknown number of points as a result. So it's often more efficient to learn by observing others, and cognitive psychologists have identified a fascinating characteristic of the way we do that. It's especially striking in young children but continues to shape how we learn even in adulthood.[14] It has been called "over-imitation."[15]

Over-imitation has been found across a wide range of human societies, and it happens much more in humans than in other primate species; it may even be unique to human beings.[16] We are *extravagant* imitators of the behavior of others. When children are trying to learn from

experimental demonstrators how to perform some task (such as opening a box or constructing a complex object), they don't imitate only the
aspects of the demonstrators' behavior whose relationship to the ultimate objective they can understand. They also make a point of imitating
any gestures or routines that accompany that behavior, even if their
purpose is completely irrelevant or obscure. Chimpanzees don't do that.
When copying a demonstrator, they'll try to figure out what the demonstrator did to open the box, and copy only the parts of the process
whose efficacy they can understand. That makes chimps effective social
learners in a jungle environment, but they're easily beaten by even
young children when dealing with challenges cooked up by researchers
in a lab. One way of putting it—and it's an idea we'll see again in chapter 6—is that human beings have a particular talent for suspending disbelief when asked to do so by someone we trust. We signal to each other
all the time: do what I'm showing you, trust me, this works—even if
you can't see why.

There are two main reasons why a tendency to suspend disbelief
when we imitate others might have spread among human beings in
prehistory—and would not have spread among chimpanzees or other
nonhuman animals. One is that human beings face more complex environmental and social challenges than those of chimps—they're more
like those in the lab, so it would pay us to copy others more faithfully,
despite the greater cognitive load involved. The second reason, which
could operate independently of the first, is that by copying others faithfully, we signal to those others that we respect them, that we trust them,
that we're on their side, that we want to belong to their group.

Researchers are still debating the relative importance of these two
explanations, but there's evidence to suggest both were important, and
may have given rise to separate mechanisms in our brains. Let's start
with the idea that over-imitation is just a more efficient way to learn
what works. Individual rituals, like playing with rosary beads, have been
shown to be effective at reducing stress.[17] Why might that tell us something about the effectiveness of learning? It's well known that various
kinds of stress can induce repetitive and ritualized behavior, which suggests that ritual is a response the brain has developed especially to

reduce stress (though it's a more open question whether the behavior reduces the stress or merely expresses it).[18] This would be consistent with the idea that stress prepares the brain and body for a risky environment. When we successfully perform a ritual in a situation of stress, we show ourselves that we have mastered socially learned ways of handling that environment, so our body can now scale back its response. The fact that a ritual lowers our stress level would therefore reflect a correlation between the ritual and the learning of the necessary skill.

It's also possible that a strong form of stress reduction may underlie another important benefit associated with some individual rituals, like meditation—the capacity to induce a sense of the numinous, of awe before the grandeur of the universe, a melting of the boundaries of the self. Alan Strathern describes the Indic practices of yoga and meditation as "telescopes for the soul, magnifying the inner landscape to an exceptional degree."[19] Only a very unstressed consciousness can afford to lower so completely all its mechanisms of physical and psychological defense.

However, many rituals demand community reinforcement, which suggests they involve more than just mastering information drawn from observing other people. As well as studies documenting a correlation between participation in ritual and measures of social cohesion,[20] there's now a large body of evidence about the psychological and physiological effects of performing activities such as singing, dance, and processional movements in *synchronization* with the actions of others.[21] A review of forty-two separate studies found that synchrony tends to increase cooperation and people's perceived connection to others. The question is why.[22] The immediate mechanisms may include the release of endorphins or other biochemical regulators, though not enough is known about this. But the ultimate causes, those that explain why we have evolved such a physiological response, are probably due to the continuous and costly effort such activities require us to exert to synchronize our actions. People who are genuinely interested in and care about others will find it easier to pay attention to them. Successful synchronization is therefore a reliable signal that the people involved care about one another. In fact, the more synchronized are the other members of the group, the more likely is the group to be successful at cooperating, and the more it pays any one member to pay attention. This might explain why some collective activities can remain "stuck" in low levels of coordination, then suddenly "click" into synchronicity as everyone realizes, in a mutually reinforcing feedback loop, how much they matter to one another.

Harvey Whitehouse has suggested that these two different explanations for over-imitation have endowed us with two distinct forms of mental activity, triggered under different sets of social conditions. These are called the "instrumental stance" and the "ritual stance" that our brains can adopt. He has tested this suggestion in a wide range of experiments with several collaborators. Conditions that make experimental subjects more aware of the need to reinforce ties with a social group tend to trigger the ritual stance, while those that make them more aware of the practical usefulness of the expertise of others tend to trigger the instrumental stance.[23] This tendency to switch stances may help to explain why outsiders find differences between rival rituals baffling even when insiders find them critical. Outsiders are adopting the instrumental stance—asking "what is the point of this ritual?"—to which they can rarely find an answer. Insiders are adopting the ritual stance, asking "what do my fellow members want me to do, and which details is it crucial for me to get right?" It's hard for people adopting one stance to put themselves mentally into the shoes of people adopting the other.

It seems likely that the human tendency for over-imitation was shaped by natural selection and is at least partly determined by genetic factors, since it is found universally in human societies and develops early in infancy. But the fact that we over-imitate has massively increased our ability to adopt the cultural traditions of other groups. It has thereby increased the importance of cultural rather than natural selection in our cognitive and behavioral evolution.[24] This may even apply to cognitive skills that we may think of as innate, such as our ability to "read the minds" of other people. Just like the literal reading of books, which can't have evolved purely by natural selection since books have been in existence for far too short a time to have influenced our genetic makeup, mind reading probably involves the repurposing through cultural selection of cognitive talents that originally evolved for other reasons. Psychologist

Cecilia Heyes calls such culturally evolved talents "cognitive gadgets."[25] They're like apps for the brain, and it seems likely that over-imitation has immensely increased the number and sophistication of the apps that our brains can support.

Modes of Religiosity

The importance of cultural evolution for the development of our societies almost certainly explains the contrast between two kinds of ritual that have been observed by many anthropologists and sociologists—"rare but emotionally intense rituals [that] bond together small groups of participants," and "high frequency rituals [that] serve to standardize a body of beliefs and practices in a large population."[26] Anthropologist Ruth Benedict, inspired by Friedrich Nietzsche's *The Birth of Tragedy*, contrasted "Dionysian" and "Apollonian" rituals, the former among the Kwakiutl First Nations group of the Pacific Northwest, and the latter among the Zuni people of New Mexico. Similar contrasts in ritual style, with different names and different nuances, were later drawn by Victor Turner, among many others.[27] Whitehouse calls these the "imagistic" and the "doctrinal" modes of religiosity, and in his account the importance of the distinction lies in our understanding of the different evolutionary pressures that shaped these modes, and the different psychological mechanisms that underlie them.

The imagistic mode is likely to have evolved much earlier in prehistory, as a social bonding mechanism—this is consistent with other current theories about the way language and group singing may have evolved together.[28] Intense emotional experiences, particularly ones that inflict physical or psychological pain and evoke fear of dying, create among participants a strong identification and impulse to collaborate.[29] That makes sense from an evolutionary point of view: only groups whose members responded like this would have survived challenges from predators and rivals. This is one way of understanding the paradoxically therapeutic effects that have been reported for some rituals involving extreme pain.[30] It's also how we can comprehend the curiously pleasurable effect of some such experiences when we relive them imaginatively later—recollections known as "flashbulb memories" give us a vivid reminder of the event, and who else was present.[31] They reinforce our ties to those others, as well as our sense of who we are, by reminding us that it's an experience we have, after all, survived. Rituals are a way of giving ourselves enhanced doses of certain chemicals that occur naturally in our environment, and the discharges of neural electricity that accompany them.[32] They affect our brains in ways we find pleasurable, because it was adaptive for us to consume them in the past.[33]

All the same, the emotional and physical toll such rituals take would be unendurable if they happened too often. As we'll see in chapter 12, rituals have sometimes become vehicles for sadistic abuse of vulnerable participants, and not all movements have been able to master the destructive impulses that imagistic rituals can provoke. There may be a fine line between rituals that induce social bonding through flashbulb memories and those that provoke post-traumatic stress disorder.[34] Social groups therefore needed more low-intensity mechanisms for enhancing solidarity in more normal times. Once ritual traditions became highly routinized, they became a way of spreading shared markers of identity among larger groups of people than could realistically come together for imagistic rituals.[35] This would work only if there was sufficiently faithful copying—which in turn explains why religious movements that adopted the doctrinal mode would insist on orthodoxy: only the correct performance of the ritual counts. Movements that don't enforce orthodoxy may still spread their ideas—but after a few generations of reproduction, the ideas that survive are no longer recognizably theirs.

Both the intense rituals in the imagistic mode and the routine ones in the doctrinal mode share what looks like a bug, but is really a feature: the fact that not everyone likes them. The rituals of doctrinal religions are often (let's face it) rather boring for many members, much of the time—but not to the same degree for everyone. And the intense rituals of the imagistic mode can be physically painful, emotionally distressing, and sometimes downright scary—though not to the same degree for everyone. If you're thinking of religions as supplying services like ordinary businesses, or even like ordinary clubs, it's hard to understand why they'd want to do that. But if you think of them as platforms, it suddenly makes sense. A fellow member who can sit through a long recitation of the teachings of a religious prophet or guru looks like a person with impressive powers of patience, concentration, self-mastery—someone, perhaps, who could separate the essential from the trivial, who could resist the siren call of worldly temptations, someone who could teach you wisdom. A fellow member who can tolerate, survive, perhaps even enjoy an intense, painful, or upsetting ritual is not someone ordinary— but someone you can admire, or wish to emulate, or even love. Of course, a fellow member who outsources the ritual performance to a prayer wheel or robot is not going to be quite so convincing, so it's not surprising that we find such mechanical aids more often in communities where the importance of the ritual is agreed by all concerned.

Here at last we have a coherent account of why rituals are so important to religious platforms. Platforms create relationships—but not in the banal sense of giving people access to one another's phone numbers or TikTok handles. They create what you can think of as a performance space, in which people can create an identity, both as individuals and as members of a group. They can build their relationships within that community on the strength of that shared performance. The doctrinal elements, boring though they often are, serve to give people a sense of shared heritage—we are one because, regularly and reliably, we perform the same ritual. The imagistic elements, scary though they may be, reinforce survivors' euphoria and collective bonding. It was an evolutionarily adaptive response when the scary threats came from outside, but it's one that continues to operate even for scary threats we fabricate for ourselves. By gravitating toward our fellow members whose responses to these challenges we can admire, we develop a sense that the platform is linking us up with some very special people.

Religious movements are not alone in this. Sports teams, armies, and political movements can all provide some of these same psychic rewards, but religious platforms do so with the aid of some truly otherworldly allies. And this leads us to address what is perhaps the most puzzling feature of religious platforms, which is why they ask their members to adopt beliefs about the universe that most nonmembers find quite challenging. This isn't about whether scientists, or atheists, find religious beliefs challenging, because the biggest skeptics about any one religion's beliefs are usually members of a rival religion. Why do religious platforms set themselves up for doctrinal disputes you might expect them to avoid, if they want to make themselves attractive to potential members?

One way abstract metaphysical beliefs seem to follow naturally from the adoption of the ritual stance is when they concern initiation rituals. Think of marriage rituals, which exist in all societies. If we adopt only the instrumental stance, we may think that the purpose of the marriage ritual is just to signal to others that the married couple should hereafter be treated differently from how they were treated before—with more respect perhaps, or at least with more circumspection than when they were still maritally available. But if we adopt the ritual stance, it's hard not to think that the performance of the ritual also changes something metaphysical. The couple are now married, whereas before they were not. Their state has changed. This conviction may help reinforce community members' belief in the power of the community's representatives—look what the priests have just done! They've performed a transformation of the intrinsic state of these people. Rites of passage not only legitimate the individuals who undertake the passage, they also legitimate the community because it alone can validate the passage. If the couple had been married somewhere else, according to a different ritual, it wouldn't have brought about *that* change. Reasoning in this way is likely to make it natural to think that we, in this community, enjoy a privileged access to truths about the universe: there are different states of human beings, and we have an insight into them that other communities do not.

Rituals that are frequent and repetitive may also thereby become persuasive. Musicians who practice scales thereby become better at playing their instrument, but also, through their improved competence, more inclined to see the activity of music as something that makes sense for them. Many texts that teach ritual have this double aspect. They are not just manuals for becoming more competent at doing something that their readers already value, they also reinforce the message that this is something their readers *should* value. The message in turn is not just that the ritual will make the practitioner feel better, but rather that the world is so ordered (for example, that God is so present) that the increased ease with which the practitioner can perform the ritual is a confirmation of this aspect of the world. The *Spiritual Exercises* of Ignatius of Loyola, for example, accord an important place to "discernment" (*discretio*) in just this way: performing the exercises is supposed to enable the practitioner to identify more reliably the presence of good or evil spirits in the world. Becoming practiced at prayer is then interpreted as evidence of the presence of God.[36] But even a practice as little dependent on explicit theology as Zen Buddhism can see in the graceful discipline of its own exercise a kind of confirmatory fulfilment: "What Zen does is to delineate itself on the infinite canvas of time and space the way the flying wild geese cast their shadow on the water below without any intention of doing so, while the water reflects the geese just as naturally and unintentionally."[37]

Still, even with the help of ritual, outsiders can sometimes find the metaphysical commitments that tend to come with joining a religious community quite challenging. Why is it so important for many religious communities to insist on this? This is the subject of chapter 6.

CHAPTER 6

Religion and Belief

One must begin by getting the truth; and where is it to be had in the country? Or rather, there are two truths, the Catholic truth and the Protestant truth.

—William Makepeace Thackeray, *The Irish Sketch Book*

Pascal's Wager

As a young man in the first half of the twentieth century, Reme had been one of the most admired warriors in his village in northwestern Cameroon. Among the stories of his exploits was the time when he challenged the men of a nearby village to a wrestling competition. After he defeated their champion, local custom entitled him to demand tribute—not in the form of material goods, but in the defeated villagers' teaching him a complex dance. This had been a treasured part of their village culture, but after Reme's victory they would be forbidden to perform it; only Reme's own villagers could do that. Thus did a dancing tradition leave one village and come to be taken up by another.

Among Reme's other accomplishments was to find an answer to the philosophical challenge originally posed in the seventeenth century by the French philosopher Blaise Pascal.[1] Pascal had asked why it should matter whether there was compelling evidence for the truth of Christianity. Provided the benefits of accepting Christian teaching were large enough (compared to the horrendous alternative of eternal damnation),

Theological disputes: a fresco of the Council of Nicaea in the Sistine Salon at the Vatican. It depicts the debate over the future Nicene Creed.
Credit: Pvasiliadis, Wikimedia Commons.

Fresco by Raphael in the Room of the Segnatura, Vatican. It depicts Christ surrounded by the Virgin Mary, John the Baptist, and various biblical figures. The altar is flanked by theologians debating transubstantiation.
Credit: Vatican Museum, Wikimedia Commons.

even a very small chance that it was true should be enough to persuade a rational person to accept the doctrine. Without knowing about Pascal, Reme found himself grappling with just this challenge near the end of his long life. His grandson, who became my PhD student shortly after the old man's death, told me what had happened. Reme was an animist, believing in local gods of the river and forest, but his adult daughter had become a committed Christian, and when she feared he was soon to die, she came to persuade him to convert to Christianity. She faced opposition not just from her father's doubts but also from her brother, who had traveled as a young man to neighboring Nigeria and had returned a committed Muslim. He was no less determined that their father should convert to Islam before he died. Plainly the father could not do both.

Age and terminal illness had not blunted their father's keen intelligence. "You are asking me to take a terrible risk," he told his two children. "If the Christian God is as merciful as you tell me, when my daughter goes to heaven he will listen to her prayers and call to his breast her heathen father who knew no better. Likewise, if the Muslim God is as merciful as you tell me, he will surely listen to my son's entreaties and call me to be with him in paradise. But if you ask me now to make an irrevocable choice, I have an even chance of condemning myself to hell forever."[2]

What Reme had realized, though he did not express it this way, was that Pascal's wager (as the argument came to be called) made sense only when the sole alternatives between which a person was called upon to choose were the existence and the nonexistence of God, with the threat of hell attached to the second of these. Even in Pascal's day, it made only limited sense, since believing in God didn't guarantee you would escape hell. France at the time, like most of Europe, was wracked by conflicts between Catholics and Protestants, each of whom threatened the other with hellfire for believing in the wrong sort of God. And not just with hellfire—many were tortured in this life and killed because the God in whom they believed was not considered acceptable to the authorities of the society in which they lived. But to Reme in late twentieth-century Cameroon the wager made no sense at all.

Like many millions of people before and after him, Reme faced a contest for his loyalty between the religious world in which he had grown up and an assertive world religion that wanted to claim him for its own. Unlike most of those people, he faced the claims of two assertive world religions at the same time, in circumstances that made them very evenly matched, with neither of them having a greater claim to his attention than the other. Also unlike most of those others, Reme faced the claims at the very end of his life, when the religions in question had nothing worldly to offer him in return. As we've seen, most religious organizations, though they may speak about the other world, claim to offer their members some very important benefits in this world. Even when they make practical claims (such as the claim that the healing ministry can cure cancer or diabetes) they also offer their members, whether they're cured or not, a community that envelops and supports them in the distress their disease is causing them. This tendency to "package" empirical claims that are hard to verify together with more easily verifiable claims about community-based benefits means, implicitly though rarely explicitly, that members don't need to focus on the difficult claims if they don't want to. But at the end of his life there was no packaging left for Reme—he was not going to join a human community. He simply had to decide his response according to whether he could believe what these two religions were claiming about the world to come. This makes his challenge an interesting test case of what we think about the role of beliefs in religious membership. Why do religious organizations apparently require their members to believe some things for which the evidence is at best indirect? Doesn't that undercut everything they're trying to do to attract and motivate members?

Religious Beliefs and Religious Membership—What Is the Link?

Not surprisingly, there's a strong correlation between what religion people belong to and some of the things they believe.[3] According to a 2013 survey from the Pew Research Center, 97 percent of white evangelical Protestant Christians in the United States believe that Jesus was born of a virgin, while only 32 percent of religiously unaffiliated Americans do so.[4] A total of 31 percent of US Catholics believe in transubstantiation (the doctrine that during Mass, the communion bread and wine become—literally, not symbolically—the body and blood of Jesus Christ). It's hard to know whether all these people interpreted the doctrine in the same way. But the idea that anyone who is not a Catholic might believe this was considered so unlikely that the survey did not ask any non-Catholics.[5] The vast majority of the world's Muslims believe that Muhammad was considered by God to be the most important of the prophets, but few non-Muslims believe this. Most members of the Prince Philip Movement in the village of Yaohnanen in Vanuatu believe that the late husband of Queen Elizabeth II of Great Britain was a divine spirit.[6] The proportion of the rest of the world's population that believes this belongs, like the question about how many non-Catholics believe in transubstantiation, to the vast universe of questions no survey has ever thought to ask.

As these telling omissions suggest, most of the beliefs that are correlated with religious membership are the result of belonging to a religion, and not the reason why people belong to a religion in the first place. Some people may leave a religion, or resist pressure to join one, because they cannot believe its specific claims—like the unfortunate English poet, feminist, and Anabaptist preacher Anne Askew, who felt unable to adopt the Catholic religion of her husband because she found transubstantiation too incredible, but was tortured and burnt at the stake anyway in 1546 by the Protestant régime of Henry VIII, which found her version of "plain speaking" particularly threatening.[7] Or like John Ruskin, who memorably described the impact of new discoveries in science on his Christian faith in a letter to his friend Henry Acland in 1851: "If only the Geologists would let me alone, I would do very well, but those dreadful Hammers! I hear the clink of them at the end of every cadence of the Bible verses."[8] Still, their cases are unusual. The fact that (according to the same Pew survey) over two-thirds of American Catholics *do not* believe in transubstantiation suggests that members may enjoy a lot of margin in practice to stick with a religion in spite of skepticism. Belief in transubstantiation may be a frequent consequence of being a Catholic, but it's still an optional one. Optional, that is, not as a matter of doctrine but as a matter of practice. Or rather, to put it more exactly, what you believe matters enormously to *some* members of religious movements, while apparently mattering very little to others. Seeing how religious platforms work helps us to understand how both attitudes to doctrine can coexist in the same movement. Bringing together a community of members with very different approaches to belief is not a weakness of religious platforms: it's their strength and their point.

Many religious people are clear about the unbelievability of claims made by other religions than their own, and historically far more religions have been denounced as incredible by believers in rival religions than by atheists. That's why the often-heard injunction to respect the beliefs of religious people can't require us to be willing to accept all those beliefs as true—since each of them often includes the belief that rival religions are false. But in any case, these judgments of truth or falsity are rarely crucial in determining initial religious choices. Most people belong to the same religion their parents did. Even for the minority who belong to a different religion than their parents, the reasons most of them give for their religious choices have to do with what material and spiritual benefits their religion offers them—not what factual claims it asks them to believe, about this world or the next.[9] To put it more precisely, the factual claims that make a difference to whether they join a religion (or a particular church, temple, synagogue, or mosque within a religion) are those that bear on the benefits the religion offers them. Only after they've joined do other claims begin to matter. Otherworldly questions of theology, metaphysics, the meaning of rituals, and of our place in the universe are subjects for debate mainly among those who've already signed up—even if at that point they can sometimes become very intense.[10]

Pascal's wager is unusual among discussions of religious doctrine because although it's about matters of theology, it's focused very directly on the benefits of religious membership and not on the truth or otherwise of the doctrine. It's an extreme version of an argument from the benefits of a religion to the conclusion that you should join it. It's often described as being an argument in favor of Christian belief, but that's not the best way to think about it. It's better described as an argument for accepting Christianity even if you only believe in it a tiny bit. Pascal himself, in the passage describing the wager, never wrote that it was an argument in favor of belief. He wrote about "inclining" or "betting" for or against Christianity, and at one point about "travelling towards faith," but the only references to belief in that passage are when he talks to the reader about how to deal with the "impossibility of believing."[11] Rather than an argument in favor of believing, his famous passage is much better understood as reassuring the reader that you don't have to believe— at least not more than a minuscule amount—to choose to belong. And choosing to belong is what he urges his reader to do. John Ruskin was to make a similar argument in 1852 when he wrote to reassure his worried father that he would act "as if the Bible *were* true."[12]

As Reme pointed out on his deathbed (and as Denis Diderot had previously pointed out in 1762),[13] Pascal's argument breaks down if more than one religion is trying to persuade you at the same time. For our purposes, though, the key message is that most religions, in the past as well as the present, have asked new members to accept and belong rather than necessarily to believe. Asking them to believe comes later, after they've agreed to belong. This helps us to understand the most puzzling aspect of the platform view of religious competition. If religions are trying so hard to make themselves attractive to their actual and potential members, why do they make life difficult for themselves by asking members to sign up to doctrines that, on average, most nonmembers of the religion find difficult to believe?

The answer is that *accepting* doesn't require believing, and believing is optional in practice for most members, most of the time (even while it passionately preoccupies some other members). It's only after joining that most members start to shift their beliefs in the direction of the religion's doctrines—and they do it because it comes naturally to them, not because their membership requires it. Pascal recognized this in advising readers to follow the example of others who had come to belief: "it's in acting as though they believed, in taking holy water, in saying masses. Quite naturally, that will make you believe." He then added a remark that is rarely quoted but very revealing: following this advice "will make you more stupid" (vous abêtira).[14] You couldn't ask for a clearer signal that Pascal thought that his argument was not about what it was reasonable to believe, but about what it was reasonable to do. If you had to silence the misgivings of your reason to do so, so be it.

Of course, that may have been what Pascal thought, but how do we know he was right? How confident can we be that beliefs really are optional, most of the time, for membership of religions? The fact that individuals even today can affirm, in the words of podcast host Honor Levy, a recent convert to Catholicism quoted in the *New York Times*, "You just do the rituals, and then it becomes real, even if you don't [initially] believe in it," doesn't guarantee that this is standard fare for ordinary folk—she is quoted in the *New York Times*, after all, in a piece headlined "New York's Hottest Club Is the Catholic Church," which is clearly intended as clickbait, not rigorous sociology.[15] And if beliefs are optional, why do so many religions nevertheless want to induce those people who do become members to believe in doctrines that, before they became members, they would have found impossible to believe? Indeed, how is it even possible to make members hold such beliefs? How costly are they for members to hold? Does believing in the doctrines of a religion make you act in ways that, if you didn't accept the doctrine, you'd be sure to regret? What kind of a sales pitch is that, for a religious organization seeking to attract members?

These are difficult questions, which we will look at in turn, in this and in later chapters. In any case, different individuals take different views about the centrality of belief to their own religious experience. It's worth noting first another feature of many religious beliefs, which they share with a lot of secular beliefs as well—let's call it their "incompletely worked-out" character. Many people hold beliefs that have consequences that would be radical for them if they ever stopped to think about them. Except they don't, so the radical consequences never impinge on their lives, never pose a difficult challenge. When we stop to think about what those consequences might be, the result can sometimes be sobering. Science fiction writer Ted Chiang has an intriguing short story called "Hell Is the Absence of God," which is set in an imaginary country much like modern America, except that everyone shares an agreed religion, which is true.[16] A feature of that religion is that miracles occur regularly and are accompanied by angelic visitations. The angels appear at unpredictable times and places and may cure several sick or disabled people each time.

Unfortunately, the visitations otherwise obey the laws of physics, including those that predict the consequences for nearby objects of an angel's sudden appearance. The principal character is called Neil Fisk, and his wife has died because she was present at an angelic visitation. She "was hit by flying glass when the angel's billowing curtain of flame shattered the storefront window of the café in which she was eating. She bled to death within minutes."[17] Chiang's story explores the practical and emotional consequences of working out in detail what certain miracles might be like if they really happened. In the process it forces us to think about a problem posed by all beliefs in miracles, which is their essential arbitrariness—if God is prepared to intervene to save one person from the laws of physics, why that person and not another? What's interesting for our purposes is not the answer to that question—Chiang does not give us one. It's rather the attention he draws to the fact that incompletely worked-out beliefs don't challenge us as much as they might. As religious members we may sincerely believe certain things that would be much less palatable to us if only we stopped to work out what they imply—but most of the time we have no need to.

The more we reflect, the more we realize that incompletely worked-out beliefs are everywhere, and it's not just religious leaders who benefit from them. If you find it troubling that many religious members give money to leaders holding out a prospect of eternal life, ask yourself whether it's so different from marketing campaigns for cosmetics that hint at a promise of eternal youth. The customers who buy so-called "anti-aging" products do not then act as though they had stopped aging; many treat the label as irrelevant window dressing, and even those who pay more for branded products advertised by impossibly radiant and youthful models are rarely indulging in more than a little dreaming. We should not expect members of churches that hold out the promise of eternal life to act, most of the time, as though they were immortal either; they weep for their departed relatives, fear for their own safety, and even more so for that of their children. It remains a wide-open question just how much we follow through the consequences of those beliefs that apparently guide our spending decisions, and many of our others too.[18]

Some religious disputes can be seen as the consequence of different groups holding beliefs that have been worked out to different degrees. Many religious people who are opposed to abortion in all but extreme cases believe that the human soul enters the body at conception, and that killing a creature with a soul is the greatest possible evil. They accuse other religious people, who accept abortion up to a certain stage of pregnancy, of not having worked out their beliefs sufficiently clearly. According to them, it doesn't make sense to believe that the soul enters the body at conception *and* that it's wrong to kill a creature with a soul *and* that abortion of a fertilized human ovum is acceptable at any time. And they're right—if you want to defend abortion up to a certain stage of pregnancy, you really do need to think which of the other two beliefs you're willing to question.

The problem for such arguments, though, is that if you work out the beliefs all the way, the conclusions become even more challenging. For instance, many religious people opposed to abortion also believe that, because of Original Sin, it's a terrible thing for a person with a soul to die unbaptized, and that strenuous efforts should be made to baptize infants and others who are at risk of dying. In 1786, Guatemalan priest Pedro José de Arrese published a work called *Baptism through Incision*, instructing readers on their duty to perform caesarian operations on the bodies of recently deceased pregnant women, in order to extract and baptize the fetus while it was still alive.[19] Had the good father known what we now know about the proportion of fertilized ova that never achieve implantation, and the proportion of pregnancies that miscarry in the first few weeks, he would have realized that the challenge was even more daunting than he had ever imagined, requiring even precautionary baptism of the menstrual fluid. This might have led him to question the assumption that the Almighty was dependent on the intervention of fallible human agents to be able to save souls. More likely it might have led him to halt, as so many of us do in so many contexts both religious and secular, the remorseless working out of the implications of his beliefs.

Even if it's not accompanied by the absolute need for baptism, the belief that the soul enters the body at conception would imply a duty of respect toward stillborn babies or babies that die young. Yet this has often been ignored by religious authorities when the deaths were considered embarrassing or inconvenient. In 2019, the Commission of Investigation into the Roman Catholic Mother and Baby Homes in Ireland found that "more than 900 children died in Bessborough. Despite very intensive inquiries and searches, the Commission has been able to establish the burial place of only 64 children." In the Tuam Children's Home, around 800 children were buried in a structure "built within the decommissioned large sewage tank." And more than 950 bodies of children were sent to the medical schools at University College Dublin, Trinity College Dublin, and the Royal College of Surgeons in Ireland for the purpose of anatomical research.[20] Fintan O'Toole, from whose 2021 memoir *We Don't Know Ourselves* these details are cited, writes extensively of the shared national capacity for compartmentalized thinking, for simultaneously knowing and not knowing many inconvenient truths. Though he makes a powerful case for this as a way of understanding many of the developments in Ireland during the last half of the twentieth century, the phenomenon is one known to many other countries and many other systems of belief, both religious and secular.

Bearing in mind, then, the incompletely worked-out nature of so many of our beliefs, let's return to the question: How optional are religious beliefs anyway?

Are Religious Beliefs Optional for Members?

The history of Christianity has almost certainly biased us into thinking that belief is a much more compulsory marker of religious affiliation than it really is. It's true that, as historian Diarmaid MacCulloch has put it, "medieval inquisitors did not invent the concept of heresy: it is embedded in New Testament literature in a series of bilious references to 'sects.'"[21] But as MacCulloch goes on to argue, the focus of medieval inquisitors on heretical beliefs such as those allegedly held by the Albigensians was probably an attempt to stamp out a movement that sought "to extend the logic of the Gregorian reforms further than Gregorian reformers in the Church hierarchy thought appropriate. As in so many other situations, this was a dispute about authority rather than about faith itself."[22]

Let's look at an example that would seem most strongly to support the view that belief in doctrine was compulsory in practice for Christian membership. One of the main acts of the Council of Nicaea, convened by the Emperor Constantine in 325 CE, was to dispatch the Arian heresy, thereby "settling" the question whether the Son had been "begotten" by the Father and thus whether Christ was in some sense a lesser being than God the Father. The question was finally settled not only by theological arguments but also and above all by a political negotiation.[23]

It's doubtful how many of the more than a thousand attendees of the council were able to give a coherent account of whether the Son had been begotten, still less why it mattered whether the Father and Son were "consubstantial," as the Nicene Creed was to put it. But they would certainly have known, and have cared very much, which side of the argument they found themselves on, and what that meant for their alliances and their political future. Being an adherent of the Arian heresy was a matter of who your friends were—not which piece of theology you found most convincing. In any case it was not about how you interpreted the evidence, since to the ordinary person the evidence on the question was simply not visible. It was about which were the authorities to whom you were willing to defer. Imagine if someone asked you at the point of a sword whether you're a *homoousian* or a *homoiousian*. You'd probably try to find out what *they* thought and convince them you agreed. You certainly wouldn't let them see that you have no idea what the difference is between the two. And what the point of a sword can accomplish in an instant can be brought about, less rapidly but no less reliably, by the steady tug of ambition and interest.

If this was true of a great many bishops and deacons who came to the council, how much more true must it have been of the vast flocks of the faithful, who were associated thereafter with one or other of the contending factions. Though we cannot of course be certain of any interpretation at this distance in time and culture, it seems unlikely that most would have cared intrinsically about the theological niceties, as opposed to caring about whether it was their side or the other that emerged victorious from the council.[24]

The fact that reciting a "creed" (derived from the Latin "credere," meaning to believe) has become central to Christian worship since then might suggest that belief became a necessary condition of belonging to the Church after the Council of Nicaea, even if it had not been so before. But there's no reason to think that the function of a creed was to establish what someone believed. The original Greek word for a creed was σύμβολον (symbolon, as in the phrase for the Nicene creed—Σύμβολον τῆς Νικαίας), which referred originally to a mechanism for verifying someone's identity by matching two halves of a broken object. And the recitation of a creed was supposed to signal whose side the believer was on, not what piece of theology might be passing simultaneously through their mind as they were speaking.

The original Nicene creed of 325 went through many revisions before the Council of Constantinople in 381 adopted the now-standard version (sometimes called the Niceno-Constantinopolitan Creed). That doesn't mean the drafters were trying to adjust the words as if they were experimenters trying to revise a scientific theory. They were engaging in a piece of necessary factional politics, bringing on board the allies they needed, and setting up barriers against those they wanted to exclude.

Indeed, the more controversial the theology, the more bare-knuckle the politics. Consider a later controversy about the creed, the "Filioque" dispute, which contributed to the split between the Eastern and Western Churches in 1054. It was still considered important enough nearly a thousand years later, in 1995, for the Vatican to issue a clarificatory statement that while the words καὶ τοῦ Υἱοῦ ("and the Son") would indeed be heretical if used with the Greek verb ἐκπορεύομαι, the word Filioque (which means "and the Son") is not heretical when associated with the Latin verb procedo and the related word procession. Refusing to include a disputed phrase, as the Eastern Church has done and still does, is not about resisting a certain description because the description would be wrong. It's about refusing to give legitimacy to the parties that are lobbying for the phrase. For the Vatican to reply that the phrase is not heretical in Latin even if its Greek translation may indeed be heretical is evidently an exercise in constructive diplomacy, designed to heal a breach that has lasted for a millennium. If theological assertions have any claim to be factual, their truth can't depend on the language in which they are stated (so long as the translation is accurate). That maneuver is precisely what you wouldn't do if you thought the argument was really about a question of fact.

If creeds were primarily about establishing and enforcing belief, there would be a premium on including only unambiguous statements, so that everyone would know what they meant. Does the communion wine contain blood or only grape juice? Can the shaman levitate? Is the king able to cure scrofula? Will prayer bring rain? Though the Christian creeds contain some clear factual statements (albeit unverifiable ones, such as those about the resurrection of the body), they also contain statements so abstract that people would have to decide whether they agreed to them before having any idea what they meant. And that would have been precisely the point.

This doesn't at all mean that doctrine is unimportant in demarcating religious movements from one another and in shaping the way they compete. Germany in the sixteenth century, for example, was one of the most religiously competitive environments in history prior to the twentieth century, with fierce rivalry between the Catholic Church and two varieties of Protestantism (Lutheranism and Calvinism), as well as many other sects such as the Anabaptists. Differences between religious communities in many aspects of religious life became more marked—in liturgy and ritual as well as in attachment to doctrines. Historians of this process (which has been called *confessionalization*) once tended to see it as imposed from above by political rulers, but more recent research has emphasized the degree of agency that local communities enjoyed, and the extent to which they could resist the imposition of formulae they did not like.[25] But as with the Council of Nicaea, the fact that doctrine mattered does not mean that choices between doctrines were made according to which of them constituted the most convincing beliefs. The doctrine you accepted was essentially a signal of the faction to which you belonged. And, as the intervention of Protestant Sweden in

1630 in the Thirty Years' War with the support of Catholic France was to illustrate, doctrine could be flexibly asserted or downplayed according to the demands of Realpolitik. As historian Peter Wilson puts it, "Protestantism featured in [Swedish] domestic propaganda, but was omitted from the manifesto since intervention had to be presented as confessionally neutral so as not to alienate France. . . . [Swedish chancellor Axel] Oxenstierna later admitted that religion was merely a pretext, while [Swedish king] Gustavus said that if it had been the cause he would have declared war on the pope."[26]

Factional allegiance was frequently a matter of life and death, and not only in the exceptionally bloody Thirty Years' War. When Mary Tudor succeeded to the English throne in 1553, she began a campaign to reverse the move toward Protestantism begun by her father Henry VIII and continued by her half-brother Edward VI. In a reign of only five years, she had over 280 leading Protestants executed, mainly by burning at the stake. A particularly striking case was Thomas Cranmer, Archbishop of Canterbury, who after being forced to watch the grisly executions of Bishops Ridley and Latimer, recanted Protestant theology. Under the normal rules of legal procedure, he could have expected to be reprieved, but Queen Mary refused to grant this. Outraged and terrified, he withdrew the recantation on the day of his execution. The case underlines the fact that normally recantation was enough—what mattered was what you said, and not what you might secretly believe.

Recantation is not usually enough to save people convicted under various laws relating to blasphemy. Such laws are still in force today in eighty-four countries around the world from Nigeria and Poland to Pakistan, and have been used actively for repression in forty-one of those countries. Blasphemy laws remained on the statute book in the United Kingdom until 2008 and in Ireland till 2020.[27] It's also sobering to be reminded that the notorious blasphemy laws in Pakistan owe their origins to provisions of the Indian penal code imposed by the British in 1860 (and originally drafted by Lord Macaulay in 1837).[28] It's not really a surprise that recantation is no defense—the blasphemer's alleged offense is never considered to be what they believe, but the supposed insult they offer to the faith in question, to the founder of the faith, or to its followers.

If belief as such, rather than factional allegiance, was optional (in practice if not in theory) during the most doctrinally intense periods of Christianity's history, it seems likely that it was no less optional in earlier times, when written statements of doctrine played a less important part in religious activity, and particularly when religious ritual relied on a purely oral tradition. This doesn't mean that oral traditions can't enforce uniformity—indeed, a theory known as the Parry-Lord hypothesis suggests that the Homeric poems were constructed out of formulae that conformed to a particular metric structure, and could be used for the repetitive reconstruction of a long sung poem over many recitals by the same or by different singers. This therefore constituted a technology for the preservation of oral traditions over long periods of time with higher copying fidelity than had previously been thought possible.[29] The Homeric tradition was far from unusual: as philologist Wendy Doniger reports, the central Hindu text the *Rig Veda* "was preserved orally, but it was frozen, every syllable preserved for centuries, through a process of rigorous memorization."[30]

Still, if a written creed could have been used to enforce *assent* without necessarily enforcing *belief*, even a highly formulaic technology for the copying of spoken ritual elements would not have been able to enforce belief rather than merely assent. We can imagine that demonstrations of agreement with the leader's words might have been enforced rigorously—they would have marked out those members who could be relied upon to follow their leaders' instructions. But people would have been giving assent to their membership of the group, not to any particular statement with a factual content. And the question of what they actually believed would have been beside the point. I don't know of any credible ethnographic evidence of anybody ever being refused entry to a religious ceremony with the words "we like what you say—but we don't think you really mean it."

Historically, the only instances of persecution of people for what they were suspected of believing, as distinct from what they said and which religious authorities they acknowledged, were of Jews or other minorities who had converted to Catholicism and were suspected of doing so insincerely. Puritans in Elizabethan England were angry that not enough was being done to persecute Catholics for their secret beliefs. They "suspected, quite rightly, that many leaders of the established Church, not least its Nicodemite Queen, were happy to tolerate merely formal adherence from inquisitors."[31] The key point is that it was only a minority on either the Protestant or the Catholic side who cared intrinsically about adherence to the content rather than the form of doctrine; for the rest, it was the loyalties of their members that mattered and not their beliefs per se. If this was true of Christianity, a religion that ascribed high priority to doctrine, it was certainly true of traditions such as Hinduism. As Wendy Doniger puts it, "people have been killed in India because they did or did not sacrifice animals, or because they had sex with the wrong woman, or disregarded the Vedas, or even made use of the wrong sacred texts, but no one was impaled (the Hindu equivalent of burning at the stake) for saying that god was like this rather than like that."[32] We'll return in chapter 10 to the question why certain religious movements (notably Christianity and Islam) have made disagreements over doctrine a pretext for violence, whereas this has been much less common in other world religions such as Hinduism and Buddhism (where rival factions have typically killed each other for control over economic or political resources). For now, what matters is to note that even at the most doctrinally intense periods of intra-Christian rivalry, doctrine was much more a signal of factional loyalty than of the precise beliefs that any individual might hold.

You might object that even if certain supernatural beliefs had never been an explicit precondition of religious practice in some preliterate societies, they might well have been an implicit precondition, because only if people believed the practices worked would there have been any point in engaging in them. Shamanistic rituals, for example, are often costly to the participants in various ways (costly to the shaman because of the physical ordeal involved, and costly to the other participants because they would usually have to pay the shaman in some way). Why take part in them unless you believe—really believe—that they work?

This objection ignores two important facts about shamanism.[33] The first is that the ecstatic experiences of shamanism are often profoundly transformative—they involve drugs, physical ordeals, noise, collective movement, and physical contact—independently of any interpretation in terms of the spirit world. There may be a strong attraction of participation regardless of what you believe; at the very least, we don't know to what extent beliefs play a part in making those experiences happen. The second fact about shamanism is that even in communities where there's widespread respect for the shaman's person and the tradition he or she represents, shamans never enjoyed unconditional approval. A candidate for shamanhood is always subjected to critical scrutiny[34]— are their powers as great as they claim? So are the particular interventions that the shaman proposes—will the ritual work as effectively as has been promised? Skepticism is not a modern state of mind: it's an integral part of living in a community some of whose members claim privileges on account of their supposed access to unseen spiritual insight. As historian Alan Strathern puts it in discussing immanent religions more generally, "immanentism is not characterized by an absence of skepticism but by a particular form of it."[35] Robin Briggs likewise reminds us that in most of Europe in the Middle Ages, "belief in the reality of witchcraft, and the need to provide legal means to repress it, was combined with cautious skepticism about individual cases."[36] Individuals vary in their degree of skepticism, and the more skeptical members of the shaman's community may be able to take part in the rituals regardless of what they believe—even if those who become more deeply involved in the rituals will be those who believe more strongly in their efficacy.

For the over 40 percent of the world's population who profess adherence to non-Abrahamic religions, there's even less reason to think that belief as such is what matters for belonging. It would be hard even to know what beliefs to single out as essential to being a Hindu, a Buddhist, a Parsi, or a Taoist. The aggressively skeptical might wonder what's the point in taking part in a temple ritual in front of a statue of Avalokiteshvara unless you believe something specific about the ritual and its effects, and about the real existence of this earthly manifestation of the compassionate Buddha, who is said to guard the world between the departure of the historical Buddha Gautama and the arrival of the future Buddha Maitreya. But the many millions of temple visitors who do just that every day without being able to say anything very precise about what they believe would respectfully disagree.

So, if belief is mostly optional for people to belong to a religion, why do so many religions work so hard to make their members believe things that members of rival religions find incredible?

Why Do Religions Seek to Influence Their Members' Beliefs?

Before we can even begin to understand why religions try to make their members believe things that are incompatible with rival religions, we need to think more deeply about how it's even possible for them to do so. The challenge extends well beyond the field of religion, to understanding how reasonable people can disagree about anything. The Israeli American mathematician and economist Robert Aumann (incidentally a deeply religious Jew) published in 1976 a theorem describing rational decision-makers who shared the same prior beliefs about the probability of some hypothesis being true, and who then separately observed different items of private information about that hypothesis.[37] If they shared with each other the conclusions they had reached (without sharing the private information), he showed that they could not disagree about these conclusions! The argument rests on the idea that if each decision-maker is rational, and knows the other is rational, and that the other knows this, and so on, they can't "agree to disagree" because each would know that the private information the other has observed must objectively justify the conclusion the other has reached. Iterating this reasoning, Aumann argued, showed that nothing short of full agreement between the two would adequately respect each one's recognition of the other's rationality.

Before you roll your eyes in irritation at yet another example of a mathematician telling you that something that happens every day in practice is impossible in theory, it's worth reflecting on the purpose of the exercise. Aumann's argument is a mathematical theorem, so providing the theorem is valid, the conclusion is true if the premises are true. Conversely, therefore, the fact that we see disagreement all the time, about religion and about secular matters, tells us that one or more of the premises must be false—but which ones? The point of the theorem is to focus our attention on that question.

The very simple structure of Aumann's argument (the proof in his paper is just four lines long) means that there are only three possibilities. Distinguishing them really helps us to think about the sources of religious disagreement. The first possibility is that people who disagree don't have the same prior beliefs about the subject of their disagreement—therefore their disagreement is not the result of the different evidence they've observed, since they never had the same prior beliefs to begin with. This seems plausible: people in different religions seem to have very different background assumptions about what are likely ways for the world and the universe to behave, such as about whether it contains multiple gods or just one, or how likely it is that a benevolent God would intervene through miracles to help some people and not others. But it's also not very helpful, because it leaves us wondering where these different prior beliefs come from—they can't be the result of observing different evidence, since Aumann's theorem means we would have to explain that too. Perhaps there are just deep-rooted cultural differences between members of different religions, and maybe when people choose to join a religion, or an organization within some religion, they do so according to cultural affinity, rather than on the basis of specific beliefs.

The second possibility is that people who disagree have not fully shared their conclusions (in the strong sense required by the theorem, which is that their conclusions are "common knowledge"—each one knows them, and knows that the other knows that they know them, and so on). Once again, this often makes sense, since we may not be quite sure what someone else's beliefs really involve. Thinking back to the Ted Chiang short story, if someone else believes in miracles and I don't, this might be linked to the continuing uncertainty by each of us as to what, precisely, the other thinks miracles can involve. But again, while this might explain some disagreements, it doesn't seem adequate to deal with disagreements where a simple factual issue is at stake. Take transubstantiation again: surely it's clear what someone means if they think that the communion wine has been transformed—literally, not metaphorically—into the blood of Christ?

Or is it? It may be clear what they say, but that doesn't mean it's clear what they believe. If someone is using the word "literally" literally and not metaphorically (as when a person might say "I turned my study literally upside down looking for my keys"), then the belief that the communion wine is literally the blood of Christ implies that we could take it to a medical laboratory and it would test positive for the presence of hemoglobin. Someone who believes the first part of that sentence ("the communion wine is literally the blood of Christ") and not the second ("we could take it to a medical laboratory") is not using the word "literally" in the proper way. It may be just too hard to tell whether someone who claims to believe in transubstantiation really believes it, but does not want to demonstrate it through a hemoglobin test, despite the obvious attractions of doing to so to reassure the faithful and to convince others. Might they instead not really believe it but want to assert it anyway, perhaps to demonstrate loyalty to the Catholic tradition in front of others? From that chink of uncertainty about an apparently clear statement, a whole cloud of disagreement can emerge.[38] Indeed, the further we explore the question what someone "really" believes, the harder it can become to be sure where lie the boundaries between belief, supposition, conjecture, and the lively imagination. A reader of historian Paul Veyne's famous essay *Did the Greeks Believe in Their Myths?* (well, this reader anyway) can come away quite unsure, not only about what the Greeks believed, but also about whether Veyne himself knows what he believes about what they believed.[39] And recent psychological theories to the effect that human reasoning has its foundations in "argumentative" activities rather than the intrinsic wish to communicate true statements suggest that we have to be very cautious before taking people's statements about what they believe at face value.[40]

The third way to reconcile Aumann's theorem with the presence of undeniable disagreement is to take seriously the idea that rational decision-making just doesn't adequately describe how human beings behave. In particular, Aumann's theorem requires rational decision-makers to obey Bayes' rule, and each of them to know that the other does so. Bayes' rule requires the probability of some hypothesis, after the observation of evidence, to be proportional to its prior probability, among other things. Consider, for example, a medical test that is 99 percent reliable, in the sense that it has a 99 percent probability of showing the result that corresponds to your condition. If you test positive, what is the probability you have the condition? It's not 99 percent, because it makes a difference whether the condition you're looking for is common or rare—the rarer it is, the more likely is your result to be a false positive. If the condition is so common that one person in ten has it, then when you test positive, the probability you have the condition is a little under 92 percent. If only one person in a thousand has it, the probability is only about 9 percent, and if one in a million does, the probability you have the condition is less than a hundredth of 1 percent.

Bayes' rule requires, in other words, our assessments of probabilities to be strongly "anchored" by the prior probabilities of the hypotheses we are assessing. There is now an impressive amount of experimental evidence suggesting that real human decision-makers are sensitive to prior probabilities, and that this sensitivity can be detected very early in childhood. But they are not nearly as sensitive as they should be. We overreact to recent evidence relative to the background probabilities. For instance, most of us would have difficulty keeping calm in the face of news that we have just tested positive for a very rare disease—even if the rarity of the disease means it's still very unlikely that we have it, despite the positive test. We also fail to compensate for biases in the sources of our evidence—such as the fact that we may belong to a community that has its own reasons for persuading us to think in a certain way.

There's also growing scientific evidence about the ways we try to persuade each other in practice. By that I don't mean that we use anecdotes rather than statistics. That's quite compatible with Bayesian reasoning, though it creates a wide margin for people with a stock of appropriate anecdotes to cherry-pick their anecdotes (even if they are true) to influence our actions in ways that are not necessarily in our interests. It may even make it better for us to rely on the advice of relatively uninformed people who are less likely to want to manipulate us.[41] Rather, the telling aspect of the way we argue in practice is that we do so as much by trying to influence other people's interpretation of existing evidence as by offering new evidence. As two economists have put it: "In finance, when recent market performance is better than long-term averages, bullish traders argue 'this time is different.' Stock market analysts use technical analysis to argue that patterns in prices and trading volume identify profit opportunities. In debating climate change, one side might argue that extreme weather events provide evidence of global warming, while the other might argue that they reflect 'noise' in an inherently unpredictable process."[42] We wouldn't expect to argue like this if we all knew we were rational decision-makers, who share the same prior belief and whose inferences obey Bayes' rule. If we were, we would already share our interpretations of the prior evidence, so only new evidence could be a subject for argument and discussion.

Further scientific evidence about our violations of Bayesian reasoning can be found in a phenomenon known to psychologists as the Dunning-Kruger effect, which is the observation that "poor performers in many social and intellectual domains seem largely unaware of just how deficient their expertise is."[43] For our purposes what matters is not whether there is a difference between high and low performers, but rather that all of us appear to be least capable of addressing our ignorance in precisely the areas where we most need to do so. This directly contradicts Bayes' rule, which tells us that the less we know, the more we should learn from new evidence.

Evolution and Non-Bayesian Reasoning

Can we understand why human beings have evolved to be like this? There has been a sea change in recent years in the way psychologists and anthropologists think about how natural selection has shaped the cognitive processes in the human brain. Researchers have been impressed for a long time by the astonishing ability of many animals, including human beings, to navigate their natural environment. They have stressed especially their ability to distinguish the many threats and opportunities within that environment, which can make all the difference between an animal's flourishing and leaving offspring or being eaten by a predator before it can reproduce. Human cognitive abilities, though not matching those of some nonhuman animal species in certain dimensions, have been shown to be no less remarkable, even when deployed independently of any of the skills imparted by a modern education.

Anthropologists have emphasized the impressive cognitive talents of foragers, whether it is their grasp of folk biology, including the habits of the animal and plant species they track,[44] or their overall general intelligence.[45] Researchers have been understandably keen to compensate for earlier generations' characterization of forager cultures as "primitive," and in any case the evidence is by now overwhelming that forager cognition is as sophisticated in its potential as anything to be found in larger-scale societies, even if it is not applied to such activities as advanced mathematics or theoretical physics. And in all kinds of societies, many studies have stressed the extent to which human beings behave as intuitive statisticians.[46] They have documented statistical understanding in preverbal human infants and children, as well as in nonhuman primates.[47] Furthermore, these insights extend not only to behavior but also to plausible models of cognitive architecture and function: probabilistic models of cognition assume that human cognition can be explained in terms of a rational Bayesian framework.[48]

However, in more recent times the consensus has begun to change. This is due not just to findings that, for all their impressive talents, human beings depart in very systematic ways from what normative statistical theory (including Bayes' rule) would recommend, such as by giving inadequate weight to prior probabilities when drawing inferences from evidence.[49] It's also due to the crucial role played by the *social* nature of intelligence. Anthropologists such as Robert Boyd, Peter Richerson, Joseph Henrich, Sarah Mathew, and Charles Perreault have emphasized that the content of our beliefs about our natural environment depends not just on how cognitively competent we are but also on how we integrate our intelligence with the beliefs we inherit from our social environment.[50]

For example, even highly trained scientists have had great difficulty surviving in the challenging conditions of the Arctic or the Australian outback without the help of indigenous knowledge about how to survive the cold, hunt local prey, or detoxify locally available foodstuffs.[51] It would not have been adaptive in prehistory for our ancestors to depend only on their own intelligence—they would have needed to be very attentive to what others in their communities told them. In prehistory it would have been optimal for you, by and large, to adopt the beliefs of your elders—and you couldn't choose your elders! So there was nothing to be gained by taking into account the fact that you might have had different beliefs if you had happened to be taught by different elders. Your elders in turn might have told you some colorful stories about the origins of the universe, but they would have had little to gain from teaching you that people who have different beliefs from yours are dangerous heretics and deserve to be killed. That kind of toxic teaching has arrived sufficiently recently in our evolutionary history for us to have evolved few cognitive defenses against it.

The pressure of survival in harsh environments, which required us to deploy collective and not just individual intelligence, has profoundly shaped human brains.[52] There is by now a large anthropological and developmental literature documenting the human capacity for social learning from figures of authority.[53] These include our parents and elder siblings, but also adoptive authority figures in various groups we belong to. In relatively small and egalitarian communities, at least, it's mostly adaptive to believe what our elders tell us, even if our elders have some incentive to manipulate the detail of what they tell us in their own interest. We do have an evolved capacity for skepticism—what anthropologist Dan Sperber and colleagues have called "epistemic vigilance"—but it protects us only up to a point.[54] Until the last century or so, it would have been rare for young people in any community to have access to better information on any important subject than the elders of their community did (though there's a lively debate about whether, on average today, twenty-year-olds are better informed about big questions than fifty-year-olds, this is the first time in the history of humanity when the question could realistically have been asked). This also implies that if religious leaders become figures of authority first, and only then do we grow to believe what they tell us, it won't be surprising if we eventually believe many things we wouldn't otherwise have accepted. This will reinforce the widespread human tendency, which we noted in chapter 5, to use over-imitation in learning from the behavior of others.

So this is the answer to the challenge posed by Aumann's theorem—namely, how there can be disagreement between fully Bayesian reasoners who share with each other the conclusions of their reasoning. Human beings are not fully Bayesian reasoners, and there's no reason to think natural selection would have made us so. For processing information about the natural world in relation to those of its characteristics that we can observe directly, the more Bayesian we are the better, from natural selection's point of view. But for processing information about our social world in a forager environment, or about those aspects of our natural world where finding out by ourselves is very dangerous (such as which foods are poisonous or where the predators live), there's not much value to becoming highly Bayesian. There's also little value in cultivating skepticism about the information we're given by authority figures in our environment.

Summing Up

Let's summarize what we've learned about why religious leaders might try to convince their members of the truth of beliefs that are not directly related to the benefits the religion can bring them. Just as we saw in the case of ritual, there's a difference between the outsider perspective and the insider perspective. Most outsiders don't need to believe in the doctrine of a religion in order to become a member: even religions that do emphasize doctrine—for example, by requiring catechism—don't tend to enforce the belief requirement very rigorously. Many other religious movements barely emphasize doctrine at all, as opposed to religious practice. Insiders, on the other hand, often do care about doctrine (at least in movements that make doctrine salient), and do appear to believe in the doctrine, though rarely to a uniform degree. Their willingness to believe owes a great deal to their willingness to trust the leaders of their movement. Prehistory has endowed us with brains that, for all their startlingly impressive capacity to navigate our natural world, were very open to believing the things that trusted leaders of our communities had told us.

The fact that many religions profess beliefs that outsiders find difficult to accept is therefore not the marketing disadvantage it might at first appear. Doctrine has the advantage that its impact on insiders and outsiders is asymmetric. Accepting the doctrine makes it much less likely that insiders will leave or even just reduce their commitment, not least because the doctrine often underlines the unattractiveness of the alternatives. But accepting the doctrine is something the curious outsider does not need to do right away. Most of the difficult beliefs that come with religious membership are ones that we acquire after we've become members, not before. And we'll see in chapter 8 that some beliefs can even seem attractive to us not despite their difficulty but because of it.

Let's now look at some of the beliefs that, in this trusting environment, human beings have found most compelling to share with one another. Many of them come in the form of stories. Religions have proved startlingly effective—much more effective than many secular storytellers—at weaving for us narratives about our lives, about their purpose and our place in the universe. Why are they so good at this, and why are we so hungry for the stories religion can provide? This will be the subject of chapter 7.

CHAPTER 7

Religion, Narrative, and Meaning

From the cry of a tiny insect, one can hear a vast world.

—Zhang Daye, *The World of a Tiny Insect*

Defeat and Transfiguration

On October 10 of the year 680 CE (which is also year 61 in the Muslim calendar), at a place called Karbala in present-day Iraq, a man called Hossein ibn Ali was attacked and killed, along with around twenty members of his family and a bodyguard of some fifty men. The force that attacked them was around four thousand strong, though some sources have claimed that it was much larger even than that. They were killed because Hossein, as grandson of the prophet Muhammad, was a potential rival to Yazid, the new caliph of the Ummayad dynasty, the second established after the death of Muhammad and whose legitimacy was still widely contested. Yazid offered Hossein safe conduct if he swore allegiance, but Hossein refused. Whether this was because he did not want to do so, or because he did not believe the assurances, we don't know. In that event, he and his family stood no chance.

For a new monarch (or would-be monarch) to kill relatives of a previous reigning monarch has been, historically, a feature of all known societies in which kingship is transmitted through kinship. Hereditary

A large Qajar printed cotton textile (*kalamkari*) depicting a scene from the Shi'a Muslim festival of Ashura, Iran, nineteenth century, with Persian *nasta'liq* inscription cartouches to border, depicting the martyrdom at Karbala of Hussein.
Credit: Roseberys, Wikimedia Commons.

Another poignant narrative: a leaf from the Morgan Picture Bible, *c.* 1250 CE, with the story of David and his rebellious son Absalom.
Credit: Getty Center, Wikimedia Commons.

monarchy has had the advantage of clarifying, most of the time, who should succeed the current monarch. It thereby prevents, at least some of the time, a violent contestation when a monarch dies or becomes too weak to rule effectively. But it also means that if a contestation occurs, it's likely to be even more violent than it would have been otherwise. It typically involves the slaughter of many people (including infants) who pose no threat in themselves but have merely the misfortune of their kinship. It also means that, since the killer is often also related to the previous monarch, the slaughter often takes place within families.* In one single night, January 28, 1595, the new Ottoman sultan Mehmed III had all nineteen of his brothers strangled with bow strings by deaf-mute servants (who were considered to be unable to testify to the deed); their bodies were buried in a chamber next to the Hagia Sophia mosque. Other examples of regal fratricide, though less spectacular in numbers killed at one time, are attested in a wide variety of societies in Asia, Africa, and Europe, as well as being a subject of mythological record, from the Egyptian myth of Set and Osiris to those of Cain and Abel in the Bible, Eteocles and Polyneices in Greek myth, and Karna and Arjuna in the *Mahabharata*.

By the standards of historical murder, the killing of Hossein ibn Ali and his family was a sordid but unexceptional affair, apparently destined to sink into oblivion alongside those of countless others whose killers would occupy thrones and employ historians to write up their exploits and erase those of their rivals. Indeed, Hossein's father, Ali bin Abi Talib, the Prophet's cousin and son-in-law, had himself been murdered in the year 661, and the family did not seem to have much luck outwitting assassins. Yet somehow, the death of Hossein managed to inspire enough of his followers to launch a movement, the Shi'a branch of Islam, which now commands the allegiance of around 180 million people, some 10 percent of the world's Muslims. Every year up to 8 million pilgrims visit Karbala for the festival of Ashura, commemorating the anniversary

---

*Lady Bracknell says to the suitor for her niece's hand in Oscar Wilde's *The Importance of Being Earnest*, "I would strongly advise you, Mr. Worthing, to try and acquire some relations as soon as possible" (Wilde 1898, p. 38). Many members of royal families throughout history have found relations far more of a liability than an asset.

of Hossein's death. Many more than that come to celebrate Arba'in, a festival held forty days later around the mausoleum of Hossein. Hamid Dabashi describes the scene during Ashura when he was growing up:

> Early in the morning . . . from each mosque in the city would pour out an initially jubilant but intermittently mournful procession of *sineh zanan* (those who rhythmically beat their chest), *zanjir zanan* (those who do the same with a handful of chains beating their back), *alam-daran* (heavy and powerful men carrying huge masts with flags and other religious icons), *noheh khanan* (cantors), and their respective constituencies of mosque-goers. . . . [B]lock after block, as far as the eye could see, cantors would sing moving oratorios on loudspeakers fixed on long masts. . . . An almost endless, seemingly seamless succession of colorful crowds, a combustion of operatic fervor, choreographed ballets, and tragic zeal, all with epic proportions and cosmic expanse—always sad, sometimes amusing, at times funny, and always with an overriding sense of being part of a drama in which we were actors and spectators at the same time, young and old. Through that play we felt we were part of an immense celestial gathering of our cosmic universe. We were stars dancing in the heavens.[1]

The fact that Shi'ism can bring millions onto the streets in celebration of a historic defeat would have seemed extremely strange to the leaders of religious movements in most of the ancient world. Greek and Roman religions were many things, but one thing they were emphatically not was testaments to the inspirational qualities of losers. The sculptures of the Persian god Mithras, whose cult competed for a time with Christianity in the early Roman Empire, show him slaying bulls, not suffering martyrdom.[2] The Hindu god Shiva, in his dancing form called Nataraja that inspired some of the great bronze sculptures of the Indian Chola period, is the effortless lord of all the manifestations of divine energy from creation through destruction, preservation, salvation, and illusion.[3] The religions of the pre-Columbian Americas and the societies of the precolonial Pacific, as well as many others across the world, used spectacular displays of human sacrifice to inspire terror and obedience in their audiences, not a desire to emulate the victims on the altar.[4]

The earliest exception to this parade of tributes to conquerors was Osiris, the Egyptian god who was said to have been murdered by his brother Seth. The pieces of his corpse were gathered by Isis, his sister and wife. He was restored to life by her magic and given dominion over the underworld to which his spirit had already descended. He thereafter presided over a trial that all human beings had to face after death, in which their heart would be weighed against a feather; only those for whom it balanced would enjoy an afterlife. Still, as historian Norman Cohn emphasized, this "immense reassurance . . . for individuals . . . implied no change in the world order: the tranquil realm of the blessed existed, and would always exist, alongside the troubled world of the living. That time was moving towards a universal consummation, when all things would be well for evermore and chaos would no longer threaten—that notion had no place at all in Egyptian thinking."[5] Osiris held out a slender hope for individuals of a life in the world to come, but none at all for any amelioration of conditions in this one.

Today it is no longer a surprise that Shi'ism can find inspiration in this way—Christianity has celebrated in very similar ways the judicial murder of its founder on trumped-up charges, and Judaism has turned the destruction of its main temple in the year 70 CE and the subsequent exile of its people into a galvanizing event that inspires its followers to salute one another with the hope of "next year in Jerusalem." As Hamid Dabashi puts it, Shi'ism is not only "a red marker of martyrdom, sacrifice," but also one of "renewal, resurrection."[6]

How has this astonishing reversal of fortune been achieved? And why in particular for these defeats, these sacrifices? After all, no one has thought to launch a religion inspired by any of the nineteen murdered brothers of Sultan Mehmed III. The question is not just one about political and social success, it also invites us to think how something as counterintuitive as defeat could ever manage to be so world-changingly inspirational. How can the celebration of failure be a winning strategy? To put it in a single word, how can defeat be a source of meaning?

The answer to this question can also be summed up in a single word: narrative. A well-constructed narrative, delivered with the appropriate conviction and panache, may be able to overturn normal commonsense assumptions about what can persuade, what can overcome obstacles, what can win. But we must be careful in unpacking the ideas that are freighted within this single word.

It doesn't help that narrative has become a very fashionable subject of study, a go-to answer to all sorts of questions. According to Google's N-gram tool, by 2019 the word "narrative" was appearing more than six times as often in English-language publications indexed by Google as it had done in 1950, and almost twice as often as the previous peak, back around 1850.[7] Narrative has been proposed as a method for improving treatment in medicine,[8] for helping managers recover employees' tacit knowledge in business organizations,[9] for enriching the range of sociological data analysis,[10] designing convincingly empathetic robots,[11] for managing zoos,[12] as a way of understanding regime shifts in economics,[13] as an alternative way of structuring reality (alternative to the "paradigmatic" way known to science, that is),[14] and as a way to understand the self (as a "center of narrative gravity").[15] What does it mean?

Narratives are defined by the *Oxford English Dictionary* as accounts of a series of connected events or experiences (the *Wikipedia* definition uses the term "related" instead of "connected"). There are fancier definitions around, but the *OED* captures the essence of all of them. What distinguishes narratives from mere lists is the nature of the relation or connection between the events or experiences in the series. Sometimes that connection is explicitly causal, as when the English text of the Nicene creed describes God as "maker of heaven and earth." In many cases, however, it is not just causal but also a source of meaning, purpose, point, or moral justification. Later in the Nicene creed it is written of Jesus that "for our sake he was crucified under Pontius Pilate, he suffered death and was buried, and rose again on the third day in accordance with the Scriptures." Here there are two explicit claims to meaning or justification. The first is that when Jesus died it was "for our sake," which implies both a causal claim (the death brought about some benefit for us) and a claim about meaning (the purpose or point of the death was to benefit us). The second claim is that Jesus's resurrection was "in accordance with the Scriptures," which has the causal implication that the same train of events that brought about the death also led to the resurrection.

It also makes a claim about meaning: namely, that the resurrection had been foreseen in the scriptures and was therefore the purpose or point of the death.*

A similar double interpretation can be seen in a hymn that was sung during a "revival week" at one of the Assemblies of God churches in Ghana, among which my research team and I had been undertaking the work I described in chapter 3. The refrain went:

> I had a debt I could not pay,
> He paid a debt he did not owe.
> I needed someone
> To wash my sins away.

Here the causal claims are simple, but the claims of meaning or purpose are more subtle. For me to have a debt I cannot pay implies that I have an unmet obligation to someone. For someone else to have paid a debt he did not owe implies that there is a person who has an obligation to him. It takes little imagination to infer (though it is not strictly implied) that I am the person who has an obligation to the person who paid that debt. But the nature of the obligation is pleasingly smoothed over by the suggestion that what I may receive in return for fulfilling my obligation is far more consequential (the washing away of my sins) than any merely monetary sum I may offer in payment. All in all, the refrain is a useful text for persuading a congregation to take out their purses to donate to the church.

Narrative forms a central part of the discourse of most if not all of the world's religions, whether in the form of written scripture, the text of liturgy, the material of sermons, or even just the things that believers say about their spiritual and organizational journey. More interesting than this banal observation is to understand what purpose narrative serves. As these examples suggest, its function may be to explain an opaque

---

* The version of the Nicene creed quoted here is that used by the Roman Catholic Church (see *Wikipedia* contributors, "English Versions of the Nicene Creed," *Wikipedia, the Free Encyclopedia*, last revised June 25, 2023, https://en.wikipedia.org/w/index.php?title=English_versions _of_the_Nicene_Creed&oldid=1161868377). This wording is not found in all versions; in particular, the phrase "for our sake" does not occur in the 1662 Book of Common Prayer.

universe to its inhabitants, to console them for the inevitable distress they find within it, and—especially—to persuade them to follow the injunctions of the religion's leaders. But why should narrative be particularly helpful at doing this? Why go to these lengths instead of just saying things like "the church needs a new roof, and the only way we can afford one is if you donate"? To understand this, we need to dig deeper into the structure of narratives as these have been passed from speakers, writers, and creators of images to listeners, readers, and viewers throughout the ages.

The Common Structure of Compelling Narratives

Fascination with common themes in folktales goes back at least to the work of the anthologists Charles Perrault in the late seventeenth century and Johann Musäus, Achim von Arnim, Clemens Brentano, and the Brothers Grimm in the late eighteenth and early nineteenth centuries. James Frazer's *The Golden Bough* became a best seller on publication in 1890, exploring parallels between myths across many different cultures. It eventually stretched to twelve volumes, which were then condensed by the author into an abridged edition of a mere 756 pages published in 1922 (and which begins with one of the most modest opening sentences ever to appear in a world-changing work: "The primary aim of this book is to explain the remarkable rule which regulated the succession to the priesthood of Diana at Aricia").[16] It had a major influence on the work of Sigmund Freud, Carl Jung, Otto Rank, Bronislaw Malinowski, and many others. Frazer is well known for his view that "the movement of the higher thought has, on the whole, been from magic through religion to science."[17] Less often quoted is his more ruminative penultimate paragraph, ending in the questions:

> Will the great movement which for centuries has been slowly altering the complexion of thought be continued in the near future? Or will a reaction set in which may arrest progress and even undo much of what has been done? ... [W]hat will be the color of the web which the Fates are now weaving on the humming loom of time? Will it be

white [science] or red [religion]? We cannot tell. A faint glimmering light illuminates the backward portion of the web. Clouds and thick darkness hide the other end.[18]

One of those most powerfully influenced by Frazer's work was Joseph Campbell, author of *The Hero with a Thousand Faces*, a best-selling book published in 1949. It argued that many of the most compelling stories in the corpus of the world mythology share a common structure, in the form of a heroic journey.[19] He was particularly interested in the stories of Krishna, the Buddha, and Jesus, as well as in lesser known figures such as the Greek philosopher Apollonius of Tyana (a near-contemporary of Jesus). Many of the details of Campbell's account are now disputed, and his choice of sources has been criticized as unduly selective.[20] His underlying view of the mechanism by which differing societies have come to share an attachment to such stories rests on a version of Jungian psychology (particularly the notion of archetypes) that now has little scientific credibility. Nevertheless, the book (which has sold over a million copies) helped to popularize the discipline of comparative mythology—not always to the approval of researchers who had long been working in that discipline—and has spawned a voluminous follow-up literature.[21]

One of the best-known popular books following in Campbell's tracks is Christopher Booker's *The Seven Basic Plots: Why We Tell Stories*, published in 2004. As its title suggests, this argues that all important stories across a wide range of cultures could be considered to fit into one of seven structures.[22] Like Campbell, Booker has been criticized for ignoring stories that don't fit his framework, or at least diminishing their claim to be considered compelling literature (one hostile review was entitled "*Terminator 2* Good, *The Odyssey* Bad").[23] Still, it's not necessary for our purposes to decide whether the number of basic plots in the corpus of compelling stories is one, or seven, or thirty-six (for all of which tallies some good arguments have been made).[24] We can instead note that some recurrent kinds of narrative structure are more systematically represented than would happen by chance—a hypothesis that has recently been demonstrated for a large compilation of folklore from the oral traditions of around one thousand societies, which also showed that the motifs of folk stories systematically reflect salient features of the societies' physical environments.[25] We can ask why these recurrent structures seem to make stories more compelling to their readers, hearers, or viewers—what is it about us that makes us particularly keen on consuming stories like these? In recent years there has been an impressive amount of research on exactly this question.[26]

There seem to be two main elements to the answer. The first, which is less obvious than it sounds, is that narrative stories need to conform to some notions of commonsense causality. These are generally accepted hypotheses about everyday cause and effect. They usually focus on life cycle events and predicaments—birth, childhood, wandering, struggle, work, love, parenthood, aging, sickness, and death—or on events that disrupt the life cycle, most obviously violence and murder (but also more general forms of betrayal and intrigue). It makes sense to us that Macbeth might want to kill Duncan to seize the crown of Scotland. It also makes sense that, while he's hesitating, his wife might want to urge him to get on with it, that she might worry that he lacked the resolve, and also that she should taunt him about his sexuality to make him take up the challenge. These are themes we know about, and with which we have some familiarity (though we may have to translate from ambition about monarchy to ambition in other contexts). It would make no sense if instead we were told that Macbeth kills Duncan because he's bored, or because he'd rather play chess than talk to the king—at least, the backstory would have to be rich and convincing for us to find those narratives compelling. Stories about people whose motivations are nothing like ours just don't seem to grip us.

This doesn't imply that "common sense" is culturally invariant, or that it remains constant over time. We need only reflect how ideas from Freudian psychology about unconscious motivation (or related notions like Alfred Adler's theory of the "inferiority complex") have spread among the public over the course of the twentieth century. What seem like self-evident motives to us may be quite different from what our predecessors would have accepted two centuries ago.

But common sense can get us only so far. The second element of the answer to our question about why narratives are so compelling is that the most effective stories also have something counterintuitive to them. It's not just that they often feature dragons, or spirits who can see through walls or fly above mountains—though indeed they often do. It's also that they usually mess with our notions of probability, in several ways. First of all, there are features of narrative structure that predict how much readers or viewers will enjoy them: for example, studies have established (unsurprisingly, perhaps) that narratives in which the story develops more slowly at the beginning than at the end are preferred to ones in which the story develops more slowly at the end, though sequences of events in life are as likely to do the one as the other.[27] Similarly, people who recount important events in their lives may construct narratives in which bad events are succeeded by good events, or ones in which good events are succeeded by bad events. The two sequences are equally probable in life, but in the narratives of relatively happy people the former occur much more often.[28]

The second way in which compelling narratives mess with probability is that certain rare events (good events in comedic or epic narratives, bad events in tragic ones) happen far too often to be plausible. Heroes sometimes enjoy a psychologically and sociologically incredible rate of success in overcoming obstacles to their ambitions and fulfilment. At other times (when the narrative is in a tragic frame) they face an implausible risk of failure, usually seen as payback for their moral failings, and often foretold by someone at the start of the story. This is true not just of narratives that come to us in the form of explicitly fictional stories—like novels, fairy stories, or movies. Many religions tell stories about the improbable things that have happened to their founders, and even to their ordinary members. Cults everywhere recount miracle cures of ailments large and small, and describe the hand of God as swiftly punishing sins that, mostly, people continue to commit with impunity. Churches preaching the "prosperity gospel" tell stories of how some of their members have become rich through devotion to God,[29] though it would be enough for most people to look around at their fellow members to realize that these cases are exceptional. Why do storytellers everywhere do this? And why do we seem to prefer their stories to ones that represent the world more realistically? Do we actually take their probability-stretching versions of reality for the truth?

It won't be enough to suggest that we like such stories because they conform to ones we've heard many times before. Apart from just pushing the question one stage further back (why have we heard them so often?), they run up against a powerful psychological tendency—namely, habituation. Habituation typically weakens, rather than strengthens, our response to various stimuli (think how you "tune out" certain noises, like those of traffic, that you hear regularly). Having heard the "basic plots" many times, we should find stories that fit the pattern less compelling, not more so. However, if the prevalence of "basic plots" reflects the possibility that they performed some function that was adaptive for us during our biological or social evolution, we may have evolved mechanisms that incline us toward hearing those basic plots again and again.

Two notes of caution are necessary at this point. The first is that, of all the questions we are tackling in this book, this is the one for which the answers are the most speculative. The reason is simple: many aspects of human behavior in prehistory have left traces in our DNA, in our skeletons, among our artifacts, and on our physical surroundings. We can use these traces to test claims about how and why those aspects of our behavior evolved. The stories we told each other in prehistoric societies have left none of these. The best evidence we can call upon is from much later written sources for the content of stories, and from observation and experiments in modern societies for the way in which such stories interacted with our behavior. So much of what follows is intelligent guesswork at best.

The second caveat is that, though there's good evidence that we enjoy listening, watching, or reading some kinds of story more than might be expected just by chance, we have almost no evidence that we tend systematically to believe the often improbable claims these stories embody. Most of us are quite aware that married couples don't live happily ever after, that bad deeds frequently go unpunished, and that virtue often languishes unrewarded. Is there any evidence that we treat the improbable narratives we consume so greedily as true in ways that matter? Do we make decisions about education, investments, careers, marriage, and childbearing in ways that are biased by the narratives we consume? Many people (including me) think that the fact that we hear so many improbable stories, and that the people who tell them don't often take care to remind us that they're just stories, may bias our real-life decisions in important ways. But despite mountains of anecdotes, there's little rigorous evidence to show this.[30] I predict that the next ten years will see an explosion of experimental investigations to try to find out.

Let's focus now on the more manageable (if still speculative) question: Why might it have been adaptive in prehistory for us to enjoy listening to narratives that conformed to the "basic plots"?

The Evolution of Our Love of Narrative

Sharing stories has one clear potential adaptive function: like learning to fly on a flight simulator, it may help us to practice navigating our physical and social world before we must do so for real (theories that appeal to this function are called "simulation hypotheses"). By reducing the dangers, it may make us more able and willing to take calculated risks.[31] It may also hone our skills at reading the intentions of others,[32] and may therefore have helped our ancestors cope with living in groups of gradually increasing size,[33] and promoted the kinds of cooperation for which these skills were useful.[34] But for this to work, the stories we share must represent the world accurately: a flight simulator would not do the job if it regularly overestimated the probability that the pilot would escape crashing even after flying "on a wing and a prayer," as the expression goes. It's important to note that successful narratives are not grotesquely or extravagantly implausible: they're what anthropologists Pascal Boyer, Scott Atran, and Ara Norenzayan call "minimally counterintuitive," meaning that they're implausible in only a limited number of features at any one time.[35] Still, there's no getting round it: they're implausible. As often happens in evolutionary accounts of apparently maladaptive behavioral traits, we can choose between two kinds of explanation for our love for the implausible probabilities embodied in so many narratives. The first tells us the traits are a by-product of some other, adaptive function. The second tells us the trait used to be adaptive for the environment in which it evolved, but that environment is no longer present.

Two interesting "by-product" accounts of the human fondness for statistically improbable narratives are the sympathetic joy hypothesis of anthropologist Manvir Singh, and the memory-imagination trade-off hypothesis of primatologist Tetsuro Matsuzawa and several of his colleagues at the University of Kyoto.[36] Singh focuses on the subset of narratives he calls the "sympathetic plot—featuring a goal-directed protagonist who confronts obstacles, overcomes them, and wins rewards."[37] Surveying a large body of evidence from across the world, he argues that simulation hypotheses don't work, at least on their own:

> If stories are designed to teach people how to problem-solve, then we should expect characters to resemble audiences—to be normal-looking and of average strength rather than attractive and strong. A story about how a good-looking dragon-killer procures a princess is of little adaptive value to an ordinary-looking vegetable-seller. . . . Another weakness of simulation hypotheses is that many stories are unhelpful for dealing with real-world problems. Aside from being unrealistically capable, protagonists confront problems that no audience would encounter, including battling monsters or escaping dark netherworlds.[38]

Instead Singh proposes that stories recur because they provoke pleasure associated with the exercise of psychological mechanisms involved in learning and cooperation. He calls the pleasure "sympathetic joy," which is an emotion normally triggered when people's cooperative partners are successful. This makes sympathetic joy like other anticipatory emotions, including sexual arousal. Just as we may use representations of sexuality in literature and film to award ourselves more sexual arousal than we could normally expect our social environments to provide us, we overrepresent success for our protagonists to award ourselves more sympathetic joy than the world normally affords. You can think of it as optimism porn.[39] The question whether optimism porn distorts our real decision-making is therefore like the question whether sexual porn distorts our real-life sexual relationships (a difficult question on which I shall not speculate here).

The work of Matsuzawa and his colleagues began with the observation that chimpanzees, our closest evolutionary relatives (with bonobos), "have an extraordinary photographic memory for fleeting visual events. Humans may have lost this kind of memory, in a tradeoff that saw us acquiring the power of imagination."[40] In one experiment involving drawing, chimps showed an ability surpassing that of young children to copy shapes, but children were much better than chimps at filling in the missing parts of incomplete drawings of faces.[41] The researchers suggest that human beings may have lost the ability of chimps to record information about their natural environment, because of constraints on the brain's size and capacity to process information (though that remains a speculation, since they offer no evidence for these specific constraints). Humans gained instead more ability to focus on social information, and to make informed guesses about what their fellow humans were doing, thinking, and feeling. This would naturally tend to fill our heads with an overrepresentation of certain social events that interest us, while making us less attentive to counter-evidence that doesn't present itself in story form. It wouldn't make us necessarily overoptimistic, though it might explain our fondness for stories that make human beings seem more in control of events than they really are. And in Matsuzawa's account, it also helps to explain our extreme indulgence in something we also see among the juveniles of many other species: play.[42]

Our capacity for play is a key component in a more complex evolutionary explanation, according to literary scholar and evolutionary psychologist Brian Boyd. He presents our taste for fiction ("telling one another stories that neither side believes") as a by-product of the combination of some individually highly adaptive components of the human cognitive armory: language, narrative, and play. Combining insights from his own earlier book *On the Origin of Stories* with the work of the linguist Daniel Dor (who has written that "first we invented language. Then language changed us"),[43] Boyd describes storytelling as an evolved "disposition towards subsurface explanations that both delayed science and ultimately enabled it".[44] He also reminds us that even if fiction has helped human beings "over many millennia to expand their sociality . . . that does not mean that all exposure to fiction is beneficial."[45] Storytelling may just be what we most feel like doing with the impressive cognitive kit that we've developed to better understand our natural and social world.

Let's now turn to explanations according to which storytelling might have been adaptive in the environment in which we evolved, but be rather poorly adapted for our current environment. A promising suggestion would be that stories encourage the observance of social norms by members of human social groups, and particularly tend to discourage free riding. The suggestion goes back (at least) to the anthropologist Bronislaw Malinowski, who argued that "myth fulfils in primitive culture an indispensable function: it expresses, enhances and codifies belief; it safeguards and enforces morality; it vouches for the effectiveness of ritual and contains practical rules for the guidance of man."[46] Shorn of their references to "primitive culture," such arguments are still widely accepted, including in relation to religious narratives. David Sloan Wilson suggests that cultural communities such as the Hebrew nation were held together by "cultural mechanisms . . . which often took the form of narratives that provide guides for action."[47] The historian Elaine Pagels has suggested that "successive generations found in the New Testament gospels what they did not find in many other elements of early Jesus tradition—a practical design for Christian communities."[48] Stelios Michalopoulos and Melanie Meng Xue, the authors of the large folklore study I described above, argue that their data provide evidence that "folklore may be one of the vehicles by which norms are intergenerationally transmitted."[49] On the face of it, this looks plausible, especially for those narratives that encourage effort and sacrifice on behalf of others, if we interpret the narrative as conveying to individuals that their own long-term interest lies in conforming to the norm.[50]

If this function of storytelling explains our attraction for stories, it's possible it could also explain at least some aspects of the narratives' implausibility, if there were norms to which conformity made sense long ago when conditions were very different from those of modern life. In heroic narratives, for example, an individual refuses to give up in the face of adverse shocks in their natural or social environment, struggling bravely on till eventually persistence is rewarded. In prehistoric conditions, where individuals typically had no realistic survival options outside the group, it would have made sense to keep trying even after failure. But in a modern environment, it's often a bad idea. Successful entrepreneurs often learn from initial failures and abandon projects that are failing to find alternative projects where they're more likely to succeed.

Heroic narratives are not the only examples where the advice they convey is implausible in the modern world. In many narratives about courtship, a person refuses to take no for an answer from the object of their affection, and is ultimately rewarded with acceptance. We have no idea whether this might have been adaptive in a forager community, but in the modern world it typically makes you a creep and a stalker. Similarly, in betrayal narratives, cheating on one's friends or one's colleagues brings inevitably a large penalty; we don't know how often foragers got away with betrayal, but in the modern world people get away with it pretty often. In narratives that emphasize redemption, great sacrifices win back the approval of your group or of a powerful individual, such as a person you previously disappointed or betrayed; in the modern world you often have better options than to throw yourself helplessly on the mercy of those whose disapproval you fear. But all these suggestions rely on conjectures about a difference between what made sense in forager societies and what makes sense today that we have absolutely no way to verify.

In any case, if we think carefully, this explanation for the evolution of our taste for narrative won't do. Suppose that following the norm needs reinforcing because it sacrifices our interests to those of the group. In that case, *listening* to the narrative equally sacrifices our interests to those of the group, so it's hard to see how a tendency to respond to narrative would have been favored by natural selection. If ignoring the norm increased individuals' fitness at the expense of the group, so presumably did being deaf to the appeal of such narratives. Narratives may be talking about norms, but they must be doing more than just reaffirming the need to follow them, if we can understand why it was so advantageous to us to be drawn to certain narratives during our evolutionary past.

A better suggestion—and one that would explain why we continue to be fascinated by "basic plots" even when we have heard them many times—is that while narratives may have a similar general structure across widely different contexts, it's the details that count. Instead of being designed to reinforce a norm, they help readers or listeners work out which norms apply in any given situation. That's often far from obvious, so the stories help them to know what to do. Those who seek to enforce social norms need to ensure that group members know what the norms prescribe.

This matters for two main reasons. First, though the aspects of life to which norms apply seem remarkably universal across human societies—all societies have norms about killing, fighting to defend the group, sexuality and marriage, and food preparation, for example—the specific content of the norms varies from one society to another. There are different food taboos in neighboring societies, and different rules about who can marry whom. It can be central to a group's identity that its norms are different from those of the neighbors (think how food taboos or Sabbath observance reminds Jews of their differences from their non-Jewish neighbors). Elaborate ceremonies serve to remind group members of the norms they are supposed to observe, since it's usually impossible to work these out from first principles—they're not just "obvious." The more elaborate the communication required, the more often mistakes are made, and people follow the "wrong" norm.

The second reason why communication matters is that the application of norms varies according to circumstances. Consider the norm that men should be prepared to fight and die for the defense of their families and fellow group members. No society lacks norms of this kind. But when is the right moment to fight, and who needs to make what kind of sacrifice at what point? Once again these are typically not things that anyone can just work out for themselves. In most societies there's a structure of authority that privileges certain types of communication about the application of the norms. Military leaders are privileged sources of information about what the general norm prescribes at any moment, and there are further norms about when military leaders should be obeyed. These norms are often contested, of course. But this just underlines how difficult it is to reduce the process of norm enforcement to one in which society's leaders simply observe who's in violation and then inflict the appropriate punishments. They need a communication strategy.

Arguments about the appropriate norms go back a very long way in history (and doubtless in prehistory too, though we can never know for sure). Recent analysis using what are known as phylogenetic methods has suggested that a folktale called "The Smith and the Devil" dates back to the Bronze Age.[51] The story tells of a blacksmith who makes a pact with the Devil or some other malevolent spirit, selling his soul in return for exercising magical powers, and then finds a way to trick the Devil out of his prize. What's interesting about this tale is that it pits two strong moral norms against each other. The first is the norm of truth telling, or more generally of honoring agreements, and the second is the norm of refusing to compromise with evil people. The tale is an account of how to navigate in a world in which norms appear to be in conflict. This is a theme at the heart of the *Iliad* and *Odyssey*, of the Mahabharata and the Ramayana, and of other myths from around the world; it's certainly not a product of the very modern world.

Many other examples reinforce the view that the main purpose of narratives in past societies was not simply to reinforce the dominant norms, but rather to explore complexities in their application. "Defeating the monster" stories (one of the most basic plots according to both Campbell and Booker) usually rely on the hero's finding some way to outwit the monster, not on superior strength. The message is not that the hero must hang in there rather than quit (as one might think if the purpose of the narrative were to reinforce the norm of fighting to defend the group). Instead, it's that the hero must think hard about how best to win against an adversary who is much stronger than he is.

In a similar vein, many dramas and stories contain stern authority figures whose status the hero successfully undermines, and many explore the comic and strategic possibilities of those figures' being deluded or deceived. Folklorist Alan Dundes noted this paradoxical feature of folktales when he wrote that "folklore reflects (and thereby reinforces) the value configurations of the folk, but at the same time folklore provides a sanctioned form of escape from these very same values. In fairy tales the hero or heroine is invariably told not to do something; don't look in the secret chamber, don't answer the door."[52] Central characters in stories who flout prohibitions invariably get away with it, albeit with some adventures along the way. In short, narratives do not just reinforce a given social norm but provide an imaginative exercise in applying the norm in difficult circumstances. The norms in question are often framed explicitly in response to rival norms, or rival accounts of the application of a norm.

The Uses and Abuses of Narrative

If stories, especially ones with the "basic plots" structure, were important in prehistoric societies, how would the selection process have worked? How did having a sensitivity to narrative structure help the survival and reproduction prospects of individuals? Once again, this remains speculative, but the key to the answer probably lies in those distinct terms "survival" and "reproduction." We can imagine that individuals who were prepared to stay for long hours listening to stories around the campfire would have become better at navigating their natural and social environments than those who quickly became bored and wandered off in search of other pursuits, perhaps becoming some other creature's dinner in the process. Since storytelling is a process of dialogue, being a good listener may also help you to become a good storyteller. Both a talent for listening and a talent for storytelling would have been attributes that contributed to an individual's sex appeal—just as they are today, signaling empathy and emotional intelligence in a way that's hard to fake (you can't tell good stories if you have no empathy at all).[53] Sure enough, a study of storytelling among Agta hunter-gatherer communities in the Philippines showed that communities with skilled storytellers (as rated by their listeners) were both more cooperative and more attractive places to live. The skilled storytellers themselves were rated as more attractive partners, and had on average more surviving children than those who were rated as less skilled.[54] A taste for narrative seems to have been both a guide to survival and a guide to seduction.

If narratives are perceived as persuasive, and not just enjoyable, that might explain why they appear in religious rituals not just as a means of persuading the faithful but as a means of persuading God or the gods. In a collection of Hasidic tales published in 1815, the editor reported that "in the stories . . . that people tell, there are very high and hidden things; and the Besht was able to perform yehudim [meditation] through these stories. When he saw that heavenly channels were blocked and they could not be repaired through prayer, he would fix them and unify them through telling a story."[55]

A taste for narrative, if it were also deployed to persuade, might leave some people, sometimes, vulnerable to exploitation. Think of redemption narratives—ones that speak of the virtues of throwing yourself on the mercy of your community, acknowledging your inadequacy and wretchedness, and offering to do anything (anything!) that will persuade them to welcome you back in and forgive you your transgressions, real or imagined. Sometimes that's a good and prudent thing for you to do. Sometimes it isn't, but it may suit some powerful members of your community to persuade you to do it all the same. They benefit from having penitent people around to serve them, and if they can present themselves to the penitents as agents of redemption, so much the better for them. The greater the disparities in power, status, and command of resources within a social group, the more likely there will be divergences of interest, and the more some individuals or groups might have to gain from manipulating the willingness of others to listen to their stories. And who do you think might be disproportionately disadvantaged by such stories? Surprise: it's often women. The study by Michalopoulos and Meng Xue cited above showed that "societies whose folklore portrays women as less dominant, more submissive, and more likely to engage in domestic affairs than men tend to relegate their women to inferior roles in their communities, both historically and today."[56]

In a similar way, narratives that speak of finding redemption in defeat can sometimes provide a community with the necessary solidarity to rebound from a setback, as the bewildered community of the disciples of the executed Jesus, and six centuries later the supporters of the murdered Hossein ibn Ali, were to do to such spectacular effect. But sometimes, telling people that they can find redemption in defeat may just be a way to persuade them to do what you ask, whether that helps them or not. After all, in a tough and generally unforgiving world, preaching to the defeated is one way to be sure of reaching a mass market. You might feel the same way about the story recounted in the Gospel

according to Saint Mark, where Jesus comments on the donations made
to the temple by both rich and poor:

> [41] And Jesus sat over against the treasury, and beheld how the
> people cast money into the treasury: and many that were rich
> cast in much.
> [42] And there came a certain poor widow, and she threw in two
> mites, which make a farthing.
> [43] And he called unto him his disciples, and saith unto them,
> Verily I say unto you, That this poor widow hath cast more in,
> than all they which have cast into the treasury:
> [44] For all they did cast in of their abundance; but she of her want
> did cast in all that she had, even all her living.

What we see here is a profoundly uplifting message addressed to a very
poor person, recognizing her gift for the sacrifice it represents for her
and the moral qualities to which it bears witness. It's also a message that
would inspire many religious entrepreneurs over the centuries: there's
a lot of money to be made from the poor as well as from the rich, simply
because there are so many of them. All in all, whether it's in the interest
of religious members to be so attentive to such stories depends on time,
place, and context, as well as on who's telling them. But for the religious
leaders who have discovered a talent for telling them, there's no doubt
that these stories have been very good indeed.

For good or ill, what marks out today's religious platforms from most
of their secular rivals, and what marked out the new Axial movements
(the "transcendent" religions) from the transactional businesses that
thronged the marketplaces of ancient Athens and Rome as well as many
other places around the globe (the "immanent" religions), is a willingness to tell grand and ambitious stories. Not stories as such; there was no
shortage of them among the patter deployed by transactional businesses,
which used human-interest anecdotes to drum up custom, as they still
do today. And many cultures have developed complex and evocative creation stories that speak to our curiosity about our origins. Whereas immanent religions gave their listeners a variegated tapestry of stories, the
transcendent religions wove them together into a master narrative. That

master narrative sought to link the different actors in the cosmos, to claim that their actions were part of an overall scheme, and above all to give a point to suffering, to present it as part of a necessary struggle, a step on the road to salvation. The narratives of transcendental religion included stories not just about the nature of creation but specifically about our place in it, stories about why bad things keep happening to us, stories about what we can hope for if we are patient, stories about why we have to die.[57] They expressed empathy with the suffering of others—whether that found its expression in the Hindu veneration of *ahimsa* (nonviolence) as early as the Rig Veda in 1200 BCE,[58] or much later in the New Testament invocations of "the least of your brethren" or the "two sparrows sold for a farthing . . . [who] shall not fall on the ground without your Father."[59] They gave a central place to the bitter experiences of loss and bereavement, pointing out that it happens to everyone, the mighty as well as the meek. It's impossible to read the Old Testament story of the two messengers who come to bring King David the news of his son Absalom without feeling for the impending grief of a father who draws false comfort from the first messenger even while we know the second is approaching to tell him his son is dead.[60] Though of course all known human societies have their funerary rites that help the bereaved separate themselves from the deceased,[61] weaving bereavement into narrative helps to locate the grief of the individual in a larger framework.[62] Such stories told of suffering, dispossession, and defeat, and when deployed by some gifted communicators, they could also hold out a promise that defeat could—against all reasonable secular expectation—be transformed into victory.

To be sure, there were many differences between the narratives: Buddhism and Hinduism were more likely to assert the underlying justice that governed the universe,[63] while Christianity offered to compensate the injustice of the present universe with redress in the life to come. But in all of them, there was a new vision of destitution, a new vision of death. Historian Peter Brown has drawn attention to the way in which the cult of the saints in early Christianity transgressed Roman taboos about the place of the dead in the life of the city:

The rise of the Christian cult of saints took place in the great cemeteries that lay outside the cities of the Roman world . . . and came to involve the digging up, the moving, the dismemberment—quite apart from much avid touching and kissing—of the bones of the dead, and, frequently, the placing of these in areas from which the dead had once been excluded. . . . [B]y the end of the period, the immemorial boundary between the city of the living and of the dead came to be breached by the entry of relics and their housing within the walls of many late-antique towns, and the clustering of ordinary graves around them.[64]

He has also emphasized that the Christian fascination with martyrs was only tenuously related to the Greek cult of heroes. Martyrs, who had typically died not valiantly in battle but broken bodily by cruel and overwhelming force, "enjoyed close intimacy with God . . . the martyr was a 'friend of God'. He was an intercessory in a way which the hero could never have been."[65] In Islam, saints and martyrs (known also as "friends of God") have played no less powerful a role—and a particularly central one in Sufi Islam, which is part of the reason why puritanical revival strains of Islam such as Wahabism have viewed Sufism with such intense suspicion.

Periodical waves of purification have occurred in both Christianity and Islam, with only temporary success. As Alan Strathern puts it, "just as Christianity attempted to clear away the crowded field of pagan metapersonhood only to repopulate it with saints, angels, and demons, so forms of Protestantism tried to sweep it clean once more only to leave providence howling through the landscape and battling with the devil."[66] But it would be a mistake to see the recurrence of saint cults as just a resurgence of an irrepressible instinct for immanent religion. It's true that individual Christians' relations with saints could be vividly transactional—Strathern reports instances where a saint who failed to deliver on the promised benefits in return for offerings could be subjected to:

a thousand rough handlings and sacrilegious treatments . . . for example they bite it indecently on the nose, the face, the ears, the hands etc and bind it with many chains, hang it outside a window in the sun and the rain, tie it with a rope and throw it into a well or a cistern, and similar things, and they say they do this to oblige the saint to intercede for them to gain that favour.[67]

But precisely because saints were "friends of God" and not merely freelance spirits, the stories constructed around their lives were ambitious, comprehensive narratives. These promised the faithful an understanding of how God would look after them both now and in eternity, and crucially, an understanding of their place in the religious community. Here at last we can see an answer—a worldly answer, far from the one he was expecting—to the question posed by Saint Augustine in his *City of God*, a work composed to console his fellow Christians after the catastrophic defeat of the sack of Rome by the Visigoths in the year 410: "Why can the dead do such great things?"[68]

In short, religious platforms developed by the transcendent religions could deploy the human fascination with narrative with an overall ambition and coherence unknown to immanent religion. They brought consolation to the downtrodden, and thereby increased their value as allies to a privileged elite. It was the inspired conjunction of an organizational innovation—the religious platform, which underscored the way in which all the components of the religious life fit together, and how the individual could make sense of that fit through membership of a community—and an appeal to a much more ancient human need, the need for stories. As so often in the history of humanity, the novel organizational forms that succeed in establishing themselves have done so by appealing to human susceptibilities that are not novel at all.

Their very success at mobilizing narrative to reconcile people to suffering and sacrifice has of course made religious movements the subject of envy and emulation on the part of political leaders. Narrative is no less powerful a technology of mobilization than are railways and fleets. Invocations of the New Jerusalem have accompanied all kinds of movements for political liberation, from the Anabaptist Rebellion in 1534 that took over the German city of Münster to the occupation of the Chinese city of Nanjing in 1853 by Hong Xiuquan (who had founded the Taiping movement, having converted to Protestant Christianity after failing the

Chinese civil service examination for the fourth time and becoming convinced that he was the younger brother of Jesus),[69] to the visionary socialism of William Blake and his contemporaries. Appeals to the destiny of nations have accompanied territorial conquest, from the westward expansion across the American continent ("Manifest Destiny")[70] to the eastward search for "Lebensraum" by Hitler's Germany, to the 2022 invasion of Ukraine by Putin's Russia ("passionarnost").[71] Narratives that tell the story of a nation or a political movement in terms designed to promise that initial suffering will eventually be crowned in glory have proved irresistible to ambitious leaders. Natural selection may have honed our sensibilities in small communities, but narratives can now be projected on a global scale, for good and ill. We personify the struggles of the smallest animals and the largest human communities. As memorably expressed by Zhang Daye, author of a memoir about his experiences as a child in the Taiping Rebellion, probably the most violent civil war in history, "from the cry of a tiny insect, one can hear a vast world."[72]

In the end a deep puzzle remains. Narratives may be compelling in the sense that we love to hear them and tell them, and we plunder their content for inspiration of all kinds. But do we really let them distort the way we believe the world to be—and if so, why? The current state of research leaves the question wide open. What's clear is that narratives count among our favorite tools of persuasion, and that our fascination with them goes back a very long time.[73]

The idea that we owe this fascination with narrative to the operation of natural selection is sometimes dismissed as reductionist, and therefore as lacking in an appreciation of the beauty and poetry of storytelling.[74] I find this conclusion strange. The idea is certainly reductionist. All good explanations are: they explain something we don't understand by pointing out its relation to something we do. And if the suggestion I have sketched here is true, this is what we do understand. A very long time ago, one of your distant ancestors seduced another of your distant ancestors by telling her, or by telling him, a story. This was to happen again many times over the ensuing half a million years. Sometimes, too, an influential member of some forager community told a story about people who had overcome terrible dangers by cooperating instead of fighting, and your ancestors listened, moved by the story into setting aside their quarrels for a short while. The reductionist explanation tells us that these multiple seductions and persuasions, still rare in a world in which sexual coercion and other forms of violence were even more common than they are today but steadily accumulating their influence over countless millennia, are the most important cause of the exquisite sensitivity with which you respond to the appeal of stories today, the origins of which would otherwise be completely mysterious to us. This is not a metaphor but the literal truth. What could be more beautiful and poetic than that?

CHAPTER 8

The Evolutionary Origins of Enchantment

Theory places things in a causal context wider than common sense.

—Robin Horton, "African Traditional Thought and Western Science"

Celibacy and Community Survival

On January 2, 2017, at Sabbathday Lake in the town of New Gloucester, Maine, the death at the age of eighty-nine of Sister Frances Carr left the community of Shakers with only two living members in the world.[1] The Shakers (known officially as The United Society of Believers in Christ's Second Appearing) were founded in England in 1747 as a breakaway movement from the Quakers. They were known as the Shaking Quakers because of their ecstatic behavior during services. They professed egalitarian ideals, including between men and women. Among their more unusual characteristics was the practice of celibacy by all members of the community, not just by a monastic subgroup as in mainstream Christianity.[2] The inability to increase their membership by procreation was a significant challenge, which they met by welcoming children into their community through indenture, adoption, or conversion. But, given such a self-inflicted handicap, it's a tribute to their stamina and devotion that the group survived to the twenty-first century at all.

A community of Shakers in 1830.
Credit: Library of Congress.

Though unusual, the Shakers were by no means unique in their commitment to celibacy. A study by sociologist Rosabeth Moss Kanter of thirty utopian communes founded in America between 1780 and 1860 showed that eleven of them practiced celibacy at some point in their existence (and intriguingly, those that did so lasted longer on average than those that did not).[3] Nor are the Shakers the most extreme example of a religious movement's creating obstacles to its own propagation. The Skoptsy, whose name means the "self-castrated," were a sect that broke from the Russian Orthodox Church in the eighteenth century. In the words of historian Laura Engelstein, "its members were peasants from the Russian heartland skilled in the arts of animal husbandry who turned their knives on themselves to become 'eunuchs for the kingdom of heaven's sake.'" They believed that "salvation came only with the literal excision of the instruments of sin." The community was destroyed during Stalin's Terror in the 1930s, but it is evidence of remarkable commitment and charisma that it survived (through recruitment rather than procreation) for as long as it did. As Engelstein explains, its members "became adept at concealing their sectarian identity as they interacted with their Orthodox neighbors. Interaction was necessary . . . since survival of the Skoptsy depended on recruitment of new members and on success in agriculture and trade."[4] Economist Vladimir Maltsev has argued that it was precisely the severity of the Skoptsy's repudiation of the norms of secular society that bound them together in a cooperative movement, which resulted in their becoming "one of the richest sects in Russia and abroad."[5]

Almost all religious movements have encouraged fertility rather than denied it, and historically the most effective way to recruit new members has been to create them yourselves.[6] Children don't always adopt the beliefs and practices of their parents, but their parents have a head start over almost everyone else in exercising influence through persuasion. Forgoing this option seems to cost religious movements a lot. The cases of the Shakers and the Skoptsy (as well as other less extreme cases, such as that of priestly celibacy in the Roman Catholic Church) throw into sharp relief two important questions, which have already challenged us in previous chapters: Which religious beliefs and practices seem likely to help spread the movements that espouse them? Of those that don't (and on the face of it there are many), can we explain how they nevertheless persist?

Much of this book is concerned with the cultural transmission of practices and beliefs, exploring how features of religion that might seem unattractive (the lengthy tedium or intense pain involved in rituals, and the elaborate beliefs shared by many members, to take two examples) can nevertheless be understood as part of a religious movement's appeal. In doing so I've drawn on a shared commonsense understanding of human psychology (we don't like boredom, we don't like pain, we don't like to spend energy escaping imaginary threats or pursuing chimerical goals). We've seen how religious movements can appeal to that psychology, even in counterintuitive ways. In this chapter, though, we'll ask whether our psychology may be more complex than this picture makes it seem. We've already noted a hint of this in chapter 5, where I summarized research showing how our distinctively human propensity for over-imitation underlies much of our attachment to ritual. Over-imitation had clear adaptive advantages for us in prehistory, but it may also have left us vulnerable to the influence of untrustworthy models. Perhaps the point is more general: could natural selection have shaped us in such a way that we actively seek out some of religion's most counterintuitive features? If so, why wasn't their counterintuitiveness a crippling handicap to our ancestors in the struggle for existence during prehistory?

Understanding a Counterintuitive Psychology

In answering this question, we must avoid being distracted by the fact that serious scholars of religion disagree mightily about whether there are features common to religion in all human societies, and if so what they are. For instance, philosopher Kim Sterelny has proposed that, despite the wide variety of religious beliefs and practices throughout history and across the world, all religions are characterized by "a belief in powerful hidden agents or forces" that affect human beings and can be induced to act in our interests by our prayers, rituals, and community activities.[7] Anthropologist and cognitive psychologist Dan Sperber is skeptical: he cites the Dorzé community of southern Ethiopia as an example of a people who follow various forms of divinatory rites, sacrifices, funerary rituals, and sundry other ritualized activities, without these forming any kind of system, let alone one governed by a generalized belief in hidden agents or forces.[8] For our purposes we don't need to take a stance as to whether Sperber's criticism is valid or not—the details of any community's religious practices are so massively influenced by cultural transmission that we shouldn't expect a common core of similar activities to be observed everywhere across the world, still less for it to be underpinned by a psychology that encodes precisely these features. We need only consider whether there may be a more general set of psychological tendencies, found most of the time, in most places, despite the presence of occasional exceptions. All general tendencies have exceptions—even this one.

After all, the activities of the Dorzé people do presuppose the existence of ancestors, spirits of place, and other authors of spirit possession, which require human attention from time to time. None of these are visible to the senses in the way that ordinary people are visible. If

I'm told I must go and speak to my living mother, it's enough for me to reply "I looked, and she wasn't there" to explain why I haven't done so. But in a society with ancestor rituals, that answer doesn't work for my long-departed great-grandmother. Even if I can't see her, I'm not allowed to conclude that she's not there. Nor does the excuse work for other targets of ritual in a religious community. Why doesn't it? Is this just a convention—we're allowed to use this excuse for one kind of person (the living and embodied), but not another (the departed, or the disembodied)? If so, why do virtually all societies have this kind of convention in one form or another—rather than, as with most conventions, some societies having them and others not? Is there something deeper in our psychology that makes us willing to "see" hidden agents around us? And if so, how did that psychology evolve? How was it advantageous to our ancestors to have a psychology like that? The literature on this question is vast,[9] and there's no scientific consensus about the overall answer. But there are some intriguing common features to the various answers that have been proposed.

A shared presumption in this literature is that it must have been costly for our ancestors to behave as though they saw hidden agents and forces that their ordinary senses could not perceive. The implication is that, if we start to see the influence of hidden agents anywhere, we will soon be seeing it everywhere.[10] That will leave us hopelessly ill equipped to navigate the environment, escape predators, and populate the world with our offspring—even more so if the hidden agents start telling us to do things like forgo sex or mutilate ourselves. All answers to this challenge take the form of showing how our tendency to see hidden agents and forces in the world around us is not as costly as it might appear. This may be because:

- **There's nothing to explain.** This view claims that we don't really have such a deeply inbuilt tendency to believe in hidden agents. We just tend to do what other people tell us, including perhaps saying that we perceive hidden agents, whether or not we really do. Many people feel, when they pray or take part in various rituals, that they are communicating with someone, but that's not necessary to the ritual experience. Many skeptics about evolutionary arguments would take this view. Some might add that *saying* we perceive hidden agents is functionally equivalent to perceiving them, at least after we've been saying it long enough, and in any case doesn't make much difference to how we act most of the time.

- **We're selective.** We do perceive hidden agents, and communicating with them is central to the religious experience. But we don't do so indiscriminately. In fact, we perceive only certain very specific kinds, notably those that anthropologist Pascal Boyer has described as "minimally counter-intuitive."[11] These agents are like those we perceive with our ordinary senses, except in certain precise ways, such as having survived death. Perceiving hidden agents is very rule-governed, in other words, and this prevents us from multiplying instances of their influence in an extravagantly costly way. We still need to understand why we have this tendency, but it didn't have to bring us enormous advantages to survive natural selection, because it wasn't as costly as some people have claimed.

- **It's a by-product.** This view claims that perceiving invisible agents is an unavoidable by-product of being exquisitely sensitive to the possibility that hidden predators, including our human enemies, are really there. And we're better off being oversensitive rather than undersensitive to the presence of predators. This argument appeals to what are sometimes called "hyperactive agency detection devices," and has also been called the "faces in the clouds" theory, after our supposed tendency to "see" faces in clouds and other natural shapes. It doesn't explain, of course, why we quickly correct our perception of faces in the clouds and admit that they're not there, really—while reflection often reinforces rather than undermines religious belief.[12]

- **There are group-level advantages.** According to this view, we are capable of perceiving hidden agents in a large variety of contexts, and this can sometimes be very costly to us. But these costs are offset by some very large advantages to our social groups. One version of this claim is that many societies have succeeded in persuading their members that "big gods" or "moralizing high gods" (omniscient, omnipresent, and omnipotent spirits) are watching over them. Big gods punish them if they don't behave in the interests of the group.[13] These societies, it's claimed, display such social and military cohesion that they out-compete societies that lack such tools for social discipline.[14] Other kinds of group-level advantages have also been claimed, as we'll see below (advantages that don't necessarily appeal to big gods). However, such explanations are challenging to develop rigorously. As is well known, advantages to the group can explain the evolution of traits that are costly to the individual only under certain limited circumstances (and many biologists remain skeptical that these conditions are ever observed in practice). These are that competition between groups is frequent, migration between groups is infrequent, and the traits in question make an important contribution to helping some groups prevail over others.[15] So all versions of the explanation in terms of group-level advantages must establish that these conditions held, at the appropriate moments in prehistory. They also need to establish that prosocial traits could not have been naturally or culturally selected without such theological assistance. This claim has been vigorously disputed by primatologist Frans de Waal, who points to the wide extent of prosocial behavior in other primates, which nobody claims have any tendency to believe in big gods.[16]

- **There are individual-level advantages.** On this last view, we do perceive hidden agents in many contexts, and this is sometimes very costly to us. But the costs are offset by some very large advantages to those individual people who perceive them. For example, people who believe their behavior is observed by "big gods" will be more easily trusted by others, more willing to take risks, and more often invited to join powerful and productive group activities.[17]

Kim Sterelny has noted that many of these accounts can explain why religion gets transmitted once it has started, but not how it gets started in the first place. That's particularly true of the big gods accounts, which tell us that if people in a community already believe in big gods, and trust is higher in their community as a result, the community will prosper. But this explanation makes it puzzling where such beliefs come from originally.

We can see this in a study by anthropologist Richard Sosis of 200 utopian communes that were set up in America in the nineteenth and twentieth centuries. He shows that the 88 religious communes lasted around twenty-five years on average, whereas the 112 secular communes lasted on average just over six years.[18] Survival for all these communes required them to solve problems of collective action in the supply of collective labor—to prevent free riding, in other words. His results don't tell us whether the religious communes were more effective at doing this because their members believed in supernatural punishment, or because of a self-selection process whereby relatively generous and public-spirited people were more likely to join religious communes. One detail suggests that self-selection might have been an important consideration, though. While secular communes were twice as likely as religious ones to dissolve within their first five years of existence, they were four times as likely to do so within their first two years. If the main reason for dissolution is that people become tired of the effort of collective labor, there's no reason to think that differences between the two types of commune should vary much over time. But if the main reason for dissolution of the communes was that people were discovering what kinds of fellow members they were living with, you'd expect commune dissolution to be particularly likely in the very early years, and even more likely for those communes that had less committed and public-spirited members. This matches with research results from elsewhere,[19] but in either case it leaves a puzzle unaddressed: If the religious communes were more successful because their members believed in supernatural punishment, how did they come to develop those beliefs initially? And if it was because religious communes attracted more-public-spirited members, what brought about that association between religiosity and public spirit in the first place?

One final feature of religious behavior that all evolutionary explanations need to reflect is that it's robustly universal across human societies, yet not universal within them. No known human societies have entirely lacked a world of hidden agents or forces, which might make you think that any tendency to believe in such a world must have a very strong selective advantage (in the same way that all species of vertebrates have eyes, except the very few that live where there's no light). Individuals born without functioning eyes face massive disadvantages and need major social support to survive. Indeed, eyes have evolved independently several times during the development of life on this planet, sometimes despite blatant flaws in their biological architecture (like the blind spot in the human eye).[20] This is evidence for the large individual selective advantage that eyes convey. In contrast, individuals who do not believe in a world of hidden agents have existed and functioned apparently well in most human societies (and perhaps in all, though we lack the evidence to verify this), though they've sometimes had to be discreet to avoid social sanctions. This means there's no "religious eye" like the eye that perceives visible light; a religious sensibility, if it makes sense to speak of such a thing, conveys at most a slight selective advantage to individuals. The reason why it's present in all human societies is that a religious culture has (in the past, at least) conveyed a large selective advantage to groups, which therefore have an interest in encouraging it among their members. But they can rarely afford to police it 100 percent effectively, which explains why it is not universal within societies. So convincing explanations of the religious behavior need to unite an account of our individual psychological traits with an account of their social enforcement and reinforcement. This will also be easier to do if, as I suggested in chapter 1, we think of religiosity not as a single psychological trait but rather as a disposition to apply our diverse psychological traits to various religious activities.

Kim Sterelny proposes an elegant synthesis of the different explanations outlined above, which can help to explain how religion got started initially, and can also respect its universality across societies and non-universality within them. He argues that religion could have developed without imposing large costs on its practitioners, because it involved ritual long before it involved belief. He describes a state he calls *embodied* religion (which consisted of distinctive rituals, ceremony, collective activity, material symbolism—and nothing else). Ritual was socially advantageous, for reasons we saw in chapter 5, and it was faithfully transmitted because of our human capacity for over-imitation. Belief in hidden agents arrived only gradually after this, in societies that already had long-established deep and compelling rituals. It arrived in ways that enabled both individuals and groups to reap advantages in terms of social cohesion and social trust. This account is therefore a version of the "nothing to explain" view for the origins of religion, followed by a gradualist view of the arrival of hidden agents, propelled by our propensity for over-imitation.

So How Did It Happen?

Sterelny suggests there were two distinct phases to this arrival of hidden agents. In the first, the initial state of embodied religion was succeeded by *articulated* religion, "which is a package of collective activities plus an increasingly connected and coherent story or set of linked stories, typically about who we are, why we are here, and why we have a right to be here, plus various recipes for intervention in their causally complex world." In the world of articulated religion, many compelling narratives circulated, but the beliefs they entailed about hidden agents remained modest and selective, and "minimally counter-intuitive" in the terms of Pascal Boyer. They were not therefore very costly in evolutionary terms. It was not until a second phase that articulated religion was succeeded by *ideological* religion. And it was not until then that, as Sterelny puts it, "the narrative becomes (a) elaborated, (b) compulsorily believed as true, (c) moralized, and (d) increasingly central in its role. The transition to ideological religion is when religion (i) becomes very expensive, (ii) is late in human evolutionary history, probably Neolithic, and (iii) is associated with the establishment of complex hierarchical social worlds."[21]

What made these two transitions happen? There have been various suggestions. Some researchers have cited resource stress.[22] Sterelny argues that the transitions were prompted by the increasing complexity of human social life—itself the fruit of changing natural environments that raised the likelihood of intergroup interactions, and the value of hunting in larger groups. This created a need for new social technologies to manage conflict. In this vein, psychologist and anthropologist Robin Dunbar has argued for many years that the stresses of interactions in large social groups created selective pressure for larger brains. These were needed for keeping tags on our interactions with others, recording threats and promises, and developing conditional strategies for interacting with them. But larger brains were not enough—we also needed more sophisticated behavioral technologies for keeping conflict in check. Dunbar suggests that religion was the most innovative and important such technology, at least before the invention of legal systems and other institutions in the modern world.[23]

There are two important things to notice about the two-phase evolutionary process proposed by Sterelny. The first is that many of the beliefs implicit in the narratives that characterized articulated religion, though they might seem counterintuitive to us now, were not seriously counterintuitive compared to realistically available alternatives at the time.[24] To take one example, the anatomical science of the human brain has given us an explanation for the strangely altered perception of reality that we experience in dreams. Before this was developed, it was reasonable to think our spirits could leave our bodies while we slept and fly invisibly through the world. It was reasonable to believe that things we see in dreams (like talking animals or plants) might be as real as those we see in the waking world, or that dreams could bring foreknowledge of the future. These beliefs now seem (and are) untenable, but they were not always so, because there was no credible alternative.[25] Yet their influence persists: in many religious traditions, dreams are one of the main ways in which insights, instructions, and wisdom are transmitted from the spirit to the human world.[26] Similarly, believing that thunder represents the anger of the gods was not costly to our prehistoric ancestors, since the best response to thunder is like the best response to anger—stay inside, out of sight.[27] Only with modern housing, meteorology, and various other innovations, and particularly the growing importance of interactions with strangers, did there come to be any real value in distinguishing electromagnetic meteorological phenomena from human emotions. And finally, as Richard Dawkins famously pointed out in his book *The Blind Watchmaker*, until the development of the theory of natural selection by Charles Darwin and Alfred Russell Wallace, it was not un-reasonable to think that the appearance of design in the natural world must argue in favor of a conscious but supernatural designer.[28]

The second thing to notice about this process by which religious beliefs gradually became more elaborate and ambitious is that, paradoxi-cally, it has much in common with the development of scientific beliefs. Both processes drew on a feature of human thinking we might call *cognitive extravagance*. We can do many elaborate things with our brains that natu-ral selection never shaped them to do. The best example is reading, which is a skill trained adults deploy effortlessly, but which draws on neural competences that were never selected for that purpose, since reading is far too recent and elite an activity to have an impact on the neurophysiology of the general population. Of course, the competences must have been selected for *something*, since they require a lot of expen-sive brain tissue. But it may be hard to know what exactly were the selec-tive pressures that gave us the particular skills deployed in reading.[29]

A key example of cognitive extravagance is our facility at building elaborate hypotheses to explain otherwise unconnected events, from the hypothesis that the reason why we observe many people going in and out of a building every day is that there exists a firm that employs them, to the structure of quantum theory, and the hypothesis that the 1969 moon land-ing was faked by the CIA. This facility extends and exaggerates a cognitive competence that almost certainly *was* shaped by natural selection—namely, a capacity for inferring the presence of stable underlying entities that are responsible for many of the phenomena we observe in the natural world. We saw in chapter 7 some experimental evidence comparing human children with chimpanzees, suggesting that during evolution humans may have lost the impressive abilities of chimps to recall details of their natural environment. They gained instead a greater focus on other agents, and an enhanced ability to infer the motivations underlying the actions of others. There is evidence that even infants as young as two and a half months can make inferences about the physical continuity of objects when they pass behind a hidden screen. They stare longer when presented with outcomes that violate this simple principle.[30] When slightly older, children can also infer the presence of stable statistical distributions underlying events they see. For example, eight-month-old infants seeing a sequence of ping-pong balls drawn from a box, in which balls of one color predominated over another, showed a surprised reaction when the box was opened to reveal balls mostly of the "wrong" color.[31] At a little older again, infants of twenty months appear capable of making inferences about the underlying mental states of others.[32]

Though these feats may seem "obvious" to adults, they testify to an impressive talent for suspending disbelief about what might seem the commonsense inference. An object that passes behind a screen does not disappear, though that's what our eyes appear to be telling us. Balls drawn from a box are expected to conform to properties of what's in the box, although we can't see inside it. The behavior of others is not just a random assortment of actions, but proceeds from mental states we know to persist over time, though we also cannot directly observe them.

Anthropologist Robin Horton has written about some features of theoretical reasoning that are shared between many African traditional societies and communities of Western scientists.[33] Almost all attempts to explain complex phenomena require us to make leaps of inference beyond what common sense normally authorizes. In a similar vein, anthropologists Aaron Lightner and Edward Hagen have recently suggested that for many interconnected systems, "when causes are uncertain, simple explanations outperform complex ones." They provide examples in which personification of the forces underlying complex weather systems can be more efficient than attempts to track the underlying physical forces:

> If floods are not a routine problem that people can repeatedly observe, then observers needing to quickly and accurately respond to one would benefit from an explanation that reduces variance by systematically ignoring physical causes and searching for patterns at a high level of abstraction. Again, this is conveniently supplied by an ability to intuitively predict a flood's behavior in terms of its "mental attributes": generally speaking, floods have a spiteful and unhelpful disposition, they "want" to destroy levees, and they "prefer" to arrive around riverbanks at certain times of the year.[34]

The talent for selectively suspending disbelief in this way is one that human beings deploy more elaborately still, in the service of prodigious feats of the imagination. It's not just that we can spin stories that make us laugh or weep, about characters who don't exist but whom we feel we know better than our closest friends (as Shakespeare makes his character Hamlet ask in bewilderment after a performance by an actor featuring the character of Hecuba, Queen of Troy: "what's Hecuba to him, or he to Hecuba, that he should weep for her?"*—a particularly unsettling reflection given how intimately audiences over the centuries have felt they knew Hamlet). We routinely invoke invisible entities, from electromagnetic fields to corporations, that underlie what would otherwise be the bewildering complexity that we observe in the world. And among the most remarkable such feats is our human ability to believe in promises that are backed by no visible evidence.

Our cognitive extravagance carries huge risks, but it's also the foundation of much of the complexity of the modern world. The explosive growth in human brain size during our evolution did more than just give us the capacity to solve increasingly complex social and environmental problems. It also turned our brains into a marketplace for competing ideas about ourselves and our place in the world.[35] In that marketplace, just as in the real marketplace where human beings had begun to develop complex systems of trade and cooperation, the key to success lay in the creative suspension of disbelief about the everyday evidence of our senses. The establishment of elaborate networks of cooperation with other unrelated individuals has required the ability to override the evidence of our immediate senses in the interests of distant and invisible objectives. We need to work out when we can afford to trust someone who has no intrinsic reason to help us, and who offers us nothing we can immediately use.

This capacity is much more sophisticated than just the ability to exchange items of value. Monkeys and apes typically trade with each other in pursuit of immediate advantages—but human beings are prepared every day to exchange promises of future rewards they cannot

*Hamlet, act 2, scene 2, 561–62.

see, taste, or touch.[36] This ability to suspend ordinary disbelief—in a structured rather than a purely whimsical fashion—is what enabled our ancestors to survive in the harsh conditions of the Upper Paleolithic, spreading out from Africa to colonize a range of habitats quite different from those in which they first evolved.[37] It then enabled them to adopt agriculture, settle in towns and cities, and found large civilizations. It enabled the development of abstract constructions such as the modern limited liability corporation.[38] Just as with the ability to read, the ability to imagine corporations was of enormous benefit to some of those who exercised it, even though that benefit was not the reason why the ability had evolved.

This talent for suspending disbelief in the ordinary evidence of the senses also meant that human beings would be forever solicited by entrepreneurs with projects, secular or spiritual, that appeal to rewards beyond the perceptible horizon. Our talent and taste for social learning makes us ready targets for the solicitations of others. That doesn't mean we respond indiscriminately—indeed, as we saw in the case of shamans, most societies past and present have seen a complex skeptical tango between persuaders and their targets, in which the question of how much we can believe what we are told pervades interpersonal interactions at all levels. Still, this tango is absorbing only because the ability to override ordinary sensual evidence is an intrinsic function of the healthy human brain. But it's one that other human beings have learned to influence and manipulate, for good ends and bad. Such manipulation was already present in forager societies, and human beings appear to have become aware of the dangers of manipulation of their credulity from the earliest times.[39] But modern societies offer opportunities for manipulation on a larger scale than in earlier times, and these pose ever-evolving challenges for social trust.

"Canals without Water": Reassurance versus Suspicion

With great powers come great obligations. Whether or not it's a function that explains their evolution, the great doctrinal religions are heavily preoccupied with how to build and maintain trust.[40] A verse at the beginning of the fifth chapter of the Quran says bluntly: "Oh believers! Honor your obligations"—the word for obligations in Arabic (*'aqd*) refers to all binding undertakings between people, not just commercial agreements. A sentence in the following verse enjoins the faithful to "cooperate with one another in goodness and righteousness, and do not cooperate in sin and aggression." In case anyone should take this for a merely pious exhortation, the verse concludes: "And be mindful of Allah. Surely Allah is severe in punishment."[41]

The belief that one's coreligionists can be held to a higher standard than other people has historically been an important facilitator of relationships in the secular as well as the strictly religious sphere, as we saw in chapter 4.[42] Sure enough, an important theme in many religious teachings has been reassurance: because God is taking care of many of the most stressful interactions of daily life, believers can feel confident in going out into the world. "Take therefore no thought for the morrow: for the morrow shall take thought for the things of itself. Sufficient unto the day is the evil thereof," says Jesus, according the Gospel of Saint Matthew.[43] The Quran tells Muslims that "whoever is mindful of Allah, he will make a way out for them, and provide for them from sources they could never imagine. And whoever puts their trust in Allah, he alone is sufficient for them."[44] The injunctions work: Luigi Guiso, Paola Sapienza, and Luigi Zingales have shown that individual religiosity is associated with "societal attitudes . . . conducive to higher productivity and growth."[45] Robert Barro and Rachel McCleary have shown a robust, and probably causal, association between religious beliefs and economic growth across countries.[46] Several other researchers have argued that such optimistic ideas can be self-sustaining in society.[47]

Similar ideas underlie the reassuring character of many secular institutions: on this view, by emphasizing the trustworthiness of one's fellow citizens, we encourage everyone to take risks, contribute to the collective good, and avoid a self-fulfilling pessimism that will hurt everyone. This requires faith in the common interests of all: we all have something to gain if we all cooperate—for example, by paying our taxes, respecting the environment, and obeying the law. Religious messages in this tradition emphasize that we are all brothers and sisters, and that the most trustworthy people are those who are most like us. If we work together, we can do great things. But alongside this optimistic view of the gains from cooperation, there has always been the potential to preach a much darker view: that social life is a zero-sum game, that others are out to cheat us or kill us. As Kim Sterelny has written, human beings' attitudes to trust were shaped by the fact that, in the woodland savannah in which we spent the longest part of our evolution, our most dangerous predators were one another.[48] In such a world, the cleverest strategy was to study our enemies, to anticipate their actions, to become like them, even paradoxically to empathize with them so we could predict what they would do—and then out-maneuver them. And they, of course, were doing the same to us. In such a world, it's the people who are most like us, who seem the most trustworthy, whom we can trust the least.[49]

This deep suspicion can be either a shrewd survival strategy, if life really is a zero-sum game, or a destructive paranoia if it isn't. The messages of the great doctrinal religions have not always been reassuring; they too have sometimes been active propagators of distrust. Just as societies in wartime can become obsessed with spies and fifth columnists, when religions have passed through periods of hunting for heretics and witches their language has emphasized that it's the people who seem the most innocent who are guiltiest of all. Thomas More's *Dialogue concerning Heresies* (written in 1529) is full of such passages, as historian David Loewenstein describes:

> Conjuring up a world of religious darkness, secretive book circulation, and transgressive reading, More's *Dialogue* warns of heretics who are "wonte to resorte to theyr redyngys / in a chamber at mydnyghte". . . . When it comes to the behavior of evangelical brethren, Satanic forces have been operating with great subtlety, as More suggests when he describes a seemingly meek evangelical who acknowledged his heretical errors but then, despite his deceptive appearance, revoked his revocation. . . . Protean behavior made it much harder to discern the sin and inward deviance hidden in the heart of this heretic. . . . More's depiction of wily evangelicals engaged in theatrical performance as they preach to the people suggests that they are

particularly skilled, to borrow the language of Milton, at putting on a "saintly show" which conceals "deep malice" as they "pretende holynesse for the coloure of theyr cloked heresyes."[50]

More may have been unusually eloquent (as well as unusually paranoid) in his expression of these ideas, but they have been developed widely elsewhere. As anthropologist Harvey Whitehouse observes of the Pomio Kivung cult in Papua New Guinea, the movement:

> emerged and spread among populations whose experience of Christianity derived largely from efforts of the Catholic Mission of the Sacred Heart. . . . Pomio supporters maintain that the reason for the many similarities between mission practices and those of their movement is that Catholicism deliberately and cynically combines true and false elements, in order to confuse the native and undermine his chances of meriting salvation. Since some mission teachings are true, they are also persuasive and an unenlightened person can readily be tricked into thinking that if part of a message is recognizably sound, then the whole thing is credible.[51]

He also describes how the founder of a splinter group "had to tread carefully. If he claimed superiority over the orators he ran the risk of being denounced by them as a man possessed by Satan, masquerading as an ancestor."[52]

The underlying message of such deep suspicion is this: *the world is not what it seems.* In such a disquieting world, the message bearer is presented as the only person the hearer can truly trust. It is a sentiment that has given rise to entire schools of theology, such as Gnosticism. As historian Hartmut Leppin records, Gnostics believed themselves "to have superior knowledge to that of other Christians. They were convinced, for example, that the real Christ had not been crucified; rather he had stood beside the cross laughingly, as Peter is supposed to have seen in contrast to other eyewitnesses. They did not trust church institutions as bearers of the apostolic tradition." A Gnostic text called the Apocalypse of Saint Peter, generally dated to the first half of the third century, warns Christians against those who masquerade as men of faith, usually by presenting themselves as bishops: "There shall be others of those who are outside of our number, who call themselves bishop—and also deacons—as if they have received their authority from God, while they bend themselves under the judgement of the first seats. Those are the canals without water."[53] Such suspicion has also appealed to many political leaders, in history as in our own time (Richard Hofstadter famously identified in 1964 what he called the "Paranoid Style in American Politics").[54] It taps into a powerful current in our evolved psychology, one that ideological entrepreneurs of all stripes have managed to develop in the pursuit of objectives that go far beyond anything our ancestors can have imagined. In addition to equipping us with a heightened sensitivity to the presence of potential enemies that surround us, it can even bring us pleasure, as our fear of these enemies is offset by the anticipation of our triumph over them. There is evidence from neurophysiology that punishing others for perceived transgressions against us stimulates powerful reward centers in the brain, ones that have been shown to respond also to the consumption of cocaine.[55] It should come with a health warning: righteous indignation is a highly additive recreational drug. It's a drug that equips us for survival in a truly hostile world. But it can seriously warp our perception of a world that contains as many potential collaborators as enemies. Traditional communities can be very aware of the damage it can do, and some (like the Turkana pastoralists of Kenya studied by anthropologist Sarah Mathew) have evolved sophisticated mechanisms for ensuring it is not overused; they are only too aware that punishment of a society's perceived transgressors can easily spiral out of control.[56]

To sum up, what can we conclude about the nature of the psychology with which natural selection has equipped us? In a nutshell, the answer to our question about how human beings evolved a capacity to believe in the existence of invisible spirits is that counterempirical beliefs of this kind have had few adaptive costs during the great part of our evolution. Since the growth of modern hierarchical civilizations, such counterempirical beliefs have become much more elaborate, and potentially much more costly compared with reasonable alternatives, because they are the product of a process of cumulative persuasion. Other people benefit from our willingness to suspend disbelief in the evidence of the senses, and they do all they can to encourage us in this direction. Sometimes they do so in pursuit of a shared benefit, and sometimes the benefit is all theirs; it is often hard for us to tell the difference.

The point about a facility for suspending disbelief is that it cannot be calibrated in advance to ensure it operates only in instances that deserve it. It will operate in response to cues, cues that can in principle be imitated and manipulated by others. Thus a willing suspender of disbelief will be both a readier collaborator in various collective projects and a more frequent subscriber to extravagant cosmologies, if there are others around to propose them. A thoroughgoing skeptic will rarely trust anybody. After all, the hypothesis that the world is full of thieves and charlatans—"canals without water"—is so much simpler and more elegant than the alternative that someone who has nothing to show you is someone you should trust. Yet the hypothesis that you should trust what you can't see is sometimes really true, and it is on this fragile truth that all of modern society has been constructed.

Does this mean that the evolution of religion, or something like it, was in some way inevitable in the history of humanity? Religion was certainly not inevitable in the way eyes, or something like them, were inevitable. We have no convincing evidence for the existence of a religious sensibility prior to around a hundred thousand years ago, though we cannot of course rule it out. Many of the features of human social living, including sophisticated tool manufacture and the taming of fire, which go back to perhaps half a million years ago, seem to have been possible in a world without religion. It's also imaginable that some of the collective benefits of ritual in human societies might instead have been assured by other activities, like the grooming behavior that boosts group solidarity in many species of monkeys and apes. Was religion perhaps an unexpected side effect of our loss of body hair, which made grooming less important?

On the other hand, once we grant human beings their command of language and storytelling, and once we take on board the massive co-operative advantages that have come about through the invention of fictive persons such as nation-states and multinational corporations, it's hard to think the adaptive advantages of a shared commitment to hidden agents and forces would long have remained unexploited. The presence of religion in society, even if not all individuals are religious, does seem intrinsically bound up with the kinds of cooperative, talkative, narratively minded, entrepreneurial animals that we are.

What about transcendental religion, the kind that emerged in the middle of the first millennium BCE (in the Axial Age), in the form of Taoism, Confucianism, Hinduism, Buddhism, Zoroastrianism, Judaism, and then Christianity and Islam a few centuries later? Was that inevitable too? An intriguing analogy here is with agriculture, which was independently invented at least seven times, at close intervals, in different parts of the world, beginning around ten thousand years ago, having never been developed before in human evolution.[57] Agriculture may have been a near-inevitable consequence of prehistoric climate change. It's a little harder to be sure what was the degree of independence of invention in the Axial Age religions. On the face of it, Chinese, Indian, and Abrahamic religious families do seem like independent and near-contemporary responses to common sets of social challenges, including intensification of warfare, urbanization, and the emergence of social hierarchy (as sociologist Stephen Sanderson has argued).[58] On the other hand, the Aztec, Maya, and Inca societies of the Americas never invented transcendental religions despite having all of these conditions. Might they have done so given time?

Recent work by Peter Turchin and colleagues suggests that the appearance of separate invention of transcendental religion is misleading:

Evolution of moralizing supernatural punishment (MSP) is distinct in its mode from other aspects of the Holocene transformation, which, unlike full MSP, arose repeatedly and independently in different parts of the world. Instead, full MSP evolved in a particular world region at a particular time, and then spread from there. Furthermore, full MSP is not a necessary condition for effective functioning of large-scale societies. Large bureaucratic empires in China, for example, functioned well enough without other-worldly super-natural punishments, instead relying on this-world state-administered punishments and rewards.[59]

What is certain is that as the transcendental religions spread, they developed models of organization that were remarkably different within societies, and yet remarkably similar across very divergent regions of the world. Chapter 9 explores how the platform model of religious organization helps us understand both the variety and the similarity that underlies it.

CHAPTER 9

The Temple Society—and Other Business Models

Ignatius . . . and his successors found themselves confronted by a fundamental problem that characterizes every major social organization, but which was perceived as especially dire by the Jesuits. How was it to deal with dissatisfied or rebellious members and instill a feeling of solidarity among thousands of men pursuing the most diverse tasks scattered across the globe?

—**Markus Friedrich,** *The Jesuits: A History*

Memories of the Dance

The eighty-year-old woman in front of us had begun to dance—hesitatingly, raising her hands above her head and folding her fingers into the elaborate gestures she had not practiced in several decades. As she gained in confidence, she began to move forward, legs slightly bent, feet facing outward, a little stiffly. She smiled, the first time I had seen her do this in the several weeks she had been watching us discreetly from behind the trees that surrounded the handful of huts where we were living. Chinnamma (as I'll call her) had once been a devadasi, a professional dancer working for the temple in our village, whose large trapezoid tower stood out as a looming silhouette against the sunset each evening.

Temple dancers in Kanchipuram, Tamil Nadu, India, 1903.
Credit: Kurt Boeck, Wikimedia Commons.

The temple where they danced.
Credit: Kurt Boeck, Wikimedia Commons.

The temple had fallen on hard times. Though an unusually fine example of South Indian temple architecture that had once attracted
pilgrims from far away, its structure was crumbling, and it was rarely
visited nowadays. If it had ever had any significant bronzes, these had
long ago been stolen, or sold by its underpaid priests to visiting scouts
for the antiques trade. Its team of musicians would still meet occasionally to accompany processions on village festival days, but they had lost
the motivation that once inspired them, so their playing was frankly
terrible, and the processions attracted little interest outside this hamlet
of some thirty houses. But the team of devadasis had been disbanded
long before, in the early years of independent India when Chinnamma
was still a young woman.

There's much controversy about the devadasi system, from its historical origins to how many devadasis still exist in India today despite its
legal prohibition, to the ethics of an institution under which young girls
from certain castes were symbolically married to the temple deity at an
early age.[1] Such girls never legally married, and were often considered
sexually available to wealthy temple patrons. This tradition gave rise to
much censorious gossip about individuals, and few former devadasis
would talk about their experiences. At the same time, they usually
learned the arts of music and dancing to a high level, and in modern
India such skills are highly prized. Chinnamma had joined the temple
before Indian independence, and by the time of the legal abolition of
the devadasi system in 1947 enjoyed significant local renown as a dancer.
She had a male companion with whom she left the village after the abolition, returning to her family after he died.

When Chinnamma began to dance before us it felt as though many
ambivalent memories were being released. She was shy, but visibly delighted that we were enjoying her demonstration. She began to click her
fingers in time to the movements, and to stamp her feet rhythmically on
the ground. We were enchanted by her performance—but it lasted no
more than two or three minutes. Two teenage boys came past the trees
at the edge of the clearing, saw what she was doing, and burst into loud
scornful guffaws. Chinnamma immediately stopped, turned away from
us, and walked off. She never danced for us again.

The temple for which Chinnamma had once worked used to be the thriving economic center of the village. It owned large amounts of land, which were leased out to tenant farmers. It used the revenues to employ significant numbers of priests, musicians, and dancers. It supervised and epitomized a system of social economic exchange that involved, in one way or another, the entire village community; the devadasis were just part of a wider network of people who both supported the temple and depended upon it. It operated at a much smaller scale than the famous temples at Thanjavur, Madurai, and elsewhere, whose origins go back at least to the Chola and Pandya dynasties in the tenth to twelfth centuries CE. But at its height it was a living embodiment of what sociologists Arjun Appadurai and Carol Appadurai Breckenridge have called a "Temple Society."[2] This always involved, in their vision, a set of rituals that were a homage to the temple's reigning deity, a process of social redistribution funded by the temple endowments, and a relationship to an external royal power who could resolve the conflicts this process might generate. It was a particular form of what I've called the platform model, one you might have thought would have no equivalents outside Asia. But medieval historian Ian Wood has used the idea of a temple society to great effect to understand the growth and operation of the medieval Catholic Church.

Between the years 300 and 750 CE the Church acquired up to a third of the cultivable land of Western Europe, most of it in the form of bequests from Christians who had come to believe that leaving land to the Church would be good for their immortal souls.[3] Though there were also donations of treasure and other benefits in kind, the gifts of land were overwhelmingly the most important source of the Church's wealth in this period, not least because they generated substantial flows of income. These enabled the Church to employ priests, monks, nuns, and other functionaries, and also to own slaves, which it continued to do up till the late medieval period.[4] The total number of priests, monks, and nuns in Western Europe has been estimated to be several hundred thousand at the end of the sixth century, roughly as many as the total number of soldiers. This constituted perhaps 2 percent of the total population of some twenty to twenty-five million, and in some places like the Frankish city of Vienne may have constituted as much as 10 percent.[5] The Church's wealth made possible a regular flow of resources to various beneficiaries of its favor, including the poor, the sick, and the destitute, and the erection of buildings, from parish churches to monasteries, cathedrals, and bishops' palaces. Over the centuries it would provide working capital for many businesses with which the Church was directly and indirectly involved, from banks to pawnbroking operations, textile factories, travel agencies, breweries, and a long list of others.[6]

These features make the economic world of the medieval Christian Church conform closely to the Appadurais' model of a temple society. The donations were made in homage to a reigning deity. They gave rise to large-scale redistributions within European society.[7] And the Church depended on the protection of the ruling princes or nobles in each region for the maintenance of civil order and the protection of its wealth against envious predators—though of course there was fierce rivalry over legitimacy between Church and Crown. Similar characteristics have been documented for Hindu and Buddhist temples across Asia from Cambodia to China, and for Islamic mosques at around the same time—all of which continued to receive donations of land from wealthy benefactors over many hundreds of years. You might think that doctrinal religions enjoyed a great advantage over more ritual-based or transactional religions in this respect, with the doctrine providing the rationale for the donations. But the facts don't bear this out: temples in the Maya kingdoms of pre-Columbian Mexico (which had no doctrinal functions) operated in similar ways,[8] and there are many continuities with the way temples functioned in classical Greece and Rome.[9] Yet there must have been differences between countries, between institutions within countries, and across historical periods. How can we understand these different processes in a coherent way? What were the business models these religious institutions put in place, and how do they relate to other versions of the platform model of religion right up to the modern day? We'll look at these similarities and differences in terms of the answers to four features of each religious institution: its *mission*, its *structure*, its *strategies*, and its *message*.

Mission

Paradoxically, the mission of a religious movement is the dimension about which it's hardest to generalize historically. People have founded religious movements for all kinds of reasons, though the exact motive is often a matter of conjecture. It might be a literal vision, a desire for adventure, frustrated ambition, to save souls from damnation, compassion for the downtrodden, pursuit of a political goal, to make money, to win social esteem, to indulge a hyperactive libido, to rebound from bankruptcy, to escape oppression, to succeed in the eyes of teachers or parents, to continue the tradition of a temple or other sacred site, as another thing to do in a sequence of entrepreneurial projects—or, in the case of Ignatius of Loyola, founder of the Jesuit order, as a way of rebuilding his literally shattered life after a cannonball seriously wounded both his legs during the doomed defense of the citadel of Pamplona against the troops of the French king Francis I in 1521.[10] Of course, the reason for founding a movement is not the same thing as the movement's mission. The reason may be overt, unconscious, or conscious but hidden, or somewhere between all of these, but the mission is the explicit objective that the movement proclaims and around which it is organized. Sometimes a movement's initial mission is just to proclaim the teachings or to immortalize the spirit of a founder. Sometimes the founder proclaims the teachings of a different person (human or divine), or claims to be representing the spirit of an existing movement better than the current leaders of that movement. Sometimes it's even hard to know who best to call the founder: should we think of Christianity as founded by Jesus, or by Saint Peter, or by Saint Paul with a mission to proclaim the teachings of Jesus? Does the answer even matter, given that the movement survived and thrived?

The overwhelming majority of potential religious movements never survive for long, so the interesting question is whether we can say anything about the missions of those that do. In theory, movements don't need a founder—there's a tomb in the Terre Cabade cemetery of my home city of Toulouse whose occupant has somehow acquired a reputation for miracle working, so the marble monument is festooned with hundreds of notes requesting interventions to cure broken limbs or broken hearts, to restore jobs or joy. But unless someone else decides there's business potential here, this will no more become a movement than did the 322 crossroads cult places documented in Rome in the fourth century CE, or the accidental shrine that sprang up in twentieth-century Istanbul after a grocer lit a candle to advertise his wares near a grave that turned out to be that of a horse, not a holy man.[11]

In practice, movements need at least one founder. It's often more than one—as in the splinter group from the Pomio Kivung cult described by Harvey Whitehouse, which had two founders, one of whom specialized in having dreams and visions while the other one specialized in interpreting these for the members.[12] And the founder almost always gives a personal touch to the mission: the mission may be to propound a certain doctrine, but if so it's a doctrine filtered through the experience and perspective of the founder. More often the doctrine can hardly even be summarized without reference to "the teachings of the founder." Sometimes doctrine is even irrelevant—the mission of the movement may just be for the founder to keep receiving pilgrims for rituals performed in a sacred place. Indeed, most of the immanent religious movements have had little or no room for doctrine at all. This therefore highlights the importance of the biggest challenge facing any religious movement: What happens after the death of the founder, or the incapacitation of the founder through disability, defeat, or the discredit that comes from scandal—or simply the wish of the founder to step back from the firm's activities? What kind of mission can survive the founder's withdrawal or eclipse?

Though much has been written about succession to the founder in religious movements, this literature is dwarfed by the avalanche of writings about succession in secular businesses. It makes sense to apply the insights of the latter to the challenges of the former. The overwhelming majority of new secular businesses are and have always been family businesses. When their founders retire, they often try to pass the business on to other family members, usually to their children and most often to their sons. This happens also in many religious movements, such as the appointment in 2000 of Franklin Graham as CEO of the Billy Graham

Evangelistic Association. The advantages of a family succession usually consist in continuity—successors share many of the values and the characteristics of the founders they succeed. This may be attractive to the founders themselves, through the reassurance that the business is in safe—or at least familiar—hands. But continuity may also be appealing to other stakeholders in the business.[13] Family successors have been shown to be more likely, on average, to honor the contracts made with employees, suppliers, and creditors, and to keep the business model established by the founder.[14] Sometimes, too, family members may have specialized creative skills (in music, the arts, or design), which are often most easily transmitted in families, as the many dynasties of actors and musicians attest.

The disadvantages of a family succession usually consist in continuity as well. This is partly because the qualities that make for good leaders do not consist just in the organizational policies they implement, but also in their "soft skills," as the scientific literature in management has shown.[15] And these soft skills are not necessarily shared by their kin. Businesses often need fresh ideas and expertise after the eclipse of a founder, and the founder's kin are usually the least well equipped to provide them.[16] How can we tell whether the disadvantages of a family succession are likely to outweigh the advantages?

If we want to use systematic evidence to answer this question, we can't just compare firms that replace a founder with a family member against those who replace the founder with an outsider—the two types of firms typically differ in many other ways (the latter tend to be larger, for a start). But an ingenious way has been found to compare like with like—by using the natural experiment provided by the gender of the founders' children. Founders with sons are more likely to pass on the business to them than founders with only daughters, so we can compare family successions with otherwise similar outsider successions that are the result of founders who have daughters. And the results suggest that, on average, the disadvantages of family succession outweigh the advantages—except when firms are passing through turbulent times in which it's particularly important to maintain continuity. In more normal times, family businesses whose founders retire need external expertise, on average, more than they need continuity. And they need successors who are willing to distance themselves from the actions of the founder more than they need those who are motivated primarily by loyalty to the founder's person and the founder's vision.[17]

What might be the lessons for religious succession? Religious movements often mimic the dynamics of family firms. Some are indeed run by families, such as the Unification Church, founded in Korea in 1954 by Sun-Myung Moon. When the founder died in 2012 the family split into quarreling factions led by several of his children, over which Moon's widow Han Hak-ja attempted to assert control by proclaiming herself in 2014 "an independently born woman with no sin."[18] This had no visible effect on the acrimony of the disputes (which erupted in lawsuits over the ensuing decade). Supposedly doctrinal schisms within religious movements commonly occur after the death of a founder, suggesting that doctrine is not necessarily the sole source of division.[19]

Even movements that are not run by families tend to reproduce some of the intense relationships of families, down to using the terms "brother," "sister," "father," and "mother" to describe relationships among the movement's members. The fact of emphasizing fictitious rather than real family relationships may sometimes give them more flexibility in finding successors to the founders—they're less dependent on the accidents of kinship. Indeed, one of the innovations of the Christian Church was to transcend kinship as a determinant of succession: Saint Paul, who became the movement's de facto leader at an early stage, had not even known the founder personally. In contrast, disputes over the legitimacy of the Prophet's grandson as his successor divide Sunni and Shi'a Muslims to this day. Disputes over the legitimacy of the succession were to take place within Christianity as well (for example in the claims— revived after the English king Henry VIII's break with Rome—that the English Church had been founded by Joseph of Arimathea).[20] But these were neither as bitter nor as long-lasting as those among Muslims.

Still, even without dependence on strict kinship, religious movements remain prone to many of the failings of family firms—too much reverence for, and too little willingness to examine lucidly the ideas of the founder, not enough breadth of experience or openness to other points of view. They're also much less likely than comparable secular institutions to have raised capital from outside investors who are not actively involved in the daily work of the movement.[21] This is because, in their early days at least, religious movements tend to have lower capital requirements than many secular businesses; and these capital needs can often be met by donations from members. The resulting independence from outside investors gives them freedom—including the freedom to persist in their mistakes.

The corresponding strengths of religious movements, compared with secular businesses, include the ability credibly to promise continuity after the eclipse of a founder—and not just because their members remain deeply attached to the founder's vision. In addition to any such attachment, the platform model provides an explanation for the stability of a religious movement. The members may have come to the community historically because of the vision of the founder, but once that community has been created it provides a reason of its own for belonging, a social glue that outlasts the physical presence of the founder. You may choose to join a religious community for all kinds of spiritual reasons, but once you've done so, the human attachments you make there are threads that bind you cumulatively to the community. That's why, incidentally, people who have left those very intense religious movements that we call cults tend to compare the experience to that of physical addiction or romantic infatuation—the choice between continuing and stopping looks very different from the outside than it did from the inside. Other features of a religious movement may matter too—attachment to a physical place such as a temple, for instance, or to an iconic location ("next year in Jerusalem!"). But community is often stronger than location, as the Church of Latter-Day Saints discovered during the succession crisis caused by the murder of its founder Joseph Smith in 1844, when Brigham Young persuaded the bulk of the faithful to leave Illinois and move westward to Nebraska and eventually to Utah. Whatever the original mission of the founders, protection of the communities they created provides a powerful mission for their successors.

It's difficult to find contexts in which we can directly compare the impact of succession crises on religious movements with their impact on secular businesses. One study by Heather Havement and Mukti Khaire compared the US magazine industry from 1741 to the outbreak of the Civil War in 1861. The authors distinguished magazines that were founded with a strongly ideological (often religious) mission from the rest. Using a sample of 2,593 magazines founded over the period, they found that those with a strongly ideological mission tended to survive longer, but also were much more likely to fail after the death or retirement of the founder. This tends to support the suggestion that the advantages of continuity in religious movements only occasionally outweigh its disadvantages.[22]

Any religious movement that survives the eclipse of its founder (and the great majority do not) may soon face a new challenge: that of handling a growing number of members. If the original movement was limited by a constraint on the number of members who could interact personally with the founder, the absence of the founder removes that constraint. Many more members can now aspire to indirect rather than direct experience of the founder's spirit, however literally or metaphorically they may understand that spirit to move among them. But if the founder's spirit can be everywhere, the successors must move in real space: size creates a need for decisions about the movement's structure.

Structure

With its 1.3 billion believers subject to the authority of a single Pope, the Roman Catholic Church might seem to have the most hierarchical large-scale structure of any religious movement in the world. But appearances are deceptive. There are many, many layers of status in the organization, but in terms of authority to take decisions, the hierarchy is far flatter than you would find in any secular institution of even a fraction of the size. Individual Catholics are subject to the authority of their priests, who are subject to the authority of their bishops, who are subject to the authority of the Pope.[23] Four layers: that's it. That might appear to give the Pope much more authority over the faithful—fewer intermediate layers to soften the blow—but in practice the attention span of the Vatican is quite unable to cope with the sheer scale of the challenge of policing what the lower layers get up to. As a result, even within this apparent monolith there have always been large areas of de facto autonomy—what historian Peter Brown (writing of the early Middle Ages) called "micro-Christendoms," with "competing regional churches" and "little Romes."[24]

In practice the religious orders (organizations of monks or nuns, or movements such as the Society of Jesus or Opus Dei or the Christian Brothers) have enjoyed a great deal of liberty to manage their own affairs. This has been sometimes a source of great energy and innovation within the Church, and sometimes a dangerous source of weakness, as the abuse scandals of recent years have revealed. While it's tempting for the Church's critics to see this as a purely moral failing, it also reflects a structural weakness. There's no way for an organization with a hierarchical pyramid as flat as this one to observe and regulate what is happening at the lower levels—except through a great deal of devolved authority, plus the trust that it will be exercised wisely.[25] Reluctance to interfere routinely in the decisions of the lower levels of the hierarchy is the only way the Church could possibly have functioned. What the Church has had to do to keep this vast movement on message is to leverage its prestige and its immense resources of soft power. That very prestige has also constituted a great temptation to ignore some of the threats lurking within the body of the community, if the leadership could reason that investigating the threats might damage the Church's reputation more than ignoring them.

Exactly these considerations preoccupy many secular platforms that have grown so fast that they struggle to manage the actions of their members. Facebook is not just a platform but a confederation of platforms—that is, a platform many of whose members are themselves platforms. There is great controversy over who is responsible for the content distributed within such an ecosystem—just as there is continuing controversy over the extent to which online retailers like Amazon should be held legally liable for the quality of products sold on their platform by third-party retailers. As the Catholic Church—itself a confederation of platforms—knows only too well, the organization's official views of its own responsibility may come into sharp conflict with the expectations of its members and of secular society.

Historian Ian Forrest has shown how such a process of governing the Church with the cooperation of intermediaries (known as "trustworthy men") was developed in England during the Middle Ages. Such people "were jurors, informants, and witnesses who represented their parishes when bishops needed local knowledge or reliable collaborators." What he calls the "dark side" of trust emerged because of the inability of the Church's hierarchy to form reliable views of its own as to what was happening on the ground; it became too dependent on its collaborators and unable to question their actions. "For the church to discriminate between trustworthy and untrustworthy was not to identify the most honest Christians but to find people whose status meant that their word would not be contradicted. This meant men rather than women, and—usually—the wealthier tenants and property holders in each parish."[26] It's a telling account of the way in which the Church became unable to exercise oversight and control of the people who acted in its name. These were people whom nobody would dare to question—certainly not any of the countless victims of abuse whose stories have taken so long to come to light.

The Catholic Church's structure represents just one of many possible ways in which religious movements have faced the challenges of growth. Their leaders must take decisions about whom to involve in their management, and what autonomy those partners should enjoy. A comparative cross-country study by economists Gordon Hanson and Chong Xiang showed that religious movements with decentralized governance structures were more successful at attracting members in countries where motivating pastors was a particularly important challenge.[27] The question of how much autonomy to grant the partners is never an all-or-nothing matter, as the case of the Catholic Church has indicated. Control over what the partners do in a movement's name is a matter of explicit agreement, but it is also affected by practical challenges to monitoring and enforcement. This means that the choice of partners becomes critically important—almost all succession disputes are about whom the founder and the existing members can trust.

In the early centuries of the Christian Church, as historian Hartmut Leppin has shown, the election of bishops involved an appeal to the whole community of believers—but not (as we might anachronistically think) because an inclusive process lent legitimacy to the choice. There was nothing democratic about the institution of the bishopric. Rather, the community was involved because it mattered whom God had chosen. Listening to many believers would increase the chance of hearing God's message (this was an early appeal to what is now known as "the wisdom of crowds"). Only God could be trusted to get the succession right—but, unfortunately, there was no foolproof way to find out what God wanted. Once elected, though, bishops were expected to exert absolute authority, even if the consensus as to what exactly the bishop could impose remained fuzzy, constrained not just by disagreement on the underlying principles but also by the practical impossibility of exercising far-reaching oversight.[28]

In practice many religious organizations have opted for franchising, which is a compromise between centralized and decentralized control that has been widely adopted in secular service businesses, such as the retailing and restaurant sectors.[29] Under a franchising contract, a business that owns a branded product allows a service provider to distribute that product, usually with an assurance of exclusivity within a certain territory, in exchange for upfront fees and royalty payments. The franchisor usually also stipulates conditions under which the distribution should take place, conditions that are sometimes highly detailed. It may also provide training to employees of the franchisee. Still, subject to respecting these conditions franchisees can run the business as they like. This has the advantage of limiting the amount of oversight required to manageable proportions.

This model of religious organization often characterizes evangelical and Pentecostal Protestant churches, like the Assemblies of God. And the inspiration runs in both directions: Pentecostal churches have in turn inspired a particular kind of secular franchise operation, which deploys multilevel marketing (distributing their products through direct contact between distributors and clients, often in the clients' homes). Anthropologist Nathalie Luca has described in her study of such businesses in France, Haiti, and Korea a particular affinity between the prosperity gospel espoused by Pentecostal churches and the degree of "faith" that distributors in multilevel marketing operations need to develop in order to have any chance of succeeding. In the early days of multilevel marketing the faith was usually explicitly Christian, though in more recent times it has often incorporated elements from the New Age, environmentalist, and wellness movements.[30]

The franchise model can also be used to understand the way in which Catholic religious orders have functioned (the Rule of Saint Benedict, a book of precepts written around 530 CE for monks living communally under the authority of an abbot, can be understood as the franchise contract for the Benedictine order, even if it's unlikely that Saint Benedict himself ever envisaged its being used in this way). The franchise model predates Christianity: in his *Ecclesiastical History* written in the sixth century CE, John of Ephesus, a leader of the Syriac Orthodox Church, writes of a pagan temple at Derira, in modern Turkey, that "no less than fifteen hundred temples, situated in the neighboring provinces, were subject to its authority, and every year, at a vast assembly held, the regulations were fixed for the ensuing twelvemonth."[31] It's also a good model for understanding those religious movements that have relied on a process of discipleship to extend the influence of the founder. Disciples may not be under a formal contract with the founder (or whichever current leader claims to represent the founder). But they do consider themselves obliged to follow the model in a way that respects the founder's intentions.

Not all businesses with branded products use franchising—most of them distribute their goods through regular outlets with a minimum of contractual specificity. Some religious movements are like this—such as the Gideon Bibles organization, which places its Bibles in hotel rooms around the world by arrangement with the hotel management. But most are better understood either as franchises or as users of a formerly copyrighted product (the Bible, the Quran, the Book of Mormon, the Rig Veda, the Mahabharata . . .) whose copyright has expired. It's the claim that they use the authentic copyrighted product that is their claim to act in the spirit of the religion's founder. As these diverse examples suggest, there are very different degrees of precision implied by that claim. The Book of Mormon is used in rather specific contexts and only by a small number of churches in relatively direct descent from the founder (though there have been several schisms in the less than two centuries of the existence of the Church of Latter-Day Saints). The Bible and the Quran may be used in different translations, while the Mahabharata does not even have a single agreed text. In all cases, though, the primary enforcers of authenticity are not the parent organizations but the religious members themselves.

Monitoring what religious organizations are doing is easily outsourced to the members in the case of Muslim, Hindu, Buddhist, and some Protestant Christian religious organizations. In principle anyone can set up as an imam, priest, or pastor, and it's up to the congregations to make up their own minds about whose services are authentic. The absence of doctrine in everyday Hinduism and Buddhism makes the process relatively straightforward: there's a shared set of images (such as different avatars of Vishnu for Hindus or different bodhisattvas for Buddhists) and a shared set of rituals (notably puja, the basic devotional offering in both traditions). That's all a pious Hindu or Buddhist needs to accept. The authenticity of the services is maintained in much the same way as the authenticity of the recipe for pizza is maintained by customer vigilance: through a culture of people who know, and who care (there's no Pizza Pope, and there's no Hindu or Buddhist Pope either).

More elaborate questions about whether the bodhisattvas are avatars of the Buddha, or whether the Buddha himself is an avatar of Vishnu, are explicitly considered matters for theological experts, who of course disagree—there's no way to settle such questions empirically. They are not for the ordinary laity or even the ordinary priesthood. The amount of policing the lay members need to do is modest—they vote with their feet, and the process is usually peaceful. That's not to say there are no difficult decisions. Researcher Pattana Kitiarsa has written that in Thailand there is "harmonious coexistence of deities from diverse religious traditions, ranging from Buddha to local and royal spirits,"[32] but notes that it is driven by economic imperatives:

The abbot once told me and other monks that "we need to find some tricks (*ubai*) to attract devotees to our temple. We cannot survive without patronage from laypeople. Magic is not encouraged in Buddhist teachings and ecclesiastical laws (*vinaya*) but sometimes it is quite necessary when we have to deal with popular expectation. I have built this temple with donations generated through magical and supernatural rites as much as by adhering to Buddhist teachings."[33]

Such pragmatic compromises between the formal teachings of Buddhism and the imperatives of the market can happen in many places, as sociologist Carolyn Chen has noted in describing how some twenty-first-century Buddhist teachers of meditation have adapted their message to make it resonate for tech entrepreneurs in California's Silicon Valley:

> Their motivations were genuine and came from spiritual experiences they had had themselves. Their concern was to bring wholeness to people and to share their own spiritual transformation with the world. But because of the particular circumstances of living in the Bay Area, in the techtopian ecosystem, they have to figure out ways to monetize these teachings. . . . For that reason, they resorted to this kind of "doublespeak." They felt that in order to market their spirituality, they had to quote the science and use the PowerPoints and language legible to tech professionals. They have to present meditation in secular terms because many companies have qualms about bringing religion into the workplace. These teachers consider this "doublespeak" as "expedient means," which is a Buddhist term that justifies adjusting the teachings to make the dharma accessible to a variety of people.[34]

The policing of authenticity in Islam is much more tense and potentially violent than under Buddhism. This is because Islam is a doctrinal religion, and also because there exists a specific text, the Quran, against which the utterances of individual imams and lay believers can be measured. Historically an accusation of *zandaqa*, "a term originally denoting the dualist doctrines of the Manicheans but which came to be used for all kinds of heresy and freethinking,"[35] could cost the accused their life. As with Christianity, crucial questions arise not just about why and when violence may be inflicted on heretics and unbelievers but also about who gets to decide. Certain verses of the Quran appear to entitle ordinary believers to take the law into their own hands: "Fight those who do not believe in Allah or the Last Day, who do not forbid what Allah and His messenger have forbidden, and do not profess the religion of truth—even if they are those who have been given the Book."[36] This would evidently be a recipe for chaos if there were not also many verses in the Quran that enjoin peacemaking ("If the enemy is inclined towards peace, make peace with them"),[37] and if in practice the threat of violence had not been regulated by the political authorities, even if these have had to struggle to do so at times.

In practice, therefore, Islam no less than Christianity has lived in a state of continual compromise, both milder and messier than the more bellicose pronouncements to be found in their respective scriptures. Fiery denunciations of the Sufi cult of saints by imams preaching a more austere vision such as Wahabism have often remained just that—denunciations—without there being further consequences. Anthropologist David Parkin has described how "there is a division in East African coastal Islam between a) the higher status 'Arabo-Swahili' of Wahabi persuasion who denounce celebrations (*maulidi*) in honour of the Prophet Mohammed, regarding them as *biida* and debasing; and b) so-called 'African' Swahili who hold massive celebrations in different parts of the coast and, together, prolong them over many months, far beyond the month in which the Prophet was born."[38] Countless similar examples could be cited across the Muslim world and throughout the history of Islam. What is striking about such doctrinal divergences is not how often they spiral into violence but how rarely they do so, despite the ample margin given in the Quran for those who might seek justification for escalation. When they do, it's almost always a symptom of a breakdown in the wider society in which the religious culture is embedded.

If voting with your feet remains a far more widespread mechanism for enforcing the authenticity of a religious message than voting with a sword or a gun, there's a third option that is different from either, which can best be described as voting with your genes. All religious communities have tended to favor marriage within rather than outside the community, and in some societies this injunction has been very strictly enforced. In the temple society in southern India with which this chapter began,

Chinnamma the devadasi belonged to a special caste of musicians and dancers. These specialize in musical activities (even if they also work as farmers or as agricultural laborers), and tend to marry within the community. Their caste is just one of many groups defined by occupation (known as *jatis*, which are strictly speaking subgroups of the main castes in the traditional Indian system). Whether or not there was once a justification of endogamy (marriage within the caste) in terms of incentives to maintain occupational skills, complaints about the injustices of the caste system are nearly as old as the system itself.

For example, the Lingayat movement in South India, which dates back at least to the twelfth century CE, expressed strong opposition to existing caste distinctions within Hinduism. It sought to bring together the devout of all castes in places of collective worship (known as "halls of spiritual experience"), and even brought into question the authority of the Vedic scriptures. Though there were episodes of physical repression by the political authorities, a far more effective measure of repression was the simple refusal of many existing Hindus to allow their daughters to marry husbands who had joined the movement. The Lingayats effectively became another endogamous group. By the nineteenth century they had taken to squabbling with other castes over their relative position, and to encouraging the adoption of habits hitherto confined to the Brahmin castes.[39] The question whether Lingayats constitute a caste within Hinduism or a separate religion is not just an arcane theological matter. It has become a fraught question in modern India, since the group's members have tended to vote en bloc for India's nationalist party, the BJP, and have been lobbying for special status.[40] But although Hinduism is somewhat extreme in its mobilization of endogamy, a milder form of voting with your genes is widespread in all religious movements. The authenticity of the movement is steered in part by the fear of its members that their children will otherwise be unable to find suitable marriage partners.

The structure of a religious movement, then, is a matter of who (besides the founder) has authority to speak in the movement's name, to give legitimacy to its rituals, to authenticate its message—and, in rare but important cases, to enforce against rebellious members the sanctions in the movement's armory, up to and including the infliction of extreme violence. How does structure affect what religions do with this authority? What are the strategies they use to compete? The strategies that each movement will implement are, after all, the whole point and purpose of debates over the movement's structure.

Strategies

The two most consequential strategic decisions a religious movement must take are what types of service it will offer to its members, and what types of members it will target. Both decisions will be taken in the light not just of the preferences of potential members but also of the strategies of rival movements that may be competing for their attention, their resources, and their loyalty. For movements that are organized as platforms the second question follows from the first—connection to other members is one of the most important services a religious movement can offer. The clientele may not be explicitly restricted, of course. Although some organizations refuse to accept women, or non-Muslims, or even just outsiders of any kind, most are open to visits from interested strangers. But even simple one-person providers of such transactional religious services as fortune-telling, intercession with God, or the performance of occasional sacrifices to mark special occasions need to decide what kind of clientele to attract. A simple roadside shrine will cost little to keep up but yield little in income; a more grandiose décor may hope to bring in prosperous patrons but has a higher base of fixed costs to amortize. Similarly, the kind of relationship-management services the platform needs to propose will be very different in a rural community where most members already know one another than in a big city mosque or church where many members have no opportunity to see one another otherwise.

A major strategic decision concerns whether to try to bring many worshippers together at the same time in a single place, as in a mosque for Friday prayers or an outdoor tent for a revivalist Christian meeting, or instead to build many shrines for individual worship. Christian cathedrals have traditionally done both, but at a significant cost in the size and complexity of the building required. They have often defrayed this cost by persuading individual donors to associate their names to components of the structure—such as chapels, or the pews that rich families may sponsor at a prominent place in the church. Hindu, Buddhist, and Shinto temples have privileged a combination of shrines to particular deities with collective spaces for groups to gather. For them too, the preferences of donors will often guide architectural and landscaping choices. So will considerations about how the spaces can be given multiple uses. After all, the whole community can hardly be expected to be continuously present outside the main worship hours. Some of them may come at various times for choral practice, youth clubs, Bible study or Quranic instruction, counseling, individual prayer and meditation, consultation or purchase of books, food preparation, and more. So religious leaders will look for ways to increase the value of their premises, and the portfolio of religious services offered by many large organizations emerges as a logical consequence.

There's a difference, though, between offering a range of services to make best use of a communal space and a strategy of "thinking big," offering a whole portfolio of activities and services to give members of the community a total experience in one place. The first of these is driven just by cost considerations, while the second takes advantage of perceived synergies in demand. Whether thinking big makes sense will depend on whether the members envisage a single or a multiple version of the religious experience. This is partly about whether members stick to one venue rather than attending a range of different venues, perhaps praying at one Shinto shrine on their way to work while taking their family at the weekend to a different one, or attending different churches on different Sundays. It's also about whether members want an immersive experience of their religious community, in which they not only worship but also work, socialize, and educate their children together. They may even go travelling together: historian Jonathan Sumption has described how the Church in medieval Europe developed what were essentially the first travel agencies, dedicated to helping pilgrims travel to their destination.[41] The organization of pilgrimages remains an activity in which churches, mosques, synagogues, and temples are heavily involved.[42] But not all religious members want something so immersive; many prefer to mix and match these elements of their lives—for instance, worshipping at one church or synagogue or mosque but socializing with people from a wider range of communities. The varied world of religious platforms in the twenty-first century contains many examples of both models.

This choice is a familiar one in the domain of secular platforms. The literature on platforms has coined the terms "single-homing" and "multi-homing" to describe situations where users either stick to a single platform for a particular service or switch regularly between rival platforms. Sometimes the choice is strongly determined by cost or convenience—very few people use more than one computer or smartphone operating system or cable television provider. Sometimes it's because the platforms use pricing strategies to favor single-homing, which the established ones prefer because it weakens competition between them, and the new entrants dislike for the same reason. For example, real-estate agents typically offer you lower fees for selling your house or apartment if you give them exclusive rights than if you advertise it on multiple platforms. Digital technology often makes multi-homing possible where analog technology does not: many people who used to read a single physical newspaper now get their news from multiple online sources. A product might be offered for sale on multiple online platforms where previously it could be offered to only a single auction house.

Sometimes customer habits change. In the early days of social media, when Facebook drove out its early competitor Myspace, it became the conventional wisdom that single-homing on social media was inevitable. It was also believed that the scope of single-homing could only expand, as Facebook users increasingly got their news from it as well. But that was before the launch in 2010 of Instagram, which showed that multi-homing could work, since users really did have the time and energy to curate multiple profiles. Instagram provided a source of independent competitive pressure until it was acquired two years later by . . . Facebook.

Sometimes single- and multi-homing vary by country and culture. No platform in the Western world matches the reach of the Chinese platform WeChat, whose over one billion active users depend on it not just for communication but also for making payments, e-commerce, booking taxis and other transport, playing video games, and sharing photos and videos—activities that in other countries typically take place on several different platforms. This has given WeChat a unique hold over its members, one the Chinese government has exploited in constructing its mass surveillance network, and in censoring discussion of politically sensitive topics. It's obviously easier to do both of those things if users are single-homing. The point has long been known to religious leaders, who know they can count on greater ideological conformity among their members if they create for them a fully immersive community that meets all their needs and weakens their incentive to shop around. But this is to put the point misleadingly. Ideological conformity may of course follow the creation of a community, but that doesn't make it an afterthought. The community itself may be created, and strengthened after its creation, because its leaders develop a particularly compelling message.

Even that message is rarely crafted in isolation from the circumstances of rivalry among religious movements in each society. Messages are not just statements of conviction—they are also *strategies*. When there is little competition for members among religious movements, it's often easy for them to cooperate to send similar messages to their communities—especially in the face of communal challenges. Historian Andrew Robarts describes a village in Ottoman Bulgaria in which:

> Anti-disease rituals involved an elaborate ceremony of sacrifice to the "Goddess of Plague" (Boginiata Chuma) performed to allay the Goddess's anger and to divert her attention away from the village. On the day of the ceremony, so-called "prophets of plague" advised the villagers of Trunchovitsa to fast and avoid the use of fire. Surrounded by all the villagers and inside of a space formed by the circling of wagons and carts, religious leaders from Trunchovitsa's three confessional communities (Muslims, Catholic, and Greek Orthodox) performed a common liturgy and read aloud a common prayer to protect the village from disease.[43]

In contrast, when rivalry to recruit members is intense, each platform faces much greater pressure to differentiate its strategy from those of its rivals; otherwise it risks losing members to those rivals whose profiles seem barely distinct from its own. Economists studying competitive strategy have highlighted the key factors at work in secular businesses, and the insights are highly relevant here. When two firms offer very similar goods or services, they compete intensely by offering very attractive prices; this is good for their customers but hurts the firms' profits. They will do whatever they can to soften competition between them; the aim is to divide the market into niches in which each can be to some extent a monopolist. One of the ways they may try to do this is to start customer loyalty programs, like those for frequent flyers on airlines—these reduce the temptation for firms to compete so fiercely on price, since many of their potential customers are locked into the loyalty programs of rivals.

You might also think the firms would always try to differentiate their products from those of rivals to weaken price competition, but that's not always so. In certain special circumstances, which were described by the economist Harold Hotelling as long ago as 1929, this leads them paradoxically to make their services very similar. Those circumstances occur when two firms share a space that they can partition into two by each staying in the middle and serving one side. Think of two fast-food sellers serving customers on a beach front. If their food is the same (a point we'll return to), customers choose between them purely to minimize the time they walk along the beach front. So they will buy from the nearest stall, and the two stalls will end up located next to each other, with all the customers on the left side buying from the left stall and those on the right buying from the right stall. If either stall were to move away, it would lose customers in the middle without gaining any on the side. The outcome where they both occupy the middle ground is therefore a stable equilibrium.

This insight has been used to explain phenomena like the tendency of political programs in two-party systems to converge toward the center, to capture centrist voters without losing those at the extremes (ideological distance from the party you vote for is considered analogous to physical distance along the beachfront). In a world of religious competition with only two mainstream Churches, we might therefore expect their worship style and their theology to evolve to become very similar. One might be a little more traditional, the other slightly more modern, but they would not diverge very far. Each would hold its half of the theological space to some degree captive.

But these circumstances are unusual. Hotelling's insight is most important for helping us understand what happens when they do not hold. One possibility is that tacking to the center risks losing voters at the extremes—as when extreme left or extreme right voters lose their motivation to turn out for center left or center right parties. The two parties may therefore keep some distance from each other, each occupying the center of their own half of the ideological space. This is like a very long beach front where some of the customers are too far away to want to come all the way to the center, and it's too costly (or against regulations) for a third seller to come in to cater for them.

Another possibility, which is likely if the costs of setting up a stall are low relative to the expected demand, is that there may be three or more stalls on the beachfront; then the middle-ground equilibrium breaks down. The fast-food seller in the middle will be sandwiched, as it were, between the other two—and will do better by escaping to find a stretch of unoccupied beachfront elsewhere. Depending on the details, this might result in the different sellers fanning out along the beachfront at intervals, trying to keep enough distance from each other that they can enjoy a slightly captive clientele. Or it might result in their bunching together in the middle and trying to weaken the competition among them by differentiating their products in another dimension. One seller might offer Asian food, another Latino, a third might go for vegan specialties—then they could each hope to cater for customers from all over the beachfront who have those tastes, provided the customers care enough about those dimensions of the food more than they care about having to walk a little further. The stalls can also try to differentiate themselves from one another in other ways, such as by building up customer loyalty—frequent-fryer programs, perhaps?

What should these arguments lead us to expect in the field of religious offerings? The basic insight is that whenever it's easy for more than two movements to operate in a particular community, we should expect them to make great efforts to differentiate themselves from one another. We see this clearly in the way in which the translation of the Bible into the vernacular, and the spread of printing technology, lowered the obstacles to starting up new religious movements in the European Reformation during the sixteenth century. It seems paradoxical that no sooner had Europe's Protestants thrown off the yoke of Catholic orthodoxy than they spawned a whole ecosystem of doctrinally incompatible movements and cults, from Lutherans and Calvinists to the profusion of Anabaptist sects such as Mennonites, Hutterites, and Amish in Germany alone. As historian Randolph Head put it: "Neither the bishop and Reformed Synod nor the Diet drove the process of confessionalisation in the villages; rather, the decisive agents were well-placed religious minorities, who showed themselves willing to put religion before community solidarity."[44] The reason is that competition drove differentiation, as it does in so many other spheres of life—each religious minority was developing its strategy to attract adherents, and lack of community solidarity emerged as the unintended result of their interactions.[45] This also helps us to understand why differentiation so often took place in the complex dimensions of theology and ritual—as we saw in the discussion of ritual in chapter 5, it's the very opacity of many rituals that makes them effective as badges of community solidarity. Rituals and theological tenets that defy simple explanation but help to differentiate you from your rivals are the most effective customer loyalty programs of all.

It was not just the Protestant movements that responded to the new circumstances of competition in this way. The Catholic Church has also shown itself to be highly sensitive to the competitive threat posed by Protestant rivals. Economist Robert Barro and philosopher Rachel McCleary have studied the processes of beatification and canonization of saints and martyrs of the Catholic Church, which is one of the areas of Church activity one might have expected to be least influenced by such strategic considerations. Nevertheless, they show that, when analyzed by country, numbers beatified and canonized are correlated positively with measures of competition between Catholicism and Protestantism, and between Catholicism and no religion. They interpret these processes as—among other things—attempts to invigorate the Catholic faith and, thereby, to discourage the faithful from giving up their faith or from converting to Protestantism.[46]

Stressing the distinctiveness of what your movement offers is at the heart of any strategy to soften the competitive threat from rivals. Historically, when many rivals competed in one physical place this was often hard, so some sought to emancipate the dependence of a religious movement on a single place—just like our beachfront sellers experimenting with their styles of food. Peregrine Horden and Nicolas Purcell have described this in the medieval cult of relics: "One of the virtues of relics was to render the sanctity of holy places mobile. . . . The defining central sacred place becomes in a sense common currency, to be used anywhere." They show how this logic could even be extended to religious assets that were not normally considered mobile at all: "In an extreme instance, an attempt was made in the first century of Islam to suggest that, on one night of the year, the sacred spring of Mecca, Zamzam, abandoned its usual location and emerged instead in the pool of Siloam, in Jerusalem. The cult of the Temple Rock was being advanced at the same moment by 'Abd al-Malik, for basically political reasons, as something of an alternative to the Ka'ba in Mecca."[47]

In chapter 10 we'll consider what happens when religious movements have the option to do something much more drastic to escape the competitive threat from their rivals—namely, to turn to violence. For the moment we'll stick to examining peaceful strategies. Let's go back to the question I posed earlier about the choice to offer an immersive experience of religion rather than a set of component services. This choice, just like the others, will be shaped by the competitive landscape in which the movement operates. The more immersive the experience it seeks to offer, the more it will seek to persuade its members that no other movement offers anything like it. But its ambitions will also be tempered by realism: when a movement begins at a disadvantage compared with existing religious organizations, it will be more likely to compromise with the rituals and doctrines of its rivals than when it starts from a position of strength. Sociologist Nathan Irmiya Elawa illustrates this point nicely in comparing the behavior of Christian missionaries in medieval Ireland with those in nineteenth-century Africa:

> Christianity coexisted mostly in symbiotic ways alongside the indigenous religious system in Ireland for several centuries, beginning in the fifth and continuing even after Christianity had gained some dominance by the eighth century . . . [with] the continuing practice of Christians being buried with their pagan relatives as a form of identification with their ancestors. . . . Likewise, the practice of polygyny continued into the Christian era. . . . This Irish attitude towards marriage unions contrasts radically with those of Western missionaries to sub-Saharan Africa in the nineteenth and twentieth centuries, who made monogamy a rule for membership.[48]

When Christianity was being spread by missionaries under the protection of colonial powers, it was uncompromising in comparison with its more tentative exploration of the far-flung reaches of early medieval Europe. This brings us back, though, to what determines the degree of ambition of the overall strategy. What makes some religious movements so determined to deliver a truly comprehensive and ambitious message? Historically, they have not been the only organizations to do so.

Messages

Few secular businesses in our time (not even Google)[49] ever claim to offer an immersive experience to their employees that can rival what the Ford Motor Company created in Dearborn, Michigan, in the second decade of the twentieth century:

> After the announcement of the $5 day in January 1914, Ford wanted to ensure that employees did not squander their money. To this end the Ford Sociological (or Educational) Department was created to investigate and monitor employees' personal and work lives. In order to be considered a good employee, workers needed to be sober, thrifty and maintain a positive attitude. . . . [The department] sent investigators to make unannounced visits, evaluating the cleanliness

and safety of an employee's household. . . . [They] noted if the family had renters, checked with school attendance offices to determine if children were attending school and monitored bank records to verify that employees made regular deposits. Sociological Department investigators also assisted workers' families by teaching wives about home care, cooking and hygiene.

The company had its rituals, heavy with symbolism:

> In 1914 Ford Motor Company established the Ford English School, where the automaker's diverse immigrant employees could learn the English language and take civics lessons in preparation for becoming U.S. citizens. At the graduation ceremony, students wearing clothing from their native countries descended into a large "American Melting Pot" and emerged wearing homogenous suits and waving American flags.[50]

Ford was far from alone: mill towns such as Bournville, near Birmingham in England, or Pullman, outside Chicago, created environments in which workers were provided with comparatively high-quality housing, but were subjected to (by our standards) intrusive regimes of surveillance. In the economies of the industrialized West at least, secular businesses no longer try to shape their employees' lives with anything like the same degree of ambition (China may be another story). Religious movements, however, have being doing this for centuries, and their resolve shows no signs of weakening.

The message transmitted by religious organizations to their members has often been very ambitious indeed—especially when they have enjoyed political backing. Historian Carine van Rhijn has described how the Carolingian dynasty, which ruled over much of Europe between 750 and 900 CE, undertook an "ambitious pastoral project—initiated by the court, but taken up by diocesan bishops and many others—that was meant to bring religious knowledge to people of all social ranks, illiterate inhabitants of the countryside included."[51] It's hard for us now to appreciate the scale of the logistical challenges faced by this project— Europe was covered with forests and had few passable roads, illiteracy was almost universal, and the rule of law ran patchily through the country. Hard, too, to do justice to the mental transformation to which the project aspired. As Van Rhijn notes, the Church saw itself as battling against "the ignorance of well-meaning people who thought that a big stone in the field was not fundamentally different from an altar in a church, or of those people who lit candles near large trees and springs out of piety, or who believed that mere humans could influence the weather."[52] In the circumstances, it's remarkable that the Carolingian period saw a growing network of churches with resident priests and an explosion of manuscript production (over seven thousand Carolingian manuscripts survive today, compared with a few hundred from the preceding Merovingian period).

Of course, the hope of banishing magical thinking was never realistic; priests everywhere would continue for centuries to fulminate against superstition, to little effect (as they do to this day). The same was true all over the world where ambitious transcendental religions ran up against stubborn local tradition. Historian Alan Strathern notes how Buddhist writers in fourteenth-century Japan lamented the ignorance of the people who conflated Bodhisattvas and the deities of local shrines, explaining that the Bodhisattvas were obliged to collude in this ignorance because of the corruption of the current age of history. As he comments: "One could not wish for a more conscious or explicit commentary on the way in which transcendentalist truths must become mingled with immanentist desires in order to maintain a foothold in the popular imagination."[53] But although transcendental religions could not banish the everyday, transactional concerns of practical people, they could add a perspective that the folk religions could not. They could claim to offer their members a way of making sense of the harsh reality of their daily lives, of the apparently unending burden of poverty and the ever-present danger of losing their loved ones, and they could do so in a way that evoked community. To a peasant too sick to work and fearing starvation, to a parent distraught with grief at the death of a child, they could say, "You are not alone."

How effective was such a message in touching the hearts of the faithful? The illiterate have—of course—left few traces of their reactions, so we have to guess from what the few literate witnesses have told us. One of the most moving testimonies to the power of a religious message to soften suffering is the fourteenth-century poem *Pearl*, in which a grieving father has a dream-vision of his daughter in the heavenly Jerusalem as one of the 144,000 brides of Christ (who are not jealous of one another). His daughter speaks to him and explains her life in heaven, with utter serenity. The father is consoled, in a way that reminds us how comprehensively the Christian world view, and in particular its promise of resurrection after death, had come to pervade the lives of the inhabitants of medieval Europe. It also underlines how fragile such consoling power may appear to those in later centuries who are less convinced of the possibility of life after death.[54]

Rarely can a religious leader have had so revolutionary a command of his message, as well as a mastery of the technical means of diffusing it, than "a little-known German professor" (in the words of historian Andrew Pettegree) who on October 31, 1517, "proposed an academic disputation—an event so routine in sixteenth century universities that no one at the time thought it worth recording whether the propositions for debate were printed and posted up on the normal university billboard, the door of a local church." Pettegree records, in his aptly titled book *Brand Luther*, how the new technology of printing, allied to Luther's mastery of his message, together ensured that "a theological spat could become a great public event, embracing churchmen and laypeople over a wide span of the European landmass.... Luther created ... a new form of theological writing: lucid, accessible and above all short."[55] Luther's achievement did not consist just in exploiting the possibilities offered by the new communication technology of printing; he also transformed the technology itself. By the year 1530, "Luther and his friends had recast both the German publishing industry and the reading public."[56] He thereby offered to both allies and rivals new means of creating and transmitting their own "brands," transforming utterly the landscape of European, and eventually world, religion in the process.[57]

Alongside the messages communicated to their members, religious movements have also had to communicate with their representatives, especially when the movement outgrows the place where it was founded.

The need for such communication is often very practical: the movement's representatives must run the business. The Carolingian manuscripts just described were not merely engaged in communicating various points of doctrine or instructions for the liturgy. They also contained numerous recommendations to priests about how to organize their activities, as well as practical tips on such diverse subjects as "recipes for medical concoctions against piles or stomach aches, or ways of dealing with coughing sheep and other cattle diseases."[58] In addition to educating its flock, the Church in the eighth and ninth centuries was in the process of acquiring land, buildings, slaves, and tenant farmers, and it needed to establish a body of shared knowledge about what these assets consisted of and how they should be managed. The information communicated in the various *polyptiques* (documents describing the monastic estates) tends to be dominated by lists of holdings of lands and slaves, but a document called the *Capitulare de villis* comes closer to setting out what we might consider principles of management, albeit for a royal estate.[59] It seems likely that the Church was concerned to standardize the decision-making process in a way that foreshadowed more secular projects of economic management in later centuries.[60] It had also to evolve an ethic of responsible management, which took care to stress the importance of prudent stewardship of the Church's resources while distinguishing this from the pursuit of wealth and profit, against which Christian teaching had always been eloquently opposed.[61] When carefully expressed, this ethic could conveniently induce individuals to avoid the sinful burden of wealth by bequeathing at least some of it to the Church, which would manage it in their stead.

The founding of the Jesuit order in 1540 brought new challenges again, since the order sent out missionaries from its earliest days to some very distant destinations—among them India, Japan, China, the Philippines, Canada, Mexico, Peru, and Paraguay. Its founder Ignatius of Loyola wrote as early as 1542 with practical advice to the society's members about the importance of keeping multiple copies of their official correspondence, particularly in the light of the many obstacles to long-distance communication. As Jesuit historian Antoni Ucerler reports, "to ensure the arrival of their correspondence, the Jesuits in Japan and China would usually make three copies of each letter and send them on different ships, in the hope that at least one copy would survive and reach its final destination."[62] Ignatius's surviving correspondence "is almost exclusively preoccupied with matters of business."[63] In his comprehensive history of the Jesuit order, historian Markus Friedrich documents how the leadership of the order decided around the year 1600 to impose an increasingly rigorous standardization of business methods. For instance, a mandatory accounting form was introduced around 1700 that procurators (the local administrators of Jesuit property) were required to fill out every year. Though the Jesuit leadership agreed with the general Catholic doctrine in condemning profit seeking for its own sake, extending the order's command of and efficient management of economic resources came to be seen as an essential means of financing its spiritual mission, especially in territories far away from Europe.[64]

Just as the first commercial companies of the early modern era (such as the East India Company) set in place an understanding of shared business practices that would shape the way in which modern companies function, so the early work of churches, temples, mosques, and synagogues has continued to shape how religious movements work today. In both domains the received wisdom about how to manage a complex human organization, though subject to fads and fashions, has developed some shared practices that have stood the test of time. In addition to transmitting their know-how to their own representatives, successful organizations have often been copied by others. There's more explicit horizontal sharing of know-how between different religious organizations in the twenty-first century than there used to be—for instance, through accredited business school training for religious as well as secular managers. There are institutes, such as the Brazilian Institute for Catholic Marketing, which in 2023 held its twenty-seventh annual congress.[65] There's an abundance of more informal training courses competing on the internet for the attention (and the money) of would-be managers. Some appeal to name recognition, like those offered by the Billy Graham Evangelistic Association. Others borrow their branding from the military: a course called the "Christ for All Nations Evangelism Bootcamp" describes itself with conscious machismo as "less like a Bible School and more like the Navy Seals for Evangelists,"[66] but many softer approaches are also available online. Sometimes the lack of consensus on method appears bewildering: Googling "evangelism training" on a day in August 2022 yielded around six million search results, among which in the top five there were "7 secrets of effective evangelism training," "the three types of evangelism," and "the six styles of evangelism."[67] Perhaps none of these differences matter, and the only thing that makes a difference to the effectiveness of evangelism training is the determination of both the evangelists and their targets to take the training seriously.

Such, at least, seems to be the implication of a study published in 2021 by economists Gharad Bryan, James Choi, and Dean Karlan, which performed, in the authors' words, "a randomized evaluation of an evangelical Protestant Christian values and theology education program delivered to thousands of ultrapoor Filipino households."[68] The program appeared to raise the reported religiosity and income of the treated households six months after the program ended, though the religiosity differences were no longer significant after thirty months. The authors conjecture that the differences in income may have been due to the program's ability to increase perseverance in its subjects—the quality psychologists sometimes call "grit." The fact that the effects on religiosity do not persist after thirty months suggests a conclusion that is consistent with the platform model of religious competition: religion has lasting effects because it works on communities and not just on individuals; just comparing individuals who receive a message with those who don't may miss the most important channels through which such messages work. This doesn't mean that the message the individuals receive is unimportant—it's rather that the message works best when it anchors individuals in a community that provides reinforcement and a sense of belonging. What differentiates relatively successful from relatively unsuccessful religious organizations is less the content of their message than the social context of its delivery.

This conclusion makes sense from the melancholy perspective of the temple in South India where Chinnamma used to dance, which is now barely active. There's no fundamental difference between the theology of Hinduism that you'll find in this lonely temple and what you might find in the vibrant, boisterous activity of temples only a few miles away. Throughout the history of religion there have been many such contrasts between organizations on the rise and those on the wane. Everything depends on the energy of the leaders who choose to make something of a temple site, or a pilgrimage destination, or the charisma of a founder, and their ability to build a community around it.

We've seen how the platform model of religious competition helps us understand what gives certain religious organizations their power to persuade. We've looked at the various decisions religious movements must make—about their mission, their structure, their strategies, and their message. We've seen repeatedly how insights from secular businesses can help us understand important characteristics of religious movements throughout history. We've seen how many of the decisions taken by religious leaders—even in such apparently unworldly dimensions as theology—are shaped by their awareness of the competitive landscape in which they find themselves.

It's time now to look at what religious movements do with the power they have built. This will be the subject of part III.

Religion and the Uses of Power

Part III of this book will explore some of the ways religious organizations use the power they gain from persuading members to invest their time, energy, and money. Chapter 10 examines the relationship between religious power and political power. As we saw in earlier chapters, Adam Smith believed that successful religious movements attracted the envy of political leaders, who would often seek to offer religious leaders a deal: you lend us your legitimacy, and we will protect you from your competitors. Though there's some truth in this view, the historical relationship between religious and political power is more complex than Smith's account makes it appear.

For much of human history, politically powerful individuals would claim divine or partly divine status, or would have it thrust upon them when they did not wish to be seen to be claiming it themselves. It took the arrival of transcendental religion to establish clearly that political leaders could not properly claim divinity but could only hope to be blessed by it, and that being blessed by it would not only bring benefits but would also impose constraints. The presence of distinct centers of religious and political power whose relationship had to be continually negotiated is a feature of the world of transcendental religion. More specifically, it's a feature of the Abrahamic religions (Judaism, Christianity, and Islam) as well as those of South and Southeast Asia (Buddhism, Jainism, and Hinduism). It's not found in Confucianism, nor in Chinese religion more generally, which had some room for religious specialists but kept them strictly subordinate to royal power. Still, when it exists we can usefully ask what religious leaders hope to gain from harnessing political power and what political leaders hope to gain from harnessing religious power. Chapter 10 shows through historical examples how, in each case, the short-term benefits from sharing legitimacy come with a long-term cost. It also shows how, when religious leaders wield political power, the way they use and abuse it does not differ from the behavior of secular leaders. It's the opportunities and constraints on the exercise of power that make the difference, not the religiosity or otherwise of the leaders in question.

Chapter 11 investigates a particular form of power asymmetry—that between men and women. It's striking that religious leaders throughout the world are overwhelmingly male, while statistical measures of personal religiosity tilt slightly female, on average. As we'll see, this makes religious organizations no different from the great bulk of businesses and political movements. The explanations lie in many of the same phenomena that lead to asymmetries of power in secular contexts—there's nothing special about religion in this regard. In particular, the average tendency of women across the world to report higher levels of religiosity than men is mainly a feature of Christianity. It's probably due to historical features of the Christian religion that are likely to have appealed particularly to women. There's absolutely no evidence to indicate that religiosity as such is a significantly gendered trait, even if some dimensions of religiosity appeal more to men while other dimensions of religiosity appeal more to women.

Chapter 12 turns the spotlight on the physical and sexual abuse of children and vulnerable adults by religious leaders, a phenomenon that has come massively to public attention in recent years. It shows that such abuse takes place in many contexts, secular as well as religious. It is facilitated by organizational characteristics that are by no means confined to religious movements, but that many religious movements happen to share. The chapter concludes that, beyond the terrible human cost for its victims, abuse also strikes at the legitimacy of religious organizations, which share a strong interest in the implementation of measures that aim to make abuse less likely to occur. This opens the way to a more general discussion of the place of religious activity in public life, which will be the focus of part IV.

CHAPTER 10

Religion and Politics

The crookedness of the serpent is straight enough for the snake-hole.
The crookedness of the river is straight enough for the sea.
And the crookedness of our Lord's men is straight enough for our Lord!

—devotional poem to Siva by the twelfth-century Kannada poet Basavanna.[1]

Seeking or Fleeing Politics

What do political and religious movements have to offer each other? If Adam Smith was right that alliances between political and religious leaders are often damaging to the legitimacy of both sides, why do they continue to happen? Part of the answer is that the precise links between political and religious movements are often opaque to outsiders, so their leaders can be tempted by short-term gains while ignoring longer-term risks. When former prime minister Shinzo Abe was shot and killed during an election rally in July 2022, the motives of the gunman came as a shock to many observers both inside Japan and abroad. He claimed he was seeking revenge for the financial ruin of his mother by the Korean-based Unification Church, which in his view had secretly corrupted politicians into turning a blind eye to its rapacious fundraising practices.

Japan has long had a reputation for low religiosity (fewer than 20 percent of respondents to the World Values Survey report that religion is very important or rather important in their lives). Even when people are religious, they are usually flexible; it's common for the same

Turkish president Recep Tayyip Erdogan leading prayer at the newly opened Taksim mosque in 2021. The square also houses the *Republican Monument*, built in 1928 to commemorate the foundation of the secular Turkish Republic in 1923.
Credit: Umut Çolak, Wikimedia Commons.

Trump campaign launches "Evangelicals For Trump" coalition In Miami, January 2020. Faith leaders pray over President Donald Trump during an "Evangelicals for Trump" campaign event held at the King Jesus International Ministry.
Credit: INSTAR Images LLC / Alamy.

individual to visit Buddhist, Shinto, and Christian venues. Whether despite this background or because of it, the country has become a growth market for new religious movements in recent years, as well as outgrowths of more traditional movements that are new to Japan, such as Jainism.[2] The Unification Church, founded in Korea by Sun-Myung Moon in 1954, has been particularly controversial. This is partly for its aggressive recruitment strategies, partly for its mass blessings of the weddings of many hundreds or even thousands of couples (many arranged by the Church), and partly for the money it raises from so-called "spiritual sales."

It's hard to find evidence from disinterested parties, but the National Network of Lawyers against Spiritual Sales claims that over $10 billion was fraudulently raised from nearly thirty thousand people in the two decades up to 2007. They were allegedly persuaded to buy expensive votive items to help recently deceased relatives make spiritual progress in the afterlife.[3] In particular, the widespread resort to abortion in Japan since the 1960s has led Japanese parents to adopt many repurposed folk rituals to appease the spirits of their aborted babies.[4] The Church has admitted past liability for aggressive marketing practices, and apologized after the assassination of Abe for implying that these practices had disappeared (the National Network claims that fraudulent sums equal to over $2 million were raised in 2021).[5] The family of the assassin claimed his mother made donations worth $720,000 after the death of her husband, causing ruin to the family's finances.[6]

The Unification Church's growth model has involved diversification into many unrelated businesses including manufacturing, health care, real estate, and media in Korea and abroad (it owns the conservative US newspaper the *Washington Times*), as well as the development of nonprofit organizations in the fields of sports, education, politics, and the arts. One study describes the Church as playing the role of "star entrepreneur in Korea, troublemaker in the United States and money tree in Japan."[7] Abe's grandfather had played an important role in bringing the Unification Church to Japan, and Abe himself, though not a Church member, had spoken at meetings organized by the Church. There are widespread allegations, which are hard for outsiders to verify, that the

Church has made donations to political parties and sought to influence political leaders, both financially and through spreading a strongly anticommunist ideology to which Japan's right-of-center parties were particularly susceptible. In return, it is claimed, politicians agreed to avoid scrutinizing the money-raising activities of the Church.[8]

Whatever the truth of these claims, the close links between religion and politics they seek to expose are much more subtle than those in many countries that had historically established religious movements, whether Christian, Hindu, Buddhist, or Muslim. The Unification Church has had to move by stealth to gain a tiny fraction of the privileges that other movements have been able to assert with gusto. Its motives in doing so remain no less opaque: it's hard to know whether political influence was sought by Moon to avoid restrictions on his pursuit of converts and money, or whether it has also become an end in itself. The Abe assassination has sparked calls for greater transparency about the links between religion and politics in Japan; it remains to be seen whether such calls will have any lasting impact.

In some settings political involvement can be thrust upon religious leaders rather than sought by them. The Guatemalan civil war was a violent conflict between the state and a variety of left-wing rebel groups that is estimated to have claimed the lives of some hundreds of thousands of people between 1960 and 1996 (out of a population that rose from around five million to around ten million over this period).[9] Catholic priests and Protestant pastors frequently suffered at the hands of both government and rebel forces, because they were seen as spokesmen for their communities. Their different responses to the violence had a lasting impact on their perceived legitimacy. Philosopher Rachel McCleary, who has studied relations between Churches among the indigenous Maya population in the Department of El Quiche, particularly during the most intense violence in the early 1980s, notes that:

> In July 1980, the Catholic Church vacated El Quiche, and Pope John Paul II appointed an administrative bishop who ran the diocese *in absentia*. Only one priest and three nuns remained in El Quiche. Not until January 1987 did a new bishop assume full responsibility for the

diocese. This is telling because the Catholic Church, according to many Maya, abandoned them. During its absence, many Mayan communities converted to Protestantism or became "nones". When the Catholic Church attempted to reclaim its faithful, it faced opposition, and many will not convert back to Catholicism. The Protestant pastors remained in El Quiche during the war. According to the Primitive Methodist Church, whose only territory of evangelization is El Quiche, they had 50 pastors assassinated during the civil war. The Seventh Day Adventists told me they were persecuted but went underground.[10]

This is the context in which we need to understand current controversies over the Catholic Church's beatification in April 2021 of Juan Barrera Mendez, a twelve-year-old Maya boy who had been tortured and killed by government soldiers in 1980.[11] As McCleary notes, the Catholic Church needed a means to reestablish its legitimacy with the indigenous people, despite hesitations of both the majority ladino and the indigenous communities themselves:

> The dominant power group in Guatemala, the ladinos, is skeptical about the sanctity of the Maya beatifieds. They argue that there was no popular demand for these. In fact, ladinos within the church in Guatemala whisper of their involvement in the guerrilla movements, which makes them controversial figures. The Catholic Church constructed the biographies of the beatified Maya mostly through oral history, and not historical records. Racism and denigration of Maya cultures and languages meant that the Catholic Church, through a network of catechists and evangelists, also had to instill in Maya communities the idea that their martyred faithful could become saints. It was a top-down process of bishops coaxing Maya communities to overcome their fears of retaliation and confront painful memories. The Church had to educate Maya communities on the Catholic concept of martyrdom and its relevance for their martyred faithful. The beatifications are intended to give Maya communities a sense that their lives have worth even though the Guatemalan state and the ladino population continue to view them as less than equal. From the perspective of the universal Catholic Church, the beatification of

Maya is an attempt to raise its profile and counter the strong presence of Pentecostal, evangelical, and Protestant denominations and churches in the country. It is a strategy to regain the faithful.[12]

These two cases, so different from each other and from the cases we looked at in the introduction and chapter 2, suggest that there's unlikely to be a simple general story of what religious movements gain or lose from involvement in politics. The Unification Church actively (if discreetly) sought political support in order to make short-term financial gains, while (perhaps) threatening its long-term legitimacy. The Christian Churches of Guatemala, in contrast, had political involvement thrust violently upon them through their role as representatives of communities facing state repression. Their different approaches to that challenge continue to shape their relations more than a quarter of a century later.

It's easier to say what politicians in various countries hope to gain from courting religious leaders—notably, a degree of legitimacy that the politicians struggle to achieve through more conventionally political means. In return for that legitimacy, they offer a range of favors. As we saw in the introduction, Adam Smith believed that for religious leaders to accept those favors was to squander their legitimacy in a way they would regret. Still, it was a long time since the established Churches of his time had gained political power. Smith's view, expressed in *The Theory of Moral Sentiments*, that there had once been a primordial state of peaceful competition among a multitude of sects and cults, from which modern religion represented a lamentable decline, was at best a simplification.[13] Recent research has given us a more interesting picture of how religion and politics have been historically intertwined.

The Sun That Shone on My Cradle

The attribution of not just religious legitimacy but actual divinity to political leaders was once a routine practice. And it has not entirely died out. I once had the disconcerting experience of hearing Ferdinand Marcos, dictator of the Philippines, receive a grotesquely flattering tribute from a young acolyte.[14] Among other things, the young man told the aging tyrant that he was "the sun that shone on my cradle when I was a baby," and went on to ask rhetorically whether such genius could possibly have a solely human origin. Marcos, who only moments beforehand had delivered a shrewd, self-deprecating, and often funny analysis of his country's problems before an audience of technocrats, turned into a simpering jelly before this obsequious homily, lapping up the sycophancy and even, in reply, musing that he himself had often wondered about the mystery of his own genius. I don't think anyone in the audience believed for a moment that the young man thought Marcos was the sun, or that his genius had divine origin. And, though they must have wondered about the old man's faltering grip on reality, they almost certainly realized that the pleasure he derived from his disciple's servility lay less in any belief that the bizarre compliments were true than in exultation at the self-abasement of a follower apparently willing to utter any falsehood to please his master. In a similar spirit, Shakespeare makes King Lear thunder his anger at his daughter Cordelia's refusal to say she loves him better than she will love her future husband: "Let pride, which she calls plainness, marry her."[15] It's not the truth she asserts that angers him (for Lear is intelligent enough to know she speaks the truth); it's her pride, her refusal to sacrifice her integrity at his command. As the experience of countless tyrants down the ages attests, calling a powerful human a god is as clear a way as you can find of jettisoning all claims to rivalry.

I thought of Marcos, and of Lear, when reading *Accidental Gods*, Anna Della Subin's book about the "men unwittingly turned divine . . . the Europeans mistaken for gods, the unexpected side effect of their civilizing mission." Beginning with Columbus, who reported that he was met by people who "held our arrival to be a great marvel, believing that we came from heaven," she writes of:

> the lost explorers, the captains and militants . . . sailors, missionaries and settlers . . . the colonial officers, soldiers and bureaucrats who in going about their administrative duties were irritated to find themselves worshipped as living deities. They were surprised to find their dead colleagues appeased at tomb shrines with offerings of biscuits and gin. With the rise of nationalism and liberation movements in

the twentieth century come the politicians and activists, secularist and modernists, who were dismayed to learn of their own apotheoses, as tales of their miracles contradicted their political agenda.[16]

It was of course the Europeans' own interpretation that the people they met believed they were gods, an interpretation that suited not only their own self-importance but also their image of their conquered subjects as childlike in their credulity and general intelligence. Della Subin points out that we cannot really know "whether people believed in the unwitting gods." As the case of Marcos reminds us, storytelling about gods is a performative act that has many functions independent of conveying belief, and can be "used to exalt and to degrade."[17] Max Weber, who developed the notion of charismatic legitimation of a political system, acknowledged that "it is by no means true that every case of submissiveness to persons in positions of power is primarily (or even at all) oriented to this belief [in the legitimacy of the system]. Loyalty may be hypocritically simulated by individuals or by whole groups on purely opportunistic grounds, or carried out in practice for reasons of material self-interest. Or people may submit from individual weakness and helplessness because there is no acceptable alternative."[18] In classical antiquity, the emperors often claimed or were accorded the status of gods, and though there is much evidence that the process was surrounded with norms and taboos, it was intimately bound up with assertions of power as well as attempts to constrain that power. "One could constrain a powerful man by turning him into a god: in divinizing Julius [Caesar], the Senate also laid down what the virtues and characteristics of a god *should* be."[19] Among many later examples, Della Subin cites "the *ntambwe bwanga* cult, which began in the Congolese town of Kabinda in the early 1920s . . . [and] claimed to have created deified duplicates of all the colonial Belgians. Every adept who joined the society took the name of an individual Belgian resident, and in a trance state, appropriated their power."[20]

We should not conclude, of course, that the anonymous rock inscription praising the twelfth-century CE king Parakramabahu I of Sri Lanka as one "who surpasses the Sun in his own glory" was written by someone with the same ideas and objectives as the young acolyte of Marcos

I heard over eight centuries later, despite the obvious similarity in language.[21] Though it seems safe to say that extravagant praise of the powerful has been deployed in all known human societies, its deployment is part of a wide armory of strategies to allow the weak to protect themselves against the consequences of that power. Many historians and anthropologists have suggested that, in societies with purely immanent religion, individuals who acquired political power would acquire routinely the trappings of divinity—some sought it, while others had it pressed upon them.[22] It was not so much that, as Adam Smith thought, political leaders were jealous of the power of religious leaders. Instead, for political leaders during much of human history before the rise of transcendental religions, some claim to divine status more or less went with the job.

What divinity might mean could vary widely from one setting to another—it didn't mean that the politically powerful were exempt from sickness and death, for example. There was much variation in how the power was acquired. A military hero could acquire divine status through sheer force of military prowess. A shaman might acquire a following through a reputation for unusually effective powers, which would then be used as a lever for establishing a political following. The late Marshall Sahlins made the very strong claim that this second channel was overwhelmingly the most important: "Access to the [gods] on behalf of others is the fundamental political value in all human societies so organized. . . . [C]laims to divine power, as manifest in ways varying from the successful hunter sharing food or the shaman curing illness, to the African king bringing rain, have been the raison d'être of political power throughout the greater part of human history."[23]

Sahlins's claim seems too strong—earlier prowess in battle, for reasons of strength or tactical ability or sheer command of economic resources, could be the origin of later claims to divine status. This happened in later history—for example, with the divine status accorded to Alexander the Great in many parts of his conquered territory.[24] In a similar vein, work by economists Jeanet Bentzen and Gunes Gokmen suggests that prehistoric societies that enjoyed the ecological conditions that favored hierarchies of power (through suitability for irrigation works requiring coerced labor) tended subsequently to develop concepts of big gods, rather than the big gods preceding the stratification of the societies concerned.[25] But, overstated though it is, Sahlins's claim highlights an important feature of societies in which invisible spirits were everywhere. The ability of a man to become militarily powerful was always likely to depend not just on his physical strength and the economic resources he could command but on the stories he could tell others to induce them to collaborate— stories that were often religious ones. Even after transcendental religions had become widely established, the political success of various millenarian movements is a reminder that sometimes power comes just from perceived success at mediating with the spirit world. As Alan Strathern writes: "Thus Sufi saints could become Safavid kings; Hong Xiuquan— the leader of the quasi-Christian millenarian spirit-medium 'Heavenly Kingdom of Supreme Peace' movement behind the Taiping rebellion of 1850–1864—could end by becoming a secluded emperor-like figure in his palace in Nanjing; the prophet Yali came to style himself the King of New Guinea and twice ran for a seat in parliament in the 1960s."[26] More recently still, the ability of an individual like the Shi'a cleric Moqtada-al-Sadr to dominate Iraqi politics has been intimately bound up with his ability to mobilize hundreds of thousands of people to attend Friday prayers (despite occupying only a middling rank within the formal status hierarchy of Shi'a clerics).[27]

The spread of transcendental religions did change the picture, though, in ways that make Adam Smith's vision of the link between political and religious power more pertinent. Instead of religious and political power belonging intrinsically together, there came in most parts of the world to be distinct centers of religious and political power whose relationship had to be continually negotiated (in China it was a different story, as we'll see later). This was a matter both of organization and of ideas. In terms of organization, transcendental religion typically relied for its transmission on groups of full-time specialists. These were various kinds of priests or holy men (and sometimes women) who could master the skills required only if they were not simultaneously waging warfare or trying to govern (religious specialists are an ever-present feature of immanent religion too, but they typically have a secular occupation as well). A division of labor between religious and political power was the ineluctable consequence. And in terms of ideas, transcendental religion preached the notion of salvation through personal characteristics (not necessarily personal merit, but at least some form of personal grace). This required political leaders to claim legitimacy through possession of those characteristics rather than through naked power—but it was hard for political leaders to assert it for themselves. They needed someone else to validate their claim to spiritual legitimacy. This meant that religious and political leaders would forever be locked in a state of uneasy mutual dependence mingled with rivalry. They needed each other—and each envied what seemed like the easy route to success enjoyed by the other.

Religious power meant the ability to control the performance of religious ritual and the membership of religious communities. Political power meant the ability to command a monopoly of violence, and use it to force the payment of taxes. Both forms of power yield control over economic resources, but one uses the magic of ritual and the inducements of an unseen world, while the other uses the distinctly unmagical and very visible threat of physical coercion. This doesn't mean, though, that priests and rulers have entirely distinct motivations and world views. Even if political rulers have often cared instrumentally about the religious identity of their subjects—in order to be able to tax them better—they have often cared also about their religious identity for its own sake. Research by my Toulouse colleagues Mohamed Saleh and Jean Tirole has shown this for the poll tax imposed by Muslim rulers on their non-Muslim subjects from the first caliphate in the seventh century CE until the mid-nineteenth century. The fact that non-Muslims could avoid the tax by converting to Islam meant that large numbers of them did, and the rulers had to forgo revenue as a result. Far from being a flaw in the system, it was part of the point: the tax was set at a much higher level than would have maximized revenue, because the rulers cared not only about revenues but also about increasing the numbers of the faithful.[28] The example also shows that it's sometimes hard to draw a sharp line between religious conversion through force and conversion through persuasion. It was force that enabled the imposition of the poll tax, but many people did in fact choose to pay it rather than convert, so force was not the whole story.[29]

Ancient China chose a different trajectory. Chinese kings, and the emperors who succeeded them from the Qin dynasty in the third century BCE, did not need to have their legitimacy validated by priests. Astrologers validated each king's or emperor's claim to an auspicious birth. But they were royal employees who did what they were told, and by the time of Sima Qian, astrologer royal in 100 BCE, "so vital was it . . . for the imperial court to maintain absolute control over the calendar and the interpretation of celestial phenomena, that unauthorized dabbling in the secret 'heavenly calculations' became a capital crime."[30] Astrologers also helped their employers to plan activities to seem maximally auspicious. From the accession of King Wu, first ruler of the Zhou dynasty in 1046 BCE, legitimacy was encapsulated in the notion of the Mandate of Heaven. This was originally deployed to legitimate Wu's overthrow of the Shang dynasty, after a campaign launched to coincide with a massing of five planets in the constellation of the Vermilion Bird in 1059 BCE, which was recorded in the *Bamboo Annals* in the words: "A great scarlet bird clasping a jade scepter in its beak alighted on the Zhou altar to the soil."[31] But by making the Shang kings' vulnerability to overthrow constitute evidence of their unfitness to rule, it can also be thought of as an early form of payment by results. Success in agriculture and war would come to validate the Mandate of Heaven—and conversely, natural or military disasters could easily turn the population against a ruler.

This provided strong incentives for successive dynasties to invest in effective administration, which they supervised themselves rather than, as in medieval Europe, subcontracting much of the work to priests (as we saw of Carolingian Europe in chapter 9). The ideologies of Taoism and Confucianism were subordinated to an already-functioning system of administration, construing virtue in a worldly rather than a spiritual manner. Recruitment by examination began under the Han dynasty in 165 BCE and became more codified and rigorous over the next millennium. The fact that the bureaucracy was extensive and well paid also meant that successive emperors, beginning under the Northern Wei dynasty (386–534 CE), could use it to offer local warlords a stake in the effective governance of the empire, as recent research by Joy Chen, Erik Wang, and Xiaoming Zhang has shown.[32] Although the first five centuries CE saw apparently similar breakdowns of previously centralized authority in Europe and China, the trajectories of the two regions were thereafter strikingly different. Historian Walter Scheidel has persuasively argued that "imperial reconstruction succeeded in late sixth-century China (and would do so repeatedly on later occasions) but not (and in fact never again) in Europe." Even during those turbulent previous centuries, "Chinese polities . . . operated in a framework of elite interaction based on the at least loosely unifying traditions of Shang and Zhou. . . . Rome, by contrast, in most of its European territories created political unity where it had never existed before."[33] In a nutshell, China created an administrative caste answering to the emperor, to the needs of which the transcendental ideology was strictly subordinated.

The Costs and Benefits of a Division of Labor between Rulers and Priests

Though the emergence of a (rough-and-ready, often blurred) division of labor between religious and political leaders was a frequent consequence of the establishment of transcendental religion, it came with a heavy cost to the political authorities. When the religious leaders were organized enough to form an effective coalition, that cost was paid in wealth—as we saw in chapter 9, the Christian Church had by the year 750 CE come to own up to a third of the cultivable land of Western Europe. After the Reformation, when the coalition broke down, this was redistributed massively toward the uses favored by secular rulers, as recent research on the Dissolution of the Monasteries in England and its equivalent in Germany has shown.[34]

When instead religious leaders could not form an effective coalition, the cost of legitimacy to rulers was typically paid in the coin of political instability. It's hard enough for military rulers to defend a political territory when rebels can use technology to engage in asymmetric warfare; it's harder still when the rebels have a range of ideological weapons as well. Ever since the development of projectile weapons in prehistory, those who are theoretically stronger have been vulnerable to those who are nimbler and have the advantage of surprise. Human beings are the species par excellence in which the weakest individuals don't always lose to the strongest. The medieval inventions of the longbow and the cross-bow exposed a vulnerability of mounted armor to attack from which the massed armies of European emperors never fully recovered (their use against fellow Christians had been prohibited by the Second Lateran Council under Pope Innocent II in 1139 CE, to no effect).[35] And if this was true of military innovation, it was also true of religious innovation. Economists Emmanuelle Auriol and Jean-Philippe Platteau have shown how the absence of central religious authority in Islam from the very beginning left Muslim rulers highly vulnerable to the loss of legitimacy. Even if they managed to co-opt many of the official clerics of "high Islam" into supporting their regime, there would often be self-appointed clerics of "low Islam" who could cause instability by their ability to issue religious fatwas.[36] This contrasted with Catholic and Eastern Orthodox Christianity, where the presence of a centralized religious authority, which could be co-opted by the political authority (albeit sometimes at a high price), made political stability a little less difficult to attain.

There were exceptions, of course. The lack of centralized Muslim authority did not prevent periods of political stability under the Ottoman Empire, particularly after the Ottoman conquest of Constantinople in 1453, which yielded immense prestige to Sultan Mehmed II and his immediate successors (more than enough to compensate for any lack of bloodline to the Prophet). The importance of religious challenges to political authority had always ebbed and flowed with economic conditions, in any case,[37] and the resort to religious pretexts for military initiatives, whether by rulers or their challengers, was often economically opportunistic.[38] Conversely, the centralized power of the Catholic Church prior to the Reformation was no guarantee of political security for rulers who enjoyed its favor. The Cathar movement in southwestern France in the thirteenth century CE was eventually repressed with great brutality by the Church, following the opportunistic initiative of Simon de Montfort, who aimed to use the Crusade to become ruler of the independent County of Toulouse.

Despite exceptions, the greater stability of regimes that relied on legitimacy from centralized religious authorities does seem to hold up as a broad tendency of medieval and early modern world history. Lisa Blaydes and Eric Chaney have documented a divergence between the life expectancy of rulers in the Christian and Muslim worlds between the eighth century CE and the Reformation; though their leadership tenures had initially been similar, "Christian kings became increasingly long-lived compared to Muslim sultans."[39] Revolts, when they came, were easier to contain in the Christian world before the Reformation. The repression of the Cathars was successful, and mainly completed in about three decades, despite occasional flickers of resistance till the early fourteenth century. Repression of Protestantism two centuries later was not, and Europe paid, for over a century at least, a heavy political price.

But political stability was not the same as economic progress, and political instability was not inimical to innovation. Far from it. Walter Scheidel argues that it was the very breakdown of the Roman Empire that led to a "competitive fragmentation of power," setting Europe "on a trajectory away from the default pattern of serial imperial state formation—from the boom and bust of hegemonic powers—that we see elsewhere."[40] After the Reformation, Protestant Europe with all its instability began, on average and with exceptions, to grow gradually more prosperous than its Catholic neighbors.[41] And historians Timur Kuran and Jared Rubin have seen in the periods of stability in the Ottoman Empire the key to the subsequent economic decline of the Islamic world.[42] This was because their very success at achieving religious legitimacy made Ottoman rulers highly dependent on the goodwill of clerics. As a result, according to Kuran, they acceded to restrictions on lending at interest far more draconian than anything in the Christian world, as well as numerous other legal regulations that held back commercial initiative. Rubin argues that this same dependence on clerical goodwill also led them to implement restrictions on printing that lasted from an edict of Bayezid II in 1485 banning printing in Ottoman Turkish until the first press capable of printing in Arabic was authorized by Sultan Ahmed III in 1727—a delay of nearly a quarter of a millennium.[43] There's some controversy over this second claim, since historian Kathryn Schwartz has questioned whether the Ottomans really did promulgate and implement a printing ban.[44] But printing did not take off in the Ottoman Empire to the same extent as it did in Europe, whether due to clerical disapproval or for other reasons. The Catholic Church in Europe tried but failed to prevent the diffusion of printing, and recent studies suggest the diffusion of printing there was associated with an increase in Protestantism, a greater spread of knowledge, and a faster growth of cities.[45]

As these examples suggest, when religious leaders gain power to exercise political authority over their fellow citizens, how they choose to exercise that power depends largely on what constraints they face.[46] They're no different from political leaders who gain power by more conventional means. They use that power to reward their supporters and punish their enemies, even if their religious route to power may mean that they have accumulated different kinds of supporters and enemies along the way. Much has been written about how the conversion of the Roman emperor Constantine in the year 312 CE marked the beginning of a new assertiveness that would lead within a couple of generations to the massive destruction of pagan temples, libraries, and public spaces— including the notorious destruction of the Temple of Al-Lat in Palmyra in 385 CE, and the murder of the female philosopher and mathematician Hypatia in Alexandria by a Christian mob in the year 415.[47] Persecution of Jews was also widespread. Yet Peter Brown reminds us that "any attempt to draw a scale of religious violence in this period must place the violence of Christians towards each other at the top. . . . With the exception of the patriarch Cyril's attack on the Jewish community in Alexandria in 415, Christian violence against Jews was less bloodthirsty than was Christian violence against rival Christians."[48]

A particularly striking example was the violence that broke out after the death of Liberius, bishop of Rome, after his death in September 366, between supporters of rival candidates for his succession, costing the lives of 137 members of the Christian community.[49] Other examples of religious leaders imposing authoritarian rule existed in this period— "the successful imposition of a rabbinic interpretation of Judaism among the Jewish communities in Palestine, Mesopotamia and elsewhere, and . . . the formalization and propagation of Zoroastrianism throughout the Sasanian empire," for example—but we simply know much less about the collateral damage these processes involved.[50] Indeed, Brown concludes, startlingly for the modern reader, that "the most striking feature of the fourth century was the ability of the upper classes to muffle religious conflict." Those elites, he writes, constitute "a class in the grip of a 'lifeboat mentality'. They stood at the head of a social system that faced far more pressing dangers than those associated with religious error."[51]

This is not to say that ideology played no part; indeed, Johannes Hahn has argued that "religious violence as a phenomenon of public life is . . . peculiar to late Antiquity," and was "inconceivable without the involvement and even the initiative of the imperial court."[52] That court acted for reasons of spiritual conviction and not just political pragmatism. The claim is controversial,[53] but even if Hahn is right, it does not show there was something peculiarly inevitable about religious violence, as opposed to violence of other kinds. It shows instead that religious ideology was an instrument of statecraft that—like other instruments of statecraft—could sometimes go disastrously wrong. The violence it unleashed in late antiquity was something that civil authorities spent much of the ensuing centuries trying to rein in.

In his history of witchcraft trials in early modern Lorraine, Robin Briggs paints a similar picture, not so much of zealots in power (though there were undeniably some of those) as of the persistent lurking threat of sickness and misfortune in everyday life, which could be blamed on neighbors thought to bear grudges. Ordinary people instrumentalized religious teachings about the Devil against one another, in a period that was in any case "probably the harshest period of capital punishments in European history."[54] This created a dilemma for local magistrates, who sought to keep the process from spiraling out of control: "Witchcraft was about envy, ill-will and the power to harm others, exercised in small face-to-face communities which, although they could often contain such feelings, found it almost impossible to disperse them. . . . Witches were people you lived with, however unhappily, until they goaded someone past endurance."[55] Similar patterns have been found for witchcraft accusations in other parts of the world, such as sub-Saharan Africa, where recent research has shown that accusations were often leveled historically by same-sex competitors for resources and status.[56] In short, religious legitimation was just another strategy in the portfolio of strategies for members of society, rich and poor, powerful and weak, pious and impious, to use in negotiating with one another.

The Puzzles of Religious Violence

Religiously inspired violence has existed since the dawn of history, and it shows no sign of going away. The Pew Research Trust provides regular high-quality reports summarizing both governmental restrictions on religion and violent acts against individuals and groups. It's hard to measure total numbers of people killed or injured, since the definition of religiously motivated violence is often contestable in a way that can have a large influence on the statistics. (Should the hundreds of thousands of victims of Vladimir Putin's aggression against Ukraine all count as victims of religious violence just because his aggression has been enthusiastically supported by the patriarch of the Russian Orthodox Church?) So the reports of the Pew Trust focus instead on counting the number of countries in which there were instances of religiously motivated violence, and it is sobering to read just how widespread are such events. In 2019, the most recent year before the coronavirus pandemic, there were "crimes, malicious acts or violence motivated by religious hatred or bias" in 169 of the world's 198 countries, up from 130 in 2007. In 60 countries these involved violent assaults, and in 39 countries they led to deaths.[57] There were 49 countries that had religiously motivated terrorist groups operating within their borders. In 94 countries it was reported that "organized groups use force or coercion in an attempt to dominate public life with their perspective on religion, including preventing some religious groups from operating in the country." In 74 countries it was reported that "individuals or groups use violence or the threat of violence to enforce religious norms." Clearly, religious violence is not an occasional pathology in an otherwise healthy religious landscape, but a systematic and entrenched phenomenon. That's not to say that it's more prevalent than ordinary secular violence. There are over four hundred thousand victims of homicide in the world every year, and in 2019 there were additionally around seventy-seven thousand deaths in conflicts,[58] a number that has massively increased since then due to war in Ukraine. But religious movements whose leaders or some of whose members consciously perpetrate violence, with religious justifications as a motive or a pretext, are a central feature of both ancient and modern religious life.

Indeed, the incidence of religiously motivated violence is so massive that it would take several books to analyze it properly, and I don't propose to do so here. Still, the perspective of the platform model allows us to think carefully about some of the different motivations involved. We can distinguish among violence perpetrated by members of a religious community against members of the same community, members of a close rival community (such as a dissident group within a church or mosque), and members of a distant rival community (such as members of a different world religion). When the victims are from the same community, they are typically targeted in order to force them to comply with the norms of the movement, or some members' interpretation of those norms. Paradoxically, the more "moral" the members believe their movement to be, the more angrily they may respond to what they perceive as violations of the movement's norms.

When the victims are from a close rival community the conflict is typically over control over the religious or material assets of the community. When they are from a distant rival community the conflict is over religious, material, or political assets in the wider society. The platform model brings two main insights to bear on the nature of the rivalry over these assets. The first is that the more intense the competition between the groups concerned, the more each one will benefit from weakening or eliminating its rivals, and the greater the temptation to use violence to that end. The second insight is that when the groups are close rivals, the assets over which they are competing are usually people (members and potential members). When they are more distant rivals, they are usually competing over material assets such as land or business opportunities, or political assets such as access to power.

These insights make intuitive sense, but are they backed by historical evidence? It's often hard to find accurate measures of changes in the extent of competition between religious groups and to link them to changes in the incidence of violence. But a study by economists Sascha Becker and Luigi Pascali does exactly that for the causes of anti-Semitic violence in Europe after the Reformation. Conflict between Christians and Jews did not occur over matters of doctrine or ritual, since conversions were rare (much rarer than conversions between Catholicism and Protestantism), so the two movements were scarcely ever competing over members. Instead their rivalry was over economic matters. The Catholic Church had imposed a ban on usury, and Jews had become more literate on average than Christians (for reasons related to the economic incentives created by the diaspora, as economic historians Maristella Botticini and Zvi Eckstein have shown).[59] This meant that Jews had established a niche in the moneylending business, providing valuable services for Catholics while not competing directly with them. The Reformation changed this relationship, because Protestantism no longer banned usury. Protestants were therefore free to move into the moneylending business, which meant that they perceived Jews for the first time as direct competitors rather than providers of services. Becker and Pascali show not only that anti-Semitic persecution became more common in Protestant regions of Germany than in Catholic ones, but also that it was particularly pronounced in cities where Jews had become most established as moneylenders.[60]

Similar evidence comes from the work of economist Saumitra Jha, who has examined factors affecting the incidence of Hindu-Muslim violence in different areas of Gujarat state in Western India during the outbreak of interethnic rioting in 2002. As he describes:

> Gujarat was the home state of Mahatma Gandhi and has long traditions of *ahimsa*, or non-violence. Yet there was widespread religious rioting in erstwhile medieval capitals, mint towns and other places where, historically, Hindus and Muslims competed for political and economic patronage. In contrast, Gujarati medieval ports, like Surat and Gandhi's own hometown of Porbandar, where Hindus and Muslims enjoyed centuries of robust inter-ethnic complementarity in

overseas trade, the violence was much more muted, and they remained "oases of peace" despite often having larger Muslim minorities.[61]

A related study by economists Rohit Ticku, Anand Shrivastava, and Sriya Iyer shows that Muslim desecration of Hindu temples in medieval India was more common in periods of economic downturn caused by climatic fluctuations.[62] Such insights can even help us to understand one of the most puzzling features of religious violence over the centuries. As Peter Brown pointed out in relation to the fourth and fifth centuries CE, Christian violence against non-Christians was typically much less widespread and damaging than Christian violence against other Christians, and that has continued to be true over the centuries. Something similar is true of religious violence perpetrated by Muslims, which has almost certainly killed many more Muslims than non-Muslims. Yet it is not true of religious violence perpetrated by Hindus (nor that by Buddhists). There has been, and continues to be, regular violence perpetrated by Hindus against other Hindus they accuse of violating caste taboos—for example, those concerning intercaste marriage, or of encroaching on land that has traditionally been enjoyed by members of their own caste. And there is a terrible history of violence by Hindus against Muslims (and vice versa). But there is comparatively scant record of systematic violence by Hindus against other Hindus whom they accuse of being inauthentic Hindus. Saivites and Vaishnavites (followers of Shiva and Vishnu respectively) do not have a history of intergroup violence to match those of Catholics and Protestants, Sunnis and Shi'as, or different flavors of Sunni Islam such as Wahabis and Sufis. The reason is simply that different Hindu groups are not competing over people—you do not become a Saivite out of conviction but out of family tradition. Particular Hindu groups in particular places may compete over resources such as access to land or to political patronage.[63] But Saivites and Vaishnavites are as likely to find themselves in collaboration as in competition, so no religious entrepreneur has anything systematic to gain from promoting religiously motivated envy between the two groups.

The overall lessons of the platform model for understanding religious violence are clear and important. Religious violence is rarely an inexplicable outburst of irrationality or immorality; perhaps it might be less prevalent if it were. We need to understand it instead, most of the time, as a strategically driven use of force for economic or political ends. As the Indian poet Basavanna put it the twelfth century, "the crookedness of our Lord's men is straight enough for our Lord."[64] When groups claim to be fighting over an idea, such as the interpretation of a scripture, they are almost always fighting for control over an asset—namely, the people who have committed themselves to that idea. It is precisely their power to mobilize people in support of an idea that gives religious movements such exposure to the temptation to make war instead of peace.

Political Patronage and the Decline of Legitimacy

Let's turn now to the longer-term consequences of alliances between religious movements and political authorities. Though dependence of political rulers on religious legitimacy may often have provided short-term stability, it was not always in their long-run interests, nor was it perceived by them to be so. Some political leaders have felt that religious support was a kind of drug from which they needed to be weaned (just as Adam Smith believed that political support was a kind of drug from which religious leaders needed to be weaned). Economists Noel Johnson and Mark Koyama have argued that one of the most profound transformations in the growth of the modern nation-state was the evolution of political power from dependence on an identity-based rule of law to a rule of law that was universal. A rule of law that was based on identity treated Christians, Jews, Muslims, and others as subject to fundamentally different rules—and incidentally made their religious identity something they were powerless to change. It "prevented individuals from reaping the benefits [of] trading and sharing ideas across religious boundaries and opened the way for religious persecution." Johnson and Koyama show that persecution held back economic development, and that the ability of states to raise taxes was lower where they relied on local communities to provide tax revenue rather than investing in the capacity to raise taxes from all subjects regardless of their community. Spurred in large part by the need to raise revenue for military purposes, European states began to invest in fiscal and legal infrastructure that simplified the old identity-based systems of rules and institutions, a process that began earlier and moved faster in northwest Europe than it did in the south and east.[65] A reduction—admittedly gradual, admittedly incomplete—in religious persecution was not the intention, but it was the result. There are, of course, many other contributory factors to the economic development of northwestern Europe, and a vast literature has grown up to evaluate their relative importance,[66] but a move away from identity-based rule of law was undeniably part of the overall package.

If religious support was a kind of drug from which political leaders needed to be weaned, could the same be said of political support for religious leaders? Adam Smith clearly thought this of the Church of England in the mid-eighteenth century, and we saw in chapter 2 that a good case can be made for the Roman Catholic Church in Ireland, Spain, and more recently Poland in the late twentieth and early twenty-first centuries. Other examples can be given from across the world. In Egypt in the 1990s, "the government found that manipulating al-Azhar and silencing its opposition to state policy undermined al-Azhar's influence within Egyptian society and therefore its ability to discredit opponents of the government."[67] In Sri Lanka (also in the 1990s), the spiritual authority of the *mahanayakas* (patriarchs) of the main orders of Buddhist monks was openly challenged after their involvement in the National Sangha Council led them to take sides in a contentious argument about the peace process in the country's civil war.[68]

But can we move beyond anecdotes? Is there evidence that such a relationship, between political support for a favored religious movement and waning religiosity, holds more generally across historical periods, countries, and religions? The obstacles in the way of testing such a hypothesis empirically are immense. As we saw in chapter 2, religiosity has been measured systematically across countries only since the 1980s. Religiosity itself has multiple dimensions, and the survey questions are more appropriate for some religious traditions than others. And that's even before we get to trying to measure political support. There are also important questions about timing. Smith believed that political support for a religious movement would undermine a movement's legitimacy eventually, not that it would happen immediately. The case of Ireland suggests that the relationship is likely to be complex. For a religious movement to obtain political support may give it advantages in reaching a wider public, and these advantages may outweigh for a time the longer-term adverse impact on the incentives of its leaders to respond to the needs of members. Public religiosity (church attendance, for example) may respond differently from private religiosity. And the impact on the religiosity of a favored movement's own members may be the opposite of the impact on the religiosity of the members of its rivals (as Smith, observing the enthusiasm of the eighteenth-century Methodists, would have been the first to agree). It's far from clear that such a sophisticated set of potential relationships can be detected in the available data since 1980.

Still, some researchers have done what they can with the available evidence, and it's fair to say that Smith's theory is consistent with their findings but does not receive a ringing endorsement. Rachel McCleary and Robert Barro, using data up till the year 2000, use two measures of political support for religion and find they have opposite effects: the presence of an official state religion tends to increase religiosity, but state regulation of religions in general tends to reduce it.[69] Jonathan Fox tests many versions of the hypothesis over the same time period, finding support for some but not others.[70] In a study with Jori Breslawski using more recent data on Christian-majority countries, he shows that "state support for religion is associated with lower levels of individual confidence in government."[71] While this does not establish that it also diminishes the perceived legitimacy of religion itself, it is likely that the two processes would be linked. The ground is rich for further research using more data and with closer attention to the types of religiosity and political support measured, to the mechanisms involved, and to the impact on the religiosity of different people.

Can any of these insights help to understand the very particular (and, as chapter 2 showed, globally unusual) decline in reported religiosity in the United States in the last two or three decades? An influential book published in 2010 by Robert Putnam and David Campbell argued that whereas America was once divided, socially and politically, between religious denominations (such as Catholic and Protestant), it is increasingly divided between the religious and the irreligious.[72] The religious are increasingly homogeneous in their conservatism, and the political profile of religion has become more associated with the Republican Party. They suggested, however, that at the same time Americans have become "increasingly likely to work with, live alongside, and marry people of other religions—or people with no religion at all. It is difficult to demonize the religion, or lack of religion, of people you know and especially, those you love." They maintained that "Americans overwhelmingly, albeit not universally, identify with a religion. Identity, however, does not necessarily translate into religious activity."[73] And they concluded with an upbeat assessment of the future of religion in America because of the ability of the American religious landscape to create "a web of interlocking personal relationships among people of many different faiths."[74]

A recent study by economists Raphael Corbi and Fabio Miessi Sanches claims support for the arguments of Putnam and Campbell, through estimating a statistical model of the demand for church attendance.[75] This model claims two things: first, that churches, and the priests and pastors who lead them, are more conservative than the great majority of their members, and secondly, that the views of most Americans have become less conservative in recent decades, leading a substantial minority of the population to lose interest in religion altogether. The arguments are powerful ones, but it's important to understand what a statistical model of this kind can and can't do. In this case, the authors assume that individuals choose to attend the church whose leaders express the political views that are closest to their own. They then note that more-conservative individuals are more likely to attend church than liberal ones. They conclude that this is because, on average, liberal individuals are further away from the churches' ideology than are conservatives (and conservatives would therefore be even closer to the churches' ideology if they were more conservative than they are). If average individual views evolve over time in a liberal direction, but churches do not adapt to follow them, more and more individuals will decide that churches no longer reflect their own personal views and will lose interest in religion altogether.

There's much that seems persuasive in these arguments—notably, that it's changes in people's political identity that are driving their perceived religious identity rather than vice versa. Michele Margolis argues something very similar in her 2018 book *From Politics to the Pews*, where she attributes declining religious participation to increasing political partisanship.[76] Most Americans, whatever their political views, believe that organized religion should keep out of political matters, with three-quarters expressing the view that churches should not come out in favor of one candidate or another during elections.[77] It's also true from a longer-term historical perspective that religious movements have often been powerful forces for democracy and resistance against the instrumentalization of religion by partisan political interests.[78]

And evidence about people's religious beliefs, as opposed to their church membership, shows much less evidence of a decline over time, as we saw in chapter 2. This suggests that it's politically organized religion that is losing support, rather than religion per se. Further evidence comes from a study by sociologists Michael Hout and Claude Fischer, published in 2014. They showed that the religious beliefs of Americans had not changed much over time, ruling out secularization (at least in its conventional form) as an explanation. Instead, they argued, a gradual change in the salience of people's political identity as a liberal or conservative had sparked a backlash against the religious right, a backlash that was due less to evolution in individual attitudes as to generational succession—younger, more polarized cohorts replacing older ones.[79]

Still, there are some parts of the story that need to be modified. First, though Democrats are less religious than Republicans on average, they are still highly favorable to religion by the standards of other industrialized countries. According to the Pew Trust, 70 percent of Democrats surveyed in 2019 thought churches did more good than harm in American society, or at least thought they didn't make much difference (that figure was a whopping 82 percent among Black Democrats and

74 percent among Hispanic Democrats).[80] Secondly, the idea that church leaders are imposing their conservative religious views on their parishioners is questionable. The model of religious demand estimated by Corbi and Miessi Sanches assumes, but cannot demonstrate, that individuals choose a church for its closeness to their political views. Suppose instead that more-conservative people are more likely to believe that it's important to go to church, independently of its proximity to their political beliefs. Then the model will mistakenly tell us that churches are more conservative than even the most conservative parishioners, because it's attributing their greater willingness to attend to their being closer, but not quite close enough, to the church's political views.

Finally, evidence that churches are primarily pushing conservative views is based almost entirely on anecdotes—there are plenty of those, but in a large country like the United States you'd expect anecdotes to crop up often. In work that I did with economist Eva Raiber analyzing a sample of nearly four thousand US churches' Facebook posts during the coronavirus pandemic, we compared the posts of churches in strongly Democrat-leaning counties with those of churches in strongly Republican counties. We expected to find that churches in Republican counties had been less likely than those in Democrat counties to move their services online during the pandemic, because of the political controversy surrounding restrictions on in-person religious gatherings (culminating in the US Supreme Court decision of November 25, 2020, striking down restrictions on religious services imposed in New York by Governor Andrew Cuomo). In fact, we found absolutely no difference in willingness to move online.[81] In ongoing work, we are analyzing the text of the posts, looking specifically for markers of the expression of political views. We find a slightly greater tendency among churches in Democrat counties to publish political posts, mostly around events such as the Black Lives Matter protests in the late spring and summer of 2020. But overall political posts were extremely rare (well under 1 percent of all posts), even though this was a highly politically charged period in American life.[82] If churches were indeed pushing their conservative views down the throats of their unwilling parishioners, they left little trace of this on their Facebook pages.

A better way to describe what has been happening in America is not that churches have been instrumentalizing politics, but that politicians have been instrumentalizing religion (including through their influence on the courts, up to and including the Supreme Court). We saw in chapter 2 that, when we measure the proportion of a country's population who say that religion is somewhat important or very important in their lives, there's a perceptible tendency for there to be clusters of countries round 35–40 percent, around 70–80 percent, and around 90–95 percent. The difference between the countries in the first two groups seems to be that when religion is perceived as roughly politically neutral, it can hope to mobilize a substantial majority of the population, though rarely everyone (numbers above 90 percent probably reflect political or social pressure on survey respondents to express support for religion). When religion comes to be seen as politically partisan, it will be able to mobilize enthusiastically only those who are on the conservative side of the political spectrum in their societies. This will limit their catchment area to at most half of the population, even if most of the population continue to believe in God and to consider themselves at least somewhat religious. The United States may now be in the process of making the transition from the politically neutral to the politically partisan category; if so, we can expect to see measures of American religiosity continue to fall before they eventually stabilize at levels like those in Western Europe.

What can we conclude, then, from this inevitably superficial overview of the links between religion and politics in historical times as well as in our own day? That Adam Smith could even imagine an earlier golden age in which political leadership had not been intertwined with religious leadership was in some ways a tribute to how far the ideas of philosophers had developed since the Reformation, though he was well aware of the many obstacles lying in the way of a separation of the two realms. Even if an acolyte of Marcos in the late twentieth century could use language that looks superficially like that of a Buddhist writer of inscriptions nearly a millennium earlier, the context of legitimation has changed almost beyond recognition. Political leaders today can turn to many other ideological sources to clothe in legitimacy their exercise of naked power. Electoral democracy, nationalism, and scientific rationalism have all been used and misused by political leaders, and in some places and times they have seemed to eclipse the power of religion to convey legitimacy at all. But it would be unwise to bet that leaders in the twenty-first century will give up religion altogether. The economic success of religion shows no signs of faltering, so it seems likely that its value as a political tool will remain as strong as ever.

To the extent that religion both reflects and reinforces structures of political as well as economic power, it will also be no surprise that it reproduces many of the inequalities we see in the economic and political realms. One that has become particularly salient in recent years is the inequality between men and women. This is the subject of chapter 11.

CHAPTER 11

The Great Religion Gender Gap?

The woman ought not to possess private friends, but to share those of the man. But first and greatest are the gods, and it is therefore right for the wife to reverence or acknowledge only those gods who are recognized by the husband. Her street-door should be kept shut to out-of-the-way forms of worship and alien superstitions. No deity finds gratification in ceremonies which a woman performs in secret and by stealth.

—Plutarch, *Advice to Married Couples*[1]

Homage to Kali

There was a quiet but insistent knocking in the middle of the night on the door of my hut. I roused myself from sleep and opened the door to see Kumar, my colleague and interpreter, standing next to another man. Kumar whispered to me: "Come. They want us to see something." "I'll go and wake my wife," I said. "No!" he replied. "Apparently it's only for men."

I could see by my watch that it was 2:00 a.m. There was a full moon. We made our way out of the collection of huts toward a nearby stream, led by the young man we had chatted with several times in the last few days. My wife and I, together with Kumar and our female colleague Vasantha, were doing a detailed field study of two villages in contrasting areas of Tamil Nadu state in southern India, one full of rice paddies and sugar

John Knox, author of *The First Blast of the Trumpet against the Monstrous Regiment of Women* (1588), depicted reproving the ladies of Queen Mary's court.
Credit: William Thomas Roden / Scottish National Portrait Gallery.

People at a demonstration calling for the ordination of women, New York City, *c.* 1970.
Credit: FPG / Archive Photos / Getty Images.

cane fields irrigated by canals fed by the river Kaveri, the other in a very dry area of rain-fed agriculture a few miles to the south. Here, among the rice paddies, we were staying in a part of the village occupied by one of the Dalit castes (formerly known as untouchables), whose men provided most of the agricultural labor for the plowing and harvesting, and whose women and children did most of the planting of rice. The castes lived in separate streets, did mostly separate work, never intermarried, and would refuse to exchange food or drink or even to come close enough together to risk physical contact.

The dry village regularly held temple festivals that brought together the whole village, including all its different castes. Here, in the irrigated village, the separation of castes extended to their religious festivals, and in the neighborhood where we were living preparations had been underway for a festival that would start the next day. Households had been cooking sweets and washing festive saris. As the three of us snaked our way between the last remaining huts and toward the stream, I began to hear an excited low-level chatter, the kind of rustling sound made by a lot of people who know they are supposed to be keeping silent. I also heard a quiet lowing of water buffalo.

The young man made his way to the edge of a crowd of around a hundred men and pushed through in front of us, motioning to us to follow him, until we arrived at the edge of a large, freshly dug pit, around fifteen feet long and half as wide. We were standing beside one long edge of the pit, and at the end to our left were several men in dark lungis and colorful shirts, some carrying long drums, some carrying knives, and two wielding large machetes. Behind them stood a line of water buffalo, each tethered by a rope to the animal in front.

We did not have to wait long. The chattering around us grew to a low roar and the drums began. The first water buffalo was led to the pit and, just as it planted its front hooves in resistance at the edge, one man cut the cord tying it to the animal behind and a second brought the machete hard down upon the animal's neck. A couple of blows and the head was severed, blood spurted from the gaping neck, the animal's legs buckled beneath its weight, and two men behind it gave a timely heave that sent the body tumbling into the pit. The second buffalo was led to the edge of the pit and met the same fate. And then the third. And so it went on.

"How many buffalo are they going to kill?" I asked Kumar, trying to make myself heard without shouting. "There seems no end to this." "I don't know," he replied. "They're all young males. They keep the females for milking." "It's a sacrifice to the goddess Kali," he added. "A very secret sacrifice. The women aren't supposed to know, though they all do."

So this very male gathering was sacrificing to a female deity. I lost count of the animals being led to the pit and bloodily dispatched. It was certainly over thirty, though less than fifty. The noise grew louder, the rhythm of the drums more insistent, and quickly there came a pungent whiff of sacrifice. The bodies piled up in the pit, and two men jumped in, maneuvering the carcasses to leave room for the newly killed. Their bare torsos were soon glistening with blood in the moonlight.

As I looked around, I could see how excited all the men were. They groaned as the animals were led to the pit, and roared as they were beheaded. The smell of blood evoked something sexual, and the sheer presence of so many men roaring together made it impossible not to feel a tug that was as physical as it was emotional. There was also something about this massive slaughter, by Hindus, of Hinduism's most sacred animal, in a country where Christians and Muslims could be attacked and killed for allegedly mistreating cattle, that was indisputably, utterly transgressive. And, though they were making their devotion to a goddess, only the men were supposed to know.

The Gods Are Gendered

Of course the gods are gendered—religion is a very human enterprise and the gods reflect ourselves back to us. Rituals like the one I saw in South India are of course completely untypical of the general experience of Hindu worship. They're marginal and transgressive, but they're also interesting exactly for that reason, because of what they can tell us about the shared but often tacit assumptions about what is an appropriate activity for whom. Intense religious experience, like experience in many other domains, is often created, shaped, and interpreted differently for and by men and women. Men and women are often separated during religious rituals to let them feel these experiences even more intensely. This happens more often in Islamic and Christian rituals than in Hindu and Buddhist ones, but it's also true of many forager societies, where many secret (and mostly single-sex) cults appear in the ethnographic record.[2] Paradoxically, in these settings, traditional gender stereotypes can break down once they are no longer seen as necessary to keep men and women apart.

One of the most surprising subgenres in the field of Islamic jihadi propaganda consists of videos of fighters weeping. There is no stigma attached to this, and the fact that the fighter is weeping is often given prominence. Researcher Thomas Hegghammer, an expert on international jihadi movements who has studied this subgenre over many years, notes that "militant Islamists consider weeping an integral part of being a good *mujahid*. It is viewed as a signal of piety and hence as an indication that the person is not fighting for pecuniary or other selfish reasons." Far from detracting from a fighter's perceived manliness, he writes that "some of the most brutal fighters have been lauded for their weeping. Even the infamous Islamic State executioner 'Jihadi John' was described in *Dabiq* magazine as someone who wept. If anything, weeping features in jihadi biographies as a *correlate* of brutality."[3] Yet in other contexts jihadi propagandists mock their enemies for crying with fear, usually implying it to be unmanly behavior—mockery delivered as mercilessly by women as by men.[4]

Rather than seeing this phenomenon as just another example of incoherence or hypocrisy in the propaganda of violent religious extremism, it's worth taking its deliberateness seriously, reflecting on the kind of signal it is supposed to send, and to whom. There's no doubt that jihadi groups seek to recruit fighters who will be ruthless in carrying out their military missions, and whose actions will not only achieve those missions but will also instill fear more generally in the movement's adversaries. Brutality is therefore part of the job description. And for some potential recruits, this is no doubt attractive—but in a highly complicated way. Many, perhaps even most people may feel a certain thrill at the idea of inflicting violence.[5] But the thrill is transgressive—it derives its intense appeal precisely because it runs counter to the inhibitions that all religious traditions (Islam no less than the others) have erected against violence. So there's also a great deal of guilt and inhibition, except in a tiny minority of psychopaths. This makes sense from what we know about our evolution: the ability to inflict lethal violence, and the taste for doing so, were undoubtedly adaptive (for males at least) during our prehistory.[6] But as human social life became more complex, males who could not inhibit their violent impulses for the good of the group faced increasingly severe social sanctions.[7] Most normal human beings therefore feel a complicated mixture of emotions in relation to violence: they are drawn to it, up to a point, but that very attraction triggers inhibiting mechanisms in our psyche. Recruiting killers therefore typically requires playing to the thrill while finding a way around the guilt and inhibition. This challenge is all the greater for movements that claim the endorsement of the transcendental religions whose written texts emphasize the destructiveness and sinfulness of violence.

There are several possible strategies for meeting the challenge.[8] One is to emphasize the greater good that the killing can achieve.[9] Violent groups often engage in very visible philanthropic campaigns in parallel with their paramilitary mission.[10] Another way is to be explicit about the violence while showing what full and admirable people the perpetrators are. The weeping jihadi is a way of signaling that if the acts are brutal, the killers are not. Indeed, a common context in which their weeping is showcased is when the fighters hear of the suffering of Muslim civilians. They do so not just in staged videos but also, apparently spontaneously, in other settings—as illustrated by the case of "Ishaq Ahmed, a Norwegian-Somali foreign fighter returned from Syria who wept in court when describing an anecdote about a young girl [who] was raped by government soldiers, a story that he said had motivated him to go to Syria in the first place."[11] It's precisely by stressing the tenderness of the fighters, in a context in which this can be demonstrated not to put their manliness in question, that the violence of their desire for vengeance can be legitimated in the eyes of the targets of the propaganda.

If this is the right interpretation of the way weeping is portrayed in jihadi propaganda, we should expect to see it in the propaganda of other religions that also seek to recruit young men for violence while ostensibly preaching the sinfulness of killing. The most obvious place in the history of Christianity to look for such evidence is the Crusades. And, thanks to the work of several historians, this is precisely what we find. Recruitment emphasized the attractions of violence: Jay Rubenstein has shown how the places where the most recruits for the First Crusade were found were those that had previously organized anti-Jewish pogroms, not those where Pope Urban II traveled to preach in favor of the Crusade.[12] There is also evidence of an emphasis on the tenderheartedness of the crusaders. Stephen Spencer shows how the figure of "the lachrymose crusader" was widely present in twelfth- and thirteenth-century ecclesiastical texts: "weeping was an important religious practice that crusaders were expected to perform."[13] And this despite the fact that, as Kirsten Fenton writes, the First Crusade was conceived by the Benedictine monk William of Malmesbury, who was almost certainly reporting a widely shared interpretation, as a "male space," one that drew a strong distinction between the virile Christian and the cowardly, effeminate Turks, who (he claimed) shunned fighting at close quarters and relied on shooting arrows from afar.[14] The attribution of effeminacy was also used as an insult in the rhetoric of the thirteenth-century Albigensian crusaders against King Pedro II of Aragon, who had had the temerity to come to the defense of the besieged citizens of Toulouse.[15] This made the crusaders' tears all the more potent as a symbol. Although it's certainly true that, as the introduction to a compilation of readings on religion, gender, and sexuality puts it, "holy figures, like Christian saints . . . traverse boundaries . . . move between genders . . . often exist at the margins of masculinity and femininity, incorporating elements of both genders, or destabilizing hegemonic constructions of these altogether,"[16] that doesn't mean that their *purpose* is to blur gender norms. Sometimes their purpose, as in the case of these examples of jihadi and crusader propaganda, may be to exploit and even reinforce gender norms, in all their messy complexity, for the purposes of attracting recruits or raising money.

The Religious Gender Gap—How Universal Is It?

There's no getting away from it: across the world, statistically speaking, religious leaders are overwhelmingly male,[17] while women are reported to be, on average, somewhat more religious than men. This is one of those statistical phenomena that have been massively discussed by researchers but never convincingly explained, except with the kind of shrug that says, "the rest of society is like that, so why should religion be any different?" After all, despite some changes in recent years, men still dominate political leadership across the world (composing three-quarters of parliamentarians and nearly four out of five government ministers),[18] while women are, on balance, no less likely to vote than men and in many countries are slightly more likely to do so.[19] Despite some recent progress, men still make up the overwhelming majority of business leaders (around 85 percent of CEOs of the world's leading companies),[20] even in industries such as groceries, fashion, and cosmetics where far more of the spending decisions are undertaken by women than by men. Despite some evolution in the proportions, senior academics are still predominantly male, even though women make up close to 60 percent of students in most industrialized countries.[21] Perhaps there's just nothing to explain about the specifically religious nature of the difference.

Still, the gender asymmetry has a particularly disturbing aspect in the context of religion, because religious arguments are so often used as a pretext for measures that are discriminatory against women or downright repressive. In some respects the outlook is deteriorating. To take just one example, the Pew Research Center reports that in 2019 there were fifty-nine countries in which women were harassed for violating religious dress codes, a startling increase from only fourteen countries in 2007.[22] Nevertheless, what we've seen in chapter 10 should make it very clear where the blame belongs. Religious texts are instrumentalized for essentially political purposes. All of the world's main religious movements have texts that, reflecting as they do the times in which they were written, contain expressions of sentiments that are unacceptable today (about the role of women in society, and about many other things too).

They also contain expressions of sentiments we can find uplifting and inspiring today. It's a political choice to emphasize one extract from a religious text or another. Anyone who picks one rather than another will typically argue that the extracts they have chosen are the true essence of the tradition in question, but they're always using the text as cover for an essentially political message. As we've seen repeatedly in earlier chapters, religious traditions don't have an essence—they are all a vast patchwork of things that have been said and written at various points in the history of a movement. We saw this in chapter 9 in relation to the use of violence: it's futile to debate whether, say, Islam or Christianity is intrinsically more peaceful or more warlike, since both sets of sacred texts offer ample support to anyone who wants to send either a peaceful or a warlike message. It is equally futile to debate whether one religious tradition is intrinsically more respectful of women than another—all sets of texts offer ample support to those who want to send a repressive or an emancipatory message, and the choice between them is a political rather than a religious choice.[23]

With this in mind, we can return to the statistics about religiosity; the puzzle only deepens about its supposedly gendered nature. First, as a 2016 report from the Pew Research Center noted, there is a tendency on average for women to score higher than men on most measures of religiosity (from affiliation to a religion through attendance at religious services to private actions such as prayer). The difference is not large (for example, 83.4 percent of women around the world identify with a faith group, compared with 79.9 percent of men) but it is consistent with previous findings over many years. However, it is not present consistently across religions: in fact, it holds strongly for Christians but not for other religions. Muslim men and women tend to report similar degrees of religiosity on most measures, except for attendance at religious services, where men report significantly higher levels (as do Jews in Israel, though not Jews in other countries). Among other religious groupings there are few if any systematic differences in religiosity between men and women—in the reported statistics at least.[24] Perhaps that merely underlines the inability of statistical measures to capture something as intimate and potentially subjective as religiosity. But it still leaves us with a puzzle as to why the figures for Christianity are so strikingly different.

Part of the answer may come from a study published in 2022 of religiosity and gender in fourteen different societies by a consortium of anthropologists and psychologists. While far from representative of the diversity of cultures in the world, these societies are interesting in that they all contain both local gods and moralizing high gods (mainly Christian, with some Hindu and Buddhist gods and one example of a traditional deity much concerned with enforcing moral behavior). The authors report that "perhaps the clearest pattern in our data is the finding that women score higher than men on measures of religiosity towards moralising gods, but not towards local gods. This raises the possibility that some features of world religions and their powerful moralising deities have evolved to be more appealing to women."[25] In other words, women may respond to some features of religion more than to others, and religious movements may develop their message to take those preferences of women into account.

Religiosity as a Bundle of Traits

For our purposes here there is a general lesson to be drawn. As I already suggested in chapter 1, we should not think of religiosity as a fixed personal trait, one that characterizes people independently of their gender or sexuality (or their other personal and social characteristics). Instead, religiosity is a bundle of rather disparate traits, each of which expresses itself as the outcome of an interaction between individuals and their religious communities. It's the fruit of a strategy chosen by the community—the religious platform, as we've tried to think of it—and the response to that strategy of the various members of the community. As we've seen in the case of weeping jihadis and crusaders, recruitment to religious movements can sometimes make use of highly gendered strategies, and in these circumstances we should expect a highly gendered response. If going on a Crusade were considered a measure of religiosity it would skew highly male (though some women did join the Crusades as well). Some religious platforms, notably orders of monks or nuns but also movements such as the Freemasons, have by definition adopted recruitment strategies that were exclusively targeted to men or to women (though the Christian saint Pelagia of Antioch was renowned for having passed successfully as a man so that she could enjoy the monastic life).[26]

In most religious movements it also seems likely that the more intense and imagistic are the rituals, the more gendered is religious participation (though the evidence here is more ethnographic and anecdotal).[27] Men take part in certain very intense rituals reserved for men, and women take part in certain very intense rituals reserved for women. That makes sense of the fact that many of the more intense rituals track events in the human life cycle (birth, puberty, marriage, childbearing, death) that affect men and women very differently. But it would be surprising if religion *in general* turned out to skew very male or to skew very female— it would mean that religious platforms were failing to respond to opportunities for recruitment that lie in front of their eyes. Of course, certain religious movements come with baggage—they have a message that has resounded down the ages and that may not continue to resound as effectively with men and with women as the surrounding culture evolves. That may explain why we find some differences in religiosity at any point in time. But it would be surprising if such differences were to persist over very long periods.

There's a parallel here with other complex personal characteristics. Take intelligence, which has been the subject of heated debate, both over the science and over the political implications that have been drawn from the science. Intelligence is not a single trait but a bundle of traits, which can be captured by a range of different measures. Though much ink has been spilt over the question of whether there are differences in intelligence between men and women, the debate is futile: the science clearly indicates that there are some components of intelligence on which men tend to score on average higher than women, and others on which they tend to score lower. Any "average" measure would have to decide what components to include in the overall measure and what weight to give them, and there is no neutral theory that can allow us to do that.[28] Exactly the same is true of religiosity. If religiosity comprises some traits like a willingness to perform jihad or to go on Crusades, and others like a tendency to engage empathetically with the personality of the deity, it will be no surprise that the former component tends to skew male while the latter tends to skew female. Overall religiosity will be a weighted average of different components, and there is no neutral theory telling us which components should be included and what weight they should have. The question whether general religiosity is more female than male overall turns out to be as empty a question as whether general intelligence tends to be more female than male.

With that in mind, let's return to the question whether there's something in the nature of the Christian "package"—something that is not found, or at least not systematically, in other religious traditions—that might appeal slightly more to women than to men (remember that the differences here are clear, but not huge). It's been widely noted that in its early history the Christian Church made more converts among women than among men (which would be even more remarkable than it appears if, as some scholars argue, female infanticide was sufficiently widespread to lead to a significant excess of men in the Roman world).[29] It was widely believed that women were in general "especially attracted to the syncretic cults produced by the spread of eastern and Egyptian religions through the Mediterranean cities,"[30] Whether or not this was true in fact rather than just in perception, alarm among male moralists provoked stern injunctions like those of Plutarch that I quoted at the beginning of this chapter.

It's also well known that the Church imposed a code of restrictive sexual morality, forbidding both "fornication" between men and women and same-sex relationships. This may help explain the gender skew in recruitment to Christianity. Historians have pointed out that we need to understand such a moral code not simply as a restriction on the freedom of consenting adults. It was also a restoration of the freedom of many of those who, under the supposedly more liberal morality of the Roman Empire, were most subject to systematic assault and abuse. As Kyle Harper has written, Roman society between the later first century and the early third century CE was "a society whose moral lineaments were sculpted by the omnipresence of slaves and by the rigid stratifications of law."[31] Slaves were regarded not only as economic property but also as sexual property. In addition, Keith Hopkins showed many years ago that even free Roman women were often married off at a very young age to men much older than them, which certainly implies subjection if not strictly slavery. He noted that this was much less common among Christian than among pagan women (20 percent of Christian women had been married by the age of fourteen, compared to 44 percent of pagans).[32] In this context, a moral code that required men as well as women to remain chaste until marriage, that forbade adultery for men as well as women, that forbade all infanticide and not just infanticide of boys, was bound to seem like a strong defense of the rights of women and slaves against the sexual arrogance of Roman men.

These arguments might explain why early Christianity appealed more to women than to men two millennia ago, but why should it still speak more to women than to men today? To make an obvious point, the subjection of women to the sexual arrogance of men may be less blatant now than it was in the early Roman Empire, but it has not completely gone away (to put it mildly). The fact that, in principle if not always in practice, the Christian moral codes of chastity and fidelity apply to men and women equally is something that women are more likely than men to find appealing (just as men are more likely to find it irksome). Other world traditions are somewhat less likely to take a stern line on such matters, and certainly less likely even to claim to judge men as severely as women for lapses from their adopted sexual standards. Even on its own, such an explanation makes some sense.

It's nonetheless worth adding a dimension that would have been less relevant for Roman times, when literacy among women was rare, but which may be extremely important today. The Christian package involves a regular repetition of stories about the founder, whose personal characteristics are repeatedly emphasized to involve reliability, gentleness, and charisma, and who also embodies a personal narrative of triumph over death. These features make the package highly attractive to those for whom storytelling is an important component of their lives. Other major religions do indeed involve some stories about the founder—but listening to them makes up a less intense part of the overall package of religious observance. It's a surprise to no one that, in the twenty-first century, far more women than men are members of book clubs,[33] nor that women, on average, enjoy discussing fiction with others to a significantly greater degree than do men (the reasons for this, and extent to which they are due to social conditioning as opposed to innate affinities for articulating emotions, need not occupy us here).[34] Christian platforms have more in common with book clubs than do those of other religions, so it should not be surprising if religiosity as construed the Christian way has a slight tendency to be more appealing to women than to men.

That tells us nothing about religiosity in general, which involves, as we have seen, many different components, only some of which are fully captured in the kinds of questions that surveys tend to ask.[35] And importantly, it tells us nothing about whether, in their pursuit of the many complex benefits that religious communities can offer them, everyone gives up more power to the largely male leaders of those communities than is either necessary or wise. Chapter 12 will explore one important dimension in which that power can be abused.

CHAPTER 12

The Abuse of Religious Power

The thing that everybody knew and nobody grasped.

—Fintan O'Toole, *We Don't Know Ourselves*

John Smyth and the Iwerne Camps

On February 2 and 3, 2017, a two-part documentary broadcast on Channel 4 television in the United Kingdom detailed a sustained pattern of physical and sexual abuse of adolescent boys and young men carried out over nearly forty years by John Smyth, a renowned barrister and Church of England lay preacher.[1] Smyth had become famous in the 1970s as the barrister who helped Mary Whitehouse, a crusading antipornography campaigner and founder of the National Viewers' and Listeners' Association, bring a successful prosecution in 1977 for blasphemous libel against the magazine *Gay News* for publication of an erotic poem imagining a Roman centurion's longing for the crucified Christ. The case was front-page news in the United Kingdom for weeks, and its conclusion established the reputation of the young John Smyth as a fearless campaigner for a pure and muscular vision of Christianity in which sinful sexuality, whether homosexual or heterosexual, had no place.

Seven years after the successful conclusion of the case, in 1984, Smyth left Britain for Zimbabwe, moving to South Africa in 2001, where he lived until his death in 2018. The Channel 4 documentary revealed that he had left the United Kingdom at the urging of a group of churchmen

Seduction or sexual abuse? In this twelfth-century CE capital from a column from Saint Stephen's Cathedral in Toulouse, King Herod holds Salomé under the chin and looks steadily into her eyes. The contrast could not be greater with portrayals (such as that by Aubrey Beardsley below) in which Salomé is shown as a cruel temptress, drawn larger and set higher in the composition than Herod. This medieval craftsman (probably master sculptor Gilabertus of Toulouse) had the imagination to see her as a frightened teenage girl. Credit: Daniel Martin / Wikimedia Commons.

Aubrey Beardsley's illustration for Oscar Wilde's *Salome*. Credit: Aubrey Beardsley / British Library.

and lay Christians. They had learned in 1982 of Smyth's predilection for taking boys and young men to a soundproof shed in his garden and flogging them until they bled, with dozens and sometimes hundreds of strokes of a cane. Smyth had recruited his victims partly through his unofficial role as a spiritual counselor at Winchester College and partly through his involvement in a series of evangelical Christian summer camps for teenage boys held at a school in a small town in the south of England called Iwerne Minster. His pretext for flogging them was that he was purging them of their sins, and particularly of the masturbatory habits they had confessed to him after he had eased his way into their confidence as a trusted spiritual adviser.

One of Smyth's victims, a university student who had known Smyth since he was a pupil at Winchester College, was so distressed by the experience that he attempted suicide. His family had learned of the reasons, and, together with the headmaster of Winchester and a group of senior churchmen, had agreed to keep the events hidden but to urge Smyth to leave the country. What Smyth might get up to in Zimbabwe (where, not surprisingly, he went on to abuse scores of boys and young men, one of whom died in mysterious circumstances)[2] was, apparently, of at best minor concern to these highly Christian men.

The writer Andrew Graystone, who supplied the information that enabled producer Cathy Newman and her team to make the Channel 4 documentary, published in 2021 a book setting out this information in detail. According to him, one of the people who knew something of Smyth's proclivities at the time (though was not involved in the decision to persuade him to move to Zimbabwe), and who presided over a second, equally ineffectual attempt in 2013 to deal with the consequences, was Justin Welby, who at time of writing remains archbishop of Canterbury, head of the Church of England. Apart from making an apology and the promise of an enquiry that has yet to report, Welby has suffered no adverse consequences for his failure to act decisively on what he knew.[3]

Of the many revelations of sexual abuse in religious organizations that have been published in recent years, this one resonated with me particularly, because I had once known John Smyth. For a period of two or three years in the early 1970s, when I was between fifteen and seventeen years old and curious about evangelical Christianity, I had attended the summer camps in Iwerne Minster. John Smyth, then in his early thirties, was one of the perhaps fifteen or twenty men who ran the camps. He cut a striking figure in shorts and boating loafers and was often surrounded by admiring younger men and boys. I was never approached by him, and never heard any rumors of his sadistic proclivities, but I found him creepy. The atmosphere in the camps, despite the plentiful sporting activities, was also creepy in its own way. An ever-present emphasis on wholesome living contained a slyly persistent undercurrent of innuendo about the corrupting influence of sexuality. After my third visit, when an entire evening lecture was devoting to explaining to an audience of anxious teenage boys that masturbation was a way of hammering nails into the hands of the crucified Jesus, I had no wish to return. During the next four decades I rarely gave Iwerne, or John Smyth, any further thought. I spoke even more rarely about Iwerne to others, perhaps fearing that if I did so, people might think the experience had warped my general view of life. It was only after I learned of the scale of Smyth's abuse that I wondered whether my silence, and that of others like me, might have contributed unwittingly to his ability to continue unchecked for so long.

To say that religious organizations have a sexual abuse problem is putting it mildly. In recent years the Roman Catholic Church alone has been the subject of published reports detailing widespread abuse over many years in Australia, Canada, France, Germany, Ireland, the United Kingdom, and the United States. Press reporting and legal proceedings have alleged abuse in the Catholic Church in several other countries; *Wikipedia* lists such reports for eighteen distinct countries in Europe alone.[4] The number of victims in France has been estimated by the official enquiry to run to over two hundred thousand from 1950 to 2020.[5] Among the acknowledged perpetrators is Cardinal Jean-Pierre Ricard, former archbishop of Bordeaux, and at least nine other French bishops have been the subject of legal proceedings under accusations of varying degrees of severity.[6] The late Pope Benedict XVI admitted to providing mistaken information to an official German inquiry into abuse allegations, and acknowledged that he "did not act quickly or firmly enough to take the necessary action."[7] Widespread physical and sexual abuse over many years of children and other vulnerable individuals has been observed in many other Christian denominations, as well as in Jewish, Muslim, Buddhist, Hindu, and other organizations.[8] A recent review of publicly documented allegations of sexual abuse in yoga movements counted the founders of over forty distinct movements claiming many millions of followers between them.[9] There have been many high-profile convictions in recent years of leaders of religious movements in India, for rape, abduction, child abuse, and even murder; some of these accused have fled and are still at large.[10] Across the world, victims of abuse have included children of all ages as well as many adults, with those particularly at risk including the handicapped, the destitute, individuals branded as troublesome, and members of stigmatized minority groups. Abuse is not only a pathology of modern world religions—the ethnographic record shows many examples of traditional religious rituals that involve forced sexual acts by children for the gratification of powerful adults, and of demands by providers of religious services such as shamans to be remunerated through sexual favors.[11]

But religious movements are not alone. Abuse with similar characteristics has taken place in competitive sports, in the movie industry, in artistic institutions such as the Metropolitan Opera, the Royal Ballet, and the Indian classical music and dance system, in universities and other academic institutions, in secular schools and youth clubs, in the Boy Scouts, in humanitarian charities such as Oxfam and in areas controlled by United Nations peacekeeping missions, and in the military more generally.[12] Though it's hard to make comparisons about the prevalence of abuse in different institutions given the widely varying degrees of rigor with which allegations are investigated (and the varying definitions of abuse adopted), there seems so far no reason to think that any religious doctrines are particularly prone to encourage abuse. Nor is there any reason to place intrinsic blame on clerical celibacy, homosexuality, heterosexuality, a generally repressive culture, or a generally permissive culture.[13] This is not to deny, of course, that cultures can make a difference—but there are no simple lessons linking cultures to outcomes except in the tautological sense that cultures conducive to abuse do indeed lead to abuse.[14] Yet there do seem to be some common themes across this distressingly extensive catalogue of mistreatment—can we say anything about what it is, and what religious organizations might be able to do about it?

In trying to explain how John Smyth's abuse can have continued unchecked for so long, Andrew Graystone suggests (in the title as well as in the body of his book) that the Iwerne camps were a cult. The word "cult" used to indicate just a religious movement organized around a particular set of rituals—as in the cult of Mithras in the Roman Empire. In recent decades it has taken on more specific and more negative connotations, referring to movements that are more extreme than ordinary mainstream religions, and particularly to movements that in some way "capture" their members. Even in this extended sense, there is no universally agreed definition of a cult (and some critics have held that the main use of the term tends to be pejorative, against religions that the speaker happens not to like). But a common element in many uses of the term is that leaving the cult is particularly difficult, even for members who suffer from belonging to the movement and want to leave.

I suggested in chapter 9 that it's a general characteristic of religious platforms that "the choice between continuing and stopping looks very different from the outside than it did from the inside." If so the distinction between religions and cults will be a matter of degree not of kind. This chapter will not consider extreme cases of cults where undeniable physical as well as psychological means are used to prevent members from leaving, but such movements certainly exist.[15] But in any case, for the purposes of understanding the case of John Smyth, the notion that the Iwerne camps constituted a cult is not very helpful. Attendees at the camps were free to leave at any time, and many (like me) stopped coming when they stopped enjoying the experience. A more helpful metaphor would be that the camps were an environment that supported the development of a grooming network. In fact, there were two grooming networks: a clandestine one run by John Smyth, which exploited the prior presence of a more open one run (for different purposes) by other leaders of the camps' organization. If this is the case, the sad tale of John Smyth's abuse may have some lessons for abuse in a wider range of contexts. What do I mean by a grooming network?

A common theme running through the accounts of Smyth's activities, in Graystone's book as well as in other reports,[16] is that he would approach boys and young men individually, usually offering to act as their spiritual adviser. He benefited from his air of experience and worldly wisdom, as well as the esteem in which he appeared to be held by others. The word "grooming" is now well established to describe certain kinds of abusive relationship,[17] often though not always a sexually abusive one, but that is a secondary usage. Its principal usage, apart from describing the way in which human owners look after their pets, is to denote a type of behavior in group-living primates, in which one individual will comb through the coat of another looking for lice or other parasites. As well as being good for health through the removal of parasites, grooming is highly pleasurable for the recipient, and has been linked to the release of endorphins. It plays a crucial role in enhancing bonding in primate groups, and in dealing with the stresses that inevitably arise through dense group living. Most bird and mammal species form groups for defensive purposes, but these groups tend to be anonymous and transitory. Primate groups, in contrast, are constructed out of highly individualized relationships, each of which has a history through which past interactions influence the expectation of future ones.[18] Group living becomes sustainable through the glue provided by individual networks of reciprocity, many of which are reflected in and reinforced by grooming. When one individual grooms another, it sets up an expectation of a favor in return. The favor may be paid through reciprocal grooming or through the provision of something else; in most primates that something else is usually food, support in coalitional disputes, or sex.[19]

The main reason why "grooming" seems appropriate for the way in which John Smyth approached his victims is that he managed initially to make each of these individuals feel special—privileged, even—because of the way he singled them out. He was a famous, high-status barrister, and they were flattered that he should take an interest in them. Although the contexts in which he met them involved intense group living (a boys' boarding school and a summer camp for teenage boys), he convinced them that they were each individually important to him. A particularly heartrending detail, recorded in the witness statements, is that many of his victims remained convinced to the end of his care and compassion for them. They thanked him for the violence he inflicted on them, and for the purification he had convinced them it was imparting, even as their self-esteem collapsed under its impact. The word "cult" seems inappropriate to describe something so private, inflicted by one who did not need explicitly to discourage his victims from leaving because he had worked so insidiously to destroy their will to leave.

Though I was never approached by John Smyth, when I read these victim statements I recognized a version of something I had experienced in a much milder and briefer form. The men who ran the camps were inveterate networkers. They included founder E.J.H. Nash, who worked for the Scripture Union, and whom I remembered mainly as the retired clergyman full of passionate intensity who had preached to us about masturbation. They also included his successor as camp director David Fletcher (also of the Scripture Union), and the many earnest young men in their twenties who surrounded them. Two of these young men sought me out, with regular requests to have private talks about spiritual matters. They made polite but intrusive enquiries about my personal life (including a particular curiosity about any potential girl-friends), gave me exaggerated compliments, and displayed a persistent though entirely asymmetric attentiveness that seemed innocent enough at the time. This included sending regular Christmas and birthday cards (none of which were reciprocated), and from one of them years later a rather expensive wedding present, though we had not been in touch for some time and I had certainly never thought to invite him to the wedding. As I understood only later, these were not accidental encounters based on spontaneous affinity, but part of a strategy devised by Nash. He sought to recruit promising young men to the evangelical movement, in a Church of England that Nash believed to be straying dangerously from the path of biblical rectitude. I was not aware of such a mission, would never have been interested in one, and could not fathom why these two men kept mentioning my supposedly special talents since I could not see what use anyone might have for them. I eventually made clear to both men that I had no wish for these contacts to continue. But this was not before one of them had approached me late one night to voice his concerns that the Devil might be using me to undermine the faith of other participants with my skeptical questions during Bible study.

The strategy was unsuited to recruit me, but many men who went on to become influential in the Church of England, including Archbishop Justin Welby, had passed through the camps. John Smyth's grooming activities for his sadistic purposes therefore took place in a context in which adolescent boys were regularly approached by more senior men. This was for a different objective, but one that was never openly communicated to the targets of the attention, at least not until their suitability for recruitment had been patiently assessed and their determination tested. They might, if judged suitable, be taken gradually into the confidence of the leadership, in a way designed to make them feel flattered and grateful. Graystone's book describes in some detail the tactics used for such recruitment, and they are very familiar to me. They included the tendency to suggest to the targets that they should avoid an unwholesome interest in women. In addition to fomenting sexual guilt, these suggestions must also have convinced many recruits to discriminate later against women in their professional lives, having been persuaded to consider them a distraction.

It would often also be insinuated to potential recruits that they should be prepared for skepticism on the part of friends and family, which they should interpret as jealousy of their newfound enthusiasms. Such tactics have been reported in many other contexts, including political recruitment, recruitment of spies, recruitment to jihadi and other violent causes, and recruitment for special military missions.[20] Some movements (such as the Church of Scientology) have used them in more extreme form, such as by pressurizing some members to cut off contact with their immediate family, particularly family members who have left the movement.[21] However, it's the mark of a successful grooming strategy that it should rarely if ever need to make leaving difficult. Ideally, those who are unsuited for the movement should leave of their own accord, without ever realizing the movement's underlying mission. The fact that such tactics were used routinely in the Iwerne camps made it easy for Smyth to bend them to his own purposes. It may also have contributed to the eagerness of the Iwerne leaders, notably David Fletcher, to cover up reports of Smyth's activities when they first became aware of them in 1982, for fear that if his abuse became publicly known it would discredit the intense emotional infrastructure on which the experience of the camps was built.

Cultures of Secrecy, Cultures of Silence

If abusers are fortunately rare in most institutions, their actual or potential enablers are unfortunately much more common.[22] Understanding why this is so requires us to think about the difference between cultures of secrecy and cultures of silence. Cultures of secrecy prevent people who know something from talking about it to people who don't. They typically make information more valuable by giving insiders a strategic advantage against outsiders. Cultures of silence are different: they prevent two people who both know something from talking about it to each other. They typically make information less valuable by making it harder for insiders to act upon what they all know.

It's tempting to think that abuse flourishes in institutions that practice a culture of secrecy. It's true that many witness statements from victims of abuse report that their abusers swore them to secrecy. This seems natural to victims who are already used to there being secrets in the institution to which they belong. It's also true that when colleagues and friends discover the actions of the abuser their reaction is often to keep the matter a secret, in the supposed interest of the victims but more often to preserve the reputation of the institution. Still, more important than any of these is how often abuse has persisted despite its not being a secret at all. The essentials may be known to many people, but because of their inability to talk about it they are collectively powerless to act. It becomes, as Fintan O'Toole has said of the widespread physical and sexual abuse practiced in schools by the Christian Brothers in Ireland, "the thing that everybody knew and nobody grasped."[23] Many parents would warn their children against becoming too familiar with individual Christian Brothers, but because of the culture of silence (which extended to vast areas of intimate life), they could not discuss it with other parents, and parents collectively could not take action to prevent it. O'Toole again: "The violence of the Christian Brothers schools was itself inarticulate. Everybody knew about it, but almost no one could utter it without the stammers of euphemism and evasion."[24] Gerard Mannix Flynn wrote of his novel *Nothing to Say*, first published in 1983 and recounting in fictional form the story of a boy abused at a Christian Brothers school in Galway, that "they all knew that children were being sexually abused by those in authority; the government knew, the police knew, the clergy and religious knew, yet nobody could name it. They were afraid of their own shame, and conspired to deny and hide it."[25]

The abuse perpetrated by John Smyth was a secret initially between him and his victims, later kept a secret by the circle who had found out about it in 1982. But the atmosphere in the camps that facilitated the abuse was not a secret; instead, it was surrounded by a culture of silence. I certainly never spoke to other attendees, or to my parents or friends, about how creepy I found it. As the evidence of countless reports on abuse in other institutions has begun to reveal, while abuse may flourish in secrecy, the culture of silence enables abuse even when there are no longer any secrets. And the secrets may thereby persist for longer, since those who might have exposed them are prevented from doing so by the culture of silence. It's also likely that the strange passivity of those who knew the secret of John Smyth's behavior once he was, in their view, safely out of the country,[26] was in turn facilitated by an unspoken agreement not to discuss the matter among themselves more than was strictly necessary.[27]

Silence and secrecy are not necessarily bad. Some secrets are necessary, some are innocent and pleasurable, some (like professional secrecy) are the price to be paid for open and frank discussion among insiders. Silence may also be a welcome alternative to endless complaining about some of the difficulties and indignities of everyday life; many a trivial row between colleagues, friends, or lovers is best overcome by a tacit agreement not to speak about it again. Those who have lived through the opposite of cultures of silence—namely, cultures of denunciation, such as that which operated during China's Cultural Revolution—know that silence is too precious to be wished entirely away. But silence can also enable complicity, as John Smyth's case confirms.

Is there anything that makes religious organizations, compared with their secular equivalents, especially prone to either a culture of secrecy or a culture of silence? Nothing in the voluminous recent literature on abuse provides any reason to think so. While some have suggested (like Gerard Mannix Flynn) that certain religions cultivate shame with particular intensity, cultures of silence have enabled abuse in the movie and television industries, as well as in many other vigorously secular environments. If we want to understand what abusive environments have in common, we need to look at their organizational structure and the ordinary ways they function. Many religious organizations have structures and functions they have developed to compete very effectively for members, but which have the side-effect of making it harder to prevent abuse. Cultures of secrecy and cultures of silence, where they exist, are likely to be symptoms of other, deeper features that facilitate abuse.

Vulnerability and Power

Abuse is a type of behavior, but abusers are not a single type of person. Though there are some statistical predictors of abusive behavior (prior victims of abuse are indeed somewhat more likely than others to become abusers in turn, though the causal impact is weaker than is widely believed),[28] many people who engage in abusive behavior do so in response to opportunities. Those opportunities exist when a powerful person is placed in unsupervised proximity to another person who is vulnerable by reason of their age, of a relationship of dependence on the powerful person, or of physical or emotional weakness in relation to that person.[29] The powerful person need not be absolutely powerful in society—it could be someone like a babysitter, camp monitor, or young adult whose power exists purely relatively to the victim. The risks of abuse are greatly increased in such situations if the vulnerable person has no allies to whom they can turn, and if the powerful person enjoys legitimacy in their eyes, through status, reputation, or simply through a recognized authority to interpret rules in the community. They are also increased if the vulnerable person is represented as at fault in some way, or as belonging to a low-status or low-reputation group. The risks are

attenuated, though not removed, if the powerful person is a close biological relative (such as a parent or a sibling) of the vulnerable person. While
nuclear families are common sites of abuse, there is clear evidence that,
controlling for opportunity, stepfamilies are significantly higher sources
of risk—as are other human institutions that bring nonrelatives into
close and sustained contact.[30] Finally, though abusers are statistically
far more likely to be male than female, there are many documented
cases of female-perpetrated abuse, and the circumstances that facilitate
them do not appear to be radically different from those facilitating
abuse by men, though the motives may be.[31]

Religious organizations share with several types of secular organizations
some structural features and some ways of functioning that make abuse
particularly likely. Let's consider structural characteristics first. As we saw
in chapter 4, most religious organizations are not just clubs, delivering
services to members who enjoy them in a purely collective setting, as in
a movie theater. They are platforms, offering opportunities to their members to network with multiple other individuals—just the setting for
grooming to take place (and, freed of its abusive connotations, grooming
in the sense of close bilateral attentiveness between members of a community is an overwhelmingly positive good). Secondly, since members
opt in owing to their interest in spiritual matters, which are by nature
closely personal, many bilateral relationships involve communication
that, if not necessarily secret, tends to be discreet: people share with particular interlocutors things they would not share with just anyone, even
other members of their religious community. Thirdly, religious
organizations tend to have leaders whose power depends on their ability
to communicate and interpret a message; they therefore enjoy both charisma and legitimacy. When such leaders communicate with members
they don't do so just in plenary session. They also, and inevitably, have
many private, intimate, and therefore unsupervised conversations with
them, whether in a recognized role as a spiritual adviser or just because
members turn to them. Their charisma is precisely what makes them both
trusted and dangerous. An observation by researcher Erica Brown in relation to abuse in Jewish communities has a much wider application: "The
fact that a rabbi who abuses congregants or students in a youth group,

synagogue, or school setting may also be an acclaimed teacher or mesmerizing lecturer is not beside the point. It is the point."[32]

Next, as we saw in chapter 9, in large religious organizations (notably the Catholic Church), the higher leaders tend to give large amounts of discretion to leaders lower in the hierarchy (such as parish priests) and to be reluctant to countermand their judgment. That is not just an accidental feature of the way such organizations are structured, but one that reflects intrinsic features of the kind of work they do.[33] A related phenomenon is sometimes observed in relation to the way secular authorities interact with minority religious communities, sometimes simply "trust[ing] that the . . . community will police itself."[34] Finally, as we also saw in chapter 9, religious organizations are much less likely than businesses or other officially constituted organizations to have a structure whereby the leaders are formally accountable to outsiders—as happens routinely in large business, owing to its need to raise external capital for its operations. Formal accountability has many advantages, but one of the most important in this context is that it legitimates the asking of tough questions—and consequently enables breaches in a culture of silence. Not only do many religious organizations not have formal accountability, they often enjoy a degree of political protection from even informal accountability, through the reciprocal arrangements that we considered in chapter 10.

To these structural characteristics of religious organizations can be added several features of the way they commonly function. First, because the attraction of a religious movement is typically based on its community, there is usually much emphasis on the importance for members of maintaining the community's reputation.[35] The best way to do that is to behave in an exemplary fashion, at least according to the moral teachings of the movement—but the message easily shades into one that requires members not to speak ill of the movement, and especially not of its leaders. Thus do cultures of silence begin. Religious leaders often tend (whether unconsciously or deliberately) to interpret criticism of their conduct as hostility to their community, or even as hostility to religion itself. They may also preach obedience as an intrinsic virtue independently of the actions of the leader.

Secondly, because many religious rituals release strong emotions, leading to members' finding themselves in unusual and emotionally challenging states, participants are likely to be unable easily to judge what is "normal." Unusual or disturbing behavior toward them by a religious leader can easily be rationalized as part of the spiritually transformative process—especially when the leader is considered the legitimate interpreter of spiritual teachings. This is even more likely when the movement regularly authorizes its members to engage in ecstatic or other disinhibiting activity that authorizes overstepping what in other contexts are considered limits on respectable or appropriate behavior (to outsiders, women in the throes of charismatic possession may appear to be having an orgasm in public). In some religious traditions, certain practices may even be intentionally transgressive.[36] Even when transgression is not explicitly encouraged, there may be a convention that certain vices are no longer defiling for those who claim to have attained a level of spiritual achievement.[37] There may also be a shared understanding that, as Henry James Senior memorably expressed it, "the natural inheritance of every one who is capable of spiritual life, is an unsubdued forest where the wolf howls and every obscene bird of night chatters."[38]

Thirdly, because of the emphasis of many (though not all) religious movements on morality and sinfulness, it may be easy for some members and some leaders to think of vulnerable people as sinful, and therefore as not fully deserving the respect and compassion due to most others. Strong views of karma in the Hindu and Buddhist traditions can also lead believers to deny the possibility of undeserved suffering.[39]

Finally, there is the question of recruitment. There are two kinds of reason why individuals who are more likely than others to become abusers might find themselves in positions of responsibility in religious organizations. We can think of these as "pull" factors and "push" factors. Under "pull" factors we can include the range of motivations that drive individuals to want to work in positions of responsibility toward vulnerable people. In most cases these express empathy and compassion, but sometimes they may reflect a deliberate seeking out of potential victims. There's also a large gray area in between in which individuals who are unhappy in their sexuality may seek out the company of the young, the "innocent," and above all the unthreatening, while deceiving themselves and others about the likely consequences of prolonged interaction with such vulnerable people. Under "push" factors we can consider reasons why individuals who are uncomfortable in their sexuality might be ill at ease in standard secular occupations. Indeed, one plausible reason for the higher estimates of homosexuality among Catholic clergy than in the general population is that, in cultures that are generally intolerant of homosexuality, entering the Catholic priesthood may be the only way homosexuals can put an end to intrusive questions about why they have not yet married.[40] There's no statistical basis whatever for believing that homosexuals are more likely to be abusers than heterosexuals, but people who are sexually unhappy for whatever reason may find refuge in religion. That's no reason to question the entirely legitimate refuge that religion may provide, but it suggests that religious organizations need to be even more attentive than their secular counterparts to the risks this can pose to the vulnerable in their midst.

A moment's reflection should remind us that every one of these structural and behavioral features of religious organizations is shared by at least some secular organizations. There's certainly nothing intrinsic about abusers in religious organizations that makes them different from abusers elsewhere—so-called men of the cloth are cut from the same cloth as other men. Many artistic and sporting organizations are led by charismatic individuals whose legitimacy derives from success in the field to which the young and vulnerable now aspire. The very personal nature of coaching often leads them to have private and unsupervised interaction with the people in their care. In charitable organizations the people with whom leaders are in contact are often extremely dependent on those leaders, economically and perhaps for their physical safety. In charities, in the arts, and in team sports, maintaining reputation is often a priority, encouraging a culture of silence around the misgivings some may have about the behavior of others. The case of Jimmy Savile, subject of the Netflix documentary *A British Horror Story* in 2022,* who groomed and abused children over many decades in a context of high-profile

---

* Directed by Rowan Deacon.

charitable fundraising, illustrates in a secular setting all the characteristics that we've seen to favor abuse, including the cultures of both secrecy and silence.[41] Many more analogies could be drawn here, but the general point remains. Religious organizations are not uniquely open to abuse—far from it. But they do have characteristics that make them dangerously open to abuse. Both religious members and other members of society therefore have an interest in finding ways to reduce the risk that abuse will take place. How can this best be done?

Guidelines for Reducing the Risk of Abuse

The discussion so far suggests that, while the intrinsic characteristics of religious organizations make it unlikely the risk of abuse can ever be avoided entirely, there are many things that could be done to reduce the risk without undermining legitimate religious objectives. I'll focus on three: *denser networks, external accountability,* and *ending silence.*

Creating denser networks means giving vulnerable individuals more allies. These may be vertical allies (other people to turn to among the leadership) or horizontal allies (links to other members). There's no reason why any well-run religious organization needs to give its members access to just one spiritual adviser. Monopolies of access are harmful here just as they are harmful elsewhere. Members should be encouraged and entitled to discuss spiritual matters with more than one senior person in the organization. Senior people who have had unsupervised discussions with members should record that fact so that there is transparency about who is talking to whom. This does not avoid the risk of collusion between leaders; indeed, some abusive regimes (especially in residential institutions) have been enforced with the unflinching collaboration of all the senior staff. But it will sometimes deter abusive action before it becomes a shared habit. Similarly, in a well-run organization members will be encouraged to talk to other members, and to share with them their experiences of interacting with the leadership. This freedom should extend not just to informal discussion but also to the ability to contact, in confidence, representatives of the membership who are ready to discuss possible incidents of abuse. The leadership should let it be known without hesitation that such communication is healthy and desirable, and the sign of a well-functioning community.

Well-run organizations should do all these things, but what can members do in organizations that are badly run? This is where external accountability comes in. As we shall see in chapter 13, there's a strong case for imposing tough conditions on what religious organizations may do if they want to claim derogation from some of the duties that apply to other organizations that interact with the general public, such as firms. Among the conditions could be the establishment of an external reporting requirement. In addition to requiring religious organizations to provide information to others (about their revenues, for example), this would authorize external trustees to ask questions of the leadership, and would also authorize members with grievances to contact trustees. Not all grievances are legitimate, of course, but it's worth bearing some risk of dealing with allegations that are not well founded, in order to give adequate attention to grievances that are.

Neither of these kinds of structural reform will make much of a difference to abuse unless combined with a commitment to ending silence. No organization, religious or otherwise, should ever claim the right to be treated with unqualified awe. Open discussion among members of the organization's strengths and weaknesses should be considered the hallmark of an organization with sound values. This is easier said than done. Organizations that claim high authority should be willing to be held to high standards. But held to high standards by whom? The nature of religious organizations' responsibilities to the wider society in which they live will be one of the central themes of part IV.

Conclusion

The ground we've covered over the last twelve chapters yields a paradoxi-cal conclusion. Religion has deep roots in our evolutionary past, yet it has a remarkable capacity to change and develop in response to changes in the social environments in which it lives. It is precisely this capacity for change that has enabled religious movements to defy the skeptics who believed secularization would kill the demand for religion in the modern world. Secularization is a complex, multidimensional phenomenon, and it has undeniably left its mark on modern society. Yet religious organizations have adapted to meet its challenges. The key to their ability to do is has been their organization as *platforms*—structures that bring individuals together in mutually beneficial relationships that those individuals cannot easily bring about on their own. As individual needs evolve over time, so do the re-sources that religious organizations bring to bear upon them.

Religious organizations have shown themselves capable of winning the consent and enthusiastic participation of many billions of people across the world. In the process they have accumulated large amounts of economic, political, and social power. Sometimes that power is used wisely, sometimes not. What can we say about how the power of religious movements will interact with other forms of power in the twenty-first century? The question is too vast to answer comprehensively. Neverthe-less, in chapter 13, we look at three domains in which the history of reli-gious movements can help us to anticipate possible directions for their development in the future. These are the domains of technology, ideas, and relationships with secular sources of power—in particular, with democratic political institutions.

CHAPTER 13

The Past and Future of Religion

Due to unforeseen circumstances, clairvoyant Trisha will not be
appearing in the Kevin Bird Suite tomorrow night.

—announcement by Mansfield Town Football Club on September 15, 2016

The Challenges of Futurology

In 1969 an American Catholic priest called Andrew Greeley published
a book called *Religion in the Year 2000*, which contained several predictions about the next three decades of religion in America. Futurology
was a fashionable occupation in the 1960s, and it has become fashionable since then to mock predictions made at that time for their failure
to foresee developments that appear obvious to us in retrospect.
("Flying cars? Ridiculous! They didn't even foresee the smartphone!")
But *Religion in the Year 2000* was no ordinary book, and Greeley was
no ordinary priest. He was also a professor of sociology at the University
of Chicago, and six years after his foray into futurology he published the
first in a long series of novels that by the time of his death in 2013 led
the *National Catholic Reporter* to describe him as "probably the best-selling
priest-novelist of all time," netting an estimated $110 million in royalties
from his fiction alone.[1] Given that he also wrote more than eighty non-
fiction books, it would be natural to expect *Religion in the Year 2000* to
read in retrospect like a very lightweight work, scribbled out in an afternoon, of no interest except as a guide to the mood of the time.

Animal drawings in the Salon Noir, Grotte de Niaux, in southwest France. Though precise dating is uncertain, they appear to have been made between thirteen and fourteen thousand years ago. Note how the artists have used the natural features of the rock to add expression to the images—for example, where the cleft in the rock emphasizes the shoulder of the bison at the top right.
Credit: Jean-Marc Charles / agefotostock.

It would be natural, but it would be a mistake. *Religion in the Year 2000* contains predictions that look shrewd in retrospect, the more so because they ran against the wisdom of the time. There were predictions about the persistence of features of religion that were widely believed to be in terminal decline: "Religion will not lose its adherents . . . nor is religion likely to lose its 'influence.'"[2] "The sacred is not being replaced by the secular. . . . [R]eligious institutions will no more wither away than will the Marxist state."[3] He also predicted some changes that few others saw coming: "There will be a tremendous increase in the dialogue between religion and the social sciences."[4] "There will be much more emphasis in religion on personality development . . . and on the central role of sexuality in this development process."[5] "There will be . . . more sympathetic understanding of alternative religious traditions."[6] "There will be substantially more emphasis in religion on the nonrational . . . both the ecstatic and Dionysian nonrational and also the reflective and the contemplative and mystical nonrational. . . . [I]t will be much clearer . . . that the clergyman's role function . . . implies . . . development of his skills as an expressive and affectionate leader—a man who generates authentic personal warmth, trust, and reassurance."[7]

There were many things Greeley did not predict—notably, the increased involvement of religion in democratic as well as authoritarian politics (both in America and on the world stage), and the impact this might have on its legitimacy. He did not—in this book—foresee the crisis that would be provoked by the revelations of sexual abuse in the Church, though he did suggest that churches would be forced to adopt more "democratic and tolerant organizational theories and practices" in response to pressure from their members, and he would later become a pioneering campaigner on behalf of victims.[8] Greeley also underestimated the future importance of race and gender in shaping the interaction between religion and individual personality. Finally, his focus on America (and American Christianity at that) blinded him to many of the changes that were taking place in other religions and in the world outside North America, especially the doctrinal and organizational rifts that would open up between Churches in the global North and those in the global South.[9] Still, the points where he appears most perceptive are clearly not just due to lucky reading of the tea leaves. They arise from a reflective analysis of the weakness in the standard sociological view of secularization—which held that religion would decline because it was incompatible with science and rationality.[10] That view implied that in the modern world, increased mobility made it more and more difficult for religious believers to shield themselves from alternative views,[11] including those of rival religions. Not only competition with science but competition between religions would undermine both specific religions and religiosity in general.

Greeley observed, presciently, that many indicators of religiosity—orthodoxy rates, church membership, and church attendance rates—are higher in religiously pluralistic societies.[12] Confrontation between rival religions strengthens religiosity. He had several explanations for this, which are confirmed by arguments we've seen earlier in this book. First, independently of whether the conflict between science and religion is real, "the vast majority of human beings . . . have no desire to expose their religious convictions . . . to the threat that confrontation with a different set of convictions . . . might engender."[13] This is very much in line with what we saw in chapter 6. Secondly, Greeley believed that the functions of religion in providing a sense of meaning and a sense of belonging, functions whose importance had been emphasized by Weber and Durkheim respectively, could be provided to different degrees by secular rivals, and religion would remain strongest where secular alternatives were inadequate. For instance, countries with strong religious rivalry, where religious organizations that supplied their members with meaning also had a function in signaling identity, would have higher religiosity than countries where identity was signaled by other institutions, notably class-based ones.[14]

If secularization can be summarized as the theory that modernity leads to declining religiosity, its core weakness as a general theory of social change can be simply stated. Both modernity and religiosity are not single phenomena, but bundles of different though related phenomena, which sometimes occur together and sometimes diverge. Even if there are regular social processes underlying them, whether and how modernity affects religiosity will therefore depend on which aspects of modernity we are considering, and which aspects of religiosity. *Some* dimensions of modernity may have an impact on *some* kinds of religiosity. We saw in chapter 11 that whether gender affects religiosity depends on which aspects of religiosity we are considering, and we should expect no less when we ask the same question about modernity.

Overall, Greeley's futurology appears most accurate where he emphasizes the role of religion as conveying much more than beliefs. Religion provides people with narrative meanings and a sense of belonging to a community, delivered by powerful rituals and by carefully nurtured links between individual members, other members of their community, and religious leaders. These were, he believed, age-old functions of religion that had never lost their importance and were unlikely to do so any time soon. His forecasts were less accurate when he projected forward assumptions about other institutions and behaviors in society that interact with religion—notably, political institutions and behaviors.

That's a lesson we can take to heart today. The past can tell us about the eternal human needs to which religion speaks. What's harder to foresee is the extent to which modern societies can develop alternative ways to minister to those needs.

Sensitivity to how religion may develop in the future is necessary even to start thinking about its place in society today. Even if someone were to tell us that predicting the future has always been a waste of time, concluding that it will continue to be a waste of time in the coming decades would itself be an exercise in futurology. In a spirit of modest and careful futurology, therefore, we'll consider in the following sections three factors that will affect how the other institutions of modern societies interact with religious organizations. In each case we'll see how past developments might give us insight into future possibilities. These factors are technology, ideas, and secular political institutions. We begin with technology.

Religion and Technology

In July 2022 the writer and venture capitalist Matthew Ball published a book called *The Metaverse: And How It Will Revolutionize Everything*, which rapidly became a US and international bestseller. The Metaverse, described by *Wikipedia* as "a single, universal and immersive virtual world,"[15] has been widely acclaimed as the next fundamental stage in the evolution of the internet, one in which many forms of virtual reality become a part of everyday life. Ball's book about this unquestionably important technological and social phenomenon is a page-turner. It begins with the mystery about what the Metaverse even is. Ball tantalizes his readers through an introduction and two chapters with hints about what the Metaverse is not, or is nearly but not quite. He refers to the prophetic ideas of various earlier writers, such as Stanley G. Weinbaum, who in a short story published in 1931, entitled "Pygmalion's Spectacles," imagined "the invention of magical virtual reality-like goggles that produced a 'movie that gives one sight and sound. . . . [Y]ou are in the story, you speak to the shadows, and the shadows reply, and instead of being on a screen, the story is all about you, and you are in it.'"[16] At last, in chapter 3, Ball introduces a definition of the Metaverse: "A massively scaled and interoperable network of real-time rendered 3D virtual worlds that can be experienced synchronously and persistently by an effectively unlimited number of users with an individual sense of presence, and with continuity of data, such as identity, history, entitlements, objects, communications, and payments."[17] The definition makes up in precision what it lacks in poetry compared with Weinbaum's description, but both Weinbaum's story and Ball's definition reveal something striking. Shorn of the references to digital technologies, the experience of the Metaverse is something that religion has been offering its participants in analog form for many thousands of years.

We all enter virtual reality when we dream, which is something other mammals do, and therefore has very ancient evolutionary roots. But we have almost no control over what we do there, though we spend a lot of time trying to interpret our experiences to ourselves afterward. Building virtual worlds that we can control has a more recent heritage, and is entirely a product of cultural evolution, over thousands rather than millions of years. You can still enter—really, not virtually—one of the earliest virtual worlds we know to have been created collectively by human beings, and that can still be visited by the general public. It lies about half a mile inside a limestone hillside in the foothills of the Pyrenees in southwest France, close to a village called Niaux. Beginning around fourteen thousand years ago, and continuing over nearly a thousand years, a succession of highly talented artists came into this large complex of caves and, working by the light of flickering wooden torches, left paintings of many animals, including bison, horses, ibex, and deer. There are many mysteries about their presence in this place that are unlikely ever to be resolved, including the puzzle that we see so many highly skilled paintings (which often exploit features of the rock surface to enhance the expressiveness of the animal shapes) and no real duds. To put it simply—how did they stop incompetent novices and vandals from coming in to deface their work?

However, there's one question to which we can reasonably guess the answer, which is why they chose this particular place for their artistic expression. There's a special spot in the Salon Noir, the largest of the caves and the one that contains the most and the greatest images. If, after taking in the presence of these majestic animals in the torchlight, you stand precisely at that special spot and sing a note, you can hear its echo reverberate for many seconds. The deeper the note, the more profoundly satisfying are the echoes. They feel oceanic, and the least religious among us would have difficulty hearing them without experiencing a sense of awe. You sing to the shadows, and the shadows reply. And instead of being just on a painted wall, the story is about you, and you are in it.

The cave at Niaux is a transformative virtual world. Others even older exist, like the Chauvet cave in the Ardèche department of France, whose paintings, including images of rhinos, bears, and lions, date back some thirty-six thousand years. Unfortunately, the Chauvet cave can be seen by the general public only in replica form, which (though still a fascinating experience) makes it harder to experience the range of immersive emotions our ancestors must have felt. There's controversy, which will almost certainly never be settled, about whether the people who made such paintings shared other features of a religious sensibility, including a feeling for ritual.[18] Whether or not they did, their creativity inspired ingenious entrepreneurs throughout the world, who worked hard over the succeeding millennia to extend the possibilities of virtual reality and to bring it under greater control by its participants.

These inventors developed technological innovations in architecture, biochemistry, music and dance, writing, painting, rhetoric, and social organization to offer a range of experiences that built on those profound moments that a lucky few among their ancestors had been able to experience inside caves. In architecture they built dolmens, stone circles, temples, mosques, and cathedrals (some of them still in caves, like the Buddhist grottoes at Yungang near Datong in China, or the Hindu, Buddhist, and Jain cave temples at Ellora in India, or the monolithic Christian churches at Lalibela in Ethiopia). They discovered a wide range of mind-altering molecules, from ethanol to mescaline, that had large direct effects on the brain chemistry of those who inhaled or ingested them. They explored the possibilities of dozens more substances, from jasmine to sandalwood to incense, that stimulated taste and smell receptors in pleasurable and evocative ways. They found ways to provoke endorphin release by extreme physical stresses, including some that involved potentially life-threatening injury. They experimented with combined stimulations of the senses of sight, sound, and smell to create truly alternative experiences. They trained the voices of their participants through various collective exercises to sing in unison or harmony, and to allow the sensations induced by the singing to be deepened by triggering memories. They developed musical notation to transmit successful musical innovations to others. They combined music with movement to create dance. They learned to paint and carve in a range of media, from wood to bone to sandstone to fresh plaster to canvas to glass. They made innovations in rhetoric so their visual representations could be accompanied by commentary. They invented flexible forms of symbolic notation that could be used not just for keeping accounts or for promulgating laws but for recording that commentary. They developed ways of reproducing their notation so that instead of being carved in clay or stone it might be scratched on papyrus or parchment, and eventually printed in movable type. They used these methods to create hierarchies of texts, and they invented hypertext when these texts increasingly harbored references to other texts (known as "prophecies"). They created virtual worlds with these tools, they scaled them massively, and—despite repeated attempts to establish monopolies—they made them increasingly interoperable. One of the few things they didn't invent before the Metaverse was the silicon chip.

Virtual reality retains its power because we dive into it and return, refreshed and inspired. It's a complement to normal life, not a substitute for it. It's the more powerful for making us giddy, often unable to remember on which side of the boundary we currently float, like those delicious moments in the early mornings when we are both in our beds and out of them. It's no less real than the unvirtual kind of reality, so long as we remember that it's a form of reality we navigate differently from the unvirtual kind. Our ancestors could approach a bear or a lion more safely if it was painted on a cave wall than if it had wandered into the cave looking for a meal. Contemplating the images on the wall might even have made them more respectful of the creatures they would meet outside. Plato was not the first, nor the last human being to wonder what might happen if he could manage somehow to turn his gaze away from the shadows on the wall.

Most of this book has been about the innovations in *social* organization that underlie the way in which modern religion works. It deals therefore with only a few of the *technological* innovations underlying the great analog metaverse that is religion in the modern world. But it's worth reviewing, if only briefly, just how radical some of those other technological innovations have been. Social organization is itself a form of technology, which some entrepreneurs can copy from others. Both orthodoxy and heresy can spread much faster than if they had to be reinvented afresh by every religious entrepreneur. Effective social organizations also use innovations in other technologies to extend their reach, as when the invention of printing allowed Protestant movements to escape the control of the Catholic Church in a way the Cathars had been unable to do two hundred years before.[19] Meeting together to read the Bible in the vernacular provided a focus and an inspiration for dissident groups that the Cathars had never enjoyed, as well as giving credibility to the message that religious individuals no longer needed priests as intermediaries with the Almighty. The cost of access to the word had fallen, and the Word was with God, and the Word was God, as the Gospel of Saint John reassuringly told the faithful. Technology is always disruptive, as Cuthbert Tunstall, Catholic bishop of London and then successor to Cardinal Wolsey as bishop of Durham, foretold when he said: "We must root out printing or else printing will root out us."[20]

The disruption inflicted by new technology happens because some groups in society can work well with it—their activities are complementary to what the technology does—while other groups find themselves displaced by it—the technology is a substitute for what they do. That's true of how robots will affect the future of work in the twenty-first century (they will be a complement to the work of some, and a substitute for the work of others).[21] And it was true of how printing affected the future of religion after the invention of the movable-type press by Johannes Gutenberg in Mainz, in Germany, in the mid-fifteenth century CE. In Christian Europe, printing made it cheaper to own copies of the Bible, including translations from Latin into the languages most people spoke. It therefore substituted for the work of two kinds of people who had previously enjoyed high status and demand for whose services now began to fall: the monks in their scriptoria, who had copied out the texts, and the priests, who through their ability to read Latin had conveyed the meaning of those texts to the faithful. But though ordinary people could now either read the texts or at least understand them when they were read aloud in a church service, they still needed help to interpret them and set them in the context of their daily lives. So there were other people whose skills were complementary to the new technology—religious leaders who had enough learning to read the Bible in the vernacular and who could help the faithful make sense of the texts. Demand for their services went up, sometimes dramatically so. Historian Andrew Pettegree's exploration of the creation of "brand Luther" in the years after 1517 shows how the communicative talents of this German professor proved ideally complementary to the technology of printing.[22]

All significant technological innovations favor some groups while displacing others, but some innovations are particularly disruptive because they change radically the scale at which social organizations can most effectively operate. We can see this even at the simple level of the development of language, which allowed the codification of messages that founders of religious movements could transmit to followers who could not be present with them. Describing the organizational features that gave momentum to the breakaway Pomio Kivung movement in Papua New Guinea that we saw in chapter 5, Harvey Whitehouse writes:

> If the Pomio Kiving had been based around mass gatherings, it would have disintegrated rapidly as people ran out of food and other basic necessities. Koriam [the founder] somehow had to come to the people, rather than they to him, if the movement was to be constructed on solid and enduring foundations. A particularly effective way in which a few individuals can spread a movement across dispersed populations is through words, whether in the form of sacred texts or orations (or both).[23]

It will not be surprising, therefore, to note how other technologies of communication, from writing to printing to mobile telephony, have been changing the effective structure of religious organizations along-side those of other institutions in society. Printing meant, for example, that new religious movements could now compete with the Catholic Church at a smaller scale than had been possible before.

Writing only months after the fall of the Berlin Wall in 1989, econo-mist Leonard Dudley identified eight technical innovations that had had massive historical impact through changing the effective scale at which political entities such as states and empires could operate. Four were technologies that transformed communication: writing, printing, the mass media, and the integrated circuit. He believed the first three had increased the efficient scale of the state, while the fourth was in the process of reducing it (a fact that in his view explained the changes that were leading to the breakup of the communist bloc—he was writing before the Chinese government's development of mass surveillance techniques using artificial intelligence). The other four innovations high-lighted by Dudley were technologies that had transformed warfare: metal weapons, heavy cavalry, gunpowder, and the steam engine. He believed that all of these except heavy cavalry had increased the effective scale of political organizations.[24] Dudley did not apply his insights specifically to religion, but we've already seen how writing and printing affected the structure of religious movements. As well as enabling the wider distribu-tion of primary texts such as the Bible and the Quran, they have facili-tated an explosion of secondary texts, including religious commentaries and neoscriptures such as *The Book of Mormon* and *The Divine Principle* of Sun-Myung Moon. The internet has given new energy to this profu-sion of secondary texts, along with audiovisual recordings of the sermons of rabbis, pastors, priests, and imams across the globe.

Dudley's fourth great communications innovation, the integrated circuit, is what has launched the internet and is enabling the Metaverse. It is lowering dramatically the costs of creating new religious experi-ences, including new texts: algorithms are already capable of creating neoscriptures that are indistinguishable from those written by human beings, and virtual reality will enable individuals to customize their own mystical or ritual experience without having to depend on intermediar-ies such as priests, pastors, rabbis, gurus, or imams. Important questions still arise about whether internet gatekeepers might be able to monopolize access to the Metaverse, but that doesn't mean they would find it easy to control which types of content flourish within it. The ecosystem of religious experience is about to be shaken up as radically as happened in the Reformation.

Does this mean that the days of human intermediaries are over? Not at all. The dramatic fall in the costs of making musical recordings has raised, not lowered, the price of tickets to see artists performing live. Bands used to go on tour to promote their albums; now they distribute their albums to promote their concert tours. Similarly, the improvement in the quality of affordable reproductions of artworks has seen the prices soar at auctions of authenticated originals. Digital reproductions are often complements to, not substitutes for, analog creative products. In the same way, we are likely to see that the Metaverse increases the marketability of live religious experience. Being able to meditate, pray, chant, and worship in virtual reality will make people even more excited to be present in a real religious community. Not all religious leaders, nor all religious communities, will flourish in this environment, but they will certainly not all be displaced by virtual avatars. There's every reason to think digital virtual reality is complementary to the analog virtual kind, not a substitute for it—just as virtual reality itself is a complement to everyday life, not a substitute for it. That was true in the prehistoric caves, and it's no less true today.

Because technological innovation has ambivalent effects on currently powerful people and groups, it's not easy to predict who will welcome and who will resist innovation. That explains the historical paradox that powerful religious movements have often been hostile to science and technology, but have also been responsible for a great deal of innovation (as we saw in the case of architecture, writing, and the other foundations of the analog Metaverse). Just like powerful monopolies in other secular fields, they can often deliver the resources, the focus, and the coordination that some innovations require. It's no accident, for example, that Catholicism in Europe in its centuries of monopoly produced far greater architecture than the vigorously competitive Protestant movements. With the rarest of exceptions, the Gothic revolution in church architecture was never matched by anything built under any Protestant regime—and the most obvious exception, Saint Paul's Cathedral, was built by and for the glory of a religious monopoly that happened to be Protestant. The contrast between Catholic and Protestant contributions to architecture is even more striking when we consider the churches built during the Counter-Reformation, when both movements existed side by side in German-speaking central Europe.

Similarly, for all that many influential figures in the Catholic Church were suspicious of printing, it was thanks to the monasteries (as well as to the scientific institutions of the Islamic world, particularly in Baghdad, between the ninth and twelfth centuries CE)[25] that so many texts from antiquity had survived to be printed at all.[26] But like those secular monopolies, religious movements tend to be suspicious of innovations they don't control, or whose consequences are wider than they can foresee. Their suspicion is often communicated to and shared by their members. Economists Roland Bénabou, Davide Ticchi, and Andrea Vindigni have shown that measures of personal religiosity at the country or US state level tend to be negatively correlated with the intensity of patenting (which is a measure of the success of industrial innovation). They are also negatively correlated at the individual level with a range of attitudes toward science and technology, risk-taking, and innovation.[27] Eric Chaney has documented the clear decline in the proportion of written works in scientific fields in the Islamic world after the establishment of madrasas (Islamic educational institutions) in the mid- to late eleventh century CE and an increase in the proportion of authors affiliated with them.[28] Jeanet Bentzen and Lars Harhoff Andersen have shown that Christian individuals in Europe from the fourteenth century onward who were given the names of saints or biblical figures were more likely to be religious (as measured by a greater probability of studying theology or becoming a priest). But they were *less* likely than others to become doctors, engineers, scientists, and chemists, and less likely to proceed with advanced studies.[29] What the work of these different researchers has in common is the suggestion that when religious movements find it easy to prevent technological innovation that threatens their doctrinal orthodoxy, they will tend to do so—both by explicit prohibition and by encouraging their members to regard such innovation with suspicion. If they can't prevent it, they will tend to adapt their doctrine to make it compatible with the innovation that is going to occur anyway. Their arguments corroborate Adam Smith's views that religious capture of political power is not only bad for society as a whole but also makes religious movements more sluggish and conservative than they would otherwise be.

These considerations suggest it would be futile to look for evidence of a general impact of any specific religion, let alone of religion in general, on innovation.[30] Just as modernity and religiosity are multidimensional phenomena, so is innovation. Some kinds of religion have had a positive impact on some kinds of innovation, while some other kinds of religion have had a negative impact on some other kinds of innovation. To take two examples of careful empirical studies from the recent literature by economists, a study by Yuyu Chen, Hui Wang, and Se Yan finds a persistent positive long-run effect on economic growth in China of Protestant missionary work in late nineteenth-century China, operating both through investments in health and education and through effects on social values.[31] A contrasting finding is by Mara Squicciarini, who examined the introduction of technical education in primary schools in late nineteenth-century France, where technology was becoming more dependent on worker skills, and where secular state schools competed with private Catholic schools. She found that places where Catholicism was strong had lower enrolment in state schools, slower adoption of the technical curriculum, and lower levels of industrial development (controlling for other factors) beginning around ten to fifteen years later.[32] The contrast between these findings for China and for France almost certainly has nothing to do with doctrinal differences between Protestantism and Catholicism. It has a great deal to do with the fact that Christian missionaries in China were new arrivals in a very different religious landscape, while Catholic institutions in France represented an establishment tradition with an eroding monopoly to defend.

Science and technology are often associated not just with innovation but with unpredictable or general-purpose innovation, which is the kind that monopolies, both religious and secular, fear the most. Specific innovations like vaccines, which have a predictable application with little risk of unforeseen consequences, can often be encouraged by religious movements, as Sheilagh Ogilvie has shown in the case of many historical pandemics.[33] As she shows, this can make a real difference to the behavior of the faithful, and in situations like pandemics that can in turn make a tangible difference to the outcomes that matter for people's health and happiness. This leads us to a more general question: How important are religious ideas anyway? It's one thing for religious leaders to promote or resist technologies in fields such as architecture, communications, or medicine. It's another for them to promote general ideas. When they do so, do they really have a major impact on society?

Religion and Ideas

It's much harder to trace the impact of new ideas on a society than to spot the presence of tangible technologies. We can count the number of printing presses or steam engines, but how can we measure attitudes like openness to innovation, especially at times in history before the development of questionnaires or experimental methods for probing such attitudes? The scholar's standby is to see how often an idea features in the work of earlier scholars, but that presupposes that the idea is influential if it is taken up by scholars, which is precisely what is in question. To illustrate the challenges of measuring the impact of ideas, we'll briefly consider three ideas that are widely thought to have marked out the modern world: the idea of atomism, the idea of individualism, and the idea of a scientific method.

Atomism, the philosophy that the physical world is composed of a vast number of indivisible units called atoms, has very ancient roots. It was a central tenet of the Charvaka school of philosophy in India in the sixth century BCE, and was developed independently in fifth-century Greece by Leucippus and his pupil Democritus, then by Epicurus in the early third century, in opposition to the view of Aristotle that matter was continuous (which was to become the dominant view in Europe in the later Middle Ages). Also apparently independently, atomism was a central tenet of the Chinese Mohist school of philosophy that flourished in the fourth century BCE.[34] Atomism died out in China, but became influential once again in Europe from around the mid-sixteenth century CE, thanks largely to the work of the Roman philosopher Lucretius, whose poem *De rerum natura* addressed, in the words of historians Monte Johnson and Catherine Wilson, "a range of scientific subjects: nutrition, perception and mental illness; cosmology, the seasons and eclipses; thunder, clouds and the magnet; the emergence and evolution of animal and vegetable life; contagion, poisoning and plague." Since the central aim of that poem "was to demolish religious belief and banish superstitious fear," the poem "provoked both fascination and alarm."[35] But how much of an impact did it have on modern thinking? And did the attitude of the Church have any influence in either resisting or assisting that impact?

There's no serious scholarly dispute that atomism in general, and Lucretius's defense of it in particular, were much cited and read by scientists and by humanist scholars from the seventeenth century onward (though evidence for Lucretius's influence before then is contested).[36] Atomism was, in that sense, enormously influential. But it's almost impossible to know whether those scientists who cited Lucretius approvingly (including such figures as Robert Boyle and Isaac Newton) were doing so because he had caused them to look favorably on atomism and to change their scientific world view in consequence. It's possible instead that they were citing him in support of views that they had reached independently for other reasons. This is what Johnson and Wilson suggest when they write that "the experimental philosophers sought specifically an ancient metaphysics upon which to declare their practices grounded in order to convey upon them the dignity of philosophy, elevating chemistry from a merely mechanical practice."[37] Furthermore, both Boyle and Newton were disturbed by the irreligious tone of Lucretius's poem, from which they sought to distance its purely scientific content. This makes it unlikely that the attitude of the Church had much influence either way on the manner in which atomism entered into their scientific thought. Boyle and Newton accepted the Church's view on Lucretius's religious arguments, but pursued his scientific arguments anyway.

Similarly, we don't know whether atomism influenced thinkers to become more innovative, or whether it was more-innovative thinkers who were more open to accepting atomism. The sinologist Joseph Needham suggested that the fading out of atomistic philosophy in China might have led scientists to become less interested in mechanical exploration of causes, and might therefore explain China's lagging technologically behind the West:

> The Chinese physical universe in ancient and medieval times was a perfectly continuous whole. *Chhi* condensed into tangible matter was not in any significant sense composed of particles, but individual objects acted and reacted with all other objects in the world. Such mutual influences could be effective over very great distances, and worked in a wave-like or vibration-like manner dependent in the last resort on the rhythmic alternation at all levels of the two fundamental forces, the Yin and the Yang. . . . So dominant in Chinese thought was the idea of wave motion that it seems sometimes to have acted as a brake on the advance of scientific knowledge.[38]

The argument seems plausible enough, until you reflect that China was more technologically advanced than Europe for much of the medieval period; there are ample reasons for its subsequent relative decline in the vagaries of imperial policy (such as the ban on seafaring missions after the last voyage of Admiral Zheng He) without appealing to the cultural impact of the Yin and the Yang. Needham was not necessarily wrong, but there are plenty of other explanations for the Chinese technological stagnation. It's hard to know what kind of evidence might serve to settle the matter.

Similar difficulties arise in assessing the impact of other widely discussed ideas, such as "individualism" and "science." Few people would contest that the citizens of a reasonably prosperous society in the twenty-first century face a spectacularly wider range of choices in their daily lives than did their forebears in, say, the eleventh century. They are also freer to decide for themselves whether to bow to religious authority in exercising such choices. To what extent is that because of the spread of an ideology called "individualism," as opposed to the word "individualism" being just an abstract noun used to sum up what has happened? The case that "individualism" was an idea whose spread caused important social changes has indeed been argued vigorously—for example, by anthropologist and historian Alan Macfarlane and economic historian Deirdre McCloskey.[39] Some of its most influential proponents have claimed that, far from resisting individualism, the Christian Church was at the origin of the value given to individual freedom, which it asserted against the received authority of the extended family (McCloskey herself is skeptical, considering bishops to have been hostile to the bourgeois values of enterprise and innovation, and the Christian record on slavery to be at best mixed).[40] Historian Larry Siedentop has argued that Christianity, both as a body of doctrine and as a social movement, shaped the ideas that would later become the philosophy of liberalism (and would often be used against the Church by its critics).[41] Paradoxically, therefore, it was a philosophy grounded on religious authority that would eventually grant the individual the legitimacy to question authority, and to demand that submission to authority should be justified. Other historians have claimed, following an argument due originally to anthropologist Jack Goody, that the critical innovations were not ideas as such but the imposition of a set of rules governing the family, initiated by Pope Gregory I in the late sixth century CE.[42] These rules encouraged late female marriage, high female celibacy, the prohibition of marriage between cousins, and the formation of nuclear households after marriage, features that have come to be known as the European marriage pattern. This second set of claims has been much debated,[43] and the debate illustrates the difficulty of ascribing causality to a set of ideas rather than to a form of behavior that may not be the result of the adoption of the ideas at all.

In the same spirit, we can ask to what extent the decline of certain beliefs in magic since the Middle Ages has to do with the development of science.[44] The alternative is that the development of science is a term we use to describe a family of practices that includes a shift in the kinds of explanation people are willing to envisage for everyday phenomena. In the closing sentence of his book *Religion and the Decline of Magic*, Keith Thomas writes that "if magic is to be defined as the employment of ineffective techniques to allay anxiety when effective ones are not available, then we must recognize that no society will ever be free from it."[45] If we take his suggestion seriously, we should conclude that magic does not decline throughout history so much as regroup. It's a word that changes its reference over time to describe a different set of behaviors. Asking to what extent religion advances or retards science in general is equally unlikely to yield much insight. Religion has not so much retreated before science as regrouped, addressing questions that the progress of science (which is real, and of massive importance)[46] has failed to address adequately in the eyes of its adherents, questions of which there is an inexhaustible supply. Religious organizations have sometimes encouraged developments in science, and have sometimes been their enemy. But the two are destined to cohabit the earth for the foreseeable future.

Summing up, therefore, we can identify historical examples of religious organizations either helping or hindering technological innovation, which they did according to their own interests, in much the same way as secular organizations did. It's much harder to discern a systematic impact of religion on ideas such as atomism, individualism, and science. The problem lies in the fact that such ideas were also profoundly shaped by underlying economic and social phenomena like migration, the development of trading networks, education, and the development of modern states. It's fun—absorbing and fascinating, even—to speculate about such developments, but at this state of knowledge to speculate is the most it's possible to do.

We now consider the way in which religion has been and will be shaped by interactions with the secular authority of the modern state.

Religion and Secular Authority: How Can Religious Power Become More Accountable?

Human social life is a continual negotiation between those who want to impose obligations on others and those who want to resist them. These may be obligations to work (or otherwise offer the pain of one's body or mind), pay taxes (or other valuable resources), and grant esteem (or otherwise engage in symbolic submission). It's made more complicated than a simple trial of force when the obligations are imposed in the name of a general principle from which all will benefit. Human beings are more likely to accept obligations if they can be persuaded that the general principle is reasonable, and applies to others as well as themselves. We don't know exactly why this is so, but even capuchin monkeys become angry when they see themselves doing less well out of a transaction than their fellow animals,[47] and human beings have a similar sensitivity to injustice, to a highly developed degree.

Knowing this, powerful people who want to profit from imposing obligations on others know they will find it easier to do so if they appeal to general principles (though they often find ways to claim that the principles do not apply to themselves). Less powerful people can defend themselves not individually but in coalition, and human beings show a particular talent, compared with other animal species, for forming coalitions to limit the depredations of the powerful.[48] Those coalitions are often inspired by general principles too, since the people taking part in them are often exposed to significant personal risk. A world in which a gangster takes money by threatening to kill a victim is different from a world in which a ruler takes money by appealing to the legitimacy of that demand. Legitimacy is established under a general principle that also imposes some obligations—usually different ones—on the ruler, obligations that someone other than the ruler will have to ensure are respected. The world of the gangster and the world of the legitimate ruler have a fuzzy boundary between them, as Clausewitz and many others observed, but only the second can properly be described as the domain of politics.

Much of the political life of human societies in the last half millennium has involved negotiations around principles that were *transactional*. People become citizens by submitting to the authority of political leaders, and by doing so they expect to be better off than if nobody agreed to submit. Obligations are justified in return for benefits. This idea underlies the tradition in political theory that began with Thomas Hobbes. It was a tradition that argued vigorously over the precise principles, and especially about how to think of people who were not doing well out of the status quo—slavery provided the most glaring anomaly, since slaves had not chosen their state. But the condition of the working classes in the crowded cities of industrializing Europe provided a glaring contrast to the fortunes made by their employers, even if migration to the cities was evidence that urban squalor was preferred to rural misery.

Soon after Hobbes, who had argued that submission to the monarchy (any monarchy) was preferable to the state of nature—the "war of all against all"—other writers realized that it was also important to think about how the powerful might be constrained. It was all very well for them to promise benefits in exchange for the citizens' fulfilling their obligations, but what if they never delivered? The result is that general principles that are transactional rest not just on a moral foundation but on a practical and political one. If you accept the authority of certain leaders, it's because they offer a reasonable bargain from which citizens can benefit, and the system is set up so that they will keep their side of the bargain. In democratic systems, for example, if you don't think they've done so, you can vote to throw them out. This does not presuppose that voters are transactional in their decision-making—indeed, the evidence is strong that many citizens exercise their vote in ways that express their identity rather than seek to make themselves better off.[49] It claims only that the justification of obligations in terms of general principles must appeal to the benefits that such principles can bring, not to some other mystical source of authority.

The point that powerful leaders needed to be constrained applied also to leaders who were economically powerful, whether or not they were politically powerful as well (though of course they often were). It came to be considered unacceptable that a landowner should enjoy a vastly better standard of living than the peasants who worked on the land. Solutions to the disparity could come in the form of taxes if landowners were cooperative, and expropriation or the guillotine if they were not. The unacceptability extended not just to results but to processes and behaviors: the powerful could not use their power in whatever way they wanted—for example, in evicting tenants for nonpayment of rent after a failed harvest. As industrialization proceeded, it became clear that owning or managing a business could give some people even more power than owning or managing land. So the project of controlling the powerful extended both to the results (taxation of high incomes) and to the processes that generated those results (regulating the way in which workers in those businesses were treated). Control of powerful businesses and their leaders is, of course, an eternal struggle, in which the powerful find ever-more ingenious ways to evade taxes and regulations, or turn them to their advantage (for example, by using them to exclude competitors), especially if those taxes and regulations have been poorly conceived and designed. But the basic legitimacy of political control of businesses and their leaders is broadly agreed across the political spectrum, except on the radical fringes.

Political systems constructed on transactional general principles have become ubiquitous in the modern world. It's easy to forget that, for centuries before the world of Thomas Hobbes, the relations between rulers and their subjects were governed by general principles that were not transactional at all. We can call these principles *consecrational* (according to the *Oxford English Dictionary* the word does not exist, but it should). Subjects were supposed to submit to rulers not just because the rulers had the power to command it but because it was legitimate for them to command it, as their power was blessed (consecrated) by God, or the gods. And how were people supposed to know that God (or the gods) had blessed the rulers' power? They had it on the authority of the rulers themselves, of course, or of those religious leaders who had agreed to lend the rulers their legitimacy. It's easy for the modern reader to scoff at the circularity and self-serving nature of these justifications. But to the inhabitants of a turbulent and unpredictable world through which the apocalyptic horsemen thundered daily, anything that promised stability, however fleeting, must have been hard to refuse. That's not to say they were credulous—as we've seen, they faced a dizzying array of spiritual entrepreneurs in their daily lives, many of whom were inevitably tricksters and charlatans or simply incompetent even by their own standards, so they had to be skeptical to survive. But the skepticism they could afford was very different from what the modern reader can take for granted. Consecrational general principles of political legitimacy could be accepted, in part because transactional principles had not become philosophically or politically available—although, as Larry Siedentop argued, it was perhaps through prior religious jurisprudence that the very idea of transactional principles could ever have been developed.[50]

Surprisingly, though, consecrational principles are still widely held to apply to businesses that operate in the domain of religion even today, and consecrational arguments are used in debates about the policies that modern states should adopt. Let's look first at the status of religious businesses. In all industrialized countries and in most others, any group of people who organize themselves to take money from the general public must adopt a legal form that justifies this activity. If they don't, the money they receive risks being treated as their personal income, liable to tax at much higher rates than businesses typically pay. The legal form may be that of a limited-liability corporation, a particularly effective mechanism for encouraging investment in the activity, since it avoids the investors' being held personally liable for the risks the corporation undertakes and the debts it incurs. It may take the form of a partnership, or a sole proprietorship. It may take the form of a not-for-profit organization or foundation. This last is a somewhat misleading terminology, since what distinguishes not-for-profit organizations is not that they don't make profits (they do, once profits are defined as the excess of revenues over costs), but rather that they're not allowed to distribute profits to their owners or trustees. These and other legal forms vary in the kinds of obligations they impose on the activities concerned. But they share the notion that taking money from the general public justifies imposing obligations on the people who run the activities. These obligations sometimes include the payment of taxes, and always include some duty of transparency, in the form of reporting information about their activities, and the publishing of accounts. Unless, that is, the activities are religious.

The exemption for religion varies from country to country, and applies differently to questions of taxation and to questions of reporting. In all countries that have a tax exemption for charities, religious organizations can apply for charitable status. This means they never need to pay tax on their revenues, and are typically exempt from paying other levies such as property taxes, as well as being exempt from paying sales taxes on their purchases. In nine European countries including Germany, Sweden, and Iceland, not only do churches pay no tax but the government actively collects taxes on their behalf, most commonly by asking citizens to indicate their religious affiliation on a tax declaration. Often it's only the official churches that benefit from this, but in some countries, such as Iceland, any registered religion can benefit. This has led to some incongruous outcomes, including the establishment of an Icelandic movement called Zuism, which claims to be a religion whose members are exclusively atheists and agnostics opposed to the payment of taxes.[51]

In many countries there is an additional exemption enjoyed by churches, which other charities do not enjoy: exemption from any obligation to register their activities or to publish accounts. In the United States, there is a blanket exemption for "churches"—which are organizations (not necessarily Christian) that have a distinct legal form and established places of worship, as well as satisfying a range of other intuitive criteria.[52] The exemption does not apply to lobbying organizations or to unrelated businesses that happen to be owned by churches. Churches are not required to register with the Internal Revenue Service (IRS), nor to provide it with any information about their activities, unless they want to apply formally for tax-exempt status. This means that it's difficult for the IRS (or any other public body) to investigate activities of organizations that claim to be churches but do not apply for tax-exempt status. It may sometimes come under outside pressure to do so, as in the case of an organization called the Family Research Council, which in 2020 sought and received reclassification from a standard tax-exempt charity to an "association of churches," prompting a complaint to the IRS from forty members of Congress).[53] The IRS has successfully prosecuted some particularly flagrant cases of tax fraud,[54] and has been involved in controversies about the tax status of other kinds of religious organization, such as communal groups.[55]

The exemption of churches and other religious organizations from taxation on their revenues is typically justified on the grounds that religious activities fall under the general category of charitable activities, and there's no reason to treat churches differently from other charities. While there are some reasons to question tax exemption for charities, the case for treating religions like other charities is strong. It conforms to a set of transactional general principles for taxation policy (on the grounds that there's no reason to distort charitable giving either toward or away from charities that happen to be organized around religion).

However, exempting churches and other religious organizations from the reporting duties that all other charities are required to observe is a quite different matter. There's no transactional justification that can reasonably be given for this; it's a residue of consecrational thinking. Religion is thought to deserve special treatment because, well, religion is special. There are strong reasons for opposing such special treatment, which shields religion from the scrutiny that all other organizations in society must undergo in return for being allowed to operate in the public square. Religions are, after all, businesses. They're not *just* businesses, but most secular businesses are not just businesses either. Religious movements, like most secular businesses, flourish when they provide goods or services that their users, members, or customers want. The most successful religious movements have a talent for sensing what their members want. When they become successful, they not only receive large revenues, they also acquire a great deal of power over those members. That power may be legitimately acquired, but that doesn't mean every exercise of it is legitimate. Secular businesses must observe transparency about their activities, in return for receiving money from the general public. That not only allows outsiders to know more about what those businesses do, it also empowers insiders (employees, customers, shareholders) to ask questions in an informed way. There's no reason to think that religious members deserve any less.

There are historical reasons why religious leaders have successfully argued they should be exempt from such transparency requirements. Many of the first post-Columbian settlers in the United States of America were fleeing religious persecution in their home countries, and the

First Amendment to the US Constitution protected the free exercise of religion and prohibited laws respecting its establishment. The painful memory of the wars of religion in Europe made it understandable to wish to err on the side of respecting the wishes of religious movements to operate as they pleased, and to do so on an equal basis, without favoring one religion over another. Similar considerations underlie the drafting of more recent constitutions such as that of India, which guarantees freedom of religion. India's painful experience with religious violence during Partition in 1947 ensured that for a long time none of the major political forces in the country sought to disturb this equilibrium, though as memories of Partition have faded that constitutional even-handedness is being increasingly challenged.

For a long time, constitutional jurisprudence in the United States reinforced religious exceptionalism, though the right of the government to impose limits on what religious movements could do was upheld by the courts—they could not practice human sacrifice, for example. But the limits of what government could do were continually tested. A 1963 Supreme Court judgment established the need for a "compelling interest" for any imposition of a "substantial burden" on an individual's free exercise of religion. A 1990 judgment reasserted the ability of the government to impose restrictions if the burden they might impose on the free exercise of religion was an unintended by-product of laws that applied to everyone. Legislative and judicial decisions since then have partially restored the compelling interest in some US states but not in others. The details don't matter for our purposes here, but they demonstrate that the tension between transactional and consecrational principles in thinking about the place of religious organizations in society continues into the twenty-first century, although it has largely vanished from discussions about how to constrain the exercise of power in virtually all other domains. Sometimes, paradoxically, transactional arguments have been deployed to justify granting a consecrational right to religious exceptionalism (on the grounds that we need to give religion special status otherwise anarchy will ensue). But this observation suggests that conflicts over religious exceptionalism are likely to continue, and perhaps even intensify, in the decades to come. And religious exceptionalism will continue to be asserted, not just in respect of the transparency requirements around the activities of religious organizations, but also whenever public policy is discussed in a way that pits the interests of people with different religious convictions against each other. There will always be a temptation to argue: "Society should do this because the scriptures of my religion require it."

What's at stake is not a set of dry issues about charity tax law. It's a choice between conflicting visions of the place of religion in a society that respects the right of its citizens to practice any religion or none. Human societies since prehistory have struggled to make collective life tolerable by constraining the power of some to exploit the vulnerability of others. The struggle has been all the more important because those inequalities of power have typically been increased by technological innovations that have the potential to serve the well-being of all. Unlike slavery, which was not chosen by its victims, religion is a state that, in the modern world, most people are free to choose (with the exception, as we saw in the introduction, of some countries with laws against apostasy and blasphemy). Even if they live in societies with a compulsory state religion, the intensity of their devotion is something they can adjust. Religions become successful, by and large, by providing what their members are seeking rather than through imposition by force. The twenty-first century will therefore not see religion disappear, because it will continue to minister to real human needs more effectively than most available alternatives. But precisely because its success is legitimately acquired, powerful political interests will continue to manipulate religion to send soldiers to the battlefield and voters to the ballot box, and some of their citizens will continue to be intoxicated by the call. Constraining religion to wear its power more lightly than it has done so often in the past is therefore a project that ought to unite all reasonable people of any faith or of none.

CHAPTER 14

Conclusion

When preachers with light in their eyes
Inspire you to unexplored skies,
They may come robed in scarlet—
But could be just charlat-
Ans, holograms running AIs.

—limerick not generated by AI

The Uncanny Valley

How can the faithful tell the difference between true and false gods, between true and false prophets? All religious movements have been preoccupied with this question. They never found it easy, and it's becoming harder every day. Research in artificial intelligence, which had previously achieved its greatest successes in specific domains such as chess and Go, demonstrated a spectacular new achievement in late 2022, when the first of a series of large language models (LLMs), called ChatGPT, became the fastest-adopted new technology in history. LLMs, producing text that reads as if it were produced by extremely well-read human beings, can hold forth on religious subjects no less fluently than on secular ones. If you doubt it, ask an LLM of your choice to write a poem in the style of your favorite religious poet comparing artificial intelligence to a dangerous demon, and another poem comparing it to the true and mysterious word of God. Your LLM will move

Students of Amir Kabir University protest against the hijab and the Islamic Republic.
Credit: Darafsh, Wikimedia Commons.

from one task to the other without missing a beat. Both visions will sound disconcertingly plausible. Sincere but rhetorically challenged preachers have a new source of inspiration ready to hand. So do many other entrepreneurs with an exuberant variety of projects and ambitions. And the speed of progress in developing such models means they may soon come to seem more intelligent and better informed than even the most intelligent and best-informed human beings. More godlike than human, you could say.

Contrary to what you might conclude from the more panic-stricken commentaries, LLMs do not constitute a new wave of impostors in a previously calm sea of mostly authentic communication. For as long as we have records, human communication has involved claims and counterclaims attributed to sources whose authenticity has been the subject of continual argument and negotiation. Parents, teachers, prophets, elders, storytellers, wise folk, poets, political leaders, departed ancestors,

saints, gods, demons, oracles—dispensing advice, issuing orders, recounting fables or cautionary tales at first-, second-, or third-hand—it's
rare for any of us to receive a simple message from our physical or social
world. Nearly everything we hear or read is filtered through multiple
levels of appeal to authority, and the exact human status of those different levels is often undecided, even undecidable. We are surrounded by
message bearers who seem to be cleverer and better informed than we
are. There's no foolproof method to be sure whether their messages
make sense for us; we must decide this for ourselves. Religious movements have been putting such challenges to their members for thousands of years. Amid the exuberance, whom can you really trust?

We don't necessarily need to decide whether a text has been written
by a computer before responding to the ideas it contains. That's just as
well, because researchers in artificial intelligence have been noting challenges to our sense of the boundaries of the human since at least the
middle of the 1960s, when a computer program called ELIZA was able
to generate responses to (typed) conversational inputs that were trou-
blingly similar to those of a psychotherapist.[1] For instance, in reply to the
statement "I am unhappy," the program might reply, "Why do you think
that coming here will help you not to be unhappy?" and in reply to "My
father is afraid of everybody" it might reply, "What else comes to mind
when you think of your father?" It was reported that "some subjects have
been very hard to convince that ELIZA is *not* human."[2] In 1970 a professor of robotics at the University of Tokyo called Masahiro Mori proposed the notion of the *uncanny valley* to describe the way in which a
person's response to robots would initially become more empathetic as
their resemblance to humans increased, but would abruptly shift from
empathy to a kind of eerie revulsion as the robots became almost but
not quite perfectly lifelike.[3] He noted that wooden statues of the Buddha
were usually carefully crafted so as to avoid appearing too lifelike, and
as a result avoided eliciting revulsion among the faithful.[4] However,
statues of the Buddha can often be unsettling even without inhabiting
the uncanny valley, as the poet and critic William Empson noted, attributing this (controversially) to a systematic asymmetry in their faces that
leaves the viewer unsure which emotions if any to attribute to the statue

or to the being it is supposed to represent.[5] As we saw in chapter 3 when considering an awareness of the "numinous" as one of several components of religiosity, spiritual beings can appear disturbing as well as comforting, and sometimes the comfort they bring seems to be a direct response to the unsettling emotions provoked by our sense of their presence.

Wondering whether a message is genuine is not just a matter of wondering about the reality of the sender. I may ask myself whether the compliment I have just received is written by a human being who really believes it, or by a chatbot programmed to raise my morale. But I may equally wonder whether a friend, a colleague, or a therapist is telling me the truth when they praise my work or my character or my resilience in dealing with some challenge. I may doubt the message of a politician who claims to have understood the suffering of the voters in my community. These questions aren't new, and members of religious movements have been used to dealing with them for as long as religion has been around. Every person has their own way of coping—many Christians would feel that it doesn't really matter whether the Good Samaritan in the parable told by Jesus was a real person, but that it matters a lot whether the Jesus who told the parable (according to the Bible) was a real person. But we can learn lessons from the parable without resolving either question.

Because artificial intelligence intensifies the impact on communications of earlier advances in printing, computing, and telecommunications, recent advances in artificial intelligence may portend the kind of turbulence for religious movements that followed the invention of printing. The cost of sending plausible religious messages has fallen precipitously, so we can count on receiving many more of them. Still, everything we've seen in this book suggests that organized religion will ride out this challenge as it has ridden out so many that came before. When I asked an LLM in all seriousness how LLMs might be helpful to religious believers in telling the difference between true and false religious messages, it provided various pieces of advice, noting that it could help "research the source . . . evaluate the message content," and so forth. But its main advice was to "seek input from others. Talk to other members of your religious community and seek their opinions on the message." It concluded: "Remember, evaluating the truthfulness of religious messages can be complex and requires careful consideration. If you are still uncertain about a message, seek guidance from a trusted religious leader or scholar." You could not wish for a clearer affirmation of the theme of this book: religious movements are about creating trusted communities. Artificial intelligence is not going to change that business model—what it will do is to increase the intensity with which rival movements compete. It will also increase uncertainty about which messages most accurately represent which communities—and thereby raise the premium on finding communities whose communication can be trusted.

The intensity of religious competition has been increasing across the world for several decades, as migration, economic development, the spread of education, and above all the falling costs of information processing and transmission have made it easier for people to choose between alternative religious offerings, and easier for religious movements to reach out to populations beyond those they have traditionally served. This has made it easier for some people to manage their lives without any place for organized religion at all. But religious movements have adapted and evolved—notably, by developing more explicitly the platform model of religious organization. By focusing explicitly on the creation of communities, and listening to what those communities want, the most innovative religious organizations are expanding their reach. Far from being threatened by the advance of secular activity, their place in human society in the twenty-first century seems as secure as ever.

And Now, the Answers . . .

In the introduction to this book, I promised that understanding religions as platforms would help to answer many otherwise puzzling questions about how religious movements function. It's now time to come back to those questions and see what we've learned.

First, there were the personal questions: What are the needs in individual human beings to which religious movements speak? The answer is that there's no single need—it's all the needs that we have as social animals, but that we can express toward a community and its spiritual representatives. Religious movements create a performative space within which we can articulate those needs to ourselves and to others, and in articulating them to others we can aspire to find communal ways to meet those needs.

I asked whether religiosity is a distinct psychological trait; in fact, it's a bundle of diverse traits that have little in common. Religious platforms have found very varied ways to appeal to them. The activities of religion have historically included everything from private prayer and meditation through collective spectacle to violent crusades and jihad. They have channeled such diverse emotions as awe, fear, devotion, anger, excitement, and love. They cater to needs for ritual and transcendence, needs for peace and for striving to overcome a challenge, to needs for private and selfish fulfilment as well as the need to be needed by others. There's no reason to think the psychological characteristics that respond to these activities have any core features in common.

I asked how religion can claim to bring order to the unweeded garden of human perceptions and desires. The answer is that those perceptions and desires are shaped by our interactions with others; they respond to other people's awareness of us, and their hopes and expectations of us. Even in private meditation we are using techniques of psychological mastery or transcendence of the self that are validated through community participation.

How, I asked, can religion give so many people a sense of purpose in their lives that secular institutions often struggle to articulate? The answer is that human beings find purpose in activities that have a collective dimension. Religious platforms create communities that powerfully articulate that collective dimension to our lives. Some secular institutions can do that too—political parties, for instance. But religious platforms have access to historical traditions, and stories from those traditions, that give them a powerful edge.

I asked why, if religion really does speak to universal human needs and longings, it has been claimed that women are on average more religious than men. The answer is that the apparently greater religiosity of women shows up only in the statistics about Christianity. It has its roots in the way Christianity historically appealed to the downtrodden and exploited of the Roman Empire. In the rest of the world, religious platforms have found many ways to adapt their message to men as well as to women, and there's no reason to think they will cease to appeal just as much to men in the future.

Why, I asked, is religion booming in many parts of the world when observers in Europe and North America are convinced it's in terminal decline? The answer is that as secular civilization has developed, religion in turn has developed to respond its challenges. Platforms have adapted and modified what they offer their members to address the many real needs that secular institutions struggle to meet. It's only when they start to be seen as partisan political actors that they lose the authority this gives them. Ordinary religious believers overwhelmingly think that political leaders need to earn their legitimacy instead of borrowing it from religion. And even if the protection of political authorities may give temporary advantages to religious movements, their shelter from scrutiny nearly always leads them to become corrupt and abusive over time.

The second type of question I asked was organizational. Why do religious movements take so many different forms, from tiny cults to vast international organizations? The answer is that platform business models can be generalized or niche, depending on the ecosystem of other activities within which their members find themselves. Secular platforms can be as big as Google or Facebook or as small as a farmers' market—we should expect religious platforms to be no less diverse. The many different needs to which religion ministers can be met by many kinds of platform, and the most successful platforms are often those that don't do exactly what their rivals do.

What, I asked, are the most important differences between religious platforms and secular ones? Because religious communities are focused on interactions with a god or gods who give point to their rituals and inspire the narratives that make sense of their members' lives, they can more credibly offer some of the other component services of their platform. They may credibly claim that their members are more trustworthy and are, on average, more worthwhile friends and colleagues than random members of the population. Secular platforms may have their own strategies, but they are missing this crucial ingredient.

How, I asked, does technological change affect the intensity of rivalry between religious movements? The answer is that anything that makes it easier for people to make lucid comparisons between the benefits of belonging to different movements will intensify religious rivalry. People may migrate away from where they grew up, and therefore be freer to make informed religious choices away from the watchful gaze of family and birthplace community. They may obtain an education. They may become more able to read the scriptures of their religion, because printing or digital transmission lowers the costs of obtaining books, or because they can access translations into a language they can understand. They may be better able to find a church or a mosque within traveling distance of where they live.

I asked when rivalry between religious movements remains peaceful, and when it becomes angry, even violent. The answer is that religious leaders of all affiliations behave strategically. They are, and have always been, willing to contemplate violence when they see more advantages to doing so than using more peaceful means. They may use force against their own members, those of close rivals, or those of more distant rivals, and the choice among these strategies depends on the assets for whose control they are competing. Against close rivals they are mostly competing for the loyalty of people, while against more distant rivals they are mostly competing for the control of economic or political opportunities.

Why, I asked, do religious movements so often clash over abstruse points of theology or ritual that are hard for most of their members to understand, let alone decide? The answer is that, with very few exceptions, people don't join religious movements because of their theology (though they may leave because of it). They join for other reasons, and the theology becomes important to them *after* they have become members. Indeed, theology is often part of what gives them pride in belonging— it's a marker of group membership. Insiders to a movement or a religious tradition care intensely about the theology that makes it distinctive. Outsiders mostly couldn't care less, which is precisely what marks them as outsiders.

I asked when religious movements flourish and grow, when they splinter, and when they die. The answers are as varied as those for secular businesses—they turn around questions of mission, of structure, of strategy, and of message. The ways in which religious movements make these choices bear a marked resemblance to the ways that secular businesses do.

I asked how movements as different as Islam, Hinduism, Buddhism, and Protestant Christianity maintain fidelity to their practices and rituals in the absence of centralized authorities to enforce orthodoxy. The answer is that they do so by the vigilance of their members, through their attachment to a community of practice, through voting with their feet, and sometimes with their genes. That community of practice sometimes evolves, but it recruits its own members as its most reliable ambassadors.

The third type of question is political, in the broadest sense of the word: these are questions about power, its use and its abuse. I asked why movements that affirm moral values have seen an epidemic of sexual abuse. The answer is that sexual abuse afflicts all kinds of organization, secular and religious. It's particularly common in organizations that uncritically revere leaders and figures of authority, giving them a monopoly of access to vulnerable individuals. The way to rein in such abuse is to provide denser networks, external accountability, and an end to cultures of silence. None of these are standard practice in religious movements today, but they should all be.

I asked why political leaders so often claim religious support for war and repression. The answer is that in their pursuit of such strategies, political leaders often struggle to articulate as eloquently as religious leaders the need for sacrifice that violent strategies require. Religious platforms are an appealing source of legitimacy precisely because they're so successful at doing what their members want them to do. Yet the motives that lead religious leaders to lend their support to violence and repression are often sordidly self-interested. Throughout history, religious leaders have used and abused power no differently from those who acquire power by purely secular means.

I asked when religious hostility and religious violence are directed at perceived heretics within religious movements, and when are they directed at members of different movements. The answer, as with disputes over doctrine and ritual, depends on the assets over which movements are competing—is it their own people, or economic or political assets in the wider society?

Finally, there are two questions I asked in the introduction that have not yet been explicitly addressed. The first is whether a large, centralized movement like the Catholic Church can survive in the modern world, or whether instead it is destined to break up. The second is whether authoritarian religious messages can survive in a world of increasing education, falling fertility, and female emancipation. Will religion instead provide the secret sauce for a successful authoritarian backlash against the hard-won gains of the last two centuries in equality, democracy, and freedom for minorities? The first of these questions is of intense interest to about 1.3 billion Catholics, and of limited or at most academic interest to everyone else. The second potentially affects the future of every single individual on the planet. There's no way we can answer these questions for certain, but the platform model of religion provides some valuable insights into the forces that will shape the outcomes. To these two questions we now briefly, and finally, turn.

The Future of the Catholic Church

As we saw in chapter 9, the Catholic Church is an astonishingly flat hierarchic organization for one so large. It has almost as many members as the populations of China and India, yet it functions with far fewer layers of responsibility, and much less comprehensive mechanisms of information gathering. It's impossible for the higher levels in the Church's hierarchy to monitor what is taking place at the lower levels to a degree consistent with their being held responsible for all that is done in the Church's name. Does the fact that it has survived for so long testify to its indestructibility? Or is it a structural anachronism in the modern world?

Secular organizations—whether they're businesses, political parties, nation-states, supranational organizations, or empires—have constantly changed in shape and extent throughout history. Most of the European empires formed in the nineteenth century have broken up. Most of the businesses that formed in the early to mid-twentieth century have either broken up or changed their boundaries through mergers, alliances, de-mergers, or major shifts in mission and strategy. The Catholic Church is centuries older than any of these, but has changed much less. It has seen major schisms before and will doubtless see schisms again—the question here is whether a schism is particularly likely to occur in the next few years. Though prediction would be foolish, the answer must surely be that powerful forces are tending that way. The Church managed the challenges of its flat hierarchy throughout the centuries by a strategy of live and let live, organizationally and even doctrinally. The Church proclaimed doctrine loudly enough, but sought to enforce it only when it was convenient to do so. It allowed what Peter Brown has called "micro-Christendoms" to function more or less unhindered,[6] relying on soft power to steer the immense vessel, and responding in a largely reactive fashion to the occasional grave crises that resulted. Its response came through such initiatives as the medieval Inquisition and the Albigensian Crusade; the Roman, Spanish, and Portuguese Inquisitions after the Reformation; and the various councils that hammered out doctrinal compromises between the feuding factions in the Church.

The Church faces major crises today that are largely the result of technological and social changes outside its control. Congregations are dwindling in Europe and North America, and the supply of willing clergy is declining even faster. Decisions favoring Catholic doctrine by a US Supreme Court with a majority of Catholic justices may seem like victories, but are likely to accelerate the decline of the Church's perceived legitimacy in America and perhaps elsewhere.[7] Sexual abuse has always existed within the Church, but now, thanks to the internet and social media, it is impossible for its extent to be kept hidden—and it is having a visible effect on membership and participation in the Church.[8] Doctrinal differences that were once obscure to most of the faithful are now debated openly in the print and electronic media. "Live and let live" is no longer possible when the gentleness of doctrinal privacy is invaded by interlocutors who demand that anyone who claims to speak for the Church should justify their claims. Those with a stake in what some have called "the Catholic civil war" that has broken out since the death of Pope Benedict XVI feel free to use rumor and innuendo that reach millions, where once such tactics would have reached hundreds or thousands at most.[9] Differences between countries and continents that were once discreetly elided (such as the extent to which polygamy, priestly concubinage, or homosexuality might be locally tolerated) are now brought starkly into comparative light, and the Church's leaders berated for holding double standards. Competition from Pentecostal Christianity, thanks to migration and the growth of urban centers, is fiercer in many parts of the world than it is in Europe, where the Church's leadership is located and where it feels culturally most at home.[10] Yet it's in Africa, Latin America, and Asia that Church leaders are least willing to tolerate the comfortable compromises on which the Church has traditionally survived. The fact that most of the controversial doctrinal issues (such as contraception, priestly celibacy, homosexuality, or the ordination of women) are ones for which no side can claim a biblical mandate only makes matters worse. Each side claims ownership of tradition, even though tradition itself has continually evolved (priestly marriage was widespread, though in many places controversial, in the early centuries of the Church, and there was even a married Pope, Adrian II, as late as the ninth century). It is of course normal, and in most respects desirable, that such disagreements be openly aired. What is abnormal is to expect the Church's traditional methods of discreet obfuscation to be equal to the challenge.

If the Reformation of the sixteenth century was largely the fruit of the massive fall in the costs of information transmission that resulted from the invention of printing, it's hardly reasonable to expect the twenty-first century's even greater fall in the costs of information creation, processing, and transmission to have any less radical an effect on the Catholic Church today. The question is when and how the resulting schism may happen, and what will be the terms of the compromise under which the Church's vast physical, financial, human, and intangible assets are divided among rival claimants. One of the Church's greatest assets, of course, is the legitimacy that comes from the papal succession, so any potential schismatics will hesitate before openly challenging a sitting Pope. That asset consists in the ownership of the platform, and as we've already seen, platforms create substantial lock-in effects for their members: leaving a platform means turning your back on an entire community. But the asset can be depreciated: a disputed papal election would change those calculations radically. It would create uncertainty about which subset of the Church's members represented the true community. It would make it easier for each side in the schism to see the community as persisting with them. Even without a disputed election, the precedent of papal retirement set by the late Pope Benedict XVI means that in the future there are likely to be Popes and former Popes alive at the same time, which will make legitimacy more easily divisible than it has been in the past. It will take heroic willingness to compromise for the rival factions within the Catholic Church to escape a schism soon, but of such willingness there is at present very little sign.

Religion and Authoritarianism

The powerful have always sought to appropriate the legitimacy that comes from religion, so it may seem as though there's nothing new in the threat that authoritarian regimes will use religion to consolidate their power. However, the twenty-first century has seen a rise to prominence of what Sergey Guriev and Daniel Treisman call "spin dictators"— autocrats who are attached to the superficial trappings of democratic politics. In contrast to those autocrats who rule through fear, they describe how "in recent decades a new breed of media-savvy strongmen has been redesigning authoritarian rule for a more sophisticated, globally connected world. In place of overt, mass repression, [they] control their citizens by distorting information and simulating democratic procedures. Like spin doctors in democracies, they spin the news to engineer support."[11] We have already seen how autocrats who fit this description have not hesitated to call on the support of religious leaders, even those who had never shown much previous evidence of personal religiosity.

And they have found religious leaders ready to indulge them.[12] Is this a more alarming version of the age-old problem, with technology enabling the persuasive powers of religious movements to be instrumentalized in a more sinister and dangerous way?

Everything we have seen in this book about the platform model of religious movements suggests that religion cannot command the legitimacy of most of the population if its leaders use that legitimacy to prop up political rulers, whether or not they are authoritarian. Being attracted to religion is not intrinsically related to being politically or socially conservative, still less to liking authoritarian political leaders. Once prominent leaders of religious movements start to lend their legitimacy to political leaders, the association of organized religion with social or political conservatism will reduce the natural catchment area for the movement to the more conservative half of the population. Individuals may cultivate their faith in private, but they will no longer want to belong to churches, synagogues, mosques, or temples that have abandoned their ambition to speak to universal human needs. This has happened to the Catholic Church in Ireland, Spain, and elsewhere, and appears to be happening to many Protestant and Catholic Churches in the United States. Countries like India and Iran are also undergoing such disillusionment, seeking to stifle overt expression of dissent while being powerless to staunch the ebbing of legitimacy from the religious organizations that lend the political authorities their support.

The good news is that this reaction to the politicization of religion appears to happen everywhere, in all parts of the world and in all religious traditions; people are not dupes when they see their gods being harnessed as propagandists. The bad news is that it can take a long time. Political scientist Olivier Roy was already writing in the late 1990s an article entitled "The Crisis of Religious Legitimacy in Iran," describing a "de facto secularization" that was the result of the instrumentalization of Shi'a Islam by the political regime since the Iranian revolution of two decades earlier.[13] Yet in the late 2010s World Values Survey data continued to report that 90 percent of respondents in Iran considered religion to be somewhat important or very important in their lives. Still, the fact of widespread political surveillance makes it likely that these numbers are inflated. Mosque attendance is relatively low in Iran (only 43 percent report attending once per month or more). Other, more politically independent sources of information report much lower levels of religiosity along various measures, as well as a widely shared conviction that religious prescriptions should not be subject to state legislation.[14] The protests against compulsory wearing of the hijab that have erupted at various intervals since December 2017, intensifying in the fall of 2022, are a further sign of the regime's waning legitimacy. Just as the Catholic prohibition on clerical marriage does not have biblical authority, the Iranian government's laws on veiling do not have Quranic authority, and the stance taken by the religious authorities is increasingly seen by the public as a sign of pure political conservatism rather than religious inspiration.

Though the Iranian example suggests the backlash against political instrumentalization of religion may take a long time to materialize, the spread of social media is accelerating the process. Political authoritarianism will always rely on a backstop of brute force, but it's likely that the fall in the costs of collecting, processing, and transmitting information will have an effect similar to the European Reformation—sparking much turbulence, perhaps an increase in violence, but overall an empowerment of the ordinary citizen against repressive political leaders who wish to claim God is on their side. That same fall in costs will no doubt also favor some technologies of repression as well, as it is clearly doing in China, but that arms race between the repressed and their repressors will largely depend on the usual calculation of the costs of compliance versus dissent, with religious legitimacy or its absence having little weight in the calculation.

In the end, the power of religious movements to sway populations will depend on their ability to persuade rather than coerce. Even in nonauthoritarian political systems, they will do so more effectively if they can compete in the public square just as other organizations—businesses, charities, political parties—compete for the public's consent. Their long-run legitimacy, which is clearly under threat in countries where they are seen to have abused their power, will depend on their willingness to agree to greater transparency and accountability than has been generally true so far.

The gods may be beyond all understanding, transcendent in their majesty. But the religious movements that claim to act as intermediaries in our dealings with them are not. They are thoroughly (and fortunately) earthbound. They have for too long been regarded with an odd mixture of reverence by some and scorn by others. These private reactions are no way to think about religion in public life. Religious movements enjoy privileges, and they should acknowledge obligations. It's time to treat them more pragmatically, more demandingly, not with reverence but with respect.

Religion and Secularization: What Do the Data Say?

In this appendix I do three things. First, I use data (mainly census data) from the World Religion Database (WRD) to look at developments over time since the year 1900 in the shares of the population of the world and its main regions by religious affiliation.[1] Secondly, I use survey data from the World Values Survey (WVS) to look at developments over the last forty years or so in the share of the population of various countries responding that religion is very important or somewhat important in their lives.[2] Finally, I interpret these developments in the light of the literature on the secularization hypothesis.*

I begin with the evidence about religious affiliation. At first sight, the facts at the world level seem to support the view, which we came across at the beginning of chapter 2, that Christianity is declining, caught between an expansionist Islam on the one hand and secular atheism on the other. Figure 1 shows the evolution of the global population shares of the ten major religious groups used by the WRD. Between 1900 and 2020, the share of the world's population that is Muslim almost doubled, rising from 12.4% to 24.2%. Over the same period, the share that is Christian fell from 34.5% to 32.2%, with almost all that

---

* The appendix has been written with major and excellent help from Julia Hoefer and Sunny Wang. Sunny prepared the bar charts of WRD data, and Julia prepared the figures with WVS data; both obtained and checked the data before doing so.

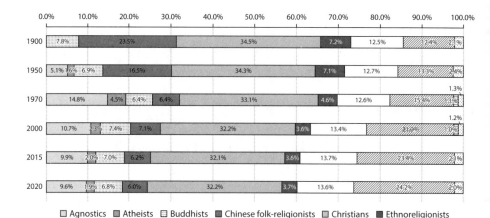

FIGURE 1   Shares of world population by major religious group.

decline coming after 1950. And the share of atheists and agnostics rose from zero to 11.5%.

These figures, though, are seriously misleading—religious trends in the world are not what they seem from looking at total numbers. To understand why, we need to explore an intriguing phenomenon known to statisticians as "Simpson's paradox." We often like to think that when a group has certain characteristics "on average," most of the individuals in that group will have those characteristics too. So, if the average amount of alcohol drunk by the American population is declining, that usually means that most individual people are drinking less than they used to. But Simpson's paradox tells us this isn't always true. Consider this: during the twenty-five years after the Second World War, the median age of the world population declined from twenty-four years old to twenty-two years old.[3] So the world was growing younger—on average, we might say. But every single person in the world was growing older, not growing younger. How can this happen? Very easily, if at the same time as everyone alive is growing older, a lot of old people are dying, and even more extremely young people are being born.

It turns out that something like Simpson's paradox has been at work when it comes to membership of the world's religious groups. The world has been growing less Christian, on average—but most regions in the

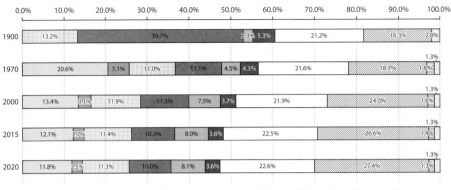

FIGURE 2 Religious proportions (Asia).

world have been growing more Christian, not less. Christianity has grown slowly overall since 1900 because in that year it was concentrated in two types of regions: those, like Europe, that were populous but growing slowly, and those, like sub-Saharan Africa, that were fast-growing but, at the beginning, still small. Islam has grown quickly since 1900 because it was concentrated in different regions, which were already populous and destined to grow fast over the next 120 years. This was particularly true in Asia (contrary to a widespread stereotype, roughly 80% of the world's Muslims are not Arabs). Figure 2 illustrates this. Christians made up only 2.3% of Asia's population in 1900. So, although this share had more than tripled by 2020, rising to 8.1%, a large fraction of the world's babies born in the intervening period were born into a highly Muslim region, and were never going to be Christian anyway.

Figure 3 shows that the share of Christians in Africa has increased dramatically from 8.9% in 1900 to 48.9% in 2020—much faster than the share of Muslims, which increased from 32.5% to 41.5% over the same period. It's in Europe and North America that the share of Christians has been declining, as figures 4 and 5 show. The reasons are subtly different in these last two continents. The share of Christians in Europe declined before 1970 owing to an increase in the reported share of atheists and agnostics. After 1970 there was an increase in the share of

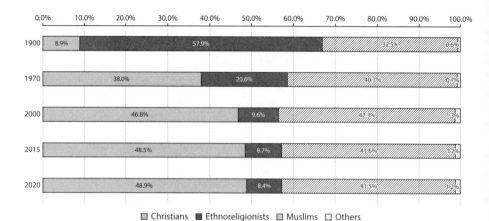

FIGURE 3   Religious proportions (Africa).

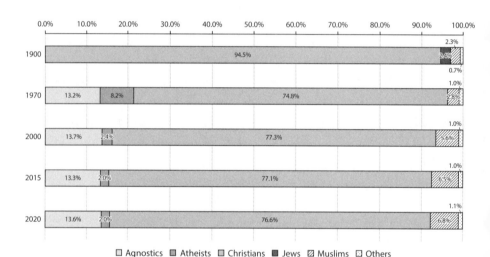

FIGURE 4   Religious proportions (Europe).

Muslims, almost entirely as a result of immigration, but it came at the expense of a decline in the share of agnostics from 21.4% to 15.6%, while the share of Christians slightly increased. The decline in the share of Christians in North America, in contrast, is not due to an increase in other religions. It's due almost entirely to a steadily increasing share over the entire period of those identifying as atheists or agnostics, which reached a record 20.3% in 2020. For those used to thinking of Europe as

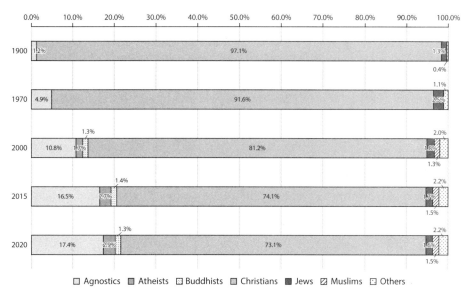

FIGURE 5   Religious proportions (North America).

a much more secular continent than North America, the results are sur-prising, to say the least.

Why should it make a difference whether religions advance or decline in numbers for demographic or for other reasons? Isn't demography the future? The reason it matters how we interpret these trends is that demography is transitory; it's the past, not the future. One of the only reliable laws governing human societies is that when women are both educated and free to work for money, they choose to have fewer children, whatever their bishops, imams, or commissars may say. Many people know that Communist China operated a one-child policy from 1980 until 2015. It's also widely believed that this policy brought about the country's rapidly falling birth rate, albeit using highly coercive methods. The num-ber of children born per woman fell from over six in 1970 to under two in 1991. Not so many people know that, a little over a decade later, fertility in Muslim-majority Iran fell even faster than in China, taking less than fifteen years to fall from six children per woman in 1986 to two children per woman in 2001—and all this without any coercion.[4] Of the many reasons for this, one of the most important was the fact that education of girls was advancing at an astonishing rate. Fifteen years before the fertility change had started, in 1975, over half of Iranian women aged between fifteen and nineteen had no education. In a mere decade and a half, this proportion had fallen to less than one woman in six.[5]

In the twenty-first century, it's reasonable to predict that demography will lose almost all its earlier importance in shaping the relative growth of the world's religions. Once countries have converged to a birth rate of two children per woman or less, there's much less room for major changes in their relative size. This doesn't mean that, once countries have been through their main demographic transition from high to low fertility, there are no differences left. There's still room, within the group of basically low-fertility societies, for things like childcare availability, public policy toward families, social norms about the participation of fathers and the organization of work, and social norms including those of different religions to make a difference to how many children women will have and at what age they will choose to have them.[6] But compared with the divergences of the past, these are small stuff. So, if we want to assess whether religions are on a growing or declining trajectory, it makes sense to look at how their membership numbers are behaving *relative to what demography would have predicted*. It's the religions that have been growing relative to their demographic projections that show the strongest future potential.

To see the importance of demography up to now, we can calculate what would have been the shares of Christianity and Islam in the world's population in 2020 if the number of each religion's adherents had simply grown at the average rate of the population in their own country since 1900. Figure 6 illustrates this. Islam would have had a share of 19.5%, so its share of 24.2% is indeed a lot higher than expected. But Christianity would have had only 25.9%, so its actual share of 32.2%, which originally looked like a retreat relative to its previous share of 34.5% in 1950, is also much higher than demography would have predicted. Higher, in fact (relative to prediction), than the share of Islam. Similar conclusions, albeit quantitatively less striking, apply if we take 1970 as the base year. This reinforces the conclusion that the strong growth in the shares of both Christianity and Islam relative to prediction applies also to the

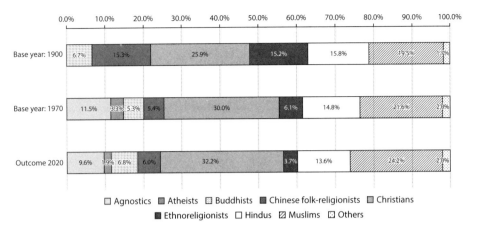

FIGURE 6   Projected religious proportions and outcome in 2020.

period since 1970, and is not just a feature of the previous period (when colonization, for example, might have been an important influence in the share of Christianity).

Figure 7 shows a breakdown of the total Christian population of each continent in 2020. The main message is that Catholics make up between around 30% and a little over 40% in all major regions of the world except Latin America, where they make up around 80% (including the doubly affiliated). Reliable shares for earlier years are hard to come by (both the WRD and the Pew Research Center formerly published estimates indicating a fall in the share of Catholics since 1970, but these sources are no longer available).

Figure 8 indicates changes in shares of Christian denominations from 2000 to 2015, which is the longest period for which the WRD now publishes data.

We now turn to data from the WVS, a large international project that has conducted repeated surveys of public opinion about values and beliefs across nearly one hundred countries, beginning in 1981.[7] We use here the share of the population of various countries reporting that religion is very or somewhat important in their lives. Figure 9 illustrates what might be called the "low religiosity stable state" that characterizes northwestern Europe, and specifically Sweden, Germany, France, and

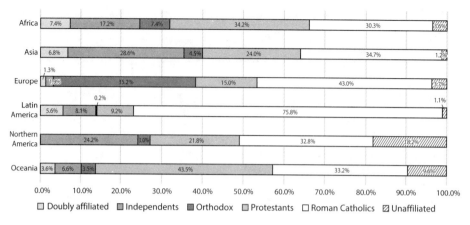

FIGURE 7   Shares of Christian denominations by region, 2020.

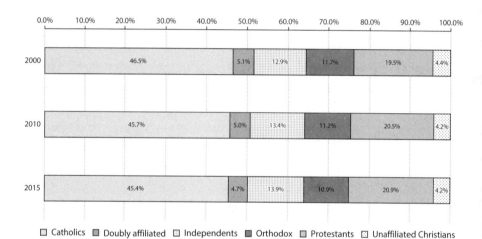

FIGURE 8   World shares of Christian denominations, 2000–2015.

Great Britain. There is variation from one round of the survey to another, but no systematic trend.

Figure 10 in contrast shows that in Catholic Europe things have been much less stable. Poland and Ireland were in a "high religiosity state" in the late 1990s, but Poland has remained in that state, while the importance of religion in Ireland has declined precipitously. In Spain it had already declined by the early 2000s, but thereafter Spain seems to have joined northwestern Europe in the low religiosity stable state. Figure 11,

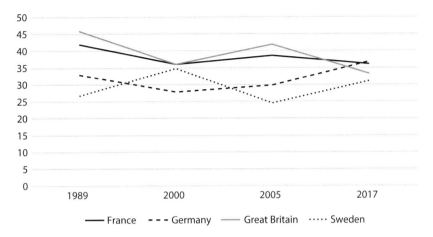

FIGURE 9 Northwestern Europe: % of population for whom religion is very or somewhat important.

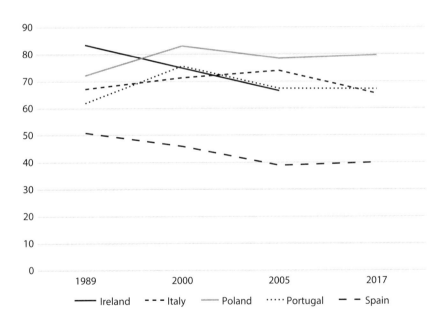

FIGURE 10 Catholic Europe: % of population for whom religion is very or somewhat important.

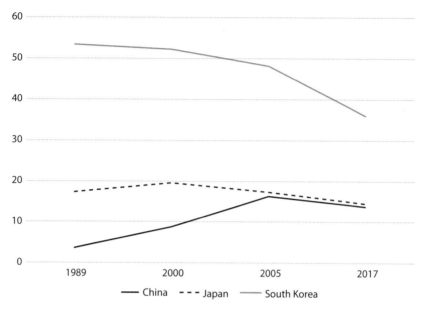

FIGURE 11 East Asia: % of population for whom religion is very or somewhat important.

for East Asia, shows China and Japan apparently in a "very low religiosity state," with levels around 10%–20%, and South Korea in a "medium
religiosity state" of around 50%—but Korea saw a large fall in the 2010s
from around 55% to around 35%, probably in reaction to scandals due
to religious involvement in politics.

Figure 12 shows that North America is undergoing a major decline in
the reported importance of religion, albeit from a high level in the
United States (over 80% as recently as the beginning of the 2000s) and
from a lower level in Canada.

A good way to get a comprehensive global picture of trends in the
reported importance of religion is to compare the numbers for the
earliest available year before 2000 with those available for the latest
available year after 2000. This is shown in figure 13, with the earlier numbers on the horizontal axis and the later ones on the vertical axis.
The 45-degree line runs through the figure—countries above the line
are those where the reported importance of religion increased during
the period of the WVS, while countries below the line are those where it
declined. Countries are grouped by the religious affiliation of the

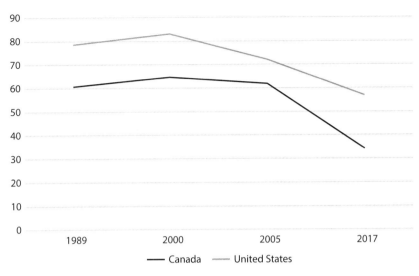

FIGURE 12 North America: % of population for whom religion is very or somewhat important.

majority. Since for some countries the data are available only in a short window around the year 2000, figure 14 repeats the analysis of figure 13, but limiting the sample to countries for which there are data at least from 1994 to 2010. The legend indicates separately for which years the data are available. What do these figures show?

The first thing to note is that in figure 13, there is no clear systematic tendency for countries to lie either above or below the 45-degree line (indeed, a regression line through the observations is statistically indistinguishable from the 45-degree line itself).[8] The average change in the importance of religion is less than half a percentage point, which is statistically indistinguishable from zero.[9] There is no overall trend toward either increasing or decreasing importance of religion, and no tendency for a different trend in countries that had initially higher or lower values. Figure 14 is very similar to figure 13 in this respect.

The second thing to note in figure 13 is that there is a tendency of countries to cluster at three points in the distribution. There is one substantial cluster around the 40% level, another somewhat smaller cluster around the 80% level, and finally one very high up the distribution, at 95%–100%. The countries at the high end are predominantly Muslim

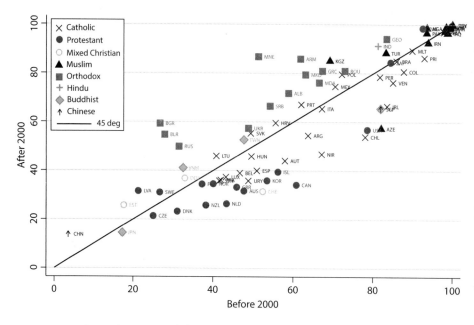

FIGURE 13 Reported importance of religion, comparing earliest year <2000 with latest year >2000.

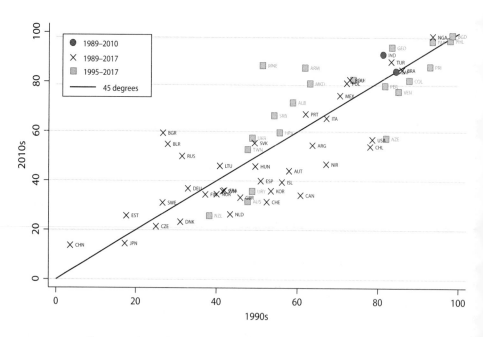

FIGURE 14 The same analysis as figure 13, limited to countries with data for at least 1994–2010.

(though the Philippines and Zimbabwe are also in the group), but otherwise there are no very clear tendencies of clustering along the line by religious category. These three clusters can also be seen, albeit less clearly, in figure 14, which removes the countries with data extending over less than fifteen years.

If we focus our attention on the countries that lie furthest above or below the 45-degree line, countries that are majority Protestant or Catholic tend to lie below the line, while countries that are majority Orthodox tend to lie above the line. On average, religion has lost 5.2 percentage points of importance in Catholic countries, lost 8.7 percentage points in Protestant countries, and gained 17.7 percentage points in Orthodox countries (these are large divergences, both absolutely and in terms of statistical significance). Muslim countries lie mostly quite close to the line, though that may partly reflect the fact that data are available for a shorter span of time. Their average change in the importance of religion, like that of all other categories of non-Christian-majority countries, is statistically indistinguishable from zero.

It's natural to ask whether other indicators of religiosity tell a similar story. Figure 15 shows the same plot as figure 13 but for the percentage of respondents reporting belief in God. Although the observations are further up the graph toward to top right than in figure 13 (because the percentages reporting belief in God are 10 to 15 points higher than those reporting religion as somewhat or very important), once again there is no systematic tendency for there to be increases or declines overall. The mean change is an increase of 1.1 percentage points, which is statistically indistinguishable from zero. Figure 16 shows the equivalent for the percentages reporting that they attend religious services at least once per month. Here there is indeed a fall on average (of 3.6 percentage points, which is more substantial and statistically less likely to be the result of chance). The largest falls are in those countries that report large falls in the importance of religion, but that often remain at high levels of belief in God (of well over 80%), such as Ireland, the USA, and Canada. Overall, it seems that there may indeed be a general tendency for a fall in religious attendance without any equivalent fall in either religious belief or attachment to religion.

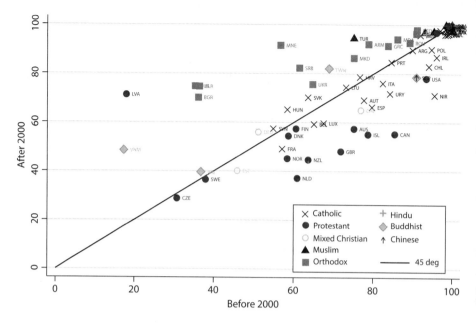

FIGURE 15 Reported belief in God, comparing earliest year <2000 with latest year >2000.

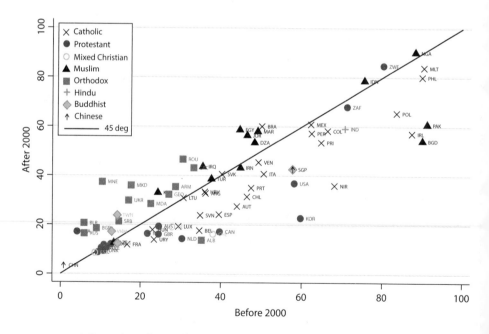

FIGURE 16 Reported attendance at religious services, comparing earliest year <2000 with latest year >2000.

What can we make of these findings in the light of the literature on secularization? The secularization hypothesis has a long pedigree; as was mentioned in chapter 1, it's probably best known from the work of Max Weber, who wrote about the "disenchantment of the world" as a consequence of modernity. Unfortunately for our purposes, it is not one hypothesis but a whole family of them. Some describe the impact of modernity on the place of religious institutions in private or public life, while others describe its impact on personal religiosity, whether this is mediated by institutions or not. Some versions are couched in terms of religious "decline," while others simply describe changes in the relationship between religion and other dimensions of life, without evaluating this as an advance or a decline. And some forms of the secularization hypothesis purport to be predictions—"modernization" means the future, whatever that may be like, and the hypotheses predict how religion will develop over time. Others are more cautious, claiming that if certain dimensions of modern life (such as scientific inquiry, or the welfare state) develop in particular ways, we can expect there to be an impact on the relevant dimensions of religion. Finally, some versions claim to be global, but limitations in the availability of comparable evidence across different countries mean that other versions confine themselves to talking about "the West," or some equivalent part of the world.

To do justice to all versions of the secularization hypothesis would take an entire book or even several, and it would take us far away from our concerns here. Still, figure 13 shows no evidence—at least over the nearly forty-year span of the WVS—for the versions of the secularization hypothesis that are global, predictive, and couched in terms of decline. Yet many people believe that religion is indeed in global decline. Can we understand why they think this?

A case in point is Ronald Inglehart's book *Religion's Sudden Decline: What's Causing It, and What Comes Next?* Inglehart, who died in the same year (2021) that his book was published, was the founding president of the WVS, and did an immense service to the research community in insisting on the importance of standardized survey methods across countries and across time. There are many other sources of excellent information about religious attitudes and behavior in particular countries or religious movements.[10] But none comes close to the geographical and temporal span of the WVS.

Inglehart used WVS data to argue in favor of a version of the secularization hypothesis, which he defined as the theory that "the economic and cultural changes linked with modernization tend to bring declining emphasis on religion." His main piece of evidence was a figure showing that the average reported importance of God in individuals' lives had declined between 2007 and 2020 (after some years of increase before then), in forty-two out of forty-nine countries that between them contained "90 percent of the world's population."[11] The particular economic and cultural changes he claimed to be responsible were "rising existential security and a shift from pro-fertility norms to individual-choice norms."[12]

However, there are serious problems with Inglehart's argument. The evidence for a decline in the importance of God holds only in a subset of (mainly rich) countries, so the explanation needs to account for what makes those different from the others. Inglehart concentrated his attention on the high-income countries as a group (he explicitly excluded Muslim-majority countries and former communist countries from this tendency). As we've seen, even among high-income countries there are large differences, notably between those where religiosity is declining and those where it's low but holding steady. But even if there were not, the fact that declining religiosity is mainly confined to rich countries makes his account of the causes even more puzzling. It's precisely in the high-income countries that rising existential security and a shift in fertility norms happened far too long ago to explain the "sudden decline" that in his view had occurred only since 2007. Prosperity has been rising on average in the world at least since the middle of the nineteenth century, and rates of interpersonal violence have been falling for several centuries.[13] Public health, as measured for example by declining child mortality, has been improving on average in the world since the second half of the nineteenth century, beginning in Europe and North America but also, by the middle of the twentieth century, in the poorest regions such as sub-Saharan Africa.[14] And "a shift from pro-fertility norms to individual-choice norms" has been underway for a very long time. Fertility fell to below replacement levels around half a century ago in the currently high-income countries—precisely the ones in which Inglehart saw secu-larization most clearly taking place after 2010. Even outside the rich world, in countries as different as China and Iran (as well as in many others) it had already fallen to below replacement levels by the mid-1990s.[15]

Overall, this suggests that, rather than looking at the decline of reli-gion as something that arises intrinsically from the process of economic development, we should look for factors whose presence may account for changes in the reported importance of religion in those countries where it has changed, and that are not present (or not to the same ex-tent) in countries where the reported importance of religion has not changed. It's important to emphasize just how widespread is the phe-nomenon of high levels of religiosity that show no visible tendency to decline over time. Countries as different as Armenia, Brazil, Colombia, and Thailand have over 80% of their citizens reporting in the 2017–20 round of the WVS that religion is very important or rather important. That rises to over 90% for a range of countries through the alphabet from Bangladesh to Zimbabwe passing through Ethiopia, Indonesia, Kenya, Myanmar, Nigeria, the Philippines, and many others on the way. The countries and regions of the world whose populations are growing most rapidly are also the ones where religiosity is higher, often dramati-cally so. Compare Europe and Africa. In Europe, responses to questions about the importance of religion tended to be divided roughly evenly among the four categories ("Very important," "Rather important," "Not very important," "Not at all important"), whereas in sub-Saharan Africa a massive majority of respondents reply that it is "Very important." In the 2017–20 round, that majority was 93% in Ethiopia, 87% in Kenya, 93% in Nigeria, and 88% in Zimbabwe.

These high numbers may of course provoke some skepticism—how do we know that people are speaking the truth when 93% of them say religion is "very important" in their lives—are we sure they're saying what they think, rather than what they feel under pressure (from their friends, their family, or their government) to say? This is a legitimate concern—and it's not the same as a generalized skepticism about the value of surveys, of the kind expressed by the primatologist Frans de Waal when he writes (of chimpanzees) that "I am . . . so skeptical of the explanations people offer for their behavior that I feel immensely lucky to work with subjects unable to fill out questionnaires."[16] Still, the pressure that some survey respondents may feel need not always lead them to exaggerate religion's importance. To see this, let's look at the case of China.

To understand this case, we need to explore in more detail how the WVS works. Around every five years (beginning at different dates in different countries), it asks a sample of one to three thousand people in that country a set of questions about their beliefs and values. These include such questions as: "On a scale of 1 (not at all important) to 10 (very important), how important is God in your life?" It asks the same question about "religion" as about "God," though it gives only four possible answers ("very important," "rather important," "not very important," and "not at all important," as well as "don't know"). The number of people surveyed can vary a lot from year to year in any one country, for reasons that are not explained. Countries that are large and internally diverse, like China and the United States, are not necessarily represented by larger numbers of survey participants. For example, in the 1990–94 round, China was represented by just 1,000 respondents, and in the 1999–2004 round, the United States was represented by 1,200 (and the United Kingdom by just 994). Not surprisingly, given these small samples, the average level of religiosity reported in most countries jumps around quite a lot from one survey cohort to the next.[17] And the way the samples of respondents are constructed may not capture the internal diversity of these large countries.

China, with its 1.4 billion citizens (nearly 18% of the world's population in 2022), makes up a big chunk of those whose religiosity has recently been declining, according to Inglehart. The evidence of decline consists in the fact that, in the 2017–20 round of the WVS, 52% of just over three thousand Chinese respondents answered that God was not at all important in their life, while in the previous 2010–14 round only 27% had answered this (out of fewer than two thousand respondents). Until then, China's reported religiosity had stayed level or increased.

Still, a decline is a decline—until you notice that 16% of respondents in the earlier round had given no answer or replied "don't know," whereas not a single respondent in the later round did so. Religion is a very sensitive political subject in China, and the government has greatly increased its surveillance and repression in recent years of Muslims (especially in Xinjiang province), as well as of Tibetan Buddhists and Christians belonging to unauthorized churches. If you were the kind of Chinese respondent who might have answered "don't know" in the years before President Xi Jinping's crackdown had gathered steam, you might feel more comfortable telling your survey enumerator (whose conversation with you is probably recorded) that religion is completely unimportant in your life. It's hard to know exactly what is happening to religiosity in China these days, but it's a safe bet that those who are religious are increasingly careful about what they are prepared to say about it, and to whom. In addition, as sociologists Chunni Zhang and Yunfeng Lu have pointed out, survey questions based on Western models are often difficult to apply in China, where "religion" (*Zongjiao*) is a foreign term, and where many people engage in religious practices, and believe in certain deities, without considering themselves members of any movement or denomination (similar reservations may apply to other countries). As they show, surveys that use different questions can yield strikingly different answers to the number of people who are counted as "nonbelievers."[18] It's safe to say that the WVS data from China cannot really be compared with those from other countries, and that the reported decline in religiosity is probably spurious.

With these caveats in mind, it's best to summarize what we've learned from survey data like this. Across the world, there's no convincing evidence that the importance of religion is declining in people's lives. It definitely *is* declining in North America. It has declined and is probably still declining in some other countries such as Ireland and Chile. It has recently declined, but may have stopped doing so, in others such as Spain. In most other countries the importance of religion appears stable—either stable and low, or stable and high. Assuming that countries where it's currently stable and high are destined to see a decline in a few years is not warranted. We need to understand more clearly what has caused the declines that have taken place.

The view that the importance of religion would inevitably decline because of modernity has in any case faced increasing challenges in recent years from many researchers, including sociologists such as Peter Berger (who was once a strong proponent of the hypothesis, but recanted in the 1990s). Sociologists Roger Finke and Rodney Stark have claimed that more systematic evidence shows religion to be either increasing or holding its own, and certainly not declining, either in the world as a whole or in specific countries such as the United States (though they wrote before the evidence from the last decade or so). Finke and Stark had previously used evidence about the numbers of available places in churches in the United States to argue that the proportion of the American population who were active church members had risen continuously, from a mere 17% at the founding of the Republic to over 60% in the late twentieth century.[19] They drew particular attention to the fact that perceptions of religious decline are often due to what can be called religious "turbulence." At any one time some religious movements are declining, while others are growing. But it's the leaders of movements in decline who can be heard most loudly complaining—the leaders of growing movements are too busy ministering to their increasing flock. And the movements in decline are more likely to be reflected in the surveys that focus on what religious people think and do. In other writings, Stark, together with sociologist William Bainbridge, acknowledged that secularizing processes were at work in modern societies. But they claimed these were counterbalanced by two other processes—namely, revival through breakaway religious movements, and religious innovation, which has been a feature of religious activity throughout recorded history, albeit much more so in some periods and societies than in others.[20]

Still, it would be wrong to think that the secularization hypothesis is discredited just because the data do not support the simple version of it that predicts a decline over time in the dimensions of religiosity measured by the WVS. After all, Max Weber saw the origins of secularization in the increasing rationalization and bureaucratization of society, which was not the same as the mechanism that preoccupied Emile Durkheim—namely, the breakdown of local institutions that provide collective meaning and solidarity. Either of them, were they alive today, might have been impressed by the ability of religious institutions to deploy rationalization and bureaucratization to respond to the demands of people cast adrift by breakdown of the traditional institutions of meaning and solidarity. They might both have acknowledged that religion has proved capable of reshaping itself to meet the challenges of modernity, even if that means it operates in a different environment from religion in earlier ages.

Many modern scholars have also written about secularization as a complex phenomenon, and it would be hard to do justice to their views here.[21] Already in the 1960s sociologist Thomas Luckmann was writing of secularization as representing a reconfiguration of religiosity as a private matter, rather than a retreat from religion as such. In the early 1980s Karel Dobbelaere was writing of secularization as a "multi-dimensional concept."[22] More recently, sociologists Grace Davie, Linda Woodhead, and Rebecca Catto distinguish three main versions of the hypothesis as implying the decline of religious institutions, the decline in the importance of religion for society, and the decline in the importance of religion for individuals. They acknowledge that there are many aspects of modernization, and each of these may have a link with some aspect of secularization, without there being any simple link between the two independently of which aspects are in question.[23] Political scientist Jonathan Fox places the most emphasis on the hypothesis of "the decline of religion as a public force," and points out that the possible mechanisms linking modernization and secularization might operate through urbanization, literacy and education, science and technology, the rationalist values of the Enlightenment, the growth of the nation-state, competing political ideologies, mass participation in politics, prosperity, mobility, social differentiation, and diversity.[24] He has written in particular about the way in which religion is deployed instrumentally in the processes of political competition.[25]

You might think the fact that this is a multidimensional problem— any of several dimensions of modernization might have a link with any of several dimensions of religion—makes it futile to hope for an answer to the question of whether religion in general is declining in the modern world. Still, there have been careful attempts to answer that question using the evidence we have. Philosopher Rachel McCleary and economist Robert Barro, for example, have used WVS data from 1980 through to 2000 to explore whether there is a tendency for personal religiosity to decline across countries as GDP increases, after controlling for many other factors, including political support for religious institutions.[26] They conclude that there is, on average and with many exceptions. And the short period over which the data are available means they are careful not to draw any conclusions about the likely trajectory of religion in the future. The relationship holds for a rather particular two-decade period in the history of the world (one that saw the breakdown of the communist bloc, among other events), and we still need to understand the underlying processes in detail. In a different study comparing Prussian counties during 1886–1911, economists Sascha Becker and Ludger Woessmann showed that an apparent negative correlation between income and church attendance disappeared once they controlled for confounding variables.[27]

One of the facets of modern religion that has attracted attention of all the scholars cited above has been the ability of religion to evolve in a changing environment. This is true not just of the so-called "new religious movements" but even of many of the old ones.[28] Some of the institutions of secular society have indeed taken over, in some societies, the functions that used to be assured by religious movements in earlier times. Researchers across the world have done impressive and detailed work documenting how the different conditions of rivalry between religious and secular organizations have given both secularization and religion a new and more interesting flavor in recent years. Some, like anthropologist Dimitris Xygalatas, who thinks that "in the modern era, the grip of religious and state institutions on ritual is diminishing," nevertheless acknowledge that new social and political challenges including the climate crisis may drive humanity to "have ever greater recourse to the powers of ritual, to give us peace of mind, foster solidarity and provide a sense of meaning and continuity."[29] This echoes the earlier predictions of Rodney Stark and William Bainbridge about the endless capacity of religion to innovate to meet new social challenges.[30] For now, let's just note that nothing in the story of "religion's sudden decline," which applies at best to North America and a small number of countries elsewhere, gives us any reason to doubt the robust health of religion in much of the rest of the world.

NOTES

Notes to Introduction

1. Moscow Patriarchate 2022. Patriarch Kirill's vision of the Russian invasion as a step in a spiritual war was not an exception or eccentric interpretation of the relation between religious and military objectives in the eyes of the Russian regime—see a series of analyses by Lucian Leustean (2022a, b, 2023).

2. RFE/RL 2022.

3. Whalen 2022; Rosguard 2022.

4. See Mackey (2022) for just one gift of over 10,000 rosaries from a church group in Texas. And Guzik (2022) for the role played by the papal almoner Cardinal Konrad Krajewski.

5. Nunn and Sanchez de la Sierra 2017, p. 585.

6. See Humanists International 2022, p. 12. As of 2022 there were 11 countries in this category.

7. Marshall 1890, book 1, chapter 1, §1.

8. Walsh 1972, pp. 223, 220.

9. Ibid., p. 220.

10. The full passage reads:

> The [clergy] may either depend altogether for their subsistence upon the voluntary contributions of their hearers; or they may derive it from some other fund to which the law of their country may entitle them; such as a landed estate, a tythe or land tax, an established salary or stipend. Their exertion, their zeal and industry, are likely to be much greater in the former situation than in the latter. In this respect the teachers of new religions have always had a considerable advantage in attacking those ancient and established systems of which the clergy, reposing themselves upon their benefices, had neglected to keep up the fervour of faith and devotion in the great body of the people; and having given themselves up to indolence, were become altogether incapable of making any vigorous exertion in defence even of their own establishment. The clergy of an established and well-endowed religion frequently become men of learning and elegance, who possess all the virtues of gentlemen, or which can recommend them to the esteem of gentlemen; but they are apt gradually to lose the qualities, both good and bad, which gave them authority and influence with the inferior ranks of people, and which had perhaps been the original causes of the success and establishment of their religion. (Smith [1776] 1904, book 5, chapter 1)

11. On the Huguenots, see McCloy (1951).

12. Voltaire 1763.

13. Smith's visit to Toulouse is discussed in detail (including the impact of the Calas affair) in Alcouffe and Massot-Bordenave (2020).

14. Thirty years earlier, Voltaire had argued something similar in his *Lettres philosophiques*, where he wrote that "If one religion only were allowed in England, the government would very possibly become arbitrary; if there were but two, the people would cut one another's throats; but as there are such a multitude, they all live happy and in peace" (Voltaire 1734, letter 6).

15. If politics had never called in the aid of religion, had the conquering party never adopted the tenets of one sect more than those of another when it had gained the victory, it would probably have dealt equally and impartially with all the different sects, and have allowed every man to choose his own priest and his own religion as he thought proper. There would in this case, no doubt have been a great multitude of religious sects.... The interested and active zeal of religious teachers can be dangerous and troublesome only where there is either but one sect tolerated in the society, or where the whole of a large society is divided into two or three great sects; the teachers of each acting by concert, and under a regular discipline and subordination. But that zeal must be altogether innocent where the society is divided into two or three hundred, or perhaps into as many thousand small sects, of which no one could be considerable enough to disturb the public tranquility. (A. Smith [1776] 1904, book 5, chapter 1)

Smith's view of the relation between religion and politics is developed at length and used to provide a fascinating interpretation of the Reformation by Ekelund et al. (2006).

16. Grim and Grim 2016.

17. These were estimated by PwC at $635 billion in 2016 (PwC 2017).

18. These are estimated at $766 billion in 2016 (Sheel 2017; Statista 2017).

19. Azerbaijan: Lomsadze 2015; Brazil: Paraguassu 2020; Yemen: Sudam 2011; Zimbabwe: *Premier* Journalist 2020.

20. MedyaNews 2022.

21. *TOI* Staff 2019.

22. For a perspective on this, which may be exaggerated but contains useful quotations from Sergei Lavrov and Mike Pompeo, see Schindler (2022). Patriarch Kirill, head of the Russian Orthodox Church, preached in support of the Russian invasion, though other religious groups were strongly opposed (Luxmoore 2022). That support continued even as the costs of the war mounted (Ivanova 2022).

23. Euractiv with Reuters 2020.

24. Johnson 2017; Kim and Bailey 2020; Margalit 2019; Mrachek and McCrum 2019; PTI 2022.

25. Gerber et al. 2015.

26. I. Wood 2022, p. 19.

27. See James Clark (2021) for a historical account of the Dissolution of the Monasteries in England, Heldring et al. (2021) for a quantitative estimate of its long-run impact on English economic development, and Cantoni et al. (2018) for a quantitative documentation of the wealth transfer during the Reformation from religious to secular authorities in Europe, as well as an estimate of the induced reallocation of investment in physical and human capital from religious to secular uses.

28. Churches typically must obey the employment law of their respective countries for salaried employees. However, they use the unpaid or low-paid services of many volunteers in ways

that, depending on the country concerned, might be illegal for other businesses, and typically lack the protections that employment law offers.

29. *Le Monde* with AFP 2023; Sage 2022.

30. Hout and Fischer (2002) documented this phenomenon, which has been much discussed in more recent years. See the fuller discussion in chapter 2.

31. The words are those of Theseus from *A Midsummer Night's Dream*, act 5, scene 1.

Part I

1. A. Watts 1957, p. xi.

Chapter 1

1. Intriguingly, given the theme of this book, there is much controversy about whether Chief Seattle ever uttered these words at all (Jerry Clark 1985).

2. Many writers have noted that what we think of as silence very rarely involves a complete absence of sound. Nevertheless, they have tended to do so to draw attention to what Alain Corbin (2016, p. 15) called the "diverse textures of silence"—in particular, the different emotional cadences that silence can provoke—rather than to the precise minor sounds that become audible once they are no longer drowned by the strident noise of the modern world, and particularly by the plethora of communications by which the modern sensibility is besieged.

3. Strathern 2019, p. 75.

4. This assessment was reported in the *Economist* (2020). Getting reliable survey evidence on religious affiliation is particularly hard in China, for reasons illuminatingly discussed in C. Zhang and Lu (2020). Koesel et al. (2019) discuss state Protestantism in China and offer a range of estimates of the extent of unofficial Protestantism based in house churches.

5. Kim Sterelny has pointed out to me (pers. comm.—e-mail, December 2022) that "organised science has emerged just once, in Western Europe, about 400 years ago. It is not a routine feature of human social worlds, or even of large scale human social worlds, as religion seems to be."

6. Sahlins 2022, prologue, p. vii.

7. Strathern 2019. Strathern uses the terms "immanentist" and "transcendentalist," but others who have followed him have tended to leave out the last syllable, and I follow their usage here.

8. Stuart-Glennie 1873; Weber (2013) 2019.

9. Jaspers (1949) 2011. The evolutionary account of religion of Bellah (2011) made this transition an important part of its argument.

10. P. Brown 1998, p. 637.

11. See the studies collected in Hoyer and Reddish (2019).

12. On Osiris, see Cohn (1993, chapter 1).

13. Hoyer and Reddish 2019, p. 395.

14. For example, Field (2008), writing of early modern England, reports that:

> A degree of religious negligence is likely to have existed, and, in Kent, this was confirmed by the visitation of the Archdeacon of Canterbury in 1511–12, on the very eve of the Reformation. In the Deanery of Lyminge the situation had apparently become so bad

that a general warning to the laity to attend church had to be issued, accompanied by a threat of defaulters being reported to the Archbishop. In Lydd many resorted to ale-houses or conversed in the churchyard during the hours of worship. Elsewhere, Sunday trading was already causing problems. In the Deanery of Canterbury the hackney horse men stood accused of buying and selling at the time of divine service, while in the parish of Canterbury St Mary Magdalen the butchers kept their shops open during worship. A fair number of individuals were cited for seldom or never attending church, including William Mett of Canterbury St Paul, who was alleged to have been absent for four years. (p. 336)

15. Burleigh (2006, p. 29) quotes Goebbels, who in his diaries describes hearing Hitler speak in Berchtesgaden: "It sounded like prophecy. In the heavens above a white cloud took on the form of a swastika. There was a flickering light in the sky, which could not be a star—a sign of destiny?" He discusses at several points (pp. 104–5, 116, 197) the extent to which Nazism could be considered an "ersatz religion."

16. We can agree with Harvey Whitehouse (2004, p. 2) that "religion consists of any set of shared beliefs and actions appealing to supernatural agency," with the nuance that the distinction between natural and supernatural is not one that all religions accommodate easily, so it may be clearer to interpret supernatural agency to mean the actions of any invisible spirit.

17. Ian Wood (2022, p. 22) draws on the notion of a "temple society" due to Appadurai and Appadurai Breckenridge (1976) to understand the economic functioning of the Christian Church in the early Middle Ages, and emphasizes their insistence on the fact that "temple ritual makes little sense unless it is viewed as the expression of homage to the reigning deity." I discuss this further in chapter 9.

18. Marlowe 2010, p. 61.

19. See, for example, the different views expressed by B.-C. Otto (2013), who calls for abandoning the term as an intrinsic category except when discussing its use in ancient sources; Frankfurter (2019), who is aware of the misleading uses of the term but recognizes its "heuristic value"; and Sanzo (2020), who pleads for retaining the term in many contexts.

20. Quinn 1998, p.30. In a comprehensive overview of attitudes to magic in the world of early Mormonism, Quinn emphasizes (p. 27) that "the majority of early Americans were 'unchurched' and participated in folk religion."

21. Thomas 1971. An evocative account of the coexistence of religion and magic among the elite is given by Briggs (2022), writing of the summons by the unwell Pope Urban VIII in 1628 of the highly unorthodox Dominican Tommaso Campanella, a Catholic friar who was also a magician.

22. Many writers have emphasized how hard it is to distinguish the religious from the magical elements in many rituals (see Sperber 2018). Still, the fact that the two kinds of element are deeply intertwined does not mean that the distinction in principle between technology and diplomacy does not make sense.

23. Gershman 2022.

24. Luhrmann 1989.

25. See Dousset (2016) for an example.

26. See Gershman (2022) for an account of the various correlates of belief in witchcraft and an account of some of the potential consequences of witchcraft practice for societies where it is prevalent. See Singh (2021a) for a more evolutionary account.

27. Ghosh (2014, esp. chapter 6) discusses Weber's use of the word "Entzauberung," sometimes translated, less poetically but more precisely, as "demagification."

28. Durkheim 1915; Frazer 1922; Freud 1928; Nietzsche 1910; Weber (1905) 1930.

29. Of Weber, for example, Ghosh (2014) writes that:

> Writing in 1904–7 Weber was open in talking about "secularization" in what was then a novel sense of the word: that is, a general process whereby a secular sphere progressively invaded and conquered a religious one, a process that in the wider culture led to the view that in some sense religion itself was being rooted out. Thus he speaks of the "'secularization' of life"; of "that characteristic process of 'secularization' to which phenomena born out of religious conceptions have everywhere fallen victim"; of "the secularizing effect of property" on religious asceticism, and "the secularization of all the contents of life by Protestantism". But as a frequent use of "" indicates, this was a term about which he had reservations, and it was abandoned in his religious writings after 1912. While he was clear that the historical course taken by modern Occidental Kultur in regard to religion was unique and remarkable, he could have no truck with the view of secularization implied by vulgar use of the term: that there had been a discontinuity in human conduct so radical that it implied the extirpation of religion in a simple and absolute sense—a change so brutal that it tended to sever the present from the past, thereby removing it from the realm of credible historical explanation. (p. 270)

30. See Gellner and Hausner (2013) and C. Zhang and Lu (2020) for examples of this relating to Nepal and China respectively.

Chapter 2

1. I'm sad to report that, eleven years after the scene reported here, Kumbo became one of the centers of a violent struggle between armed separatists and government troops, a conflict that continues at time of writing. The conflict owes its origins to a peaceful strike by lawyers and teachers that was violently repressed. It was originally fueled by an entirely local frustration with the despotic regime of President Paul Biya, in power continuously since 1982. But an increasing inflow of cryptocurrency and arms from outside the country has kept the insurgency boiling. Globalization hit Kumbo in ways I did not expect. For a useful account of the origins of the conflict, see Lessta (2018).

2. Ndi 2014.

3. *Wikipedia* contributors, "Nso people," *Wikipedia, the Free Encyclopedia*, accessed July 12, 2023, https://en.wikipedia.org/w/index.php?title=Nso_people&oldid=1151651049.

4. Searched on August 14, 2022, at 15:42, the first yielded 4.6 million results and the second 133 million results.

5. Strictly speaking, it's the section "Hair" in the page "Donald Trump in Popular Culture" (*Wikipedia* contributors, "Donald Trump in Popular Culture," *Wikipedia, the Free Encyclopedia*, last revised May 13, 2023, https://en.wikipedia.org/w/index.php?title=Donald_Trump_in_popular_culture&oldid=1154534510).

6. Huntington 1993, 1996. The winners for Huntington were predicted to be Islam, and the Sinic civilization, based on China but also taking in the Koreas, Vietnam, Singapore, and Taiwan.

7. Camus 2011.

8. The demographic facts about changes in population shares of various groups in recent decades are not in dispute, except for minor details—see Kaufmann (2010, 2018). The issue is what follows from them, in the sense of what projections can be made for future population shares, what are the likely consequences for social well-being, and what policy recommendations can reasonably be made in response.

9. The article, by the respected correspondent David Gardner, who died in 2022, reviews gloomily the various possibilities for rapprochement between Islam and Christianity in the region, concluding: "It is not clear, however, to what extent Mohammed bin Zayed [de facto ruler of the United Arab Emirates, host to the visit by Pope Francis] can help. He is part of a double act with Mohammed bin Salman [crown prince of Saudi Arabia] that, unintentionally or not, imperils Christians and other minorities seen as fifth columnists by the region's Sunni majority" (Gardner 2019).

10. Inglehart 2021, p. ix.

11. Coy 2023.

12. D. Johnson 2015, p. 8; McCaffree 2017, p. 1.

13. Jones 2021; G. Smith 2021.

14. Figure for 2023 from *Wall Street Journal* and NORC (2023); 1962 figure reported in Coy (2023).

15. Hamid 2021.

16. Barna 2021.

17. Boscaini-Gilroy 2022; Cairns 2023.

18. This essay was one in a set of writings known collectively as *Moralia*, which survive in the form of manuscripts from the tenth to thirteenth centuries. They are published in English translation as Plutarch (1898).

19. Mather 1702, book 1, p. 14.

20. Cited in Morris (2012, p. 198).

21. Field 2008.

22. Winfield 2019.

23. Cited in Bull (2021, p. 183).

24. Both the World Religion Database and the Pew Research Center formerly published estimates indicating a fall in the share of Catholics of about 3 percentage points since 1970, but these sources are no longer available.

25. Alfonsi et al. 2022, figure 1. See McCauley (2013) for an account of the growth of Pentecostalism in Ghana, D. Maxwell (1998) for a study of Zimbabwe, and Coleman (2000) for a global overview.

26. Horden and Purcell (2000, esp. pp. 411–32) provide a detailed account of the many religious sites around the Mediterranean, pointing out the recurrence of features such as springs, pools, mountains, and woodlands among the places that hosted temples and shrines (though they resist functionalist accounts of such recurrence).

27. Ibid., p. 442.

28. Ibid., p. 449.

29. Bonnet et al. 2019; Galoppin and Bonnet 2021. Bonnet (2022) also summarizes the work of historian Hans Beck (2020) as implying that "localism has had a pervasive influence on communal experience in a world of fast-paced change. Far from existing as outliers, citizens in these

communities were deeply concerned with maintaining local identity, commercial freedom, distinct religious cults, and much more."

30. Jones 2021.

31. G. Smith 2021.

32. Cited in Corbi and Miessi (2022, p. 11).

33. Giles et al. 2023.

34. Sterling and Platt 2022.

35. Roser 2013a, section "Different Data Sets on Growth in the Last Decades," subsection "Penn World Table," chart "GDP per Capita [1950–2019]."

36. In both countries this number is obviously lower than the numbers reporting themselves as nominally Catholic.

37. A television documentary broadcast in 2021 reported the case of 53 priests imprisoned in a special "prison for priests" (*Apaiz Kartzela*, directed by Oier Aranzabal, Ritxi Lizartza, and David Pallarès [Syldavia, 2021]; see Bernal 2021).

38. See Pastor (2007) for a more detailed account of the relationship between Church and state in this period.

39. Pastor 2007, p. 278.

40. Astor (2020), Griera et al. (2021), and Ruiz Andrés (2022) cover various facets of this persistent "cultural Catholicism" and discuss the way it has become a subject of political controversy sparked by immigration and economic dislocation.

41. *Economist* 2021.

42. Turpin 2022, p. 19.

43. *Magill's Literary Annual*, volume 1, parts 1 (October 1977) and 12 (September 1978), cited in Foster (2007, chapter 2).

44. Not always successfully. Foster (2007, chapter 2, loc. 868) reports that Archbishop McQuaid "had summoned [Charles] Haughey to his palace in order to show him a copy of Edna O'Brien's scandalous novel *The Country Girls* and approvingly noted the rising politician's disgust." This did not prevent the future taoiseach (prime minister) from introducing in 1979 a bill partially liberalizing access to contraception, to the outrage of the archbishop. O'Toole (2021), who also reports this incident, recounts several others in which the archbishop's behind-the-scenes interventions were sufficient to force theaters to drop plays, broadcasters to cancel programs, and in one hilarious case, to halt the transmission of Cole Porter's song "Always True to You," with its refrain "But I'm always true to you, darling, in my fashion, Yes I'm always true to you, darling, in my way," because in the archbishop's view "it advocates the proposition that a limited form of fidelity is somehow acceptable" (O'Toole 2021, p. 28). As O'Toole also reports (chapter 11), this hypersensitivity to sexual undertones did not prevent the archbishop from knowingly protecting serial child molesters within the Church.

45. On these events, as well as the transformation of the religious landscape of Ireland in the last three decades of the century, see chapter 2 of Foster (2007), provocatively entitled "How the Catholics Became Protestants." Despite this title, Foster cites Inglis (1998, p. 206) to acknowledge that "Irish Catholics are not only becoming more Protestant . . . they are also becoming more secular." O'Toole (2021) is also an excellent, if avowedly more subjective, account of this period. Turpin (2022) is more up to date, and more grounded in ethnographic research.

46. Turpin 2022. Turpin and Willard (2022) explore some factors that predict how individuals responded to the scandals.

47. Szczerbiak 2019.

48. Gellner and Hausner 2013; Hausner and Gellner 2012.

49. McCleary forthcoming.

50. One exception to this generalization is that there was substantial demographic competition between different groups of Christian settlers in North America from the sixteenth century onward. Of course, there was also violent warfare against Native Americans, but the aim was not necessarily to convert the latter to Christianity.

51. This is the theme of Strathern (2019), to which we will return in chapter 10. There are, however, societies and historical periods where scholars have emphasized the extent to which the ability of rulers to impose a religious identity on their populations was limited by significant resistance and agency on the part of those populations themselves. This has been a theme, for example, of the debate over "confessionalization" in the German Reformation. The ability of the laity to read the Bible in the vernacular, as well as the growing centrality of the sermon in the religious liturgy, gave a degree of agency to ordinary Church members that they had not enjoyed before the Reformation, even if varieties of popular Catholicism often diverged from those favored by the Church. See the discussion of confessionalization in Deventer (2004). There are also intriguing examples of rulers converting to one religion to avoid pressure from neighbors of a different religion—the Khazars, a Turkic people of central Asia, are said by Baron (1957, p. 198) to have converted to Judaism as "the equivalent of a declaration of neutrality between . . . two rival powers," though there is controversy about the reliability of the claim. Alan Strathern (pers. comm—e-mail, December 2022) suggests that popular resistance was widespread in non-Christian transcendentalist societies as well—for instance, in Thailand and Japan.

52. Cox 2011, pp. xvii–xviii.

Chapter 3

1. The phrase (a translation of "das Opium des Volks") comes from the introduction to *A Contribution to the Critique of Hegel's Philosophy of Right*, a manuscript written by Marx in 1843 but unpublished in his lifetime. The introduction is translated as Marx (1975), and the phrase appears at p. 175. For a commentary, see Pedersen (2015), who emphasizes how widespread was the use of the opium metaphor for religion in German philosophy both before and after Marx wrote. Edmond Seabright has drawn my attention to the fact that the complete quotation is better understood as arguing that religion is the only choice available to people suffering under oppressive conditions rather than as denying its character as a reflective choice: "Religious suffering is, at one and the same time, the expression of real suffering and a protest against real suffering. Religion is the sigh of the oppressed creature, the heart of a heartless world, and the soul of soulless conditions. It is the opium of the people."

2. This is not at all the same thing as the worldly success that should, in Weber's account of the Protestant ethic, follow the rigorous adoption of a professional calling (what Weber called a *Beruf*). For Weber, success was evidence that that the calling was being exercised properly; it was not an end in itself, let alone the motivation for becoming religious in the first place. "Fun" was not supposed to be part of the package.

3. Knapp 1993, p. 29.

4. Ibid., p.30. Knapp cites many intriguing sources, such as John Northbrook's *A Treatise Wherein Dicing, Dauncing, Vaine Playes or Enterluds With Other Idle Pastimes etc. Commonly Used on the Sabboth Day, Are Reproved* (1577), whose title helpfully encapsulates its thesis.

5. Friedrich 2022, pp. 385–94.

6. Burleigh 2006, p. 167.

7. For sociology, see Berger (1963, 1967), Greeley (1962, 1969, 1989), Stark and Bainbridge (1985, 1996), Finke and Stark (2005), Warner (1993), and a critique by Lechner (2007). For economics, see Azzi and Ehrenberg (1975), Iannaccone (1988, 1992), Berman (2000), and recent surveys by Aldashev and Platteau (2014) and Iyer (2016).

8. Hicks 1935, p. 8.

9. Groskop 2019.

10. A point emphasized by K. Miller (2002) and Iannaccone and Bose (2011).

11. Thornton 2008, figure 3B.

12. Gellner 2005.

13. Carvalho 2013.

14. Shofia 2022. Jacquet and Monpetit (2023) record that the positive association between education and veiling does not hold in France, and suggest that workplace discrimination (which is unlikely to occur in Indonesia) may account for this.

15. Iyer 2018, p. 215.

16. Ibid., pp. 127–34 (services), p. 146, table 5.11 (awareness of competitors).

17. Gruber and Hungerman 2008.

18. D. Chen 2010.

19. Ager and Ciccone 2018.

20. Bentzen and Force 2023, abstract.

21. Bentzen 2019, 2021.

22. Dehejia et al. 2007.

23. Gruber and Hungerman 2007.

24. Scheve and Stasavage 2006.

25. For example, she found that (pers. comm.—e-mail, January 2023):

Religiosity increases more in response to unpredictable disasters (such as earthquakes, tsunamis, and volcanic eruptions), compared to more predictable (and equally materially harmful) ones (such as tropical storms); earthquakes in areas that are otherwise rarely hit raise religiosity more than earthquakes in areas that are often hit; and larger earthquakes strengthen religiosity more than smaller ones. In addition, the rise in religiosity occurs after removing districts that were physically hit by disaster, which one would not have expected had the effect been physical. Moreover, the intensity of beliefs rise after disaster, while the impact on church attendance is much less robust. Likewise, in my covid paper, I found that prayer searches rose much more than searches for internet churches for instance.

26. Auriol et al. 2020b.

27. Cavalcanti et al. 2022.

28. Falwell and Towns (1971), cited in Harding (2000, p.16).

29. A. Wilson 2022, p. 1.

30. Ibid., p.6.

31. Homer 1924, book 6, lines 297–312; discussed by Piera Nappi (2006).

32. J. Davies 2020.

33. C. Morgan 1989, p. 17.

34. C. Hall 2021b, quote at p. 6. However, she elsewhere (2021a) also emphasizes that the categories within which we view the classical world's religious specialties were often fluid. Ptolemy, for example, believed in meteorology as a branch of astrology, a view that was different from those of other writers such as Cicero and Sextus Empiricus.

35. Augustine of Hippo (426) 1984, 7.4. This is cited by Andrew Wilson (2009, p. 395), who quotes the sentence immediately following this citation, pointing out that it alludes to an advantage of the division of labor that prefigures Adam Smith's arguments in *The Wealth of Nations*: "But the reason why a multitude of workmen was thought necessary was so that individual workers could learn individual parts of an art quickly and easily, rather than that they should all be compelled to be perfect in one entire art, which they could only attain slowly and with difficulty." Wilson compares this with another ancient text, Xenophon's *Cyropaedia*, where he writes:

> Nor should it surprise us; for if we remember to what a pitch of perfection the other crafts are brought in great communities, we ought to expect the royal dishes to be wonders of finished art. In a small city the same man must make beds and chairs and ploughs and tables, and often build houses as well; and indeed he will be only too glad if he can find enough employers in all trades to keep him. Now it is impossible that a single man working at a dozen crafts can do them all well; but in the great cities, owing to the wide demand for each particular thing, a single craft will suffice for a means of livelihood, and often enough even a single department of that; there are shoemakers who will only make sandals for men and others only for women. Or one artisan will get his living merely by stitching shoes, another by cutting them out, a third by shaping the upper leathers, and a fourth will do nothing but fit the parts together. Necessarily the man who spends all his time and trouble on the smallest task will do that task the best.

36. MacCulloch 2009, p. 66.

37. Gabrielsen 2007, esp. pp. 195–96. He writes, for example, that "the strong and persisting emphasis on religion turned the membership of every association from notional 'citizens' to a group of ardent 'worshippers'. Whatever the origin, special qualities or ritual demands of individual cults, the fact that they were being actively worshipped by private brotherhoods made the religiosity of their membership constantly visible to the outside world. As a result, the equation between an 'associate' and a 'pious man' was becoming all the more self-evident." J. Edwards and Ogilvie (2012) have argued, however, that not all arguments to this effect are borne out by the case-study evidence.

38. Iannacone (1990) pioneered the "religious human capital" approach to preference formation, which focuses on the extent to which an individual invests in their own religiosity over their lifetime.

39. Bisin and Verdier (2000, 2001) are the pioneers in the economic approach to cultural transmission; they show how parents invest in the technology of transmitting cultural traits to their children. Carvalho and McBride (2022) survey the resulting literature and construct a model that unifies their approach with that of Iannacone (1990). Jacquet (2023) extends the

Bisin-Verdier model to take account of gender differences between parents as well as interaction with other kinds of human capital.

40. R. Otto 1923.

41. R. Horton 1993, p. 26.

42. W. James 1985, p. 28.

43. Survey results from Auriol et al. (2023).

Chapter 4

1. There's a large literature documenting the role of disagreement in leading to the breakdown of cooperation in a wide range of human societies (Brenneis 1988; Duranti 1990). Boyd and Mathew (2021) have developed an evolutionary model showing the importance of institutions of arbitration in paving the way for a restoration of reciprocity.

2. Horden and Purcell 2000, p. 453.

3. Venkatesh 2009, p. 27.

4. Ibid., pp. 22, 39.

5. Ibid., p. 28.

6. Auriol et al. 2020a.

7. Rates of kidnapping in Haiti appear to have spiked in 2021 and 2022 and are now said to be among the highest in the world (CARDH, n.d.; Mérancourt and Faiola 2021). Homicide rates, which had been comparable to those of the United States in the mid-2000s, nearly doubled after the 2010 earthquake (Roser and Ritchie 2013, chart "Homicide Rate, 2020"). Even so they remained lower in 2021 than those of many other countries in Latin America and the Caribbean (InSight Crime 2022).

8. P. Jenkins 2011; Kalu 2008; Kwabena Asamoah-Gyadu 2015.

9. Serra and Schoolman (1973) 2011.

10. I Corinthians, 12: 13–22.

11. Harper 2013; see also the discussion of this book in Peter Brown (2013b).

12. Acts of the Apostles 20: 35.

13. Mauss 1950. Seneca's essay *De beneficiis* is translated by John Basore (Seneca 1935) and has been discussed in relation to the theories of Mauss by Degand (2015).

14. Stieglitz et al. 2014, 2015.

15. Andrew Clark and Oswald 1994. Hussam et al. (2022) show that providing employment for refugees raises well-being by far more than providing the cash equivalent of the wage.

16. See P. Brown (1998), especially pp. 654–55.

17. See D. Chen (2010) for Muslim networks of financial support in Indonesia.

18. Iannaccone and Bose 2011; K. Miller 2002.

19. There are many sophisticated models of platform competition—many developed by my colleagues at the Toulouse School of Economics—in a literature going back to Rochet and Tirole (2003) and Caillaud and Jullien (2003); a recent review with reference to policy implications is by Jullien and Sand-Zantmann (2021). However, these are almost all developed to explain the behaviors characteristic of social-media platforms, payment card systems, or B2B or B2C platforms in standard consumer and service industries, and many make the digital

nature of platforms central to the business model (Calvano and Polo 2021; Goldfarb and Tucker 2019).

20. The fact that religious organizations use differentiated pricing is noted by McBride (2015).

21. Iannaccone 1992. This also helped to explain some surprising features of religion, such as violent extremism (Iannaccone and Berman 2006).

22. Aimone et al. 2013; Berman 2000; Berman and Laitin 2008; Carvalho 2016; McBride 2008, 2010, 2015. Carvalho (2019) surveys the literature on clubs, and Carvalho and Sacks (2021) extend the "club good" model in several dimensions, deriving novel empirical predictions.

23. Auriol et al. 2023.

24. Chetty et al. 2022, esp. p. 3, n. 5.

25. Brennan and Pettit 2004. Their idea is closely related to an earlier notion due to Avner Offer, which he calls "the economy of regard" (Offer 1997).

26. Luhrmann 2012.

27. Fruehwirth et al. 2019.

28. This feature of platforms has been carefully modeled by Crémer and Biglaiser (2012); see also Biglaiser et al. (2019).

29. This suggests that the concern of Hungerman (2011) that "any formal theory of religious congregations competing with each other has to decide what a congregation's objective function is" should be resolved empirically rather than theoretically (p. 259). It's an open question what motivates religious leaders, and the answer may well differ between times and places. Testing hypotheses empirically is challenging, though. Szeidl and Szucs (2021) test hypotheses about the motivations of media entrepreneurs (specifically how much they are motivated by ideology and how much by profits) using data on government allocation of advertising contracts to media organizations in Hungary; they find evidence of a mixture of both motivations. It would be good to use similar methods for testing the motivations of religious entrepreneurs, but unfortunately the necessary data (notably on church revenues) are usually unavailable. In chapter 10 I report work I am undertaking with Eva Raiber to test the role of political motivations in US churches' behavior during the Covid-19 pandemic.

Chapter 5

1. Whitehouse 1995, p. 191.

2. Dubois 2012, p. 90.

3. Xygalatas (2022) provides an overview of the functions and evolutionary origins of ritual, with many traditional and modern examples.

4. Whitehouse 2021, p. 1. On the absence of ritual behavior in great apes, see Tennie and van Schaik (2020).

5. Durkheim 2015.

6. Finke and Stark 2005, p. 135.

7. Luscombe 2022.

8. Diocese of Phoenix, n.d. The *Catechism of the Catholic Church* delves more deeply into these theological matters, and is available on the website of the United States Conference of Catholic Bishops.

9. The Diocese of Phoenix website reports that "According to St. Thomas Aquinas, God has bound Himself **to** the sacraments, but He is not bound **by** the sacraments. This means that while we can be certain that God always works through the sacraments when they are properly conferred by the minister, God is not bound by the sacraments in that He can and does extend His grace in whatever measure and manner He wills. We can be assured that all who approached God, our Father, in good faith to receive the sacraments did not walk away empty-handed." This website was accessed on June 1, 2022, but when I looked again on April 5, 2023, the website had been taken down, and a search for the name "Arango" yielded no results.

10. Lucas 2006, pp. 102–5, esp. n. 84.

11. Gould and Walters 2020, p. 279.

12. A. Watts 1957, p. 27.

13. Whitehouse (2021) is a good place to start, and Jagiello et al. (2022) cover more specifically the literature on the cognitive foundations of "the ritual stance."

14. Tomasello 1990, 1999, 2019.

15. Lyons et al. 2007.

16. Horner and Whiten 2005. The claim of uniqueness is made in Clay and Tennie (2018). The authors acknowledge that they cannot rule out the possibility of over-imitation in other species, but they claim that existing findings that appear to show this should not be interpreted in this way.

17. Bernardi et al. 2001; Lang et al. 2020.

18. Boyer and Liénard 2006; Lang et al. 2015.

19. Strathern 2019, p. 60. He has much to say on the way in which, in transcendental religion, "individual interiority rather than ritual action becomes the privileged arena of religious life" (p. 59).

20. Power 2017.

21. Launay et al. 2016; Mehr et al. 2021; Savage et al. 2021.

22. Mogan et al. 2017.

23. Summarized in Whitehouse (2021, chapter 1) and Jagiello et al. (2022).

24. A point emphasized in Heyes (2018b), summarizing her earlier work (1993, 2012, 2018a).

25. Heyes and Frith 2014.

26. Whitehouse 2021, p. 106.

27. Benedict 1934; Nietzsche 1910; Turner 1969.

28. Mithen 2005.

29. An extreme version of such collaboration is dying for the group. See Whitehouse (2018) for a developed theory.

30. Xygalatas et al. 2019. However, it is not the only candidate explanation. The body releases endorphins after physical trauma, probably an evolved response to enable the individual to escape the site of greatest danger (Valentino and Van Bockstaele 2015). Seeking this endorphin surge may explain acts that involve exposing the body intentionally to harm (Störkel et al. 2021).

31. R. Brown and Kulik 1977.

32. Baumard and Boyer 2013b.

33. Indeed, rituals may also involve the consumption of alcohol and other drugs like mescaline, with the ritual itself acting as an independent source of stimulation.

34. Tasuji et al. 2021. Boals and Schuettler (2011) draw attention to the fact that construing a traumatic event as central to one's identity can even increase the risk of PTSD. However, Atran

and Norenzayan (2004, p. 5) note that "stress sufferers who permanently lose memory and undergo reduced immune response often suffer from chronic stress and lack of effective social support. . . . By contrast, even the most severe and emotionally aversive religious initiations end in positive exhibitions of social acceptance."

35. Whitehouse 2000, 2004.

36. Ignatius of Loyola 2012. A more modern (and Protestant, indeed Anglican) set of spiritual exercises by Harrison Warren (2016) repeats the notion of the presence of God in the everyday with a regularity that is evidently intended not just to reinforce trust in the method but also in the presence. The book has become very popular, to the point that in 2019 its publishers announced that around $240,000-worth of fake copies had been sold on Amazon (Blair 2019).

37. Suzuki 2010, p. 17.

Chapter 6

1. Pascal 1669, 418-233, "Infini rien."

2. I owe this story to Reme's grandson Jibirila Leinyuy.

3. Central to the argument of Hardin (1997) is the assertion that "it is a striking fact of religious commitment that people tend to have the commitments of their community, family, and friends" (p. 269).

4. Pew Research Center 2013.

5. Pew Research Center 2019b.

6. C. Davies 2021.

7. Loewenstein 2013, chapter 2.

8. Wheeler 1999, p. 25.

9. Mohamed 2021.

10. As an example, Janet Reitman reports of her initial encounter in 2008 with a recruiter for the Church of Scientology:

> At the intake level, Scientology comes across as good, practical self-help. Rather than playing on themes that might distance a potential member—the concept that I am a "thetan," for example—members hit on topics that have universal appeal. Instead of claiming some heightened degree of enlightenment, they come across as fellow travelers: people who smoke too much, who have had bad marriages, who have had addictions they couldn't handle but have somehow managed to land on their feet. Scientology, they explain, has been a form of "recovery." As one woman I meet puts it, "Scientology *works*." (Reitman 2006)

11. Pascal 1669, 418-233, "Infini rien." I have translated "pencher" as "incline," and "parier," "gager," "jouer," and "hasarder" as "bet."

12. Wheeler, 1999, p. 25.

13. Diderot (1762) 2015.

14. Pascal 1669, 418-233.

15. Yost 2022.

16. Chiang 2002.

17. Ibid., p. 207.

18. Kim Sterelny has suggested to me that some religious beliefs share a characteristic of phobias—"they drive behavior in a very specific behavioral domain, without integration into the rest of the cognitive economy" (pers. comm.).

19. Few et al. 2020.

20. O'Toole 2021, p. 409.

21. MacCulloch 2014, p. 164.

22. Ibid., p. 165.

23. MacCulloch (2009, pp. 211–22) provides a useful summary of the Arian controversy. He is more sympathetic than I am to the view that the contending parties really cared about the theological issues, though he admits that "it may seem baffling now that such apparently rarefied disputes could have aroused the sort of passion now largely confined to the aftermath of a football match" (p. 222). He goes on to write that "apart from the propensity of human beings to become irrationally tribal about the most obscure matters ... ordinary Christians experienced their God through the Church's liturgy in a devotional intensity which seized them in holy places. Once they had experienced the divine in such particular settings, having absorbed one set of explanations about what the divine was, anything from outside which disrupted those explanations threatened their access to divine power" (ibid.). Two things are problematic in this argument. One is the use of the word "irrationally." He offers no reason why it might have been irrational for the participants in the council to prefer strongly that the faction with which they were associated should emerge victorious from the council. Indeed, in his account of the negotiations he supplies many reasons why this would have been a very sensible preference to have. The second is that he does not explain why, if belief per se rather than a sense of belonging was what mattered for devotional intensity, individuals who had already experienced devotional intensity should have felt threatened by a compromise statement hammered out by a vast committee summarizing the beliefs of others.

24. There is a much-quoted passage by Gregory, bishop of Nyssa in Cappadocia in the fourth century CE, in which he writes:

> Everywhere, in the public squares, at crossroads, on the streets and lanes, people would stop you and discourse at random about the Trinity. If you asked something of a moneychanger, he would begin discussing the question of the Begotten and the Unbegotten. If you questioned a baker about the price of bread, he would answer that the Father is greater and the Son is subordinate to Him. If you went to take a bath, the Anomoean bath attendant would tell you that in his opinion the Son simply comes from nothing.

This is commonly interpreted to mean that Gregory thought ordinary people were passionate believers in theological doctrine. In fact, the context makes it clear that Gregory thoroughly disapproved of this behavior, which was his way of saying that ordinary people were apt to subscribe to any old heresy that came along. In a later sentence he writes, "I do not know what we should call this evil, whether dementia, madness or some epidemic sickness of this kind; it produces a distortion of reason." This passage tells us less about ordinary people's grasp of theology than about an elderly bishop's paranoia about heresy. The text is apparently unavailable in English translation but is quoted in a French translation by Matthieu Cassin (2011, p. 281).

25. See the summaries of the confessionalization debate in Lotz-Heimann (2001) and Deventer (2004).

26. P. Wilson 2009, p. 462.

27. United States Commission on International Religious Freedom 2020.

28. Stanley 2018, p. 173. As Stanley points out, Macaulay's original motivation was to preserve religious harmony among different communities by preventing the giving of offence.

29. This was first set out in full detail in Lord's *Singer of Tales* ([1960] 2000). An early assessment is by Pope (1963), and a later overview by Jensen (2017) suggests the theory has broadly held up well subject to some qualifications.

30. Doniger 2009, p. 33.

31. MacCulloch 2014, pp. 175–76. "Nicodemites" (after Nicodemus, a secret follower of Jesus) was the name given to Protestants living in Catholic countries who concealed their beliefs to escape persecution; this was clearly true of Elizabeth under the reign of her sister Mary.

32. Doniger 2009, p. 46.

33. Ones evident in such ethnographic surveys as that of Mircea Eliade (1964).

34. Christopher Boehm (1999) cites an incident among the Paliyans of India reported by Peter Gardner: "when men trying to exert leadership in a crisis were manipulatively invoking the gods, the rank and file mocked both the leaders and the gods they invoked" (p. 75); and also one among the Bihor of India, when "members of a hunting party simply ignored the lead taken by an influential shaman who knew little about hunting" (p. 77).

35. Strathern 2019, p. 42.

36. Briggs 2002, conclusion, loc. 5400.

37. Aumann 1976.

38. Wittgenstein (1972, part 1, paragraph 79) uses the example of the sentence "Moses did not exist" to illustrate the notion of language games, since the meaning of the sentence depends entirely on the context in which the sentence is uttered.

39. Veyne 1983.

40. Mercier and Sperber 2011.

41. See Haghtalab et al. (2022) for a formal argument and model of this.

42. Schwartzstein and Sundaram 2021, p. 276. The authors provide a sophisticated model of the process of persuasion of this kind.

43. Dunning 2011, p. 247. The original research is reported in Kruger and Dunning (1999).

44. Atran 1998; Boyer 2001; Mithen 1996.

45. Diamond 1999.

46. Peterson and Beach 1967.

47. Preverbal infants: Denison and Xu 2010; Xu and Garcia 2008. Children: Zhu and Gigerenzer 2006. Nonhuman primates: Rakoczy et al. 2014.

48. Andy Clark 2013; Tenenbaum et al. 2011.

49. Individuals have been claimed to be excessively conservative Bayesians (W. Edwards et al. 1963) who use multiple over-simplistic heuristics and biases when making statistical inferences (see Kahneman and Tversky 1982; Tversky and Kahneman 1974, 1983). In addition, apparent statistical ability varies across experimental protocols (Lejarraga and Hertwig 2021), which draws attention to the limitations in human beings' evolved reasoning capacities when faced with some of the challenges of inference in modern life.

50. R. Boyd and Richerson 1985; Henrich 2015.

51. R. Boyd 2017. Tennie et al. (2009) emphasize what they call the "ratchet effect"—namely, the cumulative character of the evolution of human knowledge.

52. Boyer (2018) gives a comprehensive account of how this process has shaped human societies.

53. R. Maxwell and Silverman 1970; Werner 1981. Mathew and Perreault (2015) claim that social learning is "the main mode of human adaptation," accounting for a larger share of the variance in human behavior than the ecological environment.

54. Sperber et al. 2010.

Chapter 7

1. Dabashi 2011, pp. 4–5.

2. Bricault et al. (2021) provide a rich array of examples (see especially pp. 133–41).

3. Coomaraswamy 1918.

4. J. Watts et al. (2016b) summarize the evidence for this. They use phylogenetic analysis to demonstrate the role of human sacrifice in the maintenance of social control across a sample of 93 Austronesian traditional societies.

5. Cohn 1993, p. 30. Evidence for the worship of Isis exists as early as the Fifth Dynasty in the third millennium BCE. But the murder of Osiris was a setback from which he was able to return, thanks to the intervention of Isis; it had no intrinsic point. He was worshipped not as a martyr but as the eventual victor and lord of the afterlife.

6. Dabashi 2011, p. xi.

7. Searched August 22, 2022, at Google Books Ngram Viewer: https://books.google.com /ngrams/graph?content=narrativeandyear_start=1800andyear_end=2019andcorpus =26andsmoothing=3anddirect_url=t1%3B%2Cnarrative%3B%2Cc0#t1%3B%2Cnarrative% 3B%2Cc0.

8. Greenhalgh and Hurwitz 1999.

9. Savita et al. 2011.

10. Franzosi 1998.

11. Dautenhahn 2002.

12. Jordan, n.d.

13. McCloskey (1990) was a very early methodological discussion of the use of narrative in economics; Shiller (2019) and M. Morgan and Stapleford (2023) are more recent ones.

14. Bruner 1985, 1987, 1991.

15. Bhaya Nair 2002; Dennett 1992.

16. Frazer 1922, preface, p. iii.

17. Ibid., p. 711.

18. Ibid., pp. 713–14.

19. Campbell 1949.

20. The literature on comparative mythology is too vast to summarize here. Campbell was particularly strongly criticized by Alan Dundes, whose 2004 presidential address to the American Folklore Society, with many hostile references to Campbell, was republished with commentaries in Haring (2016). Toelken (1996) has produced a comprehensive introduction to

folklore studies, which argues that Campbell had been led by a misunderstanding of archetypes "to argue in an otherwise brilliant book that there is a universal hero myth—an assertion that can be maintained only by suppressing thousands of stories like 'The Sun's Myth' in which culture is threatened and destroyed, not stabilized and renewed, by the egotistical actions of a powerful male seeker" (loc. 5526).

21. The claim about the book's sales is made on the website of the Joseph Campbell Foundation on the page "The Hero with a Thousand Faces," accessed July 11, 2023, https://jcf.org/titles/the-hero-with-a-thousand-faces/. In Alan Dundes's presidential address he did not disguise his irritation that "we professional folklorists are badly outnumbered by amateurs who give our field a bad name" (Haring 2016, p.12), a phenomenon he attributed morosely to Campbell's popularity. "I cannot tell you how many students as well as applicants to the folklore program at Berkeley include in their statements of interest that they have read and enjoyed Campbell's writings" (p. 25).

22. Booker 2004.

23. Mars-Jones 2004.

24. For thirty-six, Georges Polti published *Les trente-six situations dramatiques* in 1895, saying in his introduction that he owed the idea to Carlo Gozzi and to Johann Wolfgang von Goethe.

25. Michalopoulos and Meng Xue (2021).

26. The literature is vast. Major contributions include Carroll (1995, 2004), Gottschall and Wilson (2005), Gottschall (2008), B. Boyd (2010), Baretta et al. (2009), Da Silva and Tehrani (2016), Singh (2021b), and Dubourg and Baumard (2022).

27. Dos Santos and Berger 2022.

28. McAdams et al. 2001.

29. Gifford 2004; Ukiah 2005.

30. Michalopoulous and Meng Xue (2021) "explore whether a group's level of generalized trust is influenced by how cheating is portrayed in its oral tradition" (p. 2019). They show that:

> Second-generation immigrants in European countries who trace their ancestry to oral traditions where tricksters are often unsuccessful are systematically more trusting and enjoy in the same country higher incomes than those with a heritage of an oral tradition where antisocial behavior is not prominently punished. The possibility that today's trust levels can be traced in how tricksters are portrayed in the narratives that children grow up listening to suggests the long-lasting influences of early-life environments. (pp. 2023–24).

31. Dubourg and Baumard (2022) survey and assess this causal argument. Michalopoulos and Meng Xue (2021) show that "groups with oral traditions rich with heroes who successfully tackle challenging situations tend to display more appetite for risk and appear more entrepreneurial" (p. 1996).

32. Bering 2006; Oatley 2016.

33. Dautenhahn 2002.

34. E. Hopkins 2014; Lindeman et al. 2015; Mar and Oatley 2008; Willard and McNamara 2019; Willard and Norenzayan 2013.

35. Atran 2002; Atran and Norenzayan 2004; Boyer 2001.

36. Matsuzawa 2020; Saito et al. 2014.

37. Singh 2021b.

38. Ibid., p. 186.

39. It's hard to obtain reliable estimates for the annual worldwide revenues of the sexual porn industry, since estimates by industry observers have varied by a factor of ten. Most estimates around 2020 put revenues at well above $10 billion annually, and well below $100 billion. For comparison, the world film industry generated $136 billion in 2018 (*Wikipedia* contributors, "Film Industry," *Wikipedia, the Free Encyclopedia*, last revised March 27, 2023, https://en.wikipedia.org/wiki/Film_industry#cite_note-2). Even acknowledging that not all movie storylines are optimistic, and without even counting the video gaming industry and the book industry, it is easy to conclude that optimism porn generates more revenue than sexual porn. That shouldn't be surprising—much sexual porn is available for free, and its relatively simple storyline compared to other movie content means that customers are less likely to want to pay to watch recently produced material.

40. Matsuzawa 2020, p. 543. The original work by Inoue and Matsuzawa (2007) on which this is partly based was criticized by Silberberg and Kearns (2009) for inadequately controlling for the practice time of the chimp subjects. Given the few chimp subjects available for experimentation, it is extremely difficult to resolve this issue experimentally, and the hypothesis is likely to remain speculative for the foreseeable future—like many of the other hypotheses discussed in this chapter.

41. Saito et al. 2014.

42. Matsuzawa 2020.

43. B. Boyd 2010; Dor 2015, p. 4. See also Dor 2016.

44. B. Boyd 2018, p. 13.

45. B. Boyd 2021, p. 57.

46. Malinowski (1926) 2014, p. 16. Bascom (1954) writes that "Malinowski's statement is so widely accepted today that it should require no further discussion" (p. 344).

47. D. Wilson 2005, p. 13.

48. Pagels 1995, p. 74.

49. Michalopoulos and Meng Xue 2021, p. 1996.

50. D. Smith et al. 2017. Michalopoulos and Meng Xue (2021, pp. 1993–94) show that "communities with low tolerance toward antisocial behavior, captured by the prevalence of tricksters being punished, are more trusting and prosperous today." This does not establish causality (and is not claimed by the authors to do so), but it does make plausible that narratives are elaborated in a context in which discussion of norms and their enforcement is common.

51. Da Silva and Tehrani 2016.

52. Dundes 2007, p. 59.

53. This is an important part of the argument in G. Miller (2000).

54. D. Smith et al. 2017.

55. Cited in Biale et al. (2018, p. 221). The Besht was the eighteenth-century founder of Hasidism, known by many titles including *ba'al shem*—"master of the [divine] name" (p. 3).

56. Michalopoulos and Meng Xue 2021, p. 1996.

57. Whitehouse (1995, p. 177) emphasizes that:

> At the same time as developing a new and attractive vision of political authority, dignity, and wealth for the Pomio-Baining peoples, the Pomio Kivung provided an explanation

for the present lack of these things, encompassing problems which [they] were already posing but were unable to answer. Lindstrom (1990) argues [of Melanesian cargo cults in general] that "the major concern of some movements is the achievement of wisdom in general . . . rather than some plane load of material goods."

58. Doniger 2009, pp. 9–10.

59. Matthew 25: 40, 10: 29.

60. 2 Samuel 18, esp. verses 24–33.

61. Crubézy 2019.

62. There is an enormous academic as well as literary and popular tradition identifying religiosity as a response to the fear of death, and popularized by Ernest Becker (1973). Though there is plentiful experimental evidence showing that people show more signs of religiosity when primed with ideas of death (see Norenzayan and Hansen 2006), this leaves the most interesting part of the puzzle unexplained. Why should religion be a psychologically effective response to fear of death, and which components of the varied package of services offered by religion are most important in this?

63. For example, Strathern (2019, p. 68) writes that "the process of converting villagers in far northwestern Thailand to Buddhism, as observed by Charles F Keyes, was a matter of inducting them into seeing suffering 'not as the consequence of the malevolence of spirits, though these may still be the immediate agents, but as the result of a general 'law', namely that of *kamma*."

64. P. Brown 2015, pp. 4–5.

65. Ibid., pp. 5–6. Whitehouse (1995, p. 94), cites a description of the recovery of the body of Aringawuk, one of the founding heroes of a splinter group of the Pomio Kivung movement, which "was found to be peppered with bullet holes suggestive of the mutilation of Christ's body on the Cross." The suggestiveness was clearly in the eye of the beholder, since to other observers the bullet holes might have indicated that Aringawuk had been the victim of a banal homicide.

66. Strathern 2019, pp. 100–101.

67. Ibid., p. 99.

68. The question is used as the title to Robert Bartlett's (2013) book. In a different translation it reads "how is it that the martyrs . . . have the power to work such marvels?" (Augustine of Hippo [426] 1984, book 22, p. 9).

69. Platt 2012.

70. Mountjoy 2009, p.9.

71. Eltchaninoff 2022. See also Hill and Stent 2022.

72. D. Zhang 2013, p. 35.

73. See Bloom 2010; Mercier and Sperber 2011; G. Miller 2000.

74. See Shirley Dent in the *Guardian* complaining about literary Darwinism as "literature reduced to a conglomeration of atoms. . . . I detest this attempt to lock up literature in a biological grid of causation" (Dent 2008).

Chapter 8

1. Bidgood 2017.

2. Sheilagh Ogilvie has pointed out to me that extreme Pietists did this in Wuerttemberg (southwest Germany) too in the eighteenth century, and some subsects took it to America in

the nineteenth century (Fernandez 2019). Even when Pietists were not radical, they preached extreme chastity. Sosis (2000) notes that in an earlier study of religious and secular communes by Kanter (1972), "all of the communes that survived longer than 25 years in her sample (n = 9) practiced celibacy at some point in their existence. In contrast, only two of the communes that survived less than 25 years (n = 21) ever practiced celibacy" (p. 81).

3. Kanter 1972.

4. Engelstein 2003, back cover.

5. Maltsev 2022.

6. Fieder and Huber (2016) show, in a study of data from thirty-two countries as well as from the Wisconsin Longitudinal Study in the United States, that religiously homogamous women have more children than heterogamous ones. Jacquet (2023) shows that, in France, parental religion is a strong predictor of an individual's religion, that mothers are more likely than fathers to transmit their religion to their children, and that higher education is associated with a lower probability of transmitting parental religion.

7. Sterelny 2018, p. 3.

8. Sperber 2018.

9. Sterelny (2018), including the contributions of commentators, provides an excellent starting point. Sosis (2020) argues for a systemic approach, viewing religions as "an adaptive complex of traits." Atran and Norenzayan (2004) and Atran and Henrich (2010) survey many of the key arguments. Norenzayan (2013, 2014) addresses specifically the question whether religions with Big Gods make people behave more ethically. Boyer (2018) gives a less comprehensive but very accessible and interesting overview. D. Johnson (2015) focuses on the adaptive consequences of a belief in supernatural punishment, though he acknowledges (p. 10) that not all scientists agree whether this is adaptive or a by-product of other evolutionary forces. Dunbar (2022) is a recent important contribution, which inter alia summarizes much of Dunbar's own earlier research, though it is not (and does not claim to be) a representative survey of other competing hypotheses. Lightner and Hagen (2022) have made an important recent contribution, which emphasizes the continuities between religious beliefs and other forms of explanatory account of complex phenomena. Two very different, historically focused accounts of the role of cultural evolution in the rise of world religions are Bellah (2011) and R. Wright (2009).

10. Ramanchandran and Blakeslee (1998) emphasize the widespread prevalence of perceptual delusions, including the hallucinations of Charles Bonnet syndrome and the Capgras delusion, whose subjects become convinced that friends and family members are being impersonated. Many subjects are entirely able to function despite these delusions, because they can simultaneously believe them and act as though they do not believe them. On their view, overriding the evidence of our senses is not an exceptional case but our default mode of operation.

11. Boyer 2001. Atran (2002) makes similar arguments, independently researched. Norenzayan et al. (2006) provide experimental evidence in favor of the selective advantage of minimally counterintuitive narratives.

12. Guthrie (1980) makes an early statement, including a reference to the analogy of "faces in the clouds" (p. 192). Guthrie's 1993 *Faces in the Clouds* is a book-level exposition; J. Barrett (2000) gives a succinct overview.

13. Shariff and Norenzayan 2007; Shariff et al. 2016.

14. Norenzayan (2013) and Norenzayan et al. (2014) present and discuss this theory at length. See also Baumard and Boyer (2013a). Purzycki and McKay (2022) cite much of the literature that has sought to test this, and warn of the difficulties of doing so by using databases constructed by coding standardized variables by inference from ethnographic studies. Singh et al. (2021) emphasize that even "small world" religions sometimes have these preoccupations. J. Watts et al. (2015) use Bayesian phylogenetics on Austronesian data to test the moralizing high god (MHG) hypothesis against an alternative that they call "Broad Supernatural Punishment" (BSP), which encompasses "fallible localized ancestral spirits and inanimate processes like karma as well as MHGs" (p. 2). They find that BSP precedes political complexity but that political complexity precedes MHGs, leading J. Watts et al. (2016a) to call for more "clarity and causality . . . in claims about Big Gods." In line with their argument, Bentzen and Gokmen (2023) use instrumental variables estimation to argue that it was in fact the societies that achieved social stratification first that subsequently developed MHGs. Turchin et al. (2022) argue that "intergroup warfare, supported by resource availability, played a major role in the evolution of both social complexity and moralizing religions. Thus, the correlation between social complexity and moralizing religion seems to result from shared evolutionary drivers, rather than from direct causal relationships between these two variables."

15. Bowles 2006, 2009; Bowles et al. 2003; D. Wilson 1975; D. Wilson and Sober 1994.

16. De Waal 2013.

17. Ahmed 2009; Auriol et al. 2020a, 2021. Independently of religiosity, a reputation for prosociality attracts cooperation partners. Von Rueden et al. (2019, p. 1) have shown in a longitudinal study among the Tsimane forager-horticulturalists in the Bolivian Amazon that "(i) higher-status individuals gain more cooperation partners, and (ii) individuals gain status by cooperating with individuals of higher status than themselves."

18. Sosis 2000.

19. For instance, in Auriol et al. (2020a) my coauthors and I show that more-religious people in Haiti are more trustworthy in experimental games, and more likely to be involved in borrowing and lending networks in their communities.

20. Novella 2008.

21. Sterelny 2018, p. 14.

22. Alcorta and Sosis 2013; Rossano 2015; Sosis and Alcorta 2003.

23. Dunbar 2022.

24. Hardin (1997, pp. 267–68) points out that:

> The division of labor . . . reduces the investment that the individual must make in understanding the world. . . . How does the individual detect error on the part of knowledge specialists? Primarily by having it pointed out by others. . . . If I am in a traditional or small society, the prospects of my gaining insight into errors in our knowledge may be substantially less. There may seldom be alternative sources of information beyond our collective social knowledge as it has been more or less received from the past. The apparent conservatism of such societies need not be a matter of psychological disposition but merely of lack of opportunity to learn on the cheap that their ways are not as effective as they might be. This may be especially true of our religious knowledge. One of the great advantages of large, plural societies is that they offer up criticism of practices and knowledge very much on the cheap.

25. Robin Horton (1993) expresses the point well: "in traditional cultures there is no developed awareness of alternatives to the established body of theoretical tenets; whereas in scientifically oriented cultures, such awareness is highly developed. It is this difference we refer to when we say that traditional cultures are 'closed' and scientifically oriented cultures are 'open'" (p. 222). Sterelny (2007) offers an illuminating discussion of some ways in which cultural evolution can lead to maladaptive beliefs and practices.

26. Whitehouse (1995, chapter 4, esp. pp. 106–7) reports how dreams played a key role in legitimating the breakaway movement from the cult.

27. Kim Sterelny has commented (pers. comm.—e-mail, December 2022) that "one thing that continues to puzzle me is a very culturally widespread, perhaps universal, refusal to recognise and admit ignorance. There are no ethnographic reports of, say, communities being asked about the cause of thunder and answering that they have no idea, though in fact, it's true of all of them that they have no idea." My response is that I agree with his observation, but I have no idea why this is so.

28. Dawkins 1986.

29. Heyes (2018b) argues that reading is just one of many cognitive skills that evolved through cultural rather than natural selection, and indeed uses reading as a motivating example to persuade us that other distinctively human skills such as "theory of mind" may be products of cultural evolution as well.

30. Spelke et al. 1992, 1994.

31. Gopnik 2012, p. 1624. In a control condition in which the prior display was not drawn from the box, infants did not show the surprise reaction.

32. Kushnir et al. 2010.

33. See particularly his essay "African Traditional Thought and Western Science," chapter 7 of *Patterns of Thought in Africa and the West* (R. Horton 1993).

34. Lightner and Hagen 2022, p. 441.

35. Lightner and Hagen (ibid.) emphasize that what they call "knowledge specialists" play an important part in encouraging the spread of explanatory stories, including supernatural ones, in any society.

36. This statement needs to be qualified to the extent that there is now observational evidence of exchanges among chimpanzees that display "memory" (Gomes and Boesch 2009, 2011). However, this does not significantly change the conclusion that the human capacity for suspension of disbelief in deferred reciprocity vastly exceeds anything we see in the nonhuman animal world.

37. This argument is central to the story developed in Harari (2014).

38. Yuval Noah Harari has claimed that belief in religion is no harder to explain than belief in corporations, which is tendentious, to put it mildly (Harari 2014); corporations as such may not be observable but they construct factories and office buildings, pay dividends, and can be sued. Corporations do not claim to be more than the fruit of certain rules of economic and legal conduct and in particular do not claim to enable their members to survive death. However, he is right that both religions and corporations involve a large degree of abstraction, and that this is in itself conducive to making such beliefs hard to refute.

39. I explore this in detail in *The Company of Strangers* (Seabright 2010).

40. See Singh et al. (2021) for an account of these preoccupations even in small world religions.

41. Translation by Dr. Mustafa Khattab on Quran.com (Surah Al-Maʾidah, https://quran
.com/5?startingVerse=1).

42. Auriol et al. 2020a; Hadnes and Schumacher 2012; Norenzayan 2014; Singh et al. 2021a.

43. Matthew 6: 34.

44. Chapter 5, verses 2, 3 (translation by Dr. Mustafa Khattab on Quran.com, Surah Al-
Maʾidah, https://quran.com/65). See Eggen (2011) for a discussion of the relation between
different conceptions of trust in the Quran, notably between *tawakkul*, which means trust in
God, and *amana*, which can stand for trust in God or in other people.

45. Guiso et al. 2003.

46. Barro and McCleary 2003. See also the large body of work collected in Barro and
McCleary (2019) for an exploration of the links between religion and economic development.

47. Bénabou and Tirole 2006, 2011; Levy and Razin 2012. Ahmed (2009) shows that highly
religious madrassa students are significantly more cooperative and generous than less religious
students.

48. Sterelny 2003.

49. Robert Wright (2009) uses a similar argument in proposing "the law of religious tolerance: people are more likely to be open to foreign gods when they see themselves as playing a
non-zero-sum game with foreigners" (p. 136). This theory "sees Israel's early monolatrists as
fierce nationalists, opponents of an internationalist foreign policy. More specifically, it sees them
as populist nationalists, drawing support from the common man's resentment of cosmopolitan
elites who profited from an internationalist foreign policy" (p. 146).

50. Loewenstein 2013, p. 31.

51. Whitehouse 1995, p. 58.

52. Ibid., p. 92.

53. Both quotations are in Leppin (2022, pp. 33–34, 33); translation by Hartmut Leppin
(pers. comm.—e-mail, September 2022).

54. Hofstadter 1964. See Peter Pomerantsev (2022) on propaganda in Putin's Russia:

> Putin's famed propaganda system has always been less about ginning up enthusiasm
> and more about spreading doubt and uncertainty, proliferating so many versions of "the
> truth" that people feel lost and turn to an authoritarian leader to guide them through
> the murkiness. In a domestic political context, these tactics make sense: They keep
> people passive, unsure of what is truly happening. But they show their limits when you
> want to move a country toward the rabid enthusiasm required for war.

55. Quervain et al. 2004.

56. Mathew 2017.

57. Richerson et al. 2001.

58. Sanderson 2018a, b. There are other purported explanations. For example, Robert Wright
(2009) suggests the rise of monotheistic religions was provoked by a renewed perception of
non-zero-sumness: "Technological evolution (wheels, roads, cuneiform, alphabets, trains, mi-
crochips) puts more and more people in non-zero-sum relationship with more and more other
people at greater and greater distances, often across ethnic, national, or religious bounds"
(p. 215). He adds to this an intellectual motor: "The more nature was seen as logical—the more
its surface irregularities dissolved into regular law—the more it made sense to concentrate

divinity into a single impetus that lay somewhere behind it all" (p. 183). It's less clear why the first half-millennium BCE should have been a particularly crucial period in this respect.

59. This is quoted from a blog post (Turchin 2023) that is condensed from "The Evolution of Moralizing Supernatural Punishment: Empirical Patterns," forthcoming in *Seshat History of Moralizing Religion*, edited by Larson et al.

Chapter 9

1. See Shingal (2015), who writes (pp. 122–23): "The devadasi tradition, once an institution that bestowed honor on women who were chosen to take part, has devolved into a system of institutionalized exploitation and prostitution of young, lower-caste girls."

2. Appadurai and Appadurai Breckenridge 1976.

3. I. Wood 2022, p. 19. There is a good deal of controversy about this estimate, though all scholars agree that the amounts were very large. As Wood goes on to emphasize, these gifts were by no means always free of strings. The founding of monasteries often included provision for the employment of founders' kin, sometimes in lucrative positions as well as those conferring spiritual authority. This was true not just in Christian but also in Hindu and Buddhist monasteries, as well as in mosques under the Islamic tradition of *waqf*. However, Wood also adds that these constraints on the property rarely persisted for more than three generations, so churches (like mosques) gained more than did the donor's family (p. 26).

4. Flechner and Fontaine (2021) note great regional variation in the extent of this. They also emphasize (p. 587) that:

> The Church encouraged pious manumissions of slaves and contributed to redefining the institution of manumission itself by introducing formal mechanisms that enabled the continual exploitation both of those who gained freedom and of their progeny. Masters could therefore be commended for their righteousness in freeing slaves while at the same time could either continue to extract dues and labour from them or hand them to a new patron, who would press the freed into service. The new patron was often the church itself.

5. I. Wood 2022, p. 48.

6. The mont-de-piété in Avignon, founded in 1608 by the congregation of Notre-Dame-de-Lorette as a pawnbroking business, found a new source of working capital after 1801, when a business was established to verify the standard of silk produced in the city and surrounding region. The fees from this business were plowed back into pawnbroking, showing just how far the Church had come in diversifying its activities from its original role as a steward of agricultural land. See Archives Municipal d'Avignon, n.d.

7. I. Wood 2022, pp. 65–77.

8. Ibid., p. 21.

9. See J. Davies 2020.

10. The story of Ignatius of Loyola is recounted by Friedrich (2022, p. 2). The conversion to Christianity of Saul of Tarsus does appear to have involved a literal vision. The motive of making money is attributed to L. Ron Hubbard, founder of the Church of Scientology, by Reitman (2013, p. 96), who writes of that "in one 1972 policy letter to his finance officers, Hubbard

summed up his philosophy: 'MAKE MONEY. MAKE MORE MONEY. MAKE OTHERS PRODUCE AS TO MAKE MONEY.'" She also reports (p. 34) that a direct spur was provided by the bankruptcy of his Dianetics movement. The motive of indulging libido was explicitly acknowledged for the Kerista utopian community, founded in New York City in 1956 by John Peltz Presmond (*Wikipedia* contributors, "Kerista," *Wikipedia, the Free Encyclopedia*, last revised May 13, 2023, https://en.wikipedia.org/wiki/Kerista) (though many other founders have in fact used their movements for sexual purposes, as discussed in chapter 12). The motive of continuing a sequence of entrepreneurial projects is reported by Venkatesh (2009).

11. Horden and Purcell 2000, p. 437.

12. Whitehouse 1995, p. 90ff.

13. Spisak et al. (2014) show that experimental subjects discriminate on the basis of age, believing that older-looking candidates for leadership represent continuity while younger-looking ones represent innovation.

14. Bach and Serrano-Velarde 2015; Stacchini and Degasperi 2015.

15. See Lazear et al. 2015; Mollick 2012.

16. This is a central assumption of the influential model of family firm succession by Burkart et al. (2003).

17. Bennedsen et al. 2007.

18. Sakurai 2019, p. 82.

19. McCleary (forthcoming) argues this for Guatemala.

20. Rée 2019, p. 34.

21. This need to raise outside capital—and the consequent dilution of ownership it entails—plays an important part in the model of Burkart et al. (2003), leading the authors to make predictions about the pattern of succession across countries that depend to an important degree on the quality of investor protection under different legal systems. This has less relevance for succession in religious movements. However, in some circumstances religious movements may receive injections of capital from outsiders (drug cartels may do this as a way of laundering the proceeds of their trafficking, for example). I am grateful to Rachel McCleary for this point.

22. Haveman and Khaire 2004.

23. Individuals at other layers in the status hierarchy—archbishops, suffragans, or deacons—play roles of helpers and consultants (respectively to the Pope, to bishops, and to priests), but individual bishops are appointed by the Pope (see Britannica, Editors of Encyclopaedia, "bishop," *Encyclopedia Britannica*, last revised May 26, 2023, https://www.britannica.com/topic/bishop-Christianity).

24. P. Brown 2013a, p.15.

25. Aghion and Tirole (1997) explore these considerations in the context of a formal economic model.

26. Forrest 2018, front inside flap.

27. Hanson and Xiang 2013.

28. Leppin 2022.

29. See Lafontaine and Slade (2015) for an overview of the economics of franchising.

30. Luca 2012. She is eloquent about the fine line that exists between some multilevel marketing operations (which are legal) and illegal pyramid schemes (which typically reward their distributors by requiring them to recruit several other new paying members).

31. John of Ephesus 1860, part 3, 3.36, p. 230.

32. Kitiarsa 2005, p. 485.

33. Kitiarsa (2012), cited in Strathern (2019, p. 94).

34. Carolyn Chen, discussing her book (2022) in an interview for *Guernica* magazine (Hertog and Chen 2022).

35. Morrissey 2021, p. 91.

36. Quran 9:29.

37. Quran 8:61.

38. Parkin 2021, p. 213.

39. Srinivas 1956, p. 482.

40. *Economist* 2017.

41. Sumption 2002.

42. See Khan 2022. Coleman (2021, p. 206) discusses "articulations between pilgrimage, mobility and economy" in the modern world.

43. Robarts 2017, p. 229. I'm grateful to Sheilagh Ogilvie for drawing my attention to this account.

44. Head 1999, p.341.

45. McCleary (forthcoming) argues this was true also for Protestant movements in Guatemala in the first half of the twentieth century: "Missionaries themselves introduced doctrinal heterodoxy to Guatemala's religion market. Through their open market approach to evangelizing, they and their national leaders evangelized crisscrossing each other's territory."

46. McCleary and Barro 2022.

47. Horden and Purcell 2000, p. 458.

48. Elawa 2020, p. 9.

49. Partridge 2022.

50. The Henry Ford, n.d.

51. Van Rhijn 2022, p. 1.

52. Ibid., p. 8.

53. Strathern 2019, p. 96.

54. *Pearl* is available in a fine modern English translation by Simon Armitage (2016). I am grateful to John Drury for drawing my attention to this work.

55. Pettegree 2015, pp. x–xii.

56. Ibid., p. 143.

57. See Maclean (2022) for an account of how, thanks to these developments, Luther's close companion Philip Melanchthon developed his own brand, which was both personal and theological.

58. Van Rhijn 2022, p. 21.

59. See the compilation of Carolingian polyptiques at the School of Historical Studies at the University of Leicester: https://www.le.ac.uk/hi/polyptyques/capitulare/site.html.

60. The later (Anglo-Saxon) document *Rectitudines singularum personarum* sets out more clearly statements of principle and not just lists of assets and obligations, for estates including ecclesiastical ones. See the University of St Andrews's site Early English Laws, https://earlyenglishlaws.ac.uk/laws/texts/rect/.

61. This is the central theme of Toneatto (2012).

62. Ucerler 2021.

63. MacCulloch 2014, p. 169. This fact leads MacCulloch to speculate about "a huge missing body of letters systematically fed into a Jesuit stove" (p. 169).

64. Friedrich 2022, esp. pp. 271–86.

65. Instituto Brasileiro de Marketing Católico, "Foz do Iguaçu: 27 encontro de marketing Católico," accessed July 11, 2023, https://www.ibmc.com.br/encontro. Einstein (2008) explores some of many ways in which commercial marketing techniques have been explicitly embraced by religious movements.

66. CfaN (Christ for all Nations), "Christ for All Nations Evangelism Bootcamp," accessed July 19, 2003, https://www.cfan.eu/bootcamp/.

67. August 18, 2022, at 12:05.

68. Bryan et al. 2021, p. 293.

Chapter 10

1. Vacana no. 144, translated by A. K. Ramanujan (1973, p. 77).

2. Chhapia 2020.

3. Sakurai 2010, p. 324.

4. Lafleur 1992; Sakurai 2019, p. 76.

5. On the Church's apology, see Kyodo (2022). On the claims of fraud, see the page for the Church on *Wikipedia* (*Wikipedia* contributors, "Unification Church," *Wikipedia, the Free Encyclopedia*, last revised May 29, 2023, https://en.wikipedia.org/wiki/Unification_Church).

6. Kyodo 2022.

7. Sakurai 2019, p. 66.

8. Fisher 2022.

9. *Wikipedia* gives an estimate of between 140,000 and 200,000 (*Wikipedia* contributors, "Guatemalan Civil War," *Wikipedia, the Free Encyclopedia*, last revised May 30, 2023, https://en .wikipedia.org/wiki/Guatemalan_Civil_War). P. Ball et al. (1999) document 37,255 killings, almost all committed by state forces or state-sponsored paramilitaries (though they acknowledge the fact of some killings by rebel groups). They add that "we hesitate to estimate total numbers of Guatemalans killed or disappeared during the conflict," but say that these were almost certainly much higher than the number they record.

10. Rachel McCleary, pers. comm.—e-mail, June 2022.

11. VaticanNews.va 2021.

12. Rachel McCleary, pers. comm.—e-mail, June 2022. She also mentions this case in her overview of child martyrs in Guatemala in McCleary (2022).

13. In part 3, chapter 5, of *The Theory of Moral Sentiments* (Smith 1759), he writes:

> During the ignorance and darkness of pagan superstition, mankind seem to have formed the ideas of their divinities with so little delicacy, that they ascribed to them, indiscriminately, all the passions of human nature, those not excepted which do the least honour to our species, such as lust, hunger, avarice, envy, revenge. They could not fail, therefore, to ascribe to those beings, for the excellence of whose nature they still conceived the highest admiration, those sentiments and qualities which are the great ornaments of

humanity, and which seem to raise it to a resemblance of divine perfection, the love of
virtue and beneficence, and the abhorrence of vice and injustice. The man who was injured called upon Jupiter to be witness of the wrong that was done to him, and could not
doubt but that divine being would behold it with the same indignation which would
animate the meanest of mankind, who looked on when injustice was committed. The
man who did the injury felt himself to be the proper object of the detestation and resentment of mankind; and his natural fears led him to impute the same sentiments to those
awful beings, whose presence he could not avoid, and whose power he could not resist.
These natural hopes, and fears, and suspicions, were propagated by sympathy, and confirmed by education; and the gods were universally represented and believed to be the
rewarders of humanity and mercy, and the avengers of perfidy and injustice. And thus
religion, even in its rudest form, gave a sanction to the rules of morality, long before the
age of artificial reasoning and philosophy. That the terrors of religion should thus enforce
the natural sense of duty, was of too much importance to the happiness of mankind for
nature to leave it dependent upon the slowness and uncertainty of philosophical
researches.

It's hard not to see in this last sentence an inspiration for Edward Gibbon's famous later observation (Gibbon [1776] 1836, chapter 2, part 1) that "the various modes of worship, which prevailed
in the Roman world, were all considered by the people, as equally true; by the philosopher, as
equally false; and by the magistrate, as equally useful. And thus toleration produced not only
mutual indulgence, but even religious concord."

14. The occasion was a surprise audience granted to the attendees of a conference of the
International Economic Association hosted by the Philippines Economic Association, in 1982,
when I was a young graduate student recruited as rapporteur for the panel discussions. A year
or so after the conference, the assassination of opposition leader Benigno Aquino on the tarmac
at Manila airport triggered international revulsion and a political backlash in the country, culminating in the eventual downfall of Marcos, who had ordered the killing.

15. *King Lear*, act 1, scene 1, line 145.

16. Della Subin 2021, pp. 7–8.

17. Ibid., p. 10.

18. Weber (1922) 1947.

19. Ibid., emphasis in the original.

20. Della Subin 2021, p. 124.

21. Inscription cited in Strathern (2019, p. 161).

22. See Strathern (2019, chapter 3) for many examples.

23. Sahlins 2017, p. 119. A related claim (p. 91) is that: "For, Hobbes notwithstanding, something like the political state is the condition of humanity in the state of nature; there are kingly
beings in heaven even where there are no chiefs on earth."

24. There is a large literature about the reasons for this attribution of divinity. Mitchell (2013)
emphasizes that Alexander was not using it to place himself "above the law"; instead he wanted
to embody it, and "he could only be law if he had also enough virtue also to be god" (p. 91).

25. Bentzen and Gokmen 2023. This is also consistent with the findings of Turchin et al.
(2022).

26. Strathern 2019, p. 149.

27. Agence France-Presse 2022.

28. Saleh and Tirole 2021.

29. Saleh (2018) shows that those who resisted conversion were, unsurprisingly, the more educated and prosperous. Much more surprisingly, he shows that the resulting economic difference between Coptic Christians and Muslims in Egypt persisted for over a millennium, until the nineteenth century. As he notes, Max Weber (1958, p. 6) had proposed a similar selection mechanism when he suggested that converts from Hinduism to Christianity and Islam in India came from the lower castes.

30. Pankenier 1995, p. 503.

31. Ibid., p. 504.

32. J. Chen et al. 2021.

33. Scheidel 2019, pp. 223–24.

34. Cantoni et al. 2018; Heldring et al. 2021.

35. Rodriguez 2020, p. 20.

36. Platteau (2017) provides many historical illustrations. A theoretical account of the process is given in Auriol and Platteau (2017a, b).

37. Chaney (2013) has shown that such challenges increased during episodes of flooding in the Nile basin between the twelfth and fifteenth centuries CE.

38. Azam (2022) shows that the campaign of jihad waged by the Sudanese government of Omar al-Bashir in the 1990s against Christian communities in the south, in which religion was used to recruit members of otherwise disunited Muslim tribes, was reversed once the government realized that it needed to reach an agreement with the rebels in order to protect the 1,500-kilometer oil pipeline that had opened in 1999 connecting the southern oilfields to the Red Sea.

39. Blaydes and Chaney 2013, p. 16. The authors' explanation does not rely only on degrees of political centralization but also on the dependence of Muslim rulers on mamluks, or non-Muslim slaves imported from non-Muslim lands, which was less effective than Christian kings' reliance on feudal tribute. But the latter may in turn have owed something to the central support of the Church.

40. Scheidel 2019, p. 9. Ma and Rubin (2019) provide an analytical explanation for, and model of, such a divergence, based on the idea that powerful centralized regimes are unable to commit not to expropriate the fruits of the investments of their citizens, a model they apply specifically to Qing China but with evident relevance to earlier periods.

41. Cantoni et al. 2018; Heldring et al. 2021.

42. Kuran (2018) summarizes the literature about the impact of Islam on economic performance, at the level of both societies and individuals.

43. Kuran 2010, 2018; Rubin 2017, esp. chapters 4 and 5. Rubin argues that absence of demand for printed books is not the explanation, despite there being little evidence of efforts to evade the ban (pp. 107–9).

44. Schwartz 2017.

45. See Rubin (2014) for the association between Protestantism and the spread of printing, and S. Becker et al. (2021) for the association between Catholic censorship of the diffusion of knowledge and city growth.

46. Aldashev and Platteau (2014, section 5) survey the literature on "the State as a Strategic Actor" with respect to religion.

47. See Hahn 2015; Nixey 2017, prologue and chapter 9.

48. P. Brown 1998, p. 648.

49. Hahn 2015, p. 385.

50. P. Brown 1998, pp. 635–36.

51. Ibid., p. 646.

52. Hahn 2015, pp. 379–80.

53. See Van Nuffelen (2020) for a contrary view. See Lane Fox (1986) for arguments that the arrival of Christianity marked a major social, ideological, and political departure from the world of pagan antiquity, contrary to those who emphasize the importance of "pagan survivals."

54. Briggs 2002, introduction, loc. 156.

55. Ibid., conclusion, loc. 5395.

56. Peacey et al. 2023.

57. Majumdar and Villa 2021. Figures from table SHI.Q1.a.

58. Roser et al. 2016.

59. Botticini and Eckstein 2012.

60. S. Becker and Pascali 2019.

61. Jha 2023, p. 59.

62. Ticku et al. 2023.

63. See Doniger (2009, pp. 348–49) for examples of violence over Hindu temples, which she claims "had little, if anything, to do with religious persecution."

64. Vacana no. 144, translated by A. K. Ramanujan (1973, p. 77).

65. N. Johnson and Koyama 2019. Quotation at p. 4.

66. See Koyama and Rubin (2022) for an overview.

67. Moustafa 2000, p. 3.

68. Tilakaratne (2006) discusses the general challenge to the legitimacy of the Buddhist orders in Sri Lanka from the growing economic and political worldliness of some Buddhist monks. See also Silva (2006, pp. 206–8).

69. McCleary and Barro 2006a, b.

70. Fox 2008.

71. Fox and Breslawski 2023, p. 1.

72. Putnam and Campbell 2010.

73. Ibid., chapter 1, locs. 145, 177.

74. Ibid., chapter 15, loc. 8392.

75. Corbi and Miessi Sanches 2022.

76. Margolis 2018.

77. Pew Research Center 2019a.

78. See Woodberry (2012) for a study of the historical impact of Protestant missionaries on the spread of democratic ideas. Muslim and Buddhist organizations have also played a role in defending democratic movements in various countries, including Iran and Myanmar.

79. Hout and Fischer 2014.

80. Pew Research Center 2019a.

81. Raiber and Seabright 2020. We conclude that:

> We find no evidence that supply-driven ideological factors have played a substantial part in shaping the churches' responses. Size and worship style are important sources of heterogeneity, while political orientation is not. Of course, we cannot rule out that churches are using their persuasive power to advance political messages in ways that escape our analysis. But if the majority of churches were opposing public health measures on a large scale we would expect to see evidence of this in our data, and we do not. (p. 126)

82. Raiber and Seabright 2023.

Chapter 11

1. Plutarch 1898, 140D.

2. See Buckner 2018.

3. Hegghammer 2020b, pp. 369, 371.

4. Hegghammer (ibid., pp. 371–72) reports several instances of enemies being mocked on social media for weeping, including "in 2015, at the time when Islamic State executed suspected homosexuals by throwing them off tall buildings, a female sympathizer posted a picture of one of the victims on Twitter, adding the comment 'hahaha poor baby—want a tissue before you go skydiving?'"

5. Saint Augustine reports in his *Confessions* how his friend Alypius had always resisted watching gladiatorial games, but was once persuaded by friends to attend one. "For so soon as he saw that blood, he therewith drunk down savageness; nor turned away, but fixed his eye, drinking in frenzy, unawares, and was delighted with that guilty fight, and intoxicated with the bloody pastime" (Augustine of Hippo [401] 2001, book 6).

6. It's likely that males obtained both a direct adaptive advantage from violence, and an indirect advantage via sexual selection—I discuss this in more detail in *The Company of Strangers* (Seabright 2010, chapters 3 and 4), though I would now qualify that discussion to reflect the arguments of Wrangham (2019).

7. This argument is set out in detail in Wrangham (2019).

8. Space forbids a full treatment here, but I am indebted to my Toulouse colleague Jean-Paul Azam for discussion of several of these strategies (and for drawing my attention to the case of Alypius as well as to the work of Jay Rubenstein). His unpublished paper (Azam 2017) offers a wealth of arguments and evidence. Thomas Hegghammer also has a very interesting discussion in *The Caravan*, his biography of Abdallah Azzam, who assembled in Afghanistan in the 1980s "the most international volunteer force the world had ever seen," with fighters from "at least forty different countries, including every single Arab state down to the Comoros Islands" (Hegghammer 2020a, esp. chapter 10 [quotes at p. 244]).

9. Organized criminals often emphasize the extent to which their actions are carried out through motives of honor (Gambetta 2009).

10. Masera and Yousaf (2022) show how the Pakistani Taliban have engaged in natural disaster relief (for example, after floods in 2010). They also show that this is effective only when it "fills the void left by a weak state" (p. 1174).

11. Hegghammer 2020b, p. 376. Marchais et al. (2022) show that such motivations may be quite genuine. Analyzing a data set of nearly seven thousand individuals during two decades of violent collective action in the Democratic Republic of the Congo's civil conflict, they show that attacks against an individual's community are strong predictors of the likelihood that the individual joins a militia chapter, an effect that is even stronger if the individual's kin are attacked. The authors conclude that "alongside selfish strategic motivations, parochial altruism and community coercion are crucial in explaining the origins, and success, of violent collective action."

12. Rubenstein 2011, chapter 3.

13. Spencer 2019b, p. 147.

14. Fenton 2011, pp. 128–31. See also Spencer 2019a.

15. Lipton 1999, p. 109–10.

16. Boisvert and Daniel-Hughes 2017, introduction, loc. 142.

17. The Association of Religion Data Archives, https://www.thearda.com/ConQS/qs_8 .asp; Sandstrom 2016.

There is a literature emphasizing the important role that women have played historically and continue to play as leaders of religious movements, even if that role has often been overlooked in historical accounts. See Künkler and Fazaeli (2012) for the role of female theologians in twentieth-century Iran. For general discussions of this phenomenon, see Bond and Patel (2022) and Whitehead (2021).

18. UN Women 2023.

19. The literature on men's and women's propensity to vote reaches conflicting conclusions, depending on the countries chosen, the date of the study, and even the type of evidence (for instance, survey data report higher male participation than do voting records). See Dassonneville and Kostelka 2021 and Stockemer and Sundstrom 2021.

20. Buchholz 2022.

21. OECD 2008, chapter 10, table 10.1.

22. Majumdar and Villa 2021. Figures from table SHI.Q11.

23. For a good example of a plea (by Bina Agarwal) to rise to the explicitly political challenge of reformulating India's civil code to respect gender equality rather than allowing religious leaders to impose their own communitarian conceptions of the role of women, see Agarwal (2023).

24. Pew Research Center 2016.

25. Vardy et al. 2022. The remainder of the study tests various hypotheses about the reasons for this conclusion, without finding strong support for any of them.

26. See Boisvert and Daniel-Hughes (2017, introduction, loc. 139).

27. Once again, see Buckner (2018).

28. I discuss this at length in *The War of the Sexes* (Seabright 2012, chapter 5, esp. pp. 101–5).

29. P. Brown 1988; Stark 1995, pp. 232–33. However, the prevalence of female infanticide has been contested: see Kuefler (2007, p. 354, and the references cited in his footnote 50).

30. Meeks 2003, p. 25.

31. Harper 2013, p.8.

32. K. Hopkins 1965.

33. Burger 2015.

34. In *The War of the Sexes* (Seabright 2012), chapters 5 to 7, I explore the possibility that there may be systematic differences, on average, in specific dimensions of the talents and preferences of men and women. Chapter 5 explains why that does not in any way imply a general difference in talents and preferences averaged across dimensions.

35. There are many more aspects of religion and gender than we have the space to consider here. Woodhead et al. (2016) survey the question and provide valuable suggestions for further reading.

Chapter 12

1. The documentary was made by Cathy Newman and the investigations team at *Channel 4 News*, using information brought to them by the writer Andrew Graystone, whose book *Bleeding for Jesus: John Smyth and the Cult of Iwerne Camps* was published in 2021. The details of Smyth's behavior in this chapter are taken from this book unless otherwise specified. While there are many details recounted in Graystone's book that I have not been able to verify independently, where he writes about things that fall within my own knowledge I find him to be reliable, both as to facts and as to capturing the nuance and atmosphere of the Iwerne camps.

2. The Scripture Union's *John Smyth Independent Case Review* (Camina 2021) refers in paragraph 1.9 to "two confirmed deaths of boys at Camps in Zimbabwe led by John Smyth and a number of attempted suicides among his UK victims." I have not been able to establish the reasons for the discrepancy in reporting.

3. These claims are made on p. 113 ("In a casual conversation over coffee the chaplain of St. Michaels [in 1983], Peter Sertin, told Welby that word had reached him that John Smyth was a bad man and not to be trusted"), p. 182 ("Welby claimed that the church had conducted 'a rigorous enquiry' in 2013, and offered 'support for survivors'"), pp. 206–7 (where Graystone recounts the receipt by Lambeth Palace, the London home of the archbishop of Canterbury, in 2013 of a letter from the Bishop of Ely reporting detailed allegations about Smyth), p. 207 (where Welby's claim that there had been a "rigorous enquiry" in 2013 is commented "There was no rigorous inquiry—in fact, there was no inquiry at all"), p. 221 (where Welby's claim that he had had no contact with Smyth after 1978 is contrasted with the statement on p. 223 that "Welby and Smyth had exchanged Christmas cards as late as the mid-90s"), and p. 223 ("In a statement later, [Welby] admitted that the church had failed catastrophically, and that they should have reported what they knew to the police and social services in 2013. However, in the months and years that followed, for whatever reason, the Archbishop's staff failed to set up a meeting with Smyth survivors").

A report in the *New York Times* of October 14, 2017, cites "Alan Wilson, a Church of England bishop who is friends with former Iwerne members, [who] said that he found it hard to believe the archbishop's denials. 'I have no evidence, but I haven't met a single Iwerne person who thinks it's credible that Justin Welby didn't know that Smyth had left the country under a cloud connected to his behavior toward boys who had been on Iwerne camps,' he said" (Yeginsu 2017).

4. Official reports from the following countries. Australia: Royal Commission into Institutional Responses to Child Sexual Abuse 2017; Canada: CCCB Ad Hoc Committee on Child Sexual Abuse 1992; France: Ciase 2021; Germany: Frings et al. 2022; Ireland: five reports from

the Ferns Report in 2005 to the Mother-and-baby-home report in 2020: Reuters Staff 2021; United Kingdom: IICSA 2022; United States: Terry et al. 2004; 40th Statewide Investigating Grand Jury 2018; Secretariat of State of the Holy See 2020. *Wikipedia* listing: Wikipedia contributors, "Catholic Church Sexual Abuse Cases in Europe," *Wikipedia, the Free Encyclopedia*, accessed July 11, 2023, https://en.wikipedia.org/wiki/Catholic_Church_sexual_abuse_cases_in_Europe.

5. Ciase 2021.

6. AP in Paris 2022; *Le Figaro* with AFP 2022.

7. Giuffrida 2022.

8. Religious movements have differed widely in the extent to which they have been willing to launch official enquiries, or resist investigation. So it is often necessary to draw on press reports, which are evidently less reliable, and individual scholarly studies, which may be more reliable but less representative. Press reports also make it harder to distinguish between abuse of children and inappropriate behavior toward adults, which may constitute abuse but is evidently more difficult to assess. Official enquiries in non-Catholic institutions include Jay et al. (2020) for the Anglican Church. Neustein's (2009) *Tempest in the Temple* is a collection of scholarly studies for Jewish communities. McGuigan and Stephenson (2015) produced a single-case study of an Old Order Amish community. Tishelman and Fontes (2017) have gathered interviews with forensic interviewers reporting cases in the following communities: "Amish, Assembly of God, Baptist, Catholic, Christian, a cloistered Christian sect, Conservative Christian, Evangelical, Fundamentalist, Jehovah's Witnesses, Hasidic, Jewish, Lakota Lutheran, Lutheran, Mennonite, Methodist, Mormon, Muslim, Orthodox Jewish, and Pentecostal" (p. 122).

Among some press reports are the following: Appiah 2021; Australian Associated Press 2021; BBC News 2018b; Borecka 2023; A. Horton 2021; Lu 2022; Pierre 2022; Pulliam Bailey 2021; Soullier 2022.

9. Parris 2024, pp. 5–9.

10. See, for example, the cases of Asaram Bapu (BBC News 2018a); Virendra Dev Dikshit (Mohan and Singh 2018); Gurmeet Ram Rahim Singh (Special correspondent 2017); Nithyananda (Mishra 2022); Ichadhari Bhimanand (India.com News Desk 2017); Swami Vikasanand (TimesofIndia.com 2018); Ganga Shashwatapada Swamy (*Express* Web Desk 2017).

11. Buckner 2018, 2019.

12. For sports, see Whyte (2022) on UK gymnastics, M. Hall (2022) on Ohio soccer. For artistic institutions, see Dhillon (2020). For schools, see Newland (2022) for the first *Federal Indian Boarding School Initiative Investigative Report* on the shocking conditions under which Native American children were interned between 1819 and 1969 in 408 boarding schools; Newsam and Ridgway (2022) on abuse of children in care homes in Oldham in the United Kingdom. For the Boy Scouts, see Milman (2020).

13. This did not prevent the *New York Times* columnist Ross Douthat, writing in 2014, from blaming rape and sexual assault on college campuses on "a fun, even bacchanalian lifestyle ... where teens and early-twentysomethings are barely supervised and held to no standard higher than consent ... a hard-drinking, sexually permissive culture." Nor retired Pope Benedict XVI from blaming sexual assault within the Catholic Church on the "swinging sixties" (Associated Press 2019).

14. Cultures of repression or permissiveness may still play a role in abuse in a more indirect way. For example, Julia Hoefer Martí and I have shown, theoretically and empirically, that sexual

assault on US college campuses is more likely in institutions that combine repressive attitudes to consensual sex with easy access to disinhibiting mechanisms like alcohol (Hoefer Martí and Seabright 2022). We clearly reject the simple form of the permissiveness hypothesis.

15. See Hassan (2018) and Rodríguez-Carballeira et al. (2015), among many others.

16. For example in the independent review commissioned by Winchester College and published in January 2022 (Pickles and Woods 2002); also in the Coltart Report, which was commissioned in 1993 from Messrs Webb, Low, and Barry, legal practitioners in in Bulawayo, by a group of Christian ministers in Bulawayo. The latter remained confidential until many years later, and is now available at https://static1.1.sqspcdn.com/static/f/970485/27843432/1519927496303/The+Coltart+Report+on+John+Smyth+1982.pdf.

17. See Raine and Kent (2019), who go into more detail than is possible here about strategies used for grooming children in religious organizations.

18. Dunbar 2022, p. 79.

19. See L. Barrett and Henzi 2001.

20. For recruitment to jihad, see the discussion of "fictive kin" in Atran (2003).

21. The literature on Scientology is large and controversial and cannot be adequately surveyed here. Reitman (2013) provides extensive interview material with both critics and spokespersons of the movement, and documents some cases of members' being pressured to cut off contacts with family members. L. Wright (2013) also documents such pressure. Urban's *Church of Scientology* (2011) is a history of the movement. The website of the Church of Scientology acknowledges a policy known as "disconnection" when encountering "persistent opposition from close associates," which it defends as a human right (Church of Scientology, "What Is 'Disconnection'?," FAQ, accessed July 11, 2023, https://web.archive.org/web/20120210152924/http://faq.scientology.org/discon.htm).

22. The prevalence of priestly abusers in the Catholic Church was estimated in the John Jay Report (*Wikipedia* contributors, "John Jay Report," *Wikipedia*, the Free Encyclopedia, accessed July 11, 2023, https://en.wikipedia.org/wiki/John_Jay_Report) to be around 4 percent of priests from 1950 to 2002, and a study of the German Catholic Church from 1946 to 2014 (Dressing et al. 2021) estimated a prevalence of 4.4 percent. Studies of individual orders such as the Christian Brothers have reached substantially higher estimates, in the region of 20 percent or more (Bravehearts, n.d.). Once abuse occurs, the frequency with which others enable the abuse to continue is attested in many cases. Erica Brown (2009, 2010, 2017) discusses abuse in Jewish communities but also points to many parallels in other religious communities (see footnotes 2 and 3 of her 2017 paper for the Catholic Church and the Jehovah's Witnesses). Dratch (2009) notes that remaining passive in the face of abuse by others is explicitly condemned under Jewish law.

23. O'Toole 2021, p. 235.

24. Ibid., p. 156.

25. Mannix Flynn 2003, p. 6.

26. Graystone (2021, p. 226) reports John Thorn, former headmaster of Winchester College, as saying "we got this bugger out of the country—excuse my language—into Africa and said: thank God that's gone."

27. Woodhead (2022, esp. pp. 91–92) discusses some other reasons for passivity on the part of the Church of England in various cases.

28. Kaufman and Zigler (1987) published an early study advancing this hypothesis. Later work has suggested various biases that might be responsible for the statistical association between experiencing abuse in childhood and committing abuse in adulthood (e.g., Widom et al. 2015). Madigan et al. (2019) conducted a meta-analysis concluding that the causal effect is likely real though the effect sizes modest once adjustments for bias are made. An interesting detail reported in the Scripture Union case review (Camina 2021, paragraph 5.2) is that John Smyth was raised in a strict Plymouth Brethren family in Canada, and that his family was expelled from the Fellowship, "which reportedly had a profound effect upon Smyth."

29. See Raine and Kent 2019. The final report of the Royal Commission into Institutional Responses to Child Sexual Abuse (2017, p. 10) summarizes "institutional factors that facilitated or enabled perpetrators."

30. Giles-Sims 1998. There is some controversy over the extent to which this represents a genuine difference in prevalence as opposed to other characteristics of stepfamilies, as found for child homicides by Temrin et al. (2011).

31. See Mallett 2017. The final report of the Royal Commission (2017) states bluntly (p. 19) that "there is a lack of research on female perpetrators, and no typical profile of women who sexually abuse children has been identified."

32. E. Brown 2009, p. 62.

33. As argued by Zech (2001), for example.

34. McGuigan and Stephenson 2015, p. 528.

35. A point emphasized by Woodhead (2022).

36. Parris (2022, p. 11) argues that this is true of some tantric practices.

37. Harris (2022), in her biography of Vivekananda, reports that he was considered to have been "never polluted by food that was forbidden to the other disciples" of his guru Ramakrishna, who himself claimed that "if a man keeps his mind on God, eating pork and beef is equivalent to eating the purest simple *havishyanna* [sacred food offerings] made of boiled vegetables." The two would smoke a pipe together, "enjoying a 'vice' that was no longer transgressive by virtue of their mutual purity and powers" (p. 76).

38. H. James 1863, p. 75.

39. Ibid.

40. This was a recognized phenomenon in some earlier ages too: MacCulloch (2014) reports that the professionally trained clergy constituted "Victorian England's only profession in which, thanks to the Anglo Catholics, lifelong abstention from marriage did not cause too much raising of eyebrows" (p. 187).

41. Harrison 2022; Lawson 2022.

Chapter 13

1. Allen 2013.

2. Greeley 1969, p. 168.

3. Ibid, p. 169.

4. Ibid, p. 171.

5. Ibid, pp. 171–72.

6. Ibid, p. 172.

7. Ibid, p. 173.

8. See his obituary in the *New York Times*, reporting that he "had been an early and vehement advocate for victims of abusive priests at least since 1989, when he began writing articles in Chicago newspapers demanding that the church take action against pedophile priests" (Steinfels 2013).

9. For example, the divisions in the Anglican Church over issues of sexuality. See, for one example amid many others, Sherwood (2022).

10. Swatos and Christiano (1999) provide an account of the many variants of secularization theory propounded in the twentieth century.

11. This is argued, for example, by Peter Berger in his theory of "plausibility structures." He writes (1969): "It is relatively easy, sociologically speaking, to be a Catholic in a social situation where one can readily limit one's significant others to fellow Catholics. . . . The story is quite different . . . where one is compelled to rub shoulders day by day with every conceivable variety of 'those others', is bombarded with communications that deny or ignore one's Catholic ideas, and where one has a terrible time even finding some quiet Catholic corners to withdraw into" (1969, pp. 43–44).

12. Greeley 1969, p. 97.

13. Ibid., pp. 67–68.

14. "If, in a given country, one's belief also confers upon one social- and self-definition over against others, then the belief is likely to be more elaborate and the organizational commitment flowing from the belief more vigorous" (Greeley 1969, p. 96). That would be typically true in religiously pluralistic countries, as opposed to societies "where there tends to be either officially or unofficially a single religion, or where the identification of religion and social class makes social class available as an alternative means of self-definition" (p. 97).

15. *Wikipedia* contributors, "Metaverse," *Wikipedia, the Free Encyclopedia*, accessed July 11, 2023, https://en.wikipedia.org/wiki/Metaverse.

16. Ball 2022, p. 4.

17. Ibid., p. 28.

18. Clottes and Lewis-Williams (1998) argued that caves such as Chauvet were sites of shamanistic rituals. While not universally accepted, this hypothesis has received support from other scholars—see Morriss-Kay (2010), for example, who argues (p. 169) that "the interpretation that therianthropes represent shamans has a sound basis in recently-observed societies," and that "there is considerable evidence that the cave wall (or rock surface in the case of rock art in other parts of the world) was regarded as a membrane between the human and spirit worlds." However, she adds that "although the self-induction of trance states is well documented for many extant and recent hunter-gatherer communities, it is not clear that it is an essential preliminary to the creation of rock or cave art." It's hard to know what evidence would settle the question.

19. Eisenstein (1979) produced a classic work exploring the impact of this technology, a theme developed further by Dudley (1991, esp. chapter 5).

20. Quoted in Loewenstein (2013, p. 31).

21. Acemoglu and Restrepo 2019.

22. Pettegree 2015.

23. Whitehouse 1995, p.183.

24. Dudley 1991.

25. The transmission of Greek and Arabic texts to Christian Europe in the twelfth and thirteenth centuries is surveyed by Burnett (2013). The role of Baghdad in this process is emphasized by Ragep (2013).

26. Lindberg (2013, p. 283) emphasizes that "the overwhelming majority of medieval scientific achievements were produced by scholars who subscribed to the Augustinian formula of science as the handmaiden of theology and the church. The church became the patron of the sciences through its support of schools and universities, many of which were under its authority and protection."

27. Bénabou et al. 2015, 2022.

28. Chaney 2016, esp. figure 2.

29. Andersen and Bentzen 2022. They also show that cities with a larger proportion of individuals with religious names grew more slowly over this period, though the causality is evidently more difficult to establish, since religiosity and economic growth might both be influenced by other, unobserved characteristics of cities.

30. Grajzl and Murrell (2023) report, using machine learning to identify distinct topics in the corpus of nearly fifty-eight thousand texts from sixteenth- and seventeenth-century England, that shocks to the attention devoted to religious topics were followed by increases in attention to scientific topics (and vice versa). One possibility is that this is because religious writers were not, after all, hostile to scientific innovation. Another is that writers on scientific topics saw themselves as in competition with religious writers and increased their efforts in response to an increase in the attention to religious topics. Unfortunately this study does not enable us to distinguish between these two explanations, but future analyses may be able to do so.

31. Y. Chen, Wang, and Yan 2022. This is in line with a prior literature documenting the effect of the Protestant Reformation on investments in human capital, beginning with S. Becker and Woessmann (2009). Becker et al. (2021) survey this literature. However, J. Edwards (2021) questions the econometrics underlying the Becker and Woessmann (2009) study and concludes that although Protestantism was associated with higher incomes it was not via increasing literacy. Ogilvie et al. (2022) cast doubt on whether literacy as such for the general population was likely to lead to economic productivity: "The books people owned were overwhelmingly religious, as elsewhere in pre-modern Europe. People consumed books for multifarious purposes, many of them non-economic" (abstract).

32. Squicciarini 2020. Squicciarini's results were challenged by Kelly (2021), and she has replied (Mara P. Squicciarini, "Reply to Kelly," n.d., https://d0588f21-3f05-484e-93b7 -532977ce2186.filesusr.com/ugd/08a88f_d5a58116d5b84bf0b906b5eb9d99e427.pdf).

33. Ogilvie 2023.

34. Ronan and Needham 1985, p. 326.

35. M. Johnson and Wilson 2007, p. 131.

36. Greenblatt (2011) argues that the discovery in Germany in 1417 of a manuscript of Lucretius's poem by the Italian Renaissance humanist Poggio Bracciolini was one of a series of pivotal events that helped to bring about the Renaissance. A lengthy review by Monfasani (2012) disputes the extent of the book's influence, writing that "not only did the ultra-orthodox Thomas

More make his Utopians Epicureans without the least obeisance to Lucretius, but the great Erasmus also added insult to injury by expressing several times his appreciation of Epicureanism while ignoring Lucretius entirely." However, by the seventeenth century, M. Johnson and Wilson (2007, p. 131) write, "thanks in large measure to their compelling presentation in Lucretius' poem, Epicurean ideas effectively replaced the scholastic-Aristotelian theory of nature formerly dominant in the universities." Of the Enlightenment, Baker (2007, p. 274) writes that "virtually every major figure of the period was in some way influenced by Lucretius."

37. M. Johnson and Wilson 2007, p. 140.

38. Ronan and Needham 1985, p. 327.

39. Notably in Macfarlane's *Origins of English Individualism* (1978) and in McCloskey's *Bourgeois Era* trilogy (2006, 2010, 2016a).

40. McCloskey 2016b, p. 52. In contrast, Friedman (2005, esp. pp. 32–38, 42–47, 67–72) provides many examples of religious thinkers who helped to advance ideas of economic progress.

41. Siedentop 2014.

42. Goody 1983, chapter 6.

43. For a recent book-length statement of the claim that the Christian Church caused the marriage pattern and that the marriage pattern had long-lasting effects on individualistic psychology and economic growth, see Henrich (2020). This claim has been disputed on several grounds—see McCants (2021) for a strong summary of the objections—notably that close-kin marriage was already rare in the Western Roman Empire at the time Henrich claims the Church acted to abolish it (see Shaw and Saller [1984] for some relevant evidence). For skeptical analysis of the claim that the European marriage pattern (EMP) had an impact on economic development, and of the claim that the EMP either caused or was caused by particular cultural or religious beliefs, see Dennison and Ogilvie (2014). An overview of the debate up to 2014 or so is given in Aldashev and Platteau (2014, pp. 601–4). For a view that the EMP had nothing to do with the Gregorian reforms and everything to do with the economics of land management in the presence of labor scarcity, see Hartmann (2004). For a taste of the variety in implementation of the Church's rules across Europe, see Müller (2021).

44. Hunter (2020) provides a nuanced overview of the issues and evidence for Britain.

45. Thomas 1971, p. 800.

46. It would be pointless to try to summarize the vast literature on this question. Mokyr (2002, 2017) argues for the central importance of scientific knowledge, and a set of cultural values that valued it, to the economic development of the modern world. Koyama and Rubin (2022) evaluate such arguments in the light of the overall literature on industrialization and economic growth.

47. Brosnan and de Waal 2003. The experiment can be viewed on video, as an extract from a TED talk by Frans de Waal, at YouTube (vladimerk1, "Capuchin Monkey Fairness Experiment," YouTube, April 13, 2012, https://www.youtube.com/watch?v=-KSryJXDpZo).

48. This is a central theme of Boehm's *Hierarchy in the Forest* (1999).

49. The theory of expressive voting was set out comprehensively by Brennan and Lomasky (1993), though the idea was present in the early work of many scholars, as mentioned in the comprehensive overview paper by Hamlin and Jennings (2019), especially at footnote 3.

50. Siedentop 2014.

51. Lam 2015.

52. The Internal Revenue Service's *Guide for Churches and Religious Organizations* (2015, p. 33) contains the following definition of churches:

> Certain characteristics are generally attributed to churches. These attributes of a church have been developed by the IRS and by court decisions. They include: distinct legal existence; recognized creed and form of worship; definite and distinct ecclesiastical government; formal code of doctrine and discipline; distinct religious history; membership not associated with any other church or denomination; organization of ordained ministers; ordained ministers selected after completing prescribed courses of study; literature of its own; established places of worship; regular congregations; regular religious services; Sunday schools for the religious instruction of the young; and schools for the preparation of its ministers. The IRS generally uses a combination of these characteristics, together with other facts and circumstances, to determine whether an organization is considered a church for federal tax purposes. The IRS makes no attempt to evaluate the content of whatever doctrine a particular organization claims is religious, provided the particular beliefs of the organization are truly and sincerely held by those professing them and the practices and rites associated with the organization's belief or creed are not illegal or contrary to clearly defined public policy.

53. J. Jenkins 2022.

54. R. Wood 2014.

55. See Brunson 2016; Emory and Zelenak 1982.

Chapter 14

1. Weizenbaum (1966) described and analyzed the ELIZA program.

2. Ibid. Quotes at pp. 37 and 42.

3. Mori 2012.

4. Ibid., p. 100 and figure 4.

5. Empson began to develop his ideas while living in Japan during the 1930s, but the sole text of his work was lost in the aftermath of the Second World War, and was not rediscovered until sixty years later. It was eventually edited and published with a substantial commentary by Rupert Arrowsmith (Empson 2016).

6. P. Brown 2013a.

7. For the religious demographics of the US Supreme Court, see Coyle (2022). For a statistical analysis of the decisions of the Roberts court, see Epstein and Posner (2021), who find that:

> Over the entire period, the Court ruled in favor of religion 59% of the time. . . . Across the Warren, Burger, and Rehnquist Courts the religious side prevailed about half the time, with gradually increasing success. In the Roberts Court, the win rate jumps to 83%. . . . The Roberts Court extended the Warren Court's protections for minority religions so as to encompass majority religions as well. . . . On average, Catholic Justices are significantly ($p < 0.05$) more likely to vote for religion than non-Catholic Justices are (71.1% versus 52.0%).

8. See Hungerman (2013) for evidence that abuse scandals have seen a substitution away from US Catholic churches to others, notably Baptist churches (though not to Episcopalian ones).

9. See Thompson (2023) for a recent example.

10. See McCauley (2013) for an account of the factors that fuel the growth of Pentecostalism in Ghana.

11. Guriev and Treisman 2023.

12. Even authoritarian leaders who are not elected may resort to such tactics. A particularly intriguing example of a religious leader indulging an authoritarian political leader is the Chinese Buddhist master Chin Kung, who in a widely circulated online video released in 2016 stated that Xi Jin-Ping is a reincarnation of the Buddha (Ai 2016).

13. Roy 1999.

14. The Dutch-based Group for Analyzing and Measuring Attitudes in Iran (GAMAAN), reported in 2020 that 60 percent stated that they do not pray, that 15 percent identified as atheist or agnostic, while an additional 22 percent did not identify with any religious category. "68% of the population believes that religious prescriptions should be excluded from state legislation, even if believers hold a parliamentary majority" (Maleki and Tamimi Arab 2020).

Statistical Appendix

1. T. Johnson and Grim 2023.

2. World Values Survey Association, World Values Survey, https://www.worldvaluessurvey.org/wvs.jsp.

3. Ritchie and Roser 2019, graph "Median Age, 1950 to 2100."

4. Roser et al. 2013, graph "Fertility Rate: Children per Woman."

5. The percentage of the female population aged 15–19 with no education comes from Robert J. Barro and Jong-Wha Lee's Barro-Lee Educational Attainment Dataset, accessed July 2023, http://www.barrolee.com/.

6. These factors are summarized in detail in Doepke et al. (2022).

7. Inglehart et al. 2022.

8. The coefficient of the slope is 0.92, with confidence intervals of 0.80 and 1.04. The intercept has a coefficient of 4.7, with confidence intervals of −3.1 and 12.5.

9. More precisely, the mean change in the importance of religion in figure 13 is −0.39 percentage points, and the hypothesis that this is different from zero has a p-value of 0.78. The data set and code for generating the figures are available at https://paulseabright.com/?p=2490.

10. Of particular importance are the Pew Research Center, the Association of Religion Data Archives, the International Social Survey Programme, and the World Christian Database, as well as the World Religion Database.

11. Inglehart 2021, figure 7.4. The claim about 90 percent of the world's population is stated in the first paragraph of the preface, p. ix.

12. Inglehart 2021, p. 16.

13. For prosperity, see Roser (2013a, graph "GDP per capita"). DeLong (2022) proposes 1870 as the date after which prosperity in the world really took off. On interpersonal violence, see Seabright (2010, chapter 2) and Pinker (2011).

14. On infant mortality, see historical data in Volk and Atkinson (2013, table 2). For data since 1950, see Roser (2013b). For global child mortality since 1800, see Roser et al. (2019, graph "Global Child Mortality").

15. He also mentions, in the list of possible causes of secularization, "reactions against religious fundamentalists' embrace of xenophobic authoritarian positions, against the Roman Catholic Church's long history of covering up child abuse, and against terrorism by religious extremists" (Inglehart 2021, p. 2). None of these seems like the long-term underlying causes with which the secularization hypothesis has traditionally been concerned, and none is given the extensive treatment in the text accorded to the two main causes.

16. De Waal 2013, p. 171.

17. Inglehart et al. 2022.

18. C. Zhang and Lu 2020. See especially p. 421, where they note that two surveys conducted using different types of question yielded 89.3 percent and 73 percent of nonbelievers.

19. Finke and Stark 2005, esp. as summarized in figure 1.2, p. 23.

20. Stark and Bainbridge 1985.

21. Swatos and Christiano (1999) provide an account of the many variants of secularization theory propounded in the twentieth century. Barker (2004) focuses on the distinction between religiosity and spirituality. Davie et al. (2016) summarize the state of the debate as reflected in the many contributions to Woodhead et al.'s *Religions in the Modern World* (2016). Morris (2012) gives an overview and assessment of the secularization debate in the United Kingdom.

22. Berger and Luckmann 1966; Dobbelaere 1981.

23. Davie et al. 2016, pp. 551–52.

24. Fox 2018, pp. 13–14.

25. Fox 2008.

26. McCleary and Barro 2006a, b.

27. S. Becker and Woessmann 2013.

28. See Barker (1999) as well as the other essays published in B. Wilson and Cresswell (1999).

29. Xygalatas 2022, pp. 269–70.

30. Stark and Bainbridge 1985.

BIBLIOGRAPHY

Acemoglu, Daron, and Restrepo, Pascal (2019): "The Wrong Kind of AI? Artificial Intelligence and the Future of Labor Demand," Toulouse Network for Information Technology working paper, March 5, 2019. https://www.tse-fr.eu/groups/tnit?tabs=3.

Agarwal, Bina (2023): "Uniform Civil Code: Can the Debate Be Extricated from Identity Politics and Refocused on Gender Equality?," *Indian Express*, February 9, 2023. https://indianexpress.com/article/opinion/columns/uniform-civil-code-identity-politics-gender-equality-8401706/.

Agence France-Presse (2022): "Hundreds of Protesters Storm Iraq Parliament in Support of Cleric Moqtada al-Sadr," *Guardian*, July 28, 2022. https://www.theguardian.com/world/2022/jul/28/hundreds-of-protesters-storm-iraq-parliament-in-support-of-cleric-moqtada-al-sadr.

Ager, P., and Ciccone, A. (2018): "Agricultural Risk and the Spread of Religious Communities," *Journal of the European Economic Association*, 16(4): 1021–68.

Aghion, Philippe, and Tirole, Jean (1997): "Formal and Real Authority in Organizations," *Journal of Political Economy*, 105(1): 1–27.

Ahmed, Ali M. (2009): "Are Religious People More Prosocial? A Quasi-experimental Study with Madrasah Pupils in a Rural Community in India," *Journal for the Scientific Study of Religion*, 48(2): 368–74.

Ai, John (2016): "Monks Revere Xi Jinping: A Reincarnation of the Buddha," *PIME Asia News*, April 14, 2016. https://www.asianews.it/news-en/Monks-revere-Xi-Jinping:-A-reincarnation-of-the-Buddha-37218.html.

Aimone, J. A., Iannaccone, L. R., Makowsky, M. D., and Rubin, J. (2013): "Endogenous Group Formation via Unproductive Costs," *Review of Economic Studies*, 80: 1215–36.

Alcorta, C. S., and Sosis, R. (2013): "Ritual, Religion, and Violence: An Evolutionary Perspective," in M. Jerryson, M. Juergensmeyer, and A. M. Kitts (eds.), *Oxford Handbook of Religion and Violence*, pp. 571–96. New York: Oxford University Press.

Alcouffe, A., and Massot-Bordenave, P. (2020): *Adam Smith in Toulouse and Occitania: The Unknown Years*. London: Palgrave Macmillan.

Aldashev, Gani, and Platteau, Jean-Philippe (2014): "Religion, Culture and Development," chapter 21 in Victor A. Ginsburgh and David Throsby (eds.), *Handbook of the Economics of Art and Culture*, vol. 2. Amsterdam: North-Holland.

Alfonsi, L., Bauer, M., Chytilova, J., and Miguel, E. (2022): "Human Capital Affects Religious Identity: Causal Evidence from Kenya," working paper, December 2022. https://www.liviaalfonsi.com/research.

Allen, John L. (2013): "Fr. Andrew Greeley, Sociologist and Priest-Novelist, Dies at 85," *National Catholic Reporter*, May 30, 2013. https://www.ncronline.org/news/people/fr-andrew-greeley -sociologist-and-priest-novelist-dies-85.

Andersen, Lars Harhoff, and Bentzen, Jeanet S. (2022): "In the Name of God! Religiosity and the Emergence of Modern Science and Growth," working paper, November 3, 2022. https:// www.dropbox.com/s/pwlllyfuwr772jv/Andersen_Bentzen_InTheNameOfGod_website1 .pdf?dl=0.

AP in Paris (2022): "French Cardinal Jean-Pierre Ricard Admits to Abusing 14-Year-Old Girl 35 Years Ago," *Guardian*, November 7, 2022. https://www.theguardian.com/world/2022/nov /07/french-cardinal-jean-pierre-ricard-admits-to-abusing-14-year-old-girl-35-years-ago.

Appadurai, Arjun, and Appadurai Breckenridge, Carol (1976): "The South Indian Temple: Authority, Honour and Redistribution," *Contributions to Indian Sociology*, 10(2): 187–211.

Appiah, Edwin (2021): "Darkness in a Lighthouse: Pastors Recount Abuse and Trauma (Pt.1)," Fourth Estate, April 23, 2021. https://thefourthestategh.com/2021/04/23/darkness-in-a -lighthouse-pastors-recount-abuse-and-trauma-pt-1/.

Archives Municipal d'Avignon (n.d.): "Un lieu patrimonial," accessed July 10, 2023. http:// archives.avignon.fr/4DCGI/Web_Custompage/lieu.shtm/ILUMP24835.

Armitage, Simon, trans. (2016): *Pearl*. London: Faber & Faber.

Associated Press (2019): "Ex-Pope Benedict XVI Blames Sexual Abuse on Swinging Sixties," *Guardian*, April 11, 2019. https://www.theguardian.com/world/2019/apr/11/ex-pope -benedict-xvi-blames-sexual-abuse-on-swinging-sixties.

Astor, Avi (2020): "Religion and Counter-state Nationalism in Catalonia," *Social Compass*, 67(2): 159–76.

Atran, Scott (1998): "Folk Biology and the Anthropology of Science: Cognitive Universals and Cultural Particulars," *Behavioral and Brain Sciences*, 21: 547–609.

——— (2002): *In Gods We Trust: The Evolutionary Landscape of Religion*. New York: Oxford University Press.

——— (2003): "Genesis of Suicide Terrorism," *Science*, 299(5612): 1534–39.

Atran, Scott, and Henrich, Joseph (2010): "The Evolution of Religion: How Cognitive By-Products, Adaptive Learning Heuristics, Ritual Displays, and Group Competition Generate Deep Commitments to Prosocial Religions," *Biological Theory*, 5: 18–30.

Atran, Scott, and Norenzayan, Ara (2004): "Religion's Evolutionary Landscape: Counterintuition, Commitment, Compassion, Communion," *Behavioral and Brain Sciences*, 27: 713–30.

Augustine of Hippo ([401] 2001): *The Confessions of Saint Augustine, Bishop of Hippo*, translated by E. B. Pusey. Digital edition available at https://www.gutenberg.org/files/3296/3296-h /3296-h.htm#link2H_4_0006.

——— ([426] 1984): *City of God*, translated by Henry Bettenson, Penguin Classics. Digital edition available at https://archive.org/stream/TheTeacherTheFreeChoiceOAugustineSt .RussellRobe5162_201903/City%20of%20God%20-%20St.%20Augustine%20%26%20 Henry%20Bettenson_djvu.txt.

Aumann, R. (1976): "Agreeing to Disagree," *Annals of Statistics*, 4: 1236–39.

Auriol, Emmanuelle, Delissaint, Diego, Fourati, Maleke, Miquel-Florensa, Josepa, and Seabright, Paul (2020a): "Trust in the Image of God: Religion and Respect for Norms in Haiti," *Economics of Transition and Institutional Change*, 29(1): 3–34.

——— (2021): "Betting on the Lord: Lotteries and Religiosity in Haiti," *World Development*, 144: 105441.

Auriol, Emmanuelle, Lassébie, Julie, Panin, Amma, Raiber, Eva, and Seabright, Paul (2020b): "God Insures Those Who Pay? Formal Insurance and Religious Offerings in Ghana," *Quarterly Journal of Economics*, 135(4): 1799–1848.

Auriol, Emmanuelle, Panin, Amma, Raiber, Eva, and Seabright, Paul (2023): "A Model of Religious Organizations as Competing Platforms," working paper, Toulouse School of Economics.

Auriol, Emmanuelle, and Platteau, Jean-Philippe (2017a): "The Explosive Combination of Religious Decentralization and Autocracy," *Economics of Transition*, 25(2): 313–50.

——— (2017b): "Religious Co-option in Autocracy: A Theory Inspired by History," *Journal of Development Economics*, 127: 395–412.

Australian Associated Press (2021): "Witness Feared Alleged Victims Would Sue if She Testified against Malka Leifer, Court Hears," *Guardian*, September 20, 2021. https://www.theguardian .com/world/2021/sep/20/witness-feared-alleged-victims-would-sue-if-she-testified -against-malka-leifer-court-hears.

Azam, Jean-Paul (2017): "The Sight of Blood and the Apocalypse: The Motivations of Daesh's Recruits," working paper, Toulouse School of Economics.

——— (2022): "Hasty Ethics Can Kill: How Vilified Pipelines Helped to Tame Jihad in Sudan and Chad," working paper, Toulouse School of Economics.

Azzi, C., and Ehrenberg, R. (1975): "Household Allocation of Time and Church Attendance," *Journal of Political Economy*, 83(1): 27–56.

Bach, Laurent, and Serrano-Velarde, Nicolas (2015): "CEO Identity and Labor Contracts: Evidence from CEO Transitions," *Journal of Corporate Finance* 33: 227–42.

Baker, Eric (2007): "Lucretius in the European Enlightenment," in Stuart Gillespie and Philip Hardie (eds.), *The Cambridge Companion to Lucretius*, pp. 274–88. Cambridge: Cambridge University Press.

Ball, Matthew (2022): *The Metaverse: And How It Will Revolutionize Everything*. New York: Liveright.

Ball, Patrick, Kobrak, Paul, and Spirer, Herbert (1999): *State Violence in Guatemala 1960–1996: A Quantitative Reflection*. Washington, DC: American Association for the Advancement of Science and Centro Internacional para Investigaciones en Derechos Humanos. http://shr .aaas.org/guatemala/ciidh/qr/english/en_qr.pdf.

Baretta, Luciane, Tomitch, Leda, McNair, Nicolas A., Lim, Vanessa K., and Waldie, Karen E. (2009): "Inference Making while Reading Narrative and Expository Texts: an ERP Study," *Psychology and Neuroscience*, 2(2): 137–45.

Barker, Eileen (1999): "New Religious Movements: Their Incidence and Significance," in B. Wilson and Cresswell (1999), pp. 15–32.

——— (2004): "The Church Without and the God Within? Religiosity and/or Spirituality?," in Dinka Marinović Jerolimov, Siniša Zrinščak, and Irena Borowik (eds.), *Religion and Patterns of Social Transformation*, pp. 187–202. Zagreb: Institute for Social Research.

Barna (2021): "38% of U.S. Pastors Have Thought about Quitting Full-Time Ministry in the Past Year," Leaders and Pastors, November 16, 2021. https://www.barna.com/research/pastors -well-being/.

Baron, Salo Wittmayer (1957): *A Social and Religious History of the Jews*, vol. 3. New York: Columbia University Press.

Barrett, Justin (2000): "Exploring the Natural Foundations of Religion," *Trends in Cognitive Science*, 4(1): 29–34.

Barrett, Louise, and Henzi, S. Peter (2001): "The Utility of Grooming in Baboon Troops," in R. O. Noë, J. Van Hooff, and P. Hammerstein (eds.), *Economics in Nature: Social Dilemmas, Mate Choice and Biological Markets*, pp. 119–45. Cambridge: Cambridge University Press.

Barro, Robert J., and McCleary, Rachel M. (2003): "Religion and Economic Growth across Countries," *American Sociological Review*, 68(5): 760–81.

——— (2019): *The Wealth of Religions: The Political Economy of Believing and Belonging*. Princeton, NJ: Princeton University Press.

Bartlett, Robert (2013): *Why Can the Dead Do Such Great Things? Saints and Worshippers from the Martyrs to the Reformation*. Princeton, NJ: Princeton University Press.

Bascom, William (1954): "Four Functions of Folklore," *Journal of American Folklore*, 67(266): 333–49.

Baumard, N., and Boyer, P. (2013a): "Explaining Moral Religions," *Trends in Cognitive Sciences*, 17(6): 72–280.

——— (2013b): "Religious Beliefs as Reflective Elaborations on Intuitions: A Modified Dual-Process Model," *Current Directions in Psychological Science*, 22(4): 295–300.

BBC News (2018a): "Asaram Bapu: Indian Guru Sentenced to Life for Raping Girl," India, April 25, 2018. https://www.bbc.com/news/world-asia-india-43889797.

——— (2018b): "South Korean Pastor Lee Jae-rock Jailed for Raping Followers," Asia, November 22, 2018. https://www.bbc.co.uk/news/world-asia-46299239.

Beck, Hans (2020): *Localism and the Ancient Greek City-State*. Chicago: Chicago University Press.

Becker, Ernest (1973): *The Denial of Death*. New York: Simon and Schuster.

Becker, Sascha O., and Pascali, Luigi (2019): "Religion, Division of Labor, and Conflict: Anti-Semitism in Germany over 600 Years," *American Economic Review*, 109(5): 1764–804.

Becker, Sascha O., Rubin, Jared, and Woessmann, Ludger (2021): "Religion in Economic History: A Survey," IZA Discussion paper no. 13371, IZA—Institute of Labor Economics.

Becker, Sascha O., and Woessmann, Ludger (2009): "Was Weber Wrong? A Human Capital Theory of Protestant Economic History," *Quarterly Journal of Economics*, 124(2): 531–96.

——— (2013): "Not the Opium of the People: Income and Secularization in a Panel of Prussian Counties," *American Economic Review*, 103(3): 539–44.

Bellah, R. (2011): *Religion in Human Evolution: From the Paleolithic to the Axial Age*. Cambridge, MA: Belknap Press of Harvard University Press.

Bénabou, Roland, Ticchi, Davide, and Vindigni, Andrea (2015): "Religion and Innovation," *American Economic Review: Papers and Proceedings*, 105(5): 346–51.

——— (2022): "Forbidden Fruits: The Political Economy of Science, Religion and Growth," *Review of Economic Studies*, 89(4): 1785–832.

Bénabou, Roland, and Tirole, Jean (2006): "Belief in a Just World and Redistributive Politics," *Quarterly Journal of Economics* 121(2): 699–746.

——— (2011): "Identity, Morals, and Taboos: Beliefs as Assets," *Quarterly Journal of Economics*, 126(2): 805–55.

Benedict, Ruth (1934): *Patterns of Culture*. Boston: Houghton Mifflin Harcourt.

Bennedsen, M., Meisner Nielsen, K., Perez-Gonzalez, F., and Wolfenzon, D. (2007): "Inside the Family Firm: The Role of Families in Succession Decisions and Performance," *Quarterly Journal of Economics*, 122(2): 647–91.

Bentzen, J. S. (2019): "Acts of God? Religiosity and Natural Disasters across Subnational World Districts," *Economic Journal*, 129(622): 2295–321.

——— (2021): "In Crisis, We Pray: Religiosity and the Covid-19 Pandemic," *Journal of Economic Behavior and Organization*, 192: 541–83.

Bentzen, J. S., and Force, E. (2023): "Did Seismic Activity Lead to the Rise of Religion?," Discussion Paper no. 17878, Centre for Economic Policy Research.

Bentzen, J. S., and Gokmen, G. (2023): "The Power of Religion," *Journal of Economic Growth*, 28(1): 45–78.

Berger, P. (1963): "A Market Model for the Analysis of Ecumenicity," *Social Research*, 30(1): 77–93.

——— (1967): *The Sacred Canopy: Elements of a Sociological Theory of Religion*. New York: Doubleday.

——— (1969): *A Rumor of Angels*. New York: Doubleday.

Berger, P., and Luckmann, T. (1966): *The Social Construction of Reality: A Treatise in the Sociology of Religion*. Garden City, NY: Anchor Books.

Bering, J. M. (2006): "The Folk Psychology of Souls," *Behavioral and Brain Sciences*, 29: 453–62.

Berman, E. (2000): "Sect, Subsidy and Sacrifice: An Economist's View of Ultra-Orthodox Jews," *Quarterly Journal of Economics*, 115(3): 905–53.

Berman, E., and Laitin, D. D. (2008): "Religion, Terrorism and Public Goods: Testing the Club Model," *Journal of Public Economics*, 92(10–11): 1942–67.

Bernal, Fernando (2021): "Crítica de 'Apaiz Kartzela (La cárcel de curas),'" 20minutos, December 7, 2021. https://www.20minutos.es/cinemania/criticas/critica-de-apaiz-kartzela-la -carcel-de-curas-4918062/.

Bernardi, L., Sleight, P., Bandinelli, G., Cencetti, S., Fattorini, L., Wdowczyc-Szulc, J., and Lagi, A. (2001): "Effect of Rosary Prayer and Yogic Mantras on Autonomic Cardiovascular Rhythms: Comparative Study," *British Medical Journal*, 325: 1446–49.

Bhaya Nair, Rukmini (2002): *Narrative Gravity*. New Delhi: Oxford University Press India.

Biale, D., Assaf, D., Brown, B., Gellman, U., Heilman, S., Rosman, M., Sagiv, G., and Wodzinski, M. (2018): *Hasidism: A New History*. Princeton, NJ: Princeton University Press.

Bidgood, Jess (2017): "Sister Frances Ann Carr, One of the Last Three Shakers, Dies at 89," *New York Times*, January 4, 2017. https://www.nytimes.com/2017/01/04/us/sister-frances-ann -carr-one-of-the-last-three-shakers-dies-at-89.html.

Biglaiser, G., Calvano, E., and Crémer, J. (2019): "Incumbency Advantage and Its Value," *Journal of Economics and Management Strategy*, 28: 41–48.

Bisin, A., and Verdier, T. (2000): "'Beyond the Melting Pot': Cultural Transmission, Marriage, and the Evolution of Ethnic and Religious Traits," *Quarterly Journal of Economics*, 115(3): 955–88.

——— (2001): "The Economics of Cultural Transmission and the Dynamics of Preferences," *Journal of Economic Theory*, 97: 298–319.

Blair, Leonardo (2019): "Christian Author Asks for Help, Prayers after Amazon Sells $240K Worth of Fake Copies of Her Book," *Christian Post*, July 10, 2019. https://www.christianpost .com/news/christian-author-asks-for-help-prayers-after-amazon-sells-240k-worth-of-fake -copies-of-her-book.html.

Blaydes, Lisa, and Chaney, Eric (2013): "The Feudal Revolution and Europe's Rise: Political Divergence of the Christian West and the Muslim World before 1500 CE," *American Political Science Review*, 107(1): 16–34.

Bloom, Paul (2010): "How Do Morals Change?," *Nature* 464(7288): 490.

Boals, Adriel, and Schuettler, Darnell (2011): "A Double-Edged Sword: Event Centrality, PTSD and Posttraumatic Growth," *Applied Cognitive Psychology*, 25(5): 817–22.

Boehm, Christopher (1999): *Hierarchy in the Forest: The Evolution of Egalitarian Behavior*. Cambridge, MA: Harvard University Press.

Boisvert, Donald, and Daniel-Hughes, Carly (2017): *The Bloomsbury Reader in Religion, Sexuality and Gender*, Kindle. London: Bloomsbury Academic.

Bond, Sarah E., and Patel, Shaily (2022): "Recovering the Female Clerics of the Early Church," *Los Angeles Review of Books*, January 17, 2022. https://lareviewofbooks.org/article/recovering -the-female-clerics-of-the-early-church/.

Bonnet, Corinne (2022): "From Olympus to Tibet: Religion and Globalisation: A Transdisciplinary Dialogue," presentation at Opening Session of European Association of Biblical Studies, Toulouse, July 4, 2022.

Bonnet, Corinne, Bianco, Maria, Galoppin, Thomas, Guillon, Elodie, Laurent, Antoine, Lebreton, Sylvain, and Porzia, Fabio (2019): "Mapping Ancient Gods: Naming and Embodiment beyond 'Anthropomorphism'. A Survey of the Field in Echo to the Books of M.S. Smith and R. Parker," *Mediterranean Historical Review*, 34(2): 207–20.

Booker, Christopher (2004): *The Seven Basic Plots: Why We Tell Stories*. London: Bloomsbury.

Borecka, Natalia (2023): "US Christian Group Accused of Covering Up Sexual Abuse of Minors," *Guardian*, March 19, 2023. https://www.theguardian.com/us-news/2023/mar/19 /international-churches-of-christ-lawsuits-alleged-sexual-abuse.

Boscaini-Gilroy, Giacomo (2022): "The Rise of Non-religious Britain: Only a Minority of People in England and Wales Now Identify as Christian," *New Statesman*, November 29, 2022. https://www.newstatesman.com/politics/religion/2022/11/rise-non-religious -britain-christian.

Botticini, Maristella, and Eckstein, Zvi (2012): *The Chosen Few: How Education Shaped Jewish History, 70–1492*. Princeton, NJ: Princeton University Press.

Bowles, Samuel (2006): "Group Competition, Reproductive Leveling, and the Evolution of Human Altruism," *Science*, 314(5805): 1569–72.

——— (2009): "Did Warfare among Ancestral Hunter-Gatherers Affect the Evolution of Human Altruism?," *Science*, 324(5932): 1293–98.

Bowles, Samuel, Choi, Jung-Kyoo, and Hopfensitz, Astrid (2003): "The Co-evolution of Individual Behaviors and Social Institutions," *Journal of Theoretical Biology*, 223(2): 135–47.

Boyd, Brian (2010): *On the Origin of Stories: Evolution, Cognition and Fiction*. Cambridge, MA: Harvard University Press.

——— (2018): "The Evolution of Stories: From Mimesis to Language, from Fact to Fiction," *WIREs Cognitive Science*, 9: e1444.

——— (2021): "Learning from Fiction?," *Evolutionary Studies in Imaginative Culture*, 5(1): 57–66.

Boyd, Robert (2017): *A Different Kind of Animal*. Princeton, NJ: Princeton University Press.

Boyd, Robert, and Mathew, Sarah (2021): "Arbitration Supports Reciprocity when There Are Frequent Perception Errors," *Nature Human Behaviour*, 5(5): 596–603.

Boyd, Robert, and Richerson, Peter (1985): *Culture and the Evolutionary Process*. Chicago: University of Chicago Press.

Boyer, Pascal (2001): *Religion Explained: The Evolutionary Origins of Religious Thought*. New York: Basic Books.

——— (2018): *Minds Make Societies*. New Haven, CT: Yale University Press.

Boyer, Pascal, and Liénard, Pierre (2006): "Why Ritualized Behavior? Precaution Systems and Action Parsing in Developmental, Pathological and Cultural Rituals," *Behavioral and Brain Sciences*, 29: 595–650.

Bravehearts (n.d.): "Child Sexual Abuse and Religious Organisations," Stats and Facts, accessed July 10, 2023. https://bravehearts.org.au/what-we-do/research/child-sexual-abuse-facts -stats/child-sexual-abuse-religious-organisations/.

Brennan, Geoffrey, and Lomasky, Loren (1993): *Democracy and Decision*. Cambridge: Cambridge University Press.

Brennan, Geoffrey, and Pettit, Philip (2004): *The Economy of Esteem: An Essay on Civil and Political Society*. Oxford: Oxford University Press.

Brenneis, D. (1988): "Language and Disputing," *Annual Review of Anthropology*, 17(1): 221–37.

Bricault, Laurent, Veymiers, Richard, and Amoroso, Nicolas (2021): *The Mystery of Mithras: Exploring the Heart of a Roman Cult*. Morlanwelz, Belgium: Musée Royal de Mariemont.

Briggs, Robin (2002): *Witches and Neighbours: The Social and Cultural Context of European Witchcraft*, Kindle. Oxford: Blackwell.

——— (2022): "Between the Magical Universe and die Entzauberung der Welt," presentation at the conference to honor the 50th anniversary of the publication of *Religion and the Decline of Magic*, All Souls College, Oxford, September 3, 2021.

Brosnan, S. F., and de Waal, Frans B. M. (2003): "Monkeys Reject Unequal Pay," *Nature*, 425: 297–99.

Brown, Erica (2009): "Straying the Course: Can Jewish and Secular Leadership Archetypes Rein in Religious Leaders?," in Neustein (2009), pp. 63–64.

——— (2010): *Confronting Scandal: How Jews Can Respond when Jews Do Bad Things*. Woodstock, VT: Jewish Lights.

——— (2017): "Standing Idly By: When Leaders Enable Sexual Abuse," *Tradition: A Journal of Orthodox Jewish Thought*, 50(2): 78–92.

Brown, Peter (1988): *The Body and Society: Men, Women and Sexual Renunciation in Early Christianity*. New York: Columbia University Press.

——— (1998): "Christianization and Religious Conflict," in A. Cameron and P. Garnsey (eds.), *The Cambridge Ancient History*, vol. 13, *The Late Empire, AD 337–425*, pp. 632–64. Cambridge: Cambridge University Press.

——— (2013a): *The Rise of Western Christendom: Triumph and Diversity, AD 200–1000*, tenth anniversary revised edition. Chichester, UK: Wiley Blackwell.

——— (2013b): "Rome: Sex and Freedom," *New York Review of Books*, December 19, 2013.

——— (2015): *The Cult of the Saints: Its Rise and Function in Latin Christianity*, enlarged edition. Chicago: University of Chicago Press.

Brown, R., and Kulik, J. (1977): "Flashbulb Memories," *Cognition*, 5(1): 73–99.

Bruner, Jerome (1985): "Narrative and Pragmatic Modes of Thought," *Teachers College Record*, 86(6): 97–115.

——— (1987): "Life as Narrative," *Social Research*, 54(1): 11–32.

——— (1991): "The Narrative Construction of Reality," *Critical Inquiry*, 18(1): 1–21.

Brunson, Samuel (2016): "Taxing Utopia," *Seton Hall Law Review*, 47(1): 137–96.

Bryan, G., Choi, J., and Karlan, D. (2021): "Randomizing Religion: The Impact of Protestant Evangelism on Economic Outcomes," *Quarterly Journal of Economics*, 136(1): 293–380.

Buchholz, Katharina (2022): "How Has the Number of Female CEOs in Fortune 500 Companies Changed over the Last 20 Years?," World Economic Forum, March 10, 2022. https://www.weforum.org/agenda/2022/03/ceos-fortune-500-companies-female.

Buckner, William (2018): "On Secret Cults and Male Dominance," *Traditions of Conflict* (blog), January 31, 2018. https://traditionsofconflict.com/blog/2018/1/31/on-secret-cults-and-male-dominance.

——— (2019): "Charlatanism: Realms of Deception and Religious Theater," *Traditions of Conflict* (blog), January 4, 2019. https://traditionsofconflict.com/blog/2019/1/4/charlatanism-realms-of-deception-and-religious-theater.

Bull, Christian (2021): "Prophesying the Demise of Egyptian Religion in Late Antiquity: The *Perfect Discourse* and Antoninus in Canopus," *Numen*, 68: 180–203.

Burger, Pamela (2015): "Women's Groups and the Rise of the Book Club," *JSTOR Daily*, August 12, 2015. https://daily.jstor.org/feature-book-club/.

Burkart, M., Panunzi, F., and Shleifer, A. (2003): "Family Firms," *Journal of Finance*, 58(5): 2167–201.

Burleigh, Michael (2006): *Sacred Causes: Religion and Politics in Europe from the French Revolution to the Great War*. London: Harper Collins.

Burnett, Charles (2013): "Translation and Transmission of Greek and Islamic Science to Latin Christendom," in David Lindberg and Michael Shank (eds.), *The Cambridge History of Science*, vol. 2, pp. 341–64. Cambridge: Cambridge University Press.

Caillaud, B., and Jullien, B. (2003): "Chicken and Egg: Competition among Intermediation Service Providers," *Rand Journal of Economics*, 34: 521–52.

Cairns, Madoc (2023): "Britain's Crisis of Unbelief: In a Nation That Binds Spiritual and Temporal Power, Will the End of the Old Metaphysical Order Threaten the State Itself?," *New Statesman*, February 12, 2023. https://www.newstatesman.com/the-weekend-essay/2023/02/britain-crisis-unbelief-christian-northern-ireland.

Calvano, E., and Polo, M. (2021): "Market Power, Competition and Innovation in Digital Markets: A Survey," *Information Economics and Policy*, 54: 100853.

Camina, Gill, Universal Safeguarding Solutions Ltd. (2021): *John Smyth Independent Case Review: Executive Summary*. Milton Keynes, UK: Scripture Union England and Wales.

https://content.scriptureunion.org.uk/sites/default/files/2021-03/Executive_Summary _of_SU_John_Smyth_Independent_Case_Review_March_2021.pdf.

Campbell, Joseph (1949): *The Hero with a Thousand Faces*. Princeton, NJ: Princeton University Press.

Camus, R. (2011): *Le grand remplacement*. Paris: David Reinharc.

Cantoni, Davide, Dittmar, Jeremiah, and Yuchtman, Noam (2018): "Religious Competition and Reallocation: The Political Economy of Secularization in the Protestant Reformation," *Quarterly Journal of Economics*, 133(4): 2037–96.

CARDH (Centre d'analyse et de recherche en droits de l'homme) (n.d.): "Cellule d'observation de la criminalité-COC," accessed July 10, 2023. https://cardh.org/celulle-dobservation-de -la-criminalite.

Carroll, J. (1995): "Evolution and Literary Theory," *Human Nature*, 6: 119–34.

——— (2004): *Literary Darwinism: Evolution, Human Nature, and Literature*. London: Routledge.

Carvalho, Jean-Paul (2013): "Veiling," *Quarterly Journal of Economics*, 128(1): 337–70.

——— (2016): "Identity-Based Organizations," *American Economic Review*, 106(5): 410–14.

——— (2019): "Religious Clubs: The Strategic Role of Religious Identity," in Carvalho, Sriya Iyer, and Jared Rubin (eds.), *Advances in the Economics of Religion*, pp. 25–41. Cham, Switzerland: Palgrave Macmillan.

Carvalho, Jean-Paul, and McBride, Michael (2022): "The Formation of Religious Beliefs and Preferences," in Klaus F. Zimmerman (ed.), *Handbook of Labor, Human Resources and Population Economics*. Cham, Switzerland: Springer.

Carvalho, Jean-Paul, and Sacks, Michael (2021): "The Economics of Religious Communities," *Journal of Public Economics*, 201: 104481.

Cassin, Mathieu (2011): "De deitate ilii et spiritus sancto et In Abraham," in Volker Henning Drcoll and Margitta Berghaus (eds.), *Gregory of Nyssa: The Minor Treatises on Trinitarian Theology and Apollinarism, Supplements to Vigiliae Christianae* 106, pp. 277–311. Leiden: Brill.

Catechism of the Catholic Church (2019), 2nd ed. Vatican City: Libreria Editrice Vaticana. Available on the website of the United States Conference of Catholic Bishops. https://www.usccb .org/sites/default/files/flipbooks/catechism/314/.

Cavalcanti, T., Iyer, S., Rauh, C., Roehrig, C., and Vaziri, M. (2022): "A City of God: Afterlife Beliefs and Job Support in Brazil," Discussion Paper no. 17719, Centre for Economic Policy Research.

CCCB (Canadian Conference of Catholic Bishops) Ad Hoc Committee on Child Sexual Abuse (1992): *From Pain to Hope*. CCCB. https://web.archive.org/web/20210701015412 /https://www.cccb.ca/wp-content/uploads/2017/11/From_Pain_To_Hope.pdf.

Chaney, E. (2013): "Revolt on the Nile: Economic Shocks, Religion and Political Power," *Econometrica*, 81(5): 2033–53.

——— (2016): "Religion and the Rise and Fall of Islamic Science," working paper, University of Oxford.

Chen, Carolyn (2022): *Work Pray Code*. Princeton, NJ: Princeton University Press.

Chen, D. (2010): "Club Goods and Group Identity: Evidence from Islamic Resurgence during the Indonesian Financial Crisis," *Journal of Political Economy*, 118(2): 300–354.

Chen, Joy, Wang, Erik, and Zhang, Xiaoming (2021): "Leviathan's Offer: State-Building with Elite Compensation in Early Medieval China," working paper, December 31, 2021. https://sites.duke.edu/hiscope/files/2022/04/Leviathan_Wang.pdf.

Chen, Yuyu, Wang, Hui, and Yan, Se (2022): "The Long-Term Effects of Protestant Activities in China," *Journal of Comparative Economics*, 50: 394–414.

Chetty, Raj, Jackson, Matthew O., Kuchler, Theresa, Stroebel, Johannes, Hendren, Nathaniel, Fluegge, Robert B., and Gong, Sara, et al. (2022): "Social Capital II: Determinants of Economic Connectedness," NBER Working Paper no. 30314, National Bureau of Economic Research.

Chhapia, Hemali (2020): "Thousands of Japanese Making a Smooth Transition from Zen to Jain," *Times of India*, February 23, 2020. https://timesofindia.indiatimes.com/india/thousands-of-japanese-making-a-smooth-transition-from-zen-to-jain/articleshow/74262195.cms.

Chiang, Ted (2002): "Hell Is the Absence of God," in *Stories of Your Life and Others*, pp. 205–35. New York: Tor Books.

Ciase (2021): *Rapport de la Commission indépendante sur les abus sexuels dans l'église*. https://www.ciase.fr/rapport-final/.

Clark, Andrew E., and Oswald, Andrew J. (1994): "Unhappiness and Unemployment," *Economic Journal*, 104(424): 648–59.

Clark, Andy (2013): "Whatever Next? Predictive Brains, Situated Agents, and the Future of Cognitive Science," *Behavioral and Brain Sciences*, 36: 181–204.

Clark, James (2021): *The Dissolution of the Monasteries*. New Haven, CT: Yale University Press.

Clark, Jerry (1985): "Thus Spoke Chief Seattle: The Story of an Undocumented Speech," *Prologue Magazine*, 18 (1). https://www.archives.gov/publications/prologue/1985/spring/chief-seattle.html.

Clay, Zanna, and Tennie, Claudio (2018): "Is Overimitation a Uniquely Human Phenomenon? Insights from Human Children as Compared to Bonobos," *Child Development*, 89(5): 1535–44.

Clottes, Jean, and Lewis-Williams, David (1998): *The Shamans of Prehistory*. New York: Harry N. Abrams.

Cohn, Norman (1993): *Cosmos, Chaos and the World to Come: The Ancient Roots of Apocalyptic Faith*. New Haven, CT: Yale University Press.

Coleman, Simon (2000): *The Globalisation of Charismatic Christianity: Spreading the Gospel of Prosperity*. Cambridge: Cambridge University Press.

——— (2021): *Powers of Pilgrimage: Religion in a World of Movement*. New York: New York University Press.

Coomaraswamy, Anand (1918): *The Dance of Shiva: Essays on Indian Art and Culture*. Mineola, NY: Dover.

Corbi, Raphael, and Miessi Sanchez, Fabio (2022): "What Drives Religiosity in America? Evidence from an Empirical Hotelling Model of Church Competition," Working Paper no. 2022-08, Department of Economics, FEA-USP, São Paulo.

Corbin, Alain (2016): *Histoire du silence: De la Renaissance à nos jours*. Paris: Albin Michel.

Cox, Harvey (2011): foreword to Candy Gunther Brown, *Global Pentecostal and Charismatic Healing*, xvii–xxi. New York: Oxford University Press.

Coy, Peter (2023): "Money Is Up. Patriotism and Religion Are Down," Peter Coy newsletter, *New York Times*, March 29, 2023. https://www.nytimes.com/2023/03/29/opinion/money -is-up-patriotism-and-religion-are-down.html.

Coyle, Marcia (2022): "The Justices' Faith and Their Religion Clause Decisions," *Constitution Daily Blog*, July 15, 2022. https://constitutioncenter.org/blog/the-justices-faith-and-their -religion-clause-decisions.

Crémer, Jacques, and Biglaiser, Gary (2012): "Switching Costs and Network Effects in Competition Policy," in Joseph E. Harrington Jr. and Yannis Katsoulacos (eds.), *Recent Advances in the Analysis of Competition Policy and Regulation*, pp. 13–27. Cheltenham, UK: Edward Elgar.

Crubézy, Eric (2019): *Aux origines des rites funéraires: Voir, cacher, sacraliser*. Paris: Odile Jacob.

Dabashi, Hamid (2011): *Shi'ism: A Religion of Protest*. Cambridge, MA: Belknap Press of Harvard University Press.

Da Silva, Sara, and Tehrani, Jamshid J. (2016): "Comparative Phylogenetic Analyses Uncover the Ancient Roots of Indo-European Folktales," *Royal Society Open Science*, 3(1): 150645.

Dassonneville, Ruth, and Kostelka, Filip (2021): "The Cultural Sources of the Gender Gap in Voter Turnout," *British Journal of Political Science*, 51(3): 1040–61.

Dautenhahn, Kerstin (2002): "The Origins of Narrative: In Search of the Transactional Format of Narratives in Humans and Other Social Animals," *International Journal of Cognition and Technology*, 1(1): 97–123.

Davie, Grace, Woodhead, Linda, and Catto, Rebecca (2016): "Secularism and Secularization," in Woodhead et al. (2016), pp. 551–70.

Davies, Caroline (2021): "Prince Philip: The Unlikely but Willing Pacific Deity," *Guardian*, April 10, 2021. https://www.theguardian.com/uk-news/2021/apr/10/prince-philip-south -sea-island-god-duke-of-edinburgh.

Davies, John (2020): "'Economics' and the 'Economics of Cult': Can a Marriage Be Arranged?," in Annelisa Lo Monaco (ed.), *Spending on the Gods: Economy, Financial Resources and Management in the Sanctuaries in Greece*, Annuario della Scuola Archeologica di Atene, supplement 7, pp. 15–21. Sesto Fiorentino, Italy: All'Insegna del Giglio.

Dawkins, Richard (1986): *The Blind Watchmaker*. New York: Norton.

Degand, Martin (2015): *Sénèque au risque du don*. Turnhout, Belgium: Brepols.

Dehejia, Rajeev, DeLeire, Thomas, and Luttmer, Erzo F. (2007): "Insuring Consumption and Happiness through Religious Organizations," *Journal of Public Economics*, 91(1–2): 259–79.

Della Subin, Anna (2021): *Accidental Gods: On Men Unwittingly Turned Divine*. New York: Metropolitan Books.

DeLong, J. Bradford (2022): *Slouching towards Utopia*. London: Basic Books.

Denison, S., and Xu, F. (2010): "Integrating Physical Constraints in Statistical Inference by 11-Month-Old Infants," *Cognitive Science*, 34(5): 885–908.

Dennett, Daniel C. (1992): "The Self as a Center of Narrative Gravity," in F. Kessel, P. Cole, and D. Johnson (eds.), *Self and Consciousness: Multiple Perspectives*, pp. 275–88. Hillsdale, NJ: Erlbaum.

Dennison, Tracey, and Ogilvie, Sheilagh (2014): "Does the European Marriage Pattern Explain Economic Growth?," *Journal of Economic History*, 74(3): 651–93.

Dent, Shirley (2008): "Literary Darwinism Should Be Deselected, Naturally," *Guardian*, September 5, 2008. https://www.theguardian.com/books/booksblog/2008/sep/05/literarydarwinismshouldbed.

Deventer, Jorg (2004): "'Confessionalisation'—a Useful Theoretical Concept for the Study of Religion, Politics, and Society in Early Modern East-Central Europe?," *European Review of History: Revue européenne d'histoire*, 11(3): 403–25.

De Waal, Frans (2013): *The Bonobo and the Atheist: In Search of Humanism among the Primates*. New York: W. W. Norton.

Dhillon, Amrit (2020): "India's Classical Music and Dance 'Guru' System Hit by Abuse Allegations," *Guardian*, October 1, 2020. https://www.theguardian.com/global-development/2020/oct/01/indias-classical-music-and-dance-guru-system-hit-by-abuse-allegations.

Diamond, Jared (1999): *Guns, Germs and Steel: The Fates of Human Societies*. New York: W. W. Norton.

Diderot, Denis ([1762] 2015): *Addition aux pensées philosophiques ou objections diverses contre les écrits de différents théologiens*, in *Oeuvres complètes*, edited by Assézat-Tourneux, Paris, Garnier Frères, vol. 1, pp. 158–70. Facsimile available online at Université du Québec à Chicoutimi. http://dx.doi.org/doi:10.1522/cla.did.add.

Diocese of Phoenix (n.d.): "Frequently Asked Questions," Valid Baptisms, accessed June 1, 2022 (page no longer available). https://dphx.org/valid-baptisms/#FAQ.

Dobbelaere, Karel (1981): "Secularization: A Multi-dimensional Concept," trend report, *Current Sociology*, 29(2): 3–153.

Doepke, M., Hannusch, A., Kindermann, F., and Tertilt, M. (2022): "The Economics of Fertility: A New Era," Discussion Paper no. 29948, National Bureau of Economic Research.

Doniger, Wendy (2009): *The Hindus: An Alternative History*. New York: Penguin.

Dor, D. (2015): *The Instruction of Imagination: Language as a Social Communication Technology*. New York: Oxford University Press.

———— (2016): "From Experience to Imagination: Language and Its Evolution as a Communication Technology," *Journal of Neurolinguistics*, 43(B): 107–19.

Dos Santos, Henrique Laurino, and Berger, Jonah (2022): "The Speed of Stories: Semantic Progression and Narrative Success," *Journal of Experimental Psychology: General*, 151(8): 1833–42.

Dousset, Laurent (2016): "La sorcellerie en Mélanésie: Élicitation de l'inacceptable," *L'homme*, 2(218): 85–115.

Douthat, Ross (2014): "Rape and the College Brand," *New York Times*, May 10, 2014. https://www.nytimes.com/2014/05/11/opinion/sunday/douthat-rape-and-the-college-brand.html.

Dratch, Mark (2009): "A Community of Co-enablers: Why Are Jews Ignoring Traditional Jewish Law by Protecting the Abuser?," in Neustein (2009), pp. 105–25.

Dressing, H., Dölling, D., Hermann, D., Kruse, A., Schmitt, E., Bannenberg, B., Whittaker, K., Hoell, A., Voss, E., and Salize, H. J. (2021): "Child Sexual Abuse by Catholic Priests, Deacons and Male Members of the Religious Orders in the Authority of the German Bishops' Conference 1946–2014," *Sexual Abuse*, 33(3): 274–94.

Dubois, Laurent (2012): *Haiti: The Aftershocks of History*. New York: Picador.

Dubourg, E., and Baumard, N. (2022): "Why Imaginary Worlds? The Psychological Foundations and Cultural Evolution of Fictions with Imaginary Worlds," *Behavioral and Brain Sciences*, 45: e276.

Dudley, Leonard M. (1991): *The Word and the Sword: How Techniques of Information and Violence
Have Shaped Our World*. Cambridge, MA: Blackwell.

Dunbar, Robin (2022): *How Religion Evolved—And Why It Endures*. London: Penguin Books.

Dundes, Alan (2007): "Folklore as a Mirror of Culture," in Simon Bronner (ed.), *Meaning of
Folklore: The Analytical Essays of Alan Dundes*, pp. 53–66. Logan, UT: University Press of
Colorado and Utah State University Press.

Dunning, David (2011): "Chapter Five—The Dunning-Kruger Effect: On Being Ignorant of
One's Own Ignorance," in James M. Olsen and Mark P. Zanna (eds.), *Advances in Experimental Social Psychology*, vol. 44, pp. 247–96. San Diego, CA: Academic Press.

Duranti, A. (1990): "Doing Things with Words: Conflict, Understanding and Change in a Sa-
moan Fono," in Karen Watson-Gegeo and Geoffrey White (eds.), *Disentangling: Conflict
Discourse in Pacific Societies*, pp. 459–89. Stanford, CA: Stanford University Press.

Durkheim, Emile (1915): *The Elementary Forms of the Religious Life*, translated by Joseph Ward
Swain. New York: Dover.

Economist (2017): "A Medieval Poet Bedevils India's Most Powerful Political Party," September 23, 2017. https://www.economist.com/asia/2017/09/23/a-medieval-poet-bedevils
-indias-most-powerful-political-party.

——— (2020): "Protestant Christianity Is Booming in China: President Xi Does Not Approve,"
September 15, 2020. https://www.economist.com/graphic-detail/2020/09/15/protestant
-christianity-is-booming-in-china.

——— (2021): "The Lingering Influence of Catholicism in Increasingly Secular Spain," May 1,
2021. https://www.economist.com/europe/2021/05/01/the-lingering-influence-of
-catholicism-in-increasingly-secular-spain.

Edwards, Jeremy (2021): "Did Protestantism Promote Prosperity via Higher Human Capital?
Replicating the Becker-Woessmann (2009) Results," *Journal of Applied Econometrics*, 36:
853–58.

Edwards, Jeremy, and Ogilvie, Sheilagh (2012): "Contract Enforcement, Institutions, and Social
Capital: The Maghribi Traders Reappraised," *Economic History Review*, 65(2): 421–44.

Edwards, W., Lindman, H., and Savage, L. J. (1963): "Bayesian Statistical Inference for Psychological Research," *Psychological Review*, 70(3): 193–242.

Eggen, Nora S. (2011): "Conceptions of Trust in the Quran," *Journal of Quranic Studies*, 13(2):
56–85.

Einstein, Mara (2008): *Brands of Faith: Marketing Religion in a Commercial Age*. London:
Routledge.

Eisenstein, E. (1979): *The Printing Press as an Agent of Change*. Cambridge: Cambridge University Press.

Ekelund, Robert, Héberg, Robert, and Tollison, Robert (2006): *The Marketplace of Christianity*.
Cambridge, MA: MIT Press.

Elawa, Nathan Irmiya (2020): *Understanding Religious Change in Africa and Europe: Crossing
Latitudes*. Cham, Switzerland: Springer.

Eliade, Mircea (1964): *Shamanism: Archaic Techniques of Ecstasy*. Princeton, NJ: Princeton University Press.

Eltchaninoff, Michel (2022): "What's Going on inside Putin's Mind? His Own Words Give Us a Disturbing Clue," *Guardian*, February 25, 2022. https://www.theguardian.com /commentisfree/2022/feb/25/putin-mind-words-russia-victimhood.

Emory, Meade, and Zelenak, Lawrence (1982): "The Tax Exempt Status of Communitarian Religious Organizations: An Unnecessary Controversy?," *Fordham Law Review*, 50: 1085–112.

Empson, William (2016): *The Face of the Buddha*, edited by Rupert Arrowsmith. New York: Oxford University Press.

Engelstein, Laura (2003): *Castration and the Heavenly Kingdom: A Russian Folktale*. Ithaca, NY: Cornell University Press.

Epstein, Lee, and Posner, Eric (2021): "The Roberts Court and the Transformation of Constitutional Protections for Religion: A Statistical Portrait," *Supreme Court Review*, 2021: 315–48.

Euractiv with Reuters (2020): "Erdogan Joins Thousands to Pray for First Time at Istanbul's Hagia Sophia," *Euractiv*, July 24, 2020. https://www.euractiv.com/section/global-europe /news/erdogan-joins-thousands-to-pray-for-first-time-at-istanbuls-hagia-sophia/.

Express Web Desk (2017): "Controversial Godmen of India: A List of Self-Styled 'Gurus' and Their Sexual Assault Controversies," *Indian Express*, May 20, 2017. https://indianexpress.com /article/india/predators-in-the-guise-of-godmen-a-list-of-self-styled-gurus-and-their -sexual-assault-controversies-4665328/.

Falwell, Jerry, and Towns, Elmer (1971): *Church Aflame*. Nashville, TN: Impact Books.

Fenton, Kirsten (2011): "Gendering the First Crusade in William of Malmesbury's *Gesta Regum Anglorum*," in Cordelia Beattie and Kirsten Fenton (eds.), *Intersections of Gender, Religion and Ethnicity in the Middle Ages*, pp. 125–39. Basingstoke, UK: Palgrave Macmillan.

Fernandez, Kathleen M. (2019): "The Communal, Sometimes Celibate, 19th-Century Ohio Town That Thrived for Three Generations," What It Means to Be American, December 1, 2019. https://www.whatitmeanstobeamerican.org/ideas/the-communal-sometimes -celibate-19th-century-ohio-town-that-thrived-for-three-generations/.

Few, Martha, Tortorici, Zeb, Warren, Adam, and Scott, Nina (2020): *Baptism through Incision: The Postmortem Caesarian Operation in the Spanish Empire*. University Park, PA: Penn State University Press.

Fieder, M., and Huber, S. (2016): "The Association between Religious Homogamy and Reproduction," *Proceedings of the Royal Society B*, 283: 20160294.

Field, Clive (2008): "Churchgoing in the Cradle of English Christianity: Kentish Evidence from the Sixteenth to the Twentieth Centuries," *Archaeologia Cantiana*, 128: 335–64.

Le Figaro with AFP (2022): "Violences sexuelles: 10 évêques ou anciens évêques 'mis en cause' devant la justice civile ou de l'Église," *Figaro*, November 7, 2022, last updated November 8, 2022. https://www.lefigaro.fr/actualite-france/violences-sexuelles-11-eveques-ou-anciens -eveques-mis-en-cause-devant-la-justice-civile-ou-de-l-eglise-20221107.

Finke, R., and Stark, R. (2005): *The Churching of America, 1776–2005: Winners and Losers in Our Religious Economy*, 2nd edition. New Brunswick, NJ: Rutgers University Press.

Fisher, Marc (2022): "How Abe and Japan Became Vital to Moon's Unification Church," *Washington Post*, July 12, 2022. https://www.washingtonpost.com/world/2022/07/12 /unification-church-japan-shinzo-abe/.

Flechner, Roay, and Fontaine, Janel (2021): "The Admission of Former Slaves into Churches and Monasteries: Reaching behind the Sources," *Early Medieval Europe*, 29(4): 586–611.

Forrest, Ian (2018): *Trustworthy Men: How Inequality and Faith Made the Medieval Church*. Princeton, NJ: Princeton University Press.

40th Statewide Investigating Grand Jury (2018): "Report 1: Interim—Redacted," August 14, 2018. https://web.archive.org/web/20180814185817/http://media-downloads.pacourts.us /InterimRedactedReportandResponses.pdf.

Foster, R. F. (2007): *Luck and the Irish: A Brief History of Change, 1970–2000*, Kindle. London: Penguin Books.

Fox, Jonathan (2008): "Contemporary Evidence Regarding the Impact of State Regulation of Religion on Religious Participation and Belief," *Sociology of Religion*, 69(3): 245–71.

——— (2018): *An Introduction to Religion and Politics: Theory and Practice*, 2nd edition. London: Routledge.

Fox, Jonathan, and Breslawski, Jori (2023): "State Support for Religion and Government Legitimacy in Christian-Majority Countries," *American Political Science Review*. Cambridge University Press, February 7, 2023, pp. 1–15. https://doi.org/10.1017/S000305542 2001320.

Frankfurter, David (2019): "Ancient Magic in a New Key: Refining an Exotic Discipline in the History of Religions," in Frankfurter (ed.), *Guide to the Study of Ancient Magic*, pp. 3–20. Leiden: Brill.

Franzosi, Robert (1998): "Narrative Analysis: Or Why (and How) Sociologists Should Be Interested in Narrative," *Annual Review of Sociology*, 24: 517–54.

Frazer, James (1922): *The Golden Bough*, abridged edition. London: Macmillan.

Freud, Sigmund (1928): *The Future of an Illusion*, translated by W. D. Robson-Scott. London: Hogarth.

Friedman, Benjamin (2005): *The Moral Consequences of Economic Growth*. New York: Alfred A. Knopf.

Friedrich, Markus (2022): *The Jesuits: A History*. Princeton, NJ: Princeton University Press.

Frings, Bernhard, Grossbölting, Thomas, Grosse Kracht, Klaus, Powroznik, Natalie, and Rüschenschmidt, David (2022): *Macht und sexueller Missbrauch in der katholischen Kirche: Betroffene, Beschuldigte und Vertuscher im Bistum Münster seit 1945*. Freiburg, Germany: Herder. https://www.uni-muenster.de/imperia/md/content/wwu/journalisten/macht _und_sexueller_missbrauch_im_bistum_muenster.pdf.

Fruehwirth, J. C., Iyer, S., and Zhang, A. (2019): "Religion and Depression in Adolescence," *Journal of Political Economy*, 127(3): 1178–209.

Gabrielsen, V. (2007): "Brotherhoods of Faith and Provident Planning: The Non-public Associations of the Greek World," *Mediterranean Historical Review*, 22(2): 183–210.

Galoppin, Thomas, and Bonnet, Corinne, eds. (2021): *Divine Names on the Spot: Towards a Dynamic Approach of Divine Denominations in Greek and Semitic Contexts*. Leuven, Belgium: Peeters.

Gambetta, Diego (2009): *Codes of the Underworld: How Criminals Communicate*. Princeton, NJ: Princeton University Press.

Gardner, David (2019): "Pope Francis Fights a Losing Battle in the Middle East," *Financial Times*, February 5, 2019. https://www.ft.com/content/24105df4-2893-11e9-a5ab-ff8ef2b976c7.

Gellner, David (2005): "The Emergence of Conversion in a Hindu-Buddhist Polytropy: The Kathmandu Valley, Nepal, c. 1600–1995," *Comparative Studies in Society and History*, 47(4): 755–80.

Gellner, David, and Hausner, Sondra L. (2013): "Multiple versus Unitary Belonging: How Nepalis in Britain Deal with 'Religion,'" in A. Day, G. Vincett, and C. Cotter, *Social Identities between the Sacred and the Secular*, pp. 75–88. Farnham, UK: Ashgate.

Gerber, Alan S., Gruber, Jonathan, and Hungerman, Daniel M. (2015): "Does Church Attendance Cause People to Vote? Using Blue Laws' Repeal to Estimate the Effect of Religiosity on Voter Turnout," *British Journal of Political Science*, 46(3): 481–500.

Gershman, B. (2022): "Witchcraft Beliefs around the World: An Exploratory Analysis," *PLoS ONE*, 17(11): e0276872.

Ghosh, Peter (2014): *Max Weber and the Protestant Ethic: Twin Histories*. New York: Oxford University Press.

Gibbon, Edward ([1776] 1836): *History of the Decline and Fall of the Roman Empire*. New York: Harper. Digital edition available at https://www.gutenberg.org/files/25717/25717-h/25717-h .htm.

Gifford, Paul (2004): *Ghana's New Christianity: Pentecostalism in a Globalising African Economy*. Bloomington: Indiana University Press.

Giles, T., Hungerman, D., and Oostrom, T. (2023): "Opiates of the Masses? Deaths of Despair and the Decline of American Religion," NBER Working Paper no. 30840, National Bureau of Economic Research.

Giles-Sims, Jean (1998): "Current Knowledge about Child Abuse in Stepfamilies," *Marriage and Family Review*, 26(3–4): 215–30.

Giuffrida, Angela (2022): "Former Pope Benedict Admits Making False Claim to Child Sexual Abuse Inquiry," *Guardian*, January 24, 2022. https://www.theguardian.com/world/2022 /jan/24/former-pope-benedict-statement-child-sexual-abuse-inquiry.

Goldfarb, A., and Tucker, C. (2019): "Digital Economics," *Journal of Economic Literature*, 57: 3–43.

Gomes, Cristina M., and Boesch, Christophe (2009): "Wild Chimpanzees Exchange Meat for Sex on a Long-Term Basis," *PLoS ONE*, 4(4): e5116. https://doi.org/10.1371/journal.pone .0005116.

——— (2011): "Reciprocity and Trades in Wild West African Chimpanzees," *Behavioral Ecology and Sociobiology*, 65: 2183–96. https://doi.org/10.1007/s00265-011-1227-x.

Goody, Jack (1983): *The Development of the Family and Marriage in Europe*. Cambridge: Cambridge University Press.

Gopnik, A. (2012): "Scientific Thinking in Young Children: Theoretical Advances, Empirical Research, and Policy Implications," *Science*, 337(6102): 1623–27.

Gottschall, J. (2008): *Literature, Science, and a New Humanities*. New York: Palgrave Macmillan.

Gottschall, J., and Wilson, D. S. (2005): *The Literary Animal: Evolution and the Nature of Narrative*. Evanston, IL: Northwestern University Press.

Gould, Hannah, and Walters, Holly (2020): "Bad Buddhists, Good Robots: Techno-Salvationist Designs for Nirvana," *Journal of Global Buddhism*, 21: 277–94.

Grajzl, Peter, and Murrell, Peter (2023): "A Macroscope of English Print Culture, 1530–1700, Applied to the Coevolution of Ideas on Religion, Science and Institutions," working paper. https://papers.ssrn.com/sol3/papers.cfm?abstract_id=4336537.

Graystone, Andrew (2021): *Bleeding for Jesus: John Smyth and the Cult of Iwerne Camps*. London: Darton, Longman, and Todd.

Greeley, A. (1962): "Areas of Research on Religion and Social Organizations," *American Catholic Sociological Review*, 23(2): 99–112.

——— (1969): *Religion in the Year 2000*. New York: Sheed and Ward.

——— (1989): *Religious Change in America*. Cambridge, MA: Harvard University Press.

Greenblatt, Stephen (2011): *The Swerve: How the World Became Modern*. New York: W. W. Norton.

Greenhalgh, Trisha, and Hurwitz, Brian (1999): "Why Study Narrative?," *British Medical Journal*, 318: 48–50.

Griera, Mar, Martínez-Ariño, Julia, and Clot-Garrell, Anna (2021): "Banal Catholicism, Morality Policies and the Politics of Belonging in Spain," *Religions*, 12: 293.

Grim, B., and Grim, M. (2016): "The Socio-economic Contribution of Religion to American Society: An Empirical Analysis," *Interdisciplinary Journal of Research on Religion*, 12: 1–31.

Groskop, Viv (2019): "A Refuge from Reality, à la Russe," *New York Review*, February 11, 2019. https://www.nybooks.com/online/2019/02/11/a-refuge-from-reality-a-la-russe/.

Gruber, J., and Hungerman, D. M. (2007): "Faith-Based Charity and Crowd-Out during the Great Depression," *Journal of Public Economics*, 91(5–6): 1043–69.

——— (2008): "The Church versus the Mall: What Happens when Religion Faces Increased Secular Competition?," *Quarterly Journal of Economics*, 123(2): 831–62.

Guiso, Luigi, Sapienza, Paola, and Zingales, Luigi (2003): "People's Opium? Religion and Economic Attitudes," *Journal of Monetary Economics*, 50(1): 225–82.

Guriev, Sergey, and Treisman, Daniel (2023): *Spin Dictators: The Changing Face of Tyranny in the 21st Century*. Princeton, NJ: Princeton University Press.

Guthrie, S. (1980): "A Cognitive Theory of Religion," *Current Anthropology*, 21(2): 181–203.

——— (1993): *Faces in the Clouds: A New Theory of Religion*. New York: Oxford University Press.

Guzik, Paulina (2022): "Pope's Point Man for Charity on the Road to Ukraine for Fourth Trip," *Crux*, September 9, 2022. https://cruxnow.com/church-in-europe/2022/09/popes-point-man-for-charity-on-the-road-to-ukraine-for-fourth-trip.

Hadnes, M., and Schumacher, H. (2012): "The Gods Are Watching: An Experimental Study of Religion and Traditional Belief in Burkina Faso," *Journal for the Scientific Study of Religion*, 51(4): 689–704.

Haghtalab, N., Immorlica, N., Lucier, B., Mobius, M., and Mohan, D. (2022): "Communicating with Anecdotes," working paper. https://arxiv.org/pdf/2205.13461.pdf.

Hahn, Johannes (2015): "The Challenge of Religious Violence: Imperial Ideology and Policy in the Fourth Century," in Wienand Johannes (ed.), *Contested Monarchy: Integrating the Roman Empire in the Fourth Century AD*, pp. 379–404. New York: Oxford University Press.

Hall, Claire (2021a): "Horoscopes of the Moon: Weather Prediction as Astrology in Ptolemy's *Tetrabiblos*," *Early Science and Medicine*, 26: 231–53.

——— (2021b): *Origen and Prophecy: Fate, Authority, Allegory and the Structure of Scripture*. Oxford: Oxford University Press.

Hall, Matthew (2022): "It Shattered My World: An Ohio Soccer Coach, Sexual Misconduct and the System That Has Protected Him," *Guardian*, July 6, 2022. https://www.theguardian.com/sport/2022/jul/06/brad-evans-allegations-toledo-soccer-coach-sexual-misconduct-system.

Hamid, Shadi (2021): "America without God," *Atlantic* (April 2021), published online March 10, 2021. https://www.theatlantic.com/magazine/archive/2021/04/america-politics-religion/618072/.

Hamlin, Alan, and Jennings, Colin (2019): "Expressive Voting," in R. Congleton, B. Grofman, and S. Voigt (eds.), *Oxford Handbook of Public Choice*, pp. 333–50. New York: Oxford University Press.

Hanson, G., and Xiang, C. (2013): "Exporting Christianity: Governance and Doctrine in the Globalization of US Denominations," *Journal of International Economics*, 91(2): 301–20.

Harari, Yuval Noah (2014): *Sapiens: A Brief History of Humankind*. New York: Random House.

Hardin, Russell (1997): "The Economics of Religious Belief," *Journal of Institutional and Theoretical Economics*, 153(1): 259–78.

Harding, Susan Friend (2000): *The Book of Jerry Falwell: Fundamentalist Language and Politics*. Princeton, NJ: Princeton University Press.

Haring, Lee (2016): *Grand Theory in Folkloristics*. Bloomington: Indiana University Press.

Harper, Kyle (2013): *From Shame to Sin*. Cambridge, MA: Harvard University Press.

Harris, Ruth (2022): *Guru to the World: The Life and Legacy of Vivekananda*. Cambridge, MA: Belknap Press of Harvard University Press.

Harrison, Phil (2022): "The Awful Truth of Netflix's Jimmy Savile Documentary: He Gaslit an Entire Nation," *Guardian*, April 14, 2022. https://www.theguardian.com/tv-and-radio/2022/apr/14/netflix-jimmy-savile-a-british-horror-story-documentary.

Harrison Warren, Tish (2016): *Liturgy of the Ordinary: Sacred Practices in Everyday Life*. Carol Stream, IL: Intervarsity Press.

Hartman, M. S. (2004): *The Household and the Making of History: A Subversive View of the Western Past*. Cambridge: Cambridge University Press.

Hassan, S. (2018): *Combating Cult Mind Control*. Newton, MA: Freedom of Mind.

Hausner, S., and Gellner, D. (2012): "Category and Practice as Two Aspects of Religion: The Case of Nepalis in Britain," *Journal of the American Academy of Religion*, 80(4): 1–27.

Haveman, Heather, and Khaire, Mukti (2004): "Survival beyond Succession? The Contingent Impact of Founder Succession on Organizational Failure," *Journal of Business Venturing*, 19: 437–63.

Head, Randolph (1999): "Catholics and Protestants in Graubünden: Confessional Discipline and Confessional Identities without an Early Modern State?," *German History*, 17(3): 321–45.

Hegghammer, Thomas (2020a): *The Caravan: Abdallah Azzam and the Rise of Global Jihad*. Cambridge: Cambridge University Press.

——— (2020b): "Weeping in Modern Jihadi Groups," *Journal of Islamic Studies*, 31(3): 358–87.

Heldring, Leander, Robinson, James, and Vollmer, Sebastian (2021): "The Long-Run Impact of the Dissolution of the English Monasteries," *Quarterly Journal of Economics*, 136(4): 2093–145.

Henrich, Joseph (2015): *The Secret of Our Success*. Princeton, NJ: Princeton University Press.

——— (2020): *The Weirdest People in the World: How the West Became Psychologically Peculiar and Particularly Prosperous*. New York: Farrar, Strauss, and Giroux.

The Henry Ford (n.d.): "Henry Ford: Sociological Department," accessed July 10, 2023. https://www.thehenryford.org/collections-and-research/digital-collections/expert-sets/7148/.

Hertog, Judith, and Chen, Carolyn (2022): "Carolyn Chen: 'Buddhism Has Found a New Institutional Home in the West: the Corporation,'" *Guernica*, July 11, 2022. https://www.guernicamag.com/carolyn-chen-buddhism-has-found-a-new-institutional-home-in-the-west-the-corporation/.

Heyes, Cecilia M. (1993): "Imitation, Culture and Cognition," *Animal Behaviour*, 46(5): 999–1010.

——— (2012): "What's Social about Social Learning?," *Journal of Comparative Psychology*, 126(2): 193–202.

——— (2018a): "Enquire Within: Cultural Evolution and Cognitive Science," *Philosophical Transactions of the Royal Society B*, 373(1743): 20170051.

——— (2018b): *Cognitive Gadgets: The Cultural Evolution of Thinking*. Cambridge, MA: Harvard University Press.

Heyes, Cecilia M., and Frith, C. D. (2014): "The Cultural Evolution of Mind Reading," *Science*, 344(6190). https://doi.org/10.1126/science.1243091.

Hicks, J. R. (1935): "Annual Survey of Economic Theory: The Theory of Monopoly," *Econometrica*, 3(1): 1–20.

Hill, Fiona, and Stent, Angela (2022): "The World Putin Wants: How Distortions about the Past Feed Delusions about the Future," *Foreign Affairs*, September/October 2022.

Hoefer Martí, Julia, and Seabright, Paul (2022): "Alcohol, Behavioral Norms and Sexual Violence on U.S. College Campuses," Discussion Paper no. 17147, Centre for Economic Policy Research.

Hofstadter, Richard (1964): "The Paranoid Style in American Politics," *Harper's Magazine*, November 1964. https://harpers.org/archive/1964/11/the-paranoid-style-in-american-politics/.

Homer (1924): *The Iliad, with an English Translation by A.T. Murray, Ph.D.* Cambridge, MA: Harvard University Press. Digital edition available at https://www.perseus.tufts.edu/hopper/text?doc=Perseus%3Atext%3A1999.01.0134%3Abook%3D6%3Acard%3D297.

Hopkins, E. (2014): "Competitive Altruism, Mentalizing and Signaling," *American Economic Journal: Microeconomics*, 6: 272–92.

Hopkins, Keith (1965): "The Age of Roman Girls at Marriage," *Population Studies*, 18: 309–27.

Horden, Peregrine, and Purcell, Nicholas (2000): *The Corrupting Sea: A Study of Mediterranean History*. Oxford: Blackwell.

Horner, V., and Whiten, A. (2005): "Causal Knowledge and Imitation/Emulation Switching in Chimpanzees (*Pan troglodytes*) and Children (*Homo sapiens*)," *Animal Cognition*, 8: 164–81.

Horton, Adrian (2021): "'This Is a Cult': Inside the Shocking Story of a Religious Weight-Loss Group," *Guardian*, September 29, 2021. https://www.theguardian.com/tv-and-radio/2021/sep/29/gwen-shamblin-docuseries-the-way-down-remnant-fellowship.

Horton, Robin (1993): *Patterns of Thought in Africa and the West: Essays on Magic, Religion and Science*. Cambridge: Cambridge University Press.

Hotelling, Harold (1929): "Stability in Competition," *Economic Journal*, 39(153): 41–57.

Hout, M., and Fischer, C. S. (2002): "Why More Americans Have No Religious Preference: Politics and Generations," *American Sociological Review*, 67(2): 165–90.

——— (2014): "Explaining Why More Americans Have No Religious Preference: Political Backlash and Generational Succession, 1987–2012," *Sociological Science*, 1: 423–47.

Hoyer, Daniel, and Reddish, Jenny (2019): *Seshat History of the Axial Age*. Chaplin, CO: Beresta Books.

Humanists International (2022): *The Freedom of Thought Report 2022*. New York: Humanists International. https://fot.humanists.international/wp-content/uploads/2022/12/FOTR -2022-webview.pdf.

Hungerman, D. M. (2011): "Rethinking the Study of Religious Markets," in Rachel McCleary (ed.), *The Oxford Handbook of the Economics of Religion*, pp. 257–74. New York: Oxford University Press.

——— (2013): "Substitution and Stigma: Evidence on Religious Markets from the Catholic Sexual Abuse Scandal," *American Economic Journal: Economic Policy*, 5(3): 227–53.

Hunter, Michael (2020): *The Decline of Magic: Britain in the Enlightenment*. New Haven, CT: Yale University Press.

Huntington, Samuel P. (1993): "The Clash of Civilizations?," *Foreign Affairs*, 72(3): 22–49.

——— (1996): *The Clash of Civilizations and the Remaking of the World Order*. New York: Simon and Schuster.

Hussam, R., Kelley, E. M., Lane, G. F., and Zahra, F. (2022): "The Psychosocial Value of Employment: Evidence from a Refugee Camp," *American Economic Review*, 112(11): 3694–724.

Iannaccone, L. R. (1988): "A Formal Model of Church and Sect," *American Journal of Sociology*, 94S: 241–68.

——— (1990): "Religious Practice: A Human Capital Approach," *Journal for the Scientific Study of Religion*, 29(3): 297–314.

——— (1992): "Sacrifice and Stigma: Reducing Free-Riding in Cults, Communes, and Other Collectives," *Journal of Political Economy*, 100(2): 271–91.

Iannaccone, L. R., and Berman, E. (2006): "Religious Extremism: The Good, the Bad and the Deadly," *Public Choice*, 128: 109–29.

Iannaccone, L. R., and Bose, F. (2011): "Funding the Faiths: Toward a Theory of Religious Finance," in Rachel McCleary (ed.), *The Oxford Handbook of the Economics of Religion*, pp. 323–42. New York: Oxford University Press.

Ignatius of Loyola (2012): *Spiritual Exercises*, translated by Pierre Wolff. Liguori, MO: Liguori.

IICSA (Independent Inquiry, Child Sexual Abuse) (2022): executive summary of *The Roman Catholic Church Investigation Report*, Reports and Recommendations, October 2022. https:// www.iicsa.org.uk/reports-recommendations/publications/investigation/roman-catholic -church/executive-summary.

India.com News Desk (2017): "Ichadhari Baba, Running High Profile Sex Racket in South Delhi, Gets Arrested," India.com, August 28, 2017. https://www.india.com/news /india/ichadhari-baba-running-high-profile-sex-racket-in-south-delhi-gets-arrested -2433505/.

Inglehart, R. (2021): *Religion's Sudden Decline: What's Causing It, and What Comes Next?* Oxford: Oxford University Press.

Inglehart, R., Haerpfer, C., Moreno, A., Welzel, C., Kizilova, K., Diez-Medrano, J., Lagos, M., Norris, P., Ponarin, E., and Puranen, B., eds. (2022): *World Values Survey: All Rounds— Country-Pooled Datafile*. Madrid, Spain, and Vienna, Austria: JD Systems Institute and WVSA Secretariat. Dataset Version 3.0.0. https://doi.org/10.14281/18241.17.

Inglis, Tom (1998): *Moral Monopoly: Rise and Fall of the Catholic Church in Modern Ireland*, revised edition. Dublin: University College Dublin Press.

Inoue, S., and Matsuzawa, T. (2007): "Working Memory of Numerals in Chimpanzees," *Current Biology*, 17(23): R1004–5.

InSight Crime (2022): "InSight Crime's 2021 Homicide Round-Up," News, February 1, 2022. https://insightcrime.org/news/insight-crimes-2021-homicide-round-up/.

Internal Revenue Service (2015): *Tax Guide for Churches and Religious Organizations*. https://www.irs.gov/pub/irs-pdf/p1828.pdf.

Ivanova, Polina (2022): "Russian Orthodox Church Lends Legitimacy to Vladimir Putin's War in Ukraine," *Financial Times*, April 18, 2022. https://www.ft.com/content/4c03d717-b322-4218-80d2-884d60e028c7.

Iyer, S. (2016): "The New Economics of Religion," *Journal of Economic Literature*, 54(2): 395–441.

——— (2018): *The Economics of Religion in India*. Cambridge, MA: Harvard University Press.

Jacquet, Antoine (2023): "Culture, Human Capital and Marital Homogamy in France," working paper, Toulouse School of Economics.

Jacquet, Antoine, and Monpetit, Sébastien (2023): "Veiling and Economic Integration of Muslim Women in France," working paper, Toulouse School of Economics.

Jagiello, R., Heyes, C., and Whitehouse, H. (2022): "Tradition and Invention: The Bifocal Stance Theory of Cultural Evolution," *Behavioral and Brain Sciences*, 45: e249.

James, Henry, Sr. (1863): *Substance and Shadow; Or, Morality and Religion in Their Relation to Life: An Essay upon the Physics of Creation*. Boston: Ticknor and Fields.

James, William (1985): *Varieties of Religious Experience*. Cambridge, MA: Harvard University Press.

Jaspers, K. ([1949] 2011): *The Origin and Goal of History*, translated by Michael Bullock. London: Routledge.

Jay, A., Evans, M., Frank, I., and Sharpling, D. (2020): *The Anglican Church: Safeguarding in the Church of England and the Church in Wales*. Independent Inquiry, Child Sexual Abuse, October 6, 2020. https://www.iicsa.org.uk/document/anglican-church-safeguarding-church-england-and-church-wales-investigation-report.

Jenkins, Jack (2022): "Democrats Call on IRS to Review Right-Wing Group's 'Church' Status," *Washington Post*, August 2, 2022. https://www.washingtonpost.com/religion/2022/08/02/family-research-council-irs/.

Jenkins, P. (2011): *The Next Christendom: The Coming of Global Christianity*. New York: Oxford University Press.

Jensen, M. (2017): "The Challenge of Oral Epic to Homeric Scholarship," *Humanities*, 6(4): 97.

Jha, Saumitra (2023): "Building Resilient Inter-ethnic Peace: Hindus and Muslims in South Asia," in D. Rohner and E. Zhuravskaya (eds.), *Nation Building: Big Lessons from Successes and Failures*, pp. 55–68. London: Centre for Economic Policy Research.

John of Ephesus (1860): *The Ecclesiastical History*, part 3, translated by Robert Payne Smith. Facsimile available online at https://archive.org/details/ecclesiasticalhi00johnuoft.

Johnson, Dominic (2015): *God Is Watching You: How the Fear of God Makes Us Human*. New York: Oxford University Press.

Johnson, Ian (2017): "What a Buddhist Monk Taught Xi Jinping," *New York Times*, March 24, 2017. https://www.nytimes.com/2017/03/24/opinion/sunday/chinas-communists-embrace-religion.html.

Johnson, Monte, and Wilson, Catherine (2007): "Lucretius and the History of Science," in Stuart Gillespie and Philip Hardie (eds.), *The Cambridge Companion to Lucretius*, pp. 131–48. Cambridge: Cambridge University Press.

Johnson, Noel, and Koyama, Mark (2019): *Persecution and Toleration: The Long Road to Religious Freedom*. Cambridge: Cambridge University Press.

Johnson, Todd M., and Grim, Brian J., eds. (2023): *World Religion Database*. Leiden: Brill. https://www.worldreligiondatabase.org/.

Jones, Jeffrey M. (2021): "U.S. Church Membership Falls below Majority for First Time," Gallup, March 29, 2021. https://news.gallup.com/poll/341963/church-membership-falls-below -majority-first-time.aspx.

Jordan, Drew (n.d.): "Storytelling . . . an Essential for Zoos," WDM Architects, accessed July 10, 2023. https://wdmarchitects.com/2014/10/storytelling-essential-zoos/.

Jullien, Bruno, and Sand-Zantmann, Wilfried (2021): "The Economics of Platforms: A Theory Guide for Competition Policy," *Information Economics and Policy*, 54: 100880.

Kahneman, D., and Tversky, A. (1982): "On the Study of Statistical Intuitions," *Cognition*, 11(2): 123–41.

Kalu, O. (2008): *African Pentecostalism: An Introduction*. New York: Oxford University Press.

Kanter, R. (1972): *Commitment and Community*. Cambridge, MA: Harvard University Press.

Kaufman, J., and Zigler, E. (1987): "Do Abused Children Become Abusive Parents?," *American Journal of Orthopsychiatry*, 57: 186–92.

Kaufmann, Eric (2010): *Shall the Religious Inherit the Earth? Demography and Politics in the Twenty-First Century*. London: Profile Books.

——— (2018): *Whiteshift: Populism, Immigration and the Future of White Majorities*. London: Allen Lane.

Kaul, Rhythma, and Dutt, Anonna (2021): "India's Fertility Rate Drops below 2.1, Contraceptive Prevalence Up: NFHS," *Hindustan Times*, November 5, 2021. https://www.hindustantimes .com/india-news/indias-fertility-rate-drops-below-2-1-population-stabilising-nfhs-data -101637751803433.html.

Kelly, Morgan (2021): "Devotion or Deprivation: Did Catholicism Retard French Development?," Discussion Paper no. 16241, Centre for Economic Policy Research.

Khan, Aina J. (2022): "British Muslim Travel Agencies in Uproar over Saudi Hajj Changes," *Guardian*, June 26, 2022. https://www.theguardian.com/world/2022/jun/26/british -muslim-travel-agencies-in-uproar-over-saudi-hajj-changes.

Kim, Seung Min, and Bailey, Sarah Pulliam (2020): "Trump Courts Latinos in Miami as Part of Launch of Evangelical Coalition," *Washington Post*, January 3, 2020. https://www .washingtonpost.com/politics/trump-to-court-latinos-in-miami-as-part-of-launch-of -evangelical-group/2020/01/03/db2e85b8-2dc1-11ea-be79-83e793dbcaef_story.html.

Kitiarsa, Pattana (2005): "Beyond Syncretism: Hybridization of Popular Religion in Contemporary Thailand," *Journal of Southeast Asian Studies*, 36(3): 461–87.

——— (2012): *Mediums, Monks and Amulets: Thai Popular Buddhism Today*. Chiang Mai, Thailand: Silkworm Books.

Knapp, Jeffrey (1993): "Preachers and Players in Shakespeare's England," *Representations*, 44: 29–59.

Koesel, Karrie, Hu, Yizhi, and Pine, Joshua (2019): "Official Protestantism in China," *Review of Religion and Chinese Society*, 6: 71–98.

Koyama, Mark, and Rubin, Jared (2022): *How the World Became Rich: The Historical Origins of Economic Growth*. Cambridge, UK: Polity.

Kruger, J. M., and Dunning, D. (1999): "Unskilled and Unaware of It: How Difficulties in Recognizing One's Own Incompetence Lead to Inflated Self-Assessments," *Journal of Personality and Social Psychology*, 77: 1121–34.

Kuefler, Mathew (2007): "The Marriage Revolution in Late Antiquity: The Theodosian Code and Later Roman Marriage Law," *Journal of Family History*, 32(4): 343–70.

Künkler, Mirjam, and Fazaeli, Roja (2012): "The Life of Two Mujtahidahs: Female Religious Authority in 20th Century Iran," in Masooda Bano and Hilary Kalmbach (eds.), *Women, Leadership and Mosques: Changes in Contemporary Islamic Authority*, pp. 127–60. Leiden: Brill.

Kuran, T. (2010): *The Long Divergence: How Islamic Law Held Back the Middle East*. Princeton, NJ: Princeton University Press.

———— (2018): "Islam and Economic Performance: Historical and Contemporary Links," *Journal of Economic Literature*, 56(4): 1292–359.

Kushnir, T., Xu, F., and Wellmann, H. (2010): "Young Children Use Statistical Sampling to Infer the Preferences of Other People," *Psychological Science*, 21(8): 1134–40.

Kwabena Asamoa-Gyadu, J. (2015): "Pentecostalism and the African Christian Landscape," in M. Lindhardt (ed.), *Pentecostalism in Africa: Presence and Impact of Pneumatic Christianity in Postcolonial Societies*, pp. 100–114. Leiden: Brill.

Kyodo, Jiji (2022): "Unification Church Corrects Remarks amid Scrutiny of Abe's Death," *Japan Times*, July 17, 2022. https://www.japantimes.co.jp/news/2022/07/17/national/unification -church-correction/.

Lafleur, Wiliam (1992): *Liquid Life: Abortion and Buddhism in Japan*. Princeton, NJ: Princeton University Press.

Lafontaine, Francine, and Slade, Margaret (2015): "Franchising and Exclusive Distribution: Adaptation and Antitrust," chapter 16 in Roger D. Blair and D. Daniel Sokol (eds.), *The Oxford Handbook of International Antitrust Economics*, vol. 2. New York: Oxford University Press.

Lam, Bourree (2015): "Wrestling with God, and Taxes," *Atlantic*, December 27, 2015. https:// www.theatlantic.com/business/archive/2015/12/tax-iceland-zuism/421647/.

Lane Fox, Robin (1986): *Pagans and Christians in the Mediterranean World from the Second Century AD to the Conversion of Constantine*. London: Viking Penguin.

Lang, M., Kratky, J., Shaver, J., Jerotijevic, D., and Xygalatas, D. (2015): "Effects of Anxiety on Spontaneous Ritualized Behavior," *Current Biology*, 25: 1892–97.

Lang, M., Kratky, J., and Xygalatas, D. (2020): "The Role of Ritual Behaviour in Anxiety Reduction: An Investigation of Marathi Religious Practices in Mauritius," *Philosophical Transactions of the Royal Society B*, 375(1805): 20190431.

Launay, J., Tarr, B., and Dunbar, R. (2016): "Synchrony as an Adaptive Mechanism for Large-Scale Human Social Bonding," *Ethology*, 122(10): 779–89.

Lawson, Mark (2022): "The Day I Thwarted Jimmy Savile: Mark Lawson on Trying to Stop Britain's Worst Sex Offender," *Guardian*, April 1, 2022. https://www.theguardian.com/tv-and -radio/2022/apr/01/the-day-i-thwarted-jimmy-savile-mark-lawson-on-trying-to-stop -britains-worst-sex-offender.

Lazear, E. P., Shaw, K. L., and Stanton, C. T. (2015): "The Value of Bosses," *Journal of Labor Economics*, 33(4): 823–61.

Lechner, Frank J. (2007): "Rational Choice and Religious Economics," in J. Beckford and J. Demerath (eds.), *The Sage Handbook of the Sociology of Religion*, pp. 81–97. Los Angeles: Sage.

Lejarraga, T., and Hertwig, R. (2021): "How Experimental Methods Shaped Views on Human Competence and Rationality," *Psychological Bulletin*, 147(6): 535–64.

Leppin, Hartmut (2022): "Zu den anfängen der Bischofsbestellung," in A. Fahrmeier (ed.), *Personalentscheidungen für gesellschaftliche Schlüsselpositionen*, pp. 33–54. Berlin: De Gruyter.

Lesta, Natalie (2018): "What's Driving the Conflict in Cameroon?," *Foreign Affairs*, November 8, 2018. https://www.foreignaffairs.com/articles/cameroon/2018-11-08/whats-driving -conflict-cameroon.

Leustean, Lucian N. (2022a): "Russia's Invasion of Ukraine: The First Religious War in the 21st Century," *LSE blogs*, March 3, 2022. https://blogs.lse.ac.uk/religionglobalsociety/2022 /03/russias-invasion-of-ukraine-the-first-religious-war-in-the-21st-century/.

——— (2022b): "When Will Russia's War on Ukraine End? Religion and Security Strategies," Religion Unplugged, May 23, 2022. https://religionunplugged.com/news/2022/5/23 /when-will-russias-war-on-ukraine-end-religion-and-security-strategies.

——— (2023): "Is Russia's Invasion of Ukraine Still a Religious War?," *LSE blogs*, February 8, 2023. https://blogs.lse.ac.uk/religionglobalsociety/2023/02/is-russias-invasion-of-ukraine -still-a-religious-war/.

Levy, Gilat, and Razin, Ronny (2012): "Religious Beliefs, Religious Participation, and Cooperation," *American Economic Journal: Microeconomics*, 4(3): 121–51.

Lightner, Aaron, and Hagen, Edward H. (2022): "All Models Are Wrong, and Some Are Religious: Supernatural Explanations as Abstract and Useful Falsehoods about Complex Realities," *Human Nature*, 33: 425–62.

Lindberg, David (2013): "Science and the Medieval Church," in Lindberg and Michael Shank (eds.), *The Cambridge History of Science*, vol. 2, pp. 268–85. Cambridge: Cambridge University Press.

Lindeman, Marjaana, Svedholm-Häkkinen, Annika M., and Lipsanen, Jari (2015): "Ontological Confusions but Not Mentalizing Abilities Predict Religious Belief, Paranormal Belief, and Belief in Supernatural Purpose," *Cognition*, 134: 63–76.

Lindstrom, L. (1990): "Knowledge of Cargo, Knowledge of Cult: Truth and Power on Tanna, Vanuatu," in G. W. Trompf (ed.), *Cargo Cults and Millenarian Movements: Transoceanic Comparisons of New Religious Movements*, pp. 239–62. Berlin: Mouton de Gruyter.

Lipton, Sara (1999): "'Tanquam effeminatum': Pedro II of Aragon and the Gendering of Heresy in the Albigensian Crusade," in J. Blackmore and G. Hutcheson (eds.), *Queer Iberia: Sexualities, Cultures, and Crossings from the Middle Ages to the Renaissance*, pp. 107–29. Durham, NC: Duke University Press.

Loewenstein, David (2013): *Treacherous Faith: The Specter of Heresy in Early Modern English Literature and Culture*. Oxford: Oxford University Press.

Lomsadze, Giorgi (2015): "Azerbaijan's President Ilham Aliyev Goes to Mecca," Eurasianet, April 8, 2015. https://eurasianet.org/azerbaijans-president-ilham-aliyev-goes-to-mecca.

Lord, A. B. ([1960] 2000): *The Singer of Tales*, 2nd edition, edited by Stephen Mitchell and Gregory Nagy. Cambridge, MA: Harvard University Press.

Lotz-Heimann, Ute (2001): "The Concept of 'Confessionalization': A Historiographical Paradigm in Dispute," *Memoria y civilización*, 4: 93–114.

Lu, Donna (2022): "Hillsong Church Apologises after Investigations Find Brian Houston Engaged in 'Inappropriate' Behaviour," *Guardian*, March 19, 2022. https://www.theguardian.com/world/2022/mar/19/hillsong-church-apologises-after-investigations-find-brian-houston-engaged-in-inappropriate-behaviour.

Luca, Nathalie (2012): *Y croire et en rêver: Réussir dans le marketing relationnel de multiniveaux*. Paris: L'Harmattan.

Lucas, Adam (2006): *Wind, Water, Work: Ancient and Medieval Milling Technology*. Leiden: Brill.

Luhrmann, Tanya (1989): *Persuasions of the Witch's Craft: Ritual Magic in Contemporary England*. Cambridge, MA: Harvard University Press.

———— (2012): *When God Talks Back: Understanding the American Evangelical Relationship with God*. New York: Knopf.

Luscombe, Richard (2022): "Thousands of Baptisms Invalidated by Priest's Use of One Wrong Word," *Guardian*, February 16, 2022. https://www.theguardian.com/us-news/2022/feb/16/arizona-baptisms-invalidated-priest-uses-one-wrong-word.

Luxmoore, Jonathan (2022): "Ukraine and Russian Church Leaders at Odds over Invasion," *Tablet*, February 24, 2022. https://www.thetablet.co.uk/news/15057/ukraine-and-russian-church-leaders-at-odds-over-invasion.

Lyons, D. E., Young, A. G., and Keil, F. C. (2007). "The Hidden Structure of Over-Imitation," *Proceedings of the National Academy of Sciences of the USA*, 104(50): 19751–56.

Ma, Debin, and Rubin, Jared (2019): "The Paradox of Power: Principal-Agent Problems and Administrative Capacity in Imperial China (and Other Absolutist Regimes)," *Journal of Comparative Economics*, 47: 277–94.

MacCulloch, Diarmaid (2009): *A History of Christianity: The First Three Thousand Years*. London: Penguin Books.

———— (2014): *Silence: A Christian History*. London: Penguin Books.

Macfarlane, Alan (1978): *The Origins of English Individualism: The Family, Property and Social Transition*. Oxford: Blackwell.

Mackey, Maureen (2022): "Rosaries for Ukraine Are 'Incredible Gift' of Faith, Prayer for Those under Siege," *Fox News*, March 12, 2022. https://www.foxnews.com/lifestyle/rosaries-ukraine-gift-faith-prayer.

Maclean, Ian (2022): "Brand Melanchthon, Brand Philippism. Polemics and the Book World, 1560–1620: A Prolegomenon," chapter 12 of Arthur der Weduwen and Malcolm Walsby (eds.), *Reformation, Religious Culture and Print in Early Modern Europe: Essays in Honour of Andrew Pettegree*, vol. 1. Leiden: Brill.

Madigan, Sheri, Cyr, Chantal, Eirich, Rachel, Fearon, R. M. Pasco, Ly, Anh, Rash, Christina, Poole, Julia C., and Alink, Lenneke R. A. (2019): "Testing the Cycle of Maltreatment Hypothesis: Meta-analytic Evidence of the Intergenerational Transmission of Child Maltreatment," *Development and Psychopathology*, 31(1): 23–51.

Majumdar, Samirah, and Villa, Virginia (2021): "Globally, Social Hostilities Related to Religion Decline in 2019, while Government Restrictions Remain at Highest Levels," Pew Research

Center, September 30, 2021. https://www.pewresearch.org/religion/2021/09/30/globally
-social-hostilities-related-to-religion-decline-in-2019-while-government-restrictions-remain
-at-highest-levels/.

Maleki, Ammar, and Tamimi Arab, Pooyan (2020): *Iranians' Attitudes toward Religion: A 2020
Survey Report*. Netherlands: Group for Analyzing and Measuring Attitudes in Iran
(GAMAAN). https://gamaan.org/wp-content/uploads/2020/09/GAMAAN-Iran
-Religion-Survey-2020-English.pdf.

Malinowski, Bronislaw ([1926] 2014): *Myth in Primitive Psychology*. Baltimore, MD: Angela.

Mallett, Xanthe (2017): "Women Also Sexually Abuse Children, but Their Reasons Often Differ
from Men's," *Conversation*, February 19, 2017. https://theconversation.com/women-also
-sexually-abuse-children-but-their-reasons-often-differ-from-mens-72572.

Maltsev, Vladimir (2022): "Economic Effects of Voluntary Religious Castration on the Informal
Provision of Cooperation: The Case of the Russian Skoptsy Sect," *European Economic Review*,
145: 104109.

Mannix Flynn, Gerard (2003): *Nothing to Say*. Dublin: Lilliput.

Mar, R., and Oatley, K (2008): "The Function of Fiction Is the Abstraction and Simulation of
Social Experience," *Perspectives on Psychological Science*, 3: 173–92.

Marchais, G., Mastaki Mugaraka, C., Sanchez de la Sierra, R., and Qihang Wu, D. (2022): "The
Pro-Social Determinants of Violent Collective Action: Evidence from Participation in Mi-
litias in Eastern Congo," working paper. https://raulsanchezdelasierra.com/research/.

Margalit, Ruth (2019): "How the Religious Right Transformed Israeli Education," *New Yorker*,
August 23, 2019. https://www.newyorker.com/news/letter-from-jerusalem/how-the
-religious-right-transformed-israeli-education.

Margolis, Michele (2018): *From Politics to the Pews: How Partisanship and the Political Environment Shape Religious Identity*. Chicago: University of Chicago Press.

Marlowe, F. (2010): *The Hadza: Hunter Gatherers of Tanzania*. Berkeley: University of California
Press.

Marshall, Alfred (1890): *Principles of Economics*. London: Macmillan.

Mars-Jones, Adam (2004): "*Terminator 2* Good, *The Odyssey* Bad," review of *The Seven Basic
Plots* by Christopher Booker, *Guardian*, November 20, 2004. https://www.theguardian.com
/books/2004/nov/21/fiction.features.

Marx, Karl (1975): "Contribution to the Critique of Hegel's Philosophy of Law: Introduction,"
in *Marx/Engels Collected Works*, vol. 3, pp. 175–87. London: Lawrence and Wishart.

Masera, F., and Yousaf, H. (2022): "The Charitable Terrorist: State Capacity and the Support
for the Pakistani Taliban," *Journal of Conflict Resolution*, 66: 1174–207.

Mather, Cotton (1702): *Magnalia Christi Americana; or, The Ecclesiastical History of New-England,
from Its First Planting in the Year 1620. unto the Year of Our Lord, 1698. In Seven Books*. London:
Thomas Parkhurst. Facsimile available online at https://archive.org/details/magnaliachristia
00math.

Mathew, Sarah (2017): "How the Second-Order Free-Rider Problem Is Solved in a Small-Scale
Society," *American Economic Review, Papers and Proceedings*, 107(5): 578–81.

Mathew, Sarah, and Perreault, Charles (2015): "Behavioural Variation in 172 Small-Scale Societies Indicates that Social Learning is the Main Mode of Human Adaptation," *Proceedings of
the Royal Society B*, 282: 20150061.

Matsuzawa, Tetsuro (2020): "Pretense in Chimpanzees," *Primates*, 61: 543–55.

Mauss, Marcel (1950): *Essai sur le don: Forme et raison de l'échange dans les sociétés archaïques.* Paris: Presses Universitaires de France. English translation by Ian Cunnison with an introduction by E. E. Evans-Pritchard. London: Cohen and West, 1966. Facsimile available online at https://archive.org/details/giftformsfunctio00maus.

Maxwell, D. (1998): "Delivered from the Spirit of Poverty? Pentecostalism, Prosperity and Modernity in Zimbabwe," *Journal of Religion in Africa*, 28(3): 350–73.

Maxwell, Robert, and Silverman, Philip (1970): "Information and Esteem: Cultural Considerations in the Treatment of the Aged," *Aging and Human Development*, 1(4): 361–92.

McAdams, D., Reynolds, J., Lewis, M., Patten, A., and Bowman, P. (2001): "When Bad Things Turn Good and Good Things Turn Bad: Sequences of Redemption and Contamination in Life Narrative and Their Relation to Psychosocial Adaptation in Midlife Adults and in Students," *Personality and Social Psychology Bulletin*, 27(4): 474–85.

McBride, M. (2008): "Religious Pluralism and Religious Participation: A Game Theoretic Analysis," *American Journal of Sociology*, 114(1): 77–108.

—— (2010): "Religious Market Competition in a Richer World," *Economica*, 77: 148–71.

—— (2015): "Why Churches Need Free-Riders: Religious Capital Formation and Religious Group Survival," *Journal of Behavioral and Experimental Economics*, 58: 77–87.

McCaffree, Kevin (2017): *The Secular Landscape: The Decline of Religion in America.* Cham, Switzerland: Palgrave Macmillan.

McCants, Anne (2021): "Who Is He Calling WEIRD?," *Journal of Interdisciplinary History*, 52(2): 251–61.

McCauley, J. F. (2013): "Africa's New Big Man Rule? Pentecostalism and Patronage in Ghana," *African Affairs*, 112(446): 1–21.

McCleary, R. M. (2022): "Catholic Child and Youth Martyrs, 1588–2022," *Catholic Historical Review*, 108(3): 469–508.

—— (forthcoming): "Protestant Doctrinal Heterodoxy and Heterogeneity in Guatemala, 1880s to 1950s," in Felipe Valencia Caicedo (ed.), *Roots of Underdevelopment in Latin America.* Springer.

McCleary, R. M., and Barro, R. J. (2006a): "Religion and Economy," *Journal of Economic Perspectives*, 20(2): 49–72.

—— (2006b): "Religion and Political Economy in an International Panel," *Journal for the Scientific Study of Religion*, 45(2): 149–75.

—— (2022): "Mártires de Latinoamérica, 1854–2022," *Revista fe y libertad*, 5(1): 61–93.

McCloskey, Deirdre (1990): "Storytelling in Economics," in Christopher Nash (ed.), *Narrative in Culture: The Uses of Storytelling in the Sciences, Philosophy and Literature*, pp. 5–22. London: Routledge.

—— (2006): *The Bourgeois Virtues: Ethics for an Age of Commerce*, vol. 1 of the trilogy The Bourgeois Era. Chicago: University of Chicago Press.

—— (2010): *Bourgeois Dignity: Why Economics Can't Explain the Modern World*, vol. 2 of the trilogy The Bourgeois Era. Chicago: University of Chicago Press.

—— (2016a): *Bourgeois Equality: How Ideas, Not Capital or Institutions, Enriched the World*, vol. 3 of the trilogy The Bourgeois Era. Chicago: University of Chicago Press.

—— (2016b): "Not Institutions, but Ethics and Religion: A Reply to Whaples, Hill, Fox, Oslington, and Boettke and Rosolino," *Faith and Economics*, 68: 47–62.

McCloy, Shelby T. (1951): "Persecution of the Huguenots in the 18th Century," *Church History*, 20(3): 56–79.

McGuigan, William, and Stephenson, Sarah (2015): "A Single-Case Study of Resiliency after Extreme Incest in an Old Order Amish Family," *Journal of Child Sexual Abuse*, 24: 526–37.

MedyaNews (2022): "Iran: Protests Continue after Execution of 23-Year-Old Rapper," November 12, 2022. https://medyanews.net/iran-protests-continue-after-execution-of-23-year-old -rapper/.

Meeks, Wayne A. (2003): *The First Urban Christians: The Social World of the Apostle Paul.* New Haven, CT: Yale University Press.

Mehr, Samuel A., Krasnow, Max M., Bryant, Gregory A., and Hagen, Edward H. (2021): "Origins of Music in Credible Signaling," *Behavioral and Brain Sciences*, 44: e60.

Mérancourt, Widlore, and Faiola, Anthony (2021): "Abductions by the Busload: Haitians Are Being Held Hostage by a Surge in Kidnappings," *Washington Post*, October 9, 2021. https:// www.washingtonpost.com/world/2021/10/09/haiti-kidnapping/.

Mercier, H., and Sperber, D. (2011): "Why Do Humans Reason? Arguments for an Argumentative Theory," *Behavioral and Brain Sciences*, 34: 57–74.

Michalopoulos, Stelios, and Meng Xue, Melanie (2021): "Folklore," *Quarterly Journal of Economics*, 136(4): 1993–2046.

Miller, Geoffrey (2000): *The Mating Mind: How Sexual Choice Shaped the Evolution of Human Nature.* New York: Random House.

Miller, K. (2002): "Competitive Strategies of Religious Organizations," *Strategic Management Journal*, 23(5): 435–56.

Milman, Oliver (2020): "Boy Scouts of America Files for Bankruptcy amid New Sex-Abuse Lawsuits," *Guardian*, February 18, 2020. https://www.theguardian.com/us-news/2020/feb /18/boy-scouts-of-america-files-for-bankruptcy-amid-new-sex-abuse-lawsuits.

Mishra, Ashutosh (2022): "Life in Danger: Rape-Accused Nithyananda Seeks Medical Asylum in Sri Lanka," *India Today*, September 2, 2022. https://www.indiatoday.in/india /story/rape-accused-nithyananda-seeks-medical-asylum-in-sri-lanka-1995805-2022 -09-02.

Mitchell, Lynette (2013): "Alexander the Great: Divinity and the Rule of Law," in Mitchel and Charles Melville (eds.), *Every Inch a King: Comparative Studies on Kings and Kingship in the Ancient and Medieval Worlds*, pp. 91–107. Boston: Brill.

Mithen, Steven J. (1996): *The Prehistory of the Mind: The Cognitive Origins of Art, Religion and Science.* New York: Thames and Hudson.

——— (2005): *The Singing Neanderthals.* Cambridge, MA: Harvard University Press.

Mogan, R., Fischer, R., and Bulbulia, J. (2017): "To Be in Synchrony or Not? A Meta-analysis of Synchrony's Effects on Behavior, Perception, Cognition and Affect," *Journal of Experimental Social Psychology*, 72: 13–20.

Mohamed, Besheer (2021): "Most Black Protestants Say Denominational Affiliation Is Less Important than Inspiring Sermons," Pew Research Center, April 29, 2021. https://www .pewresearch.org/short-reads/2021/04/29/most-black-protestants-say-denominational -affiliation-is-less-important-than-inspiring-sermons/.

Mohan, Anand, and Singh, Alok (2018): "Hardlook: The Cult of Self-Styled Godman Virender Dev Dikshit," *Indian Express*, June 25, 2018. https://indianexpress.com/article/india /hardlook-the-cult-of-self-styled-godman-virender-dev-dikshit-5015533/.

Mokyr, Joel (2002): *The Gifts of Athena: Historical Origins of the Knowledge Economy*. Princeton, NJ: Princeton University Press.

——— (2017): *A Culture of Growth: The Origins of the Modern Economy*. Princeton, NJ: Princeton University Press.

Mollick, Ethan R. (2012): "People and Process, Suits and Innovators: The Role of Individuals in Firm Performance," *Strategic Management Journal*, 33: 1001–15.

Le Monde with AFP (2023): "Emmanuel Macron annonce 'mettre fin' au Conseil français du culte musulman," *Le Monde*, February 16, 2023. https://www.lemonde.fr/societe/article /2023/02/16/emmanuel-macron-annonce-mettre-fin-au-conseil-francais-du-culte -musulman_6162094_3224.html.

Monfasani, John (2012): review of *The Swerve: How the Renaissance Began* by Stephen Greenblatt, *Reviews in History*, review no. 1283, accessed July 10, 2023, https://reviews.history.ac.uk /review/1283.

Morgan, Catherine (1989): "Divination and Society at Delphi and Didyma," *Hermathena*, 147: 17–42.

Morgan, Mary S., and Stapleford, Thomas A. (2023): "Narrative in Economics: A New Turn on the Past," *History of Political Economy*, 55(3): 395–421.

Mori, Masahiro (2012): "The Uncanny Valley [From the Field]," translated by K. Macdorman and N. Kageki, *IEEE Robotics and Automation Magazine*, 19(2): 98–100. Originally published in Japanese in 1970 in *Energy* 7(4): 33–35.

Morris, J. (2012): "Secularization and Religious Experience: Arguments in the Historiography of Modern British Religion," *Historical Journal*, 55(1): 195–219.

Morrissey, Fitzroy (2021): *A Short History of Islamic Thought*. London: Head of Zeus.

Morriss-Kay, Gillian (2010): "The Evolution of Human Artistic Creativity," *Journal of Anatomy*, 216: 158–76.

Moscow Patriarchate (2022): "On Defender of the Fatherland Day, His Holiness Patriarch Kirill Laid a Wreath at the Grave of the Unknown Soldier at the Kremlin Wall," News, February 23, 2022. http://www.patriarchia.ru/db/text/5903402.html.

Mountjoy, Shane (2009): *Manifest Destiny*. New York: Chelsea House.

Moustafa, Tamir (2000): "Conflict and Cooperation between the State and Religious Institutions in Contemporary Egypt," *International Journal of Middle East Studies*, 32: 3–22.

Mracheck, Alexis, and McCrum, Shane (2019): "How Putin Uses Russian Orthodoxy to Grow His Empire," Heritage Foundation, February 22, 2019. https://www.heritage.org/europe /commentary/how-putin-uses-russian-orthodoxy-grow-his-empire.

Müller, W. P. (2021): *Marriage Litigation in the Western Church, 1215–1517*. Cambridge: Cambridge University Press.

Murch, Walter (2001): *In the Blink of an Eye: A Perspective on Film Editing*. Los Angeles: Silman-James.

Ndi, Michael (2014): "Bleak Future for Christianity as Nso Fon Converts to Islam," *Guardian Post*, October 29, 2014. https://guardianpostonline.blogspot.com/2014/10/kumbo.html.

Neustein, Amy, ed. (2009): *Tempest in the Temple: Jewish Communities and Child Sex Scandals.* Brandeis Series in American Jewish History, Culture, and Life. Waltham, MA: Brandeis University Press.

Newland, Bryan (2022): *Federal Indian Boarding School Initiative Investigative Report.* US Department of the Interior.

Newsam, Malcolm, and Ridgway, Gary (2022): *Independent Assurance Review of the Effectiveness of Multi-agency Responses to Child Sexual Exploitation in Greater Manchester,* part 2: *The Review into Historic Safeguarding Practices in the Borough of Oldham.* https://www.greatermanchester-ca.gov.uk/media/6198/final-oldham-assurance-report-8-june-2022-14-digital-version.pdf.

Nietzsche, Friedrich (1910): *The Birth of Tragedy, or Hellenism and Pessimism,* translated by W. A. Haussmann. Edinburgh: T. N. Foulis. Digital edition available at https://www.gutenberg.org/files/51356/51356-h/51356-h.htm.

Nixey, Catherine (2017): *The Darkening Age: The Christian Destruction of the Classical World.* London: Macmillan.

Norenzayan, Ara (2013): *Big Gods.* Princeton, NJ: Princeton University Press.

——— (2014): "Does Religion Make People Moral?," *Behaviour,* 151(2–3): 365–84.

Norenzayan, Ara, Atran, Scott, Faulkner, Jason, and Schaller, Mark (2006): "Memory and Mystery: The Cultural Selection of Minimally Counterintuitive Narratives," *Cognitive Science,* 30: 531–53.

Norenzayan, Ara, and Hansen, Ian G. (2006): "Belief in Supernatural Agents in the Face of Death," *Personality and Social Psychology Bulletin,* 32(2): 174–87.

Norenzayan, Ara, Shariff, Azim F., Gervais, Will M., Willard, Aiyana K., McNamara, Rita A., Slingerland, Edward, and Henrich, Joseph (2014): "The Cultural Evolution of Prosocial Religions," *Behavioral and Brain Sciences,* 39: 1–19.

Novella, Steven (2008): "Suboptimal Optics: Vision Problems as Scars of Evolutionary History," *Evo Edu Outreach,* 1: 493–97.

Nunn, N., and Sanchez de la Sierra, R. (2017): "Why Being Wrong Can Be Right: Magical Warfare Technologies and the Persistence of False Beliefs," *American Economic Review Papers and Proceedings,* 107(5): 582–87.

Oatley, K. (2016): "Fiction: Simulation of Social Worlds," *Trends in Cognitive Science,* 20: 618–28.

OECD (Organisation for Economic Cooperation and Development) (2008): *Higher Education to 2030,* vol. 1: *Demography.* Paris: OECD.

Ofcom (2022): "The Genuine Article? One in Three Internet Users Fail to Question Misinformation," News Centre, March 29, 2022. https://www.ofcom.org.uk/news-centre/2022/one-in-three-internet-users-fail-to-question-misinformation.

Offer, Avner (1997): "Between the Gift and the Market: The Economy of Regard," *Economic History Review,* 50(3): 450–76.

Ogilvie, Sheilagh (2023): "Epidemics and Institutions from the Black Death to COVID," manuscript in preparation, courtesy of the author.

Ogilvie, Sheilagh, Edwards, Jeremy, and Küpker, Markus (2022): "Economically Relevant Human Capital or Multi-purpose Consumption Good? Book Ownership in Pre-modern Württemberg," *Explorations in Economic History,* 83: 101418.

O'Toole, Fintan (2021): *We Don't Know Ourselves: A Personal History of Modern Ireland*. New York: Liveright.

Otto, Bernd-Christian (2013): "Towards Historicizing 'Magic' in Antiquity," *Numen*, 60: 308–47.

Otto, Rudolf (1923): *The Idea of the Holy*, translated from *Das Heilige* (1917) by John W. Harvey. Oxford: Oxford University Press.

Pagels, Elaine (1995): *The Origin of Satan: How Christians Demonized Jews, Pagans, and Heretics*. New York: Vintage Books.

Pankenier, D. W. (1995): "Astrological Origins of Chinese Dynastic Ideology," *Vistas in Astronomy*, 39: 503–16.

Paraguassu, Lisandra (2020): "Brazil's Bolsonaro Turns to Prayer in Coronavirus Crisis," Reuters, April 4, 2020. https://www.reuters.com/article/us-health-coronavirus-brazil-bolsonaro-idUSKBN21L3DL.

Parkin, David (2021): *The Transformative Materiality of Meaning-Making*. Bristol, UK : Multilingual Matters.

Parris, Brett W. (2024): "Yogic Metaethics," thesis submitted for the DPhil degree, Faculty of Theology and Religion, University of Oxford.

Partridge, Joanna (2022): "Behold London's 'Landscraper'! Google's New UK HQ—as Long as the Shard Is Tall," *Guardian*, July 1, 2022. https://www.theguardian.com/business/2022/jul/01/behold-londons-landscraper-googles-new-uk-hq-as-long-as-the-shard-is-tall.

Pascal, Blaise (1669): *Pensées sur la religion et sur quelques autres sujets*. Digital edition available at https://www.ub.uni-freiburg.de/fileadmin/ub/referate/04/pascal/pensees.pdf.

Pastor, Eugenia Relaño (2007): "Spanish Catholic Church in Franco Regime: A Marriage of Convenience," *Kirchliche Zeitgeschichte*, 20(2): 275–87.

Peacey, Sarah, Campbell, Olivia, and Mace, Ruth (2023): "Same-Sex Competition and Sexual Conflict Expressed through Witchcraft Accusations," *Scientific Reports*, 12: 6655.

Pedersen, Esther Oluffa (2015): "Religion Is the Opium of the People: An Investigation into the Intellectual Context of Marx's Critique of Religion," *History of Political Thought*, 36(2): 354–87.

Peterson, C. R., and Beach, L. R. (1967): "Man as an Intuitive Statistician," *Psychological Bulletin*, 68(1): 29–46.

Pettegree, Andrew (2015): *Brand Luther: 1517, Printing, and the Making of the Reformation*. New York: Penguin Books.

Pew Research Center (2013): "Celebrating Christmas and the Holidays, Then and Now," Lifestyle, December 18, 2013. https://www.pewresearch.org/religion/2013/12/18/celebrating-christmas-and-the-holidays-then-and-now/.

——— (2016): "The Gender Gap in Religion Around the World," Gender and Religion, March 22, 2016. https://www.pewresearch.org/religion/2016/03/22/the-gender-gap-in-religion-around-the-world/.

——— (2019a): "Americans Have Positive Views about Religion's Role in Society, but Want It Out of Politics," November 15, 2019. https://www.pewresearch.org/religion/2019/11/15/americans-have-positive-views-about-religions-role-in-society-but-want-it-out-of-politics/.

——— (2019b): "2019 Pew Research Center's American Trends Panel," February 4–19, 2019. https://www.pewresearch.org/wp-content/uploads/2019/08/FT_19.08.05_Transubstantiation_Topline.pdf.

Pickles, Jan, and Woods, Genevieve (2022): *Review into the Abuse by John Smyth of Pupils and Former Pupils of Winchester College*. Winchester College. https://www.winchestercollege.org /stories/a-statement-from-the-warden-and-fellows-of-winchester-college.

Piera Nappi, Maria (2006): "Theano—Iliade VI 297–312: Mise en scène d'une prière entre gestes et paroles," *Anatolia antiqua*, 14: 159–70.

Pierre, Angèle (2022): "En Turquie, le mariage forcé d'une fillette de 6 ans relance la polémique sur les confréries religieuses," *Le Monde*, December 27, 2022. https://www.lemonde.fr /international/article/2022/12/27/en-turquie-le-mariage-force-d-une-fillette-de-6-ans -relance-la-polemique-sur-les-confreries-religieuses_6155760_3210.html.

Pinker, Steven (2011): *The Better Angels of Our Nature: The Decline of Violence in History and Its Causes*. London: Penguin.

Platt, Stephen R. (2012): *Autumn in the Heavenly Kingdom: China, the West, and the Epic Story of the Taiping Civil War*. New York: Knopf.

Platteau, J.-P. (2017). *Islam Instrumentalized: Religion and Politics in Historical Perspective*. New York: Cambridge University Press.

Plutarch (1898): *Morals*, translated by Arthur Richard Shilleto. London: George Bell and Sons. Digital edition available at https://www.gutenberg.org/files/23639/23639-h/23639-h.htm.

Polti, Georges (1895): *Les trente-six situations dramatiques*. Paris: Mercure de France.

Pomerantsev, Peter (2022): "We Can Only Be Enemies," *Atlantic*, May 1, 2022. https://www .theatlantic.com/ideas/archive/2022/05/putin-war-propaganda-russian-support/629714/.

Pope, M.W.M. (1963): "The Parry-Lord Theory of Homeric Composition," *Acta Classica*, 6: 1–21. https://www.jstor.org/stable/24591180.

Power, Eleanor (2017): "Social Support Networks and Religiosity in Rural South India," *Nature Human Behaviour*, 1: 0057.

Premier Journalist (2020): "Zimbabwe President Leads Nation in Prayer against Covid-19," *Premier Christian News*, June 16, 2020. https://premierchristian.news/en/news/article /zimbabwe-president-leads-nation-in-prayer-against-covid-19.

PTI (2022): "PM Modi Offers Prayers at Ravidas Temple," *The Hindu*, February 16, 2022. https://www.thehindu.com/news/national/pm-modi-offers-prayers-at-ravidas-temple /article65054954.ece.

Pulliam Bailey, Sarah (2021): "Southern Baptist Leader Ronnie Floyd Resigns after Internal Fight over Sex Abuse Investigation," *Washington Post*, October 15, 2021. https://www .washingtonpost.com/religion/2021/10/14/ronnie-floyd-resigns-southern-baptist-ceo/.

Purzycki, B., and McKay, R. (2022): "Moralistic Gods and Social Complexity: A Brief History of the Problem," working paper. https://www.researchgate.net/profile/Benjamin-Purzycki /publication/357835053_Moralistic_Gods_and_Social_Complexity_A_Brief_History _of_the_Problem/links/61e280b5c5e310337595f618/Moralistic-Gods-and-Social -Complexity-A-Brief-History-of-the-Problem.pdf.

Putnam, Robert, and Campbell, David (2010): *American Grace: How Religion Divides and Unites Us*, Kindle. New York: Simon and Schuster.

PwC US (2017): "PwC's Entertainment and Media Outlook Forecasts U.S. Industry Spending to Reach $759 Billion by 2021," PR Newswire, June 6, 2017. https://www.prnewswire.com /news-releases/pwcs-entertainment--media-outlook-forecasts-us-industry-spending-to -reach-759-billion-by-2021-300469724.html.

Quervain, D. de, Fischbacher, U., Treyer, V., Schellhammer, M., Schnyder, U., Buck, A., and Fehr, E. (2004): "The Neural Basis of Altruistic Punishment," *Science*, 305(5688): 1254–58.

Quinn, D. Michael (1998): *Early Mormonism and the Magic World View*. Salt Lake City: Signature Books.

Ragep, F. Jamil (2013): "Islamic Culture and the Natural Sciences," in David Lindberg and Michael Shank (eds.), *The Cambridge History of Science*, vol. 2, pp. 27–61. Cambridge: Cambridge University Press.

Raiber, E., and Seabright, P. (2020): "US Churches' Response to Covid-19: Results from Facebook," *COVID Economics*, 61. https://cepr.org/node/391061.

——— (2023): "U.S. Churches' Communication on Social Media: Connecting with Their Members or Expressing Political Views?," working paper, Toulouse School of Economics.

Raine, Susan, and Kent, Stephen (2019): "The Grooming of Children for Sexual Abuse in Religious Settings: Unique Characteristics and Select Case Studies," *Aggression and Violent Behavior*, 48: 180–89.

Rakoczy, H., Clüver, A., Saucke, L., Stoffregen, N., Gräbener, A., Migura, J., and Call, J. (2014): "Apes Are Intuitive Statisticians," *Cognition*, 131(1): 60–68.

Ramachandran, V. S., and Blakeslee, Sandra (1998): *Phantoms in the Brain*. New York: Harper Collins.

Ramanujan, A. K. (1973): *Speaking of Śiva*. London: Penguin Classics.

Rée, Jonathan (2019): *Witcraft: The Invention of Philosophy in English*. London: Allen Lane.

Reitman, Janet (2006): "Inside Scientology: Unlocking the Complex Code of America's Most Mysterious Religion," *Rolling Stone*, February 23, 2006. https://web.archive.org/web/20080622123603/http://www.rollingstone.com/politics/story/9363363/inside_scientology/print.

——— (2013): *Inside Scientology: The Story of America's Most Secretive Religion*. New York: Mariner Books.

Reuters Staff (2021): "Factbox: Reports into Abuses in the Irish Catholic Church," Europe News, January 12, 2021. https://www.reuters.com/article/us-ireland-church-abuses-factbox-idUSKBN29H1JJ.

RFE/RL (Radio Free Europe/Radio Liberty) (2022): "Russian Patriarch Kirill Says Dying in Ukraine 'Washes Away All Sins,'" News, September 26, 2022. https://www.rferl.org/a/russia-patriarch-kirill-dying-ukraine-sins/32052380.html.

Richerson, Peter, Boyd, Robert, and Bettinger, Robert (2001): "Was Agriculture Impossible during the Pleistocene but Mandatory during the Holocene? A Climate Change Hypothesis," *American Antiquity*, 66: 387–411.

Ritchie, Hannah, and Roser, Max (2019): "Age Structure," OurWorldInData.org. https://ourworldindata.org/age-structure.

Robarts, A. (2017): "Nowhere to Run to, Nowhere to Hide? Society, State, and Epidemic Diseases in the Early Nineteenth-Century Ottoman Balkans," in: N. Varlik (ed.), *Plague and Contagion in the Islamic Mediterranean: New Histories of Disease in Ottoman Society*, pp. 221–42. Leeds, UK: Arc Humanities.

Rochet, J.-C., and Tirole, J. (2003): "Platform Competition in Two-Sided Markets," *Journal of the European Economic Association*, 1: 990–1029.

Rodriguez, R. (2020): "Game-Changing Military Technologies: Adoption and Governance," in M. Kosal (ed.), *Disruptive and Game Changing Technologies in Modern Warfare: Advanced Sciences and Technologies for Security Applications*, pp. 13–29. Cham, Switzerland: Springer.

Rodríguez-Carballeira, Á., Saldaña, O., Almendros, C., Martín-Peña, J., Escartín, J., and Porrúa-García, C. (2015): "Group Psychological Abuse: Taxonomy and Severity of Its Components," *European Journal of Psychology Applied to Legal Context*, 7(1): 31–39.

Ronan, Colin, and Needham, Joseph (1985): *The Shorter Science and Civilization in China*, vol. 2. Cambridge: Cambridge University Press.

Roser, Max (2013a): "Economic Growth," OurWorldInData.org. https://ourworldindata.org/economic-growth.

———— (2013b): "Mortality in the Past: Every Second Child Died," OurWorldInData.org, April 11, 2023. https://ourworldindata.org/child-mortality-in-the-past.

Roser, Max, Hasell, Joe, Herre, Bastian, and Macdonald, Bobbie (2016): "War and Peace," OurWorldInData.org. https://ourworldindata.org/war-and-peace.

Roser, Max, and Ritchie, Hannah (2013): "Homicides," OurWorldInData.org. https://ourworldindata.org/homicides.

Roser, Max, Ritchie, Hannah, and Dadonaite, Bernadeta (2019): "Child and Infant Mortality," OurWorldInData.org. https://ourworldindata.org/grapher/global-child-mortality-timeseries.

Roser, Max, Ritchie, Hannah, Ortiz-Ospina, Esteban, and Rodés-Guirao, Lucas (2013): "World Population Growth," OurWorldInData.org. https://ourworldindata.org/world-population-growth.

Rosguard, Federal Service of the National Guard of the Russian Federation (2022): "Army General Viktor Zolotov Received from the Hands of His Holiness Patriarch of Moscow and All Russia Kirill the Icon of the August Icon of the Mother of God for the Main Church of the Federal Guard," News, March 13, 2022, archived at The Internet Archive, accessed July 11, 2023. https://web.archive.org/web/20220418063718/https://rosguard.gov.ru/News/Article/general-armii-viktor-zolotov-prinyal-iz-ruk-svyatejshego-patriarxa-moskovskogo-i-vseya-rusi-kirilla--ikonu--avgustovskoj-ikony-bozhiej-materi-dlya-gl.

Rossano, M. J. (2015): "The Evolutionary Emergence of Costly Rituals," *PaleoAnthropology*, 2015: 78–100.

Roy, Olivier (1999): "The Crisis of Religious Legitimacy in Iran," *Middle East Journal*, 53(2): 201–16.

Royal Commission into Institutional Responses to Child Sexual Abuse (2017): final report and executive summary. https://www.childabuseroyalcommission.gov.au/sites/default/files/final_report_-_preface_and_executive_summary.pdf.

Rubenstein, Jay (2011): *Armies of Heaven: The First Crusade and the Quest for Apocalypse*. New York: Basic Books.

Rubin, J. (2014): "Printing and Protestants: An Empirical Test of the Role of Printing in the Reformation," *Review of Economics and Statistics*, 96(2): 270–86.

———— (2017): *Rulers, Religion, and Riches: Why the West Got Rich and the Middle East Did Not*. New York: Cambridge University Press.

Ruiz Andrés, Rafael (2022): "Historical Sociology and Secularisation: The Political Use of 'Culturalised Religion' by the Radical Right in Spain," *Journal of Historical Sociology*, 35: 250–63.

Sage, Adam (2022): "Macron Seeks to Tackle Radical Islam with Launch of 'Moderate' Muslim Council," *The Times*, February 3, 2022. https://www.thetimes.co.uk/article/macron-seeks-to-tackle-radical-islam-with-launch-of-moderate-muslim-council-7wzrz2zmw.

Sahlins, M. (2017): "The Original Political Society," *HAU: Journal of Ethnographic Theory*, 7(2): 91–128.

——— (2022): *The New Science of the Enchanted Universe*. Princeton, NJ: Princeton University Press.

Saito, A., Hayashi, M., Takeshita, H,. and Matsuzawa, T. (2014): "The Origin of Representational Drawing: A Comparison of Human Children and Chimpanzees," *Child Development*, 85(6): 2232–46.

Sakurai, Yoshihide (2010): "Geopolitical Mission Strategy: The Case of the Unification Church in Japan and Korea," *Japanese Journal of Religious Studies*, 37: 317–34.

——— (2019): "A Management Perspective on the Mission Strategies and Global Organizational Structure of the Unification Church," in Hirochika Nakamaki, Louella Matsunaga, Tamasin Ramsay, and Wendy Smith (eds.), *Globalizing Asian Religions: Management and Marketing*, pp. 65–84. Amsterdam: Amsterdam University Press.

Saleh, Mohamed (2018): "On the Road to Heaven: Taxation, Conversions, and the Coptic-Muslim Socioeconomic Gap in Medieval Egypt," *Journal of Economic History*, 78(2): 394–434.

Saleh, Mohamed, and Tirole, Jean (2021): "Taxing Identity: Theory and Evidence from Early Islam," *Econometrica*, 89(4): 1881–919.

Sanderson, Stephen K. (2018a): "From Paganism to World Transcendence: Religious Attachment Theory and the Evolution of the World Religions," chapter 27 in Rosemary Hopcroft (ed.), *Oxford Handbook of Evolution, Biology and Society*. New York: Oxford University Press.

——— (2018b): *Religious Evolution and the Axial Age: From Shamans to Priests to Prophets*. London, Bloomsbury Academic.

Sandstrom, Aleksandra (2016): "Women Relatively Rare in Top Positions of Religious Leadership," Pew Research Center, March 2, 2016. https://www.pewresearch.org/fact-tank/2016/03/02/women-relatively-rare-in-top-positions-of-religious-leadership/.

Sanzo, J. E. (2020): "Deconstructing the Deconstructionists: A Response to Recent Criticisms of the Rubric 'Ancient Magic,'" in A. Mastrocinque, J. Sanzo, and M. Scapini (eds.), *Ancient Magic: Then and Now*, pp. 25–46. Stuttgart: Franz Steiner Verlag.

Savage, P., Loui, P., Tarr, B., Schachner, A., Glowacki, L., Mithen, S., and Fitch, T. (2021): "Music as a Coevolved System for Social Bonding," *Behavioral and Brain Sciences*, 44: e59.

Savita, K. S., Hazwani, H., and Kalid, K. S. (2011): "The Development of a Narrative Management System: Storytelling in Knowledge Management," *International Scholarly and Scientific Research and Innovation*, (5): 262–66.

Scheidel, Walter (2019): *The Great Leveler: Violence and the History of Inequality*. Princeton, NJ: Princeton University Press.

Scheve, K., and Stasavage, D. (2006): "Religion and Preferences for Social Insurance," *Quarterly Journal of Political Science*, 1: 255–86.

Schindler, John (2022): "Putin's Attack on Ukraine Is a Religious War," Top Secret Umbra, February 24, 2022. https://topsecretumbra.substack.com/p/putins-attack-on-ukraine-is-a-religious?.

Schwartz, Kathryn (2017): "Did Ottoman Sultans Ban Print?," *Book History*, 20: 1–39.

Schwartzstein, Joshua, and Sunderam, Adi (2021): "Using Models to Persuade," *American Economic Review*, 111(1): 276–323.

Seabright, Paul (2010): *The Company of Strangers: A Natural History of Economic Life*, 2nd edition. Princeton, NJ: Princeton University Press.

——— (2012): *The War of the Sexes: How Conflict and Cooperation Have Shaped Men and Women from Prehistory to the Present*. Princeton, NJ: Princeton University Press.

Secretariat of State of the Holy See (2020): *Report on the Holy See's Institutional Knowledge and Decision-Making Related to Former Cardinal Theodore Edgar McCarrick (1930 to 2017)*. Vatican City: Secretariat of State of the Holy See. https://www.vatican.va/resources/resources _rapporto-card-mccarrick_20201110_en.pdf.

Seneca (1935): *Moral Essays Volume III: De Beneficiis*, translated by John Basore. Loeb Classical Library. Cambridge, MA: Harvard University Press:

Serra, Richard, and Schoolman, Carlota Fay ([1973] 2011): *Television Delivers People* (short film), posted on YouTube by KunstSpektrum, February 2, 2011. https://www.youtube.com/watch ?v=LvZYwaQlJsg.

Shariff, A. F., and Norenzayan, A. (2007): "God Is Watching You: Priming God Concepts Increases Prosocial Behavior in an Anonymous Economic Game," *Psychological Science*, 18(9): 803–9.

Shariff, A. F., Willard, A. K., Andersen, T., and Norenzayan, A. (2016): "Religious Priming: A Meta-analysis with a Focus on Prosociality," *Personality and Social Psychology Review*, 20(1): 27–48.

Shaw, Brent D., and Saller, Richard P. (1984): "Close-Kin Marriage in Roman Society?," *Man*, 19: 432–44.

Sheel, Atul (2017): "2016–2017 Restaurant Industry Performance and the *JHFM* Index," *Journal of Hospitality Financial Management*, 25(1): 1–3.

Sherwood, Harriet (2022): "Justin Welby 'Affirms Validity' of 1998 Gay Sex Is Sin Declaration," *Guardian*, August 2, 2022. https://www.theguardian.com/uk-news/2022/aug/02/justin -welby-affirms-validity-of-1998-declaration-that-gay-sex-is-a-sin.

Shiller, Robert (2019): *Narrative Economics: How Stories Go Viral and Drive Major Economic Events*. Princeton, NJ: Princeton University Press.

Shingal, A. (2015): "The Devadasi System: Temple Prostitution in India," *UCLA Women's Law Journal*, 22(1): 107–23.

Shofia, Naila (2022): "Why Veil? Religious Headscarves and the Public Role of Women," working paper. https://papers.ssrn.com/sol3/papers.cfm?abstract_id=4196553.

Siedentop, Larry (2014): *Inventing the Individual: The Origins of Western Liberalism*. London: Penguin.

Silberberg, Alan, and Kearns, David (2009): "Memory for the Order of Briefly Presented Numerals in Humans as a Function of Practice," *Animal Cognition*, 12(2): 405–7.

Silva, Chandra de (2006): "Buddhist Monks and Peace in Sri Lanka," in Mahinda Deegalle (ed.), *Buddhism, Conflict and Violence in Modern Sri Lanka*, pp. 202–9. London: Routledge.

Singh, Manvir (2021a): "Magic, Explanations, and Evil: The Origins and Design of Witches and Sorcerers," *Current Anthropology*, 62(1): 2–29.

———— (2021b): "The Sympathetic Plot, Its Psychological Origins, and Implications for the Evolution of Fiction," *Emotion Review*, 13: 183–98.

Singh, Manvir, Kaptchuk, Ted J., and Henrich, Joseph (2021): "Small Gods, Rituals, and Cooperation: The Mentawai Water Spirit Sikameinan," *Evolution and Human Behavior*, 42(1): 61–72.

Smith, Adam (1759): *"The Theory of Moral Sentiments" and "On the Origins of Languages" (Stewart ed.)*. London: Henry G. Bohn. Digital edition available at https://oll.libertyfund.org/title /smith-the-theory-of-moral-sentiments-and-on-the-origins-of-languages-stewart-ed.

———— ([1776] 1904): *"An Inquiry into the Nature and Causes of the Wealth of Nations" by Adam Smith, Edited and with an Introduction, Notes, Marginal Summary and an Enlarged Index by Edwin Cannan*. London: Methuen. Digital edition available at https://oll.libertyfund .org//title/smith-an-inquiry-into-the-nature-and-causes-of-the-wealth-of-nations-cannan -ed-in-2-vols.

Smith, Daniel, Schlaepfer, Philip, Major, Katie, Dyble, Mark, Page, Abigail E., Thompson, James, Chaudhary, Nikhil, et al. (2017): "Cooperation and the Evolution of Hunter Gatherer Storytelling," *Nature Communications*, 8: 1853.

Smith, Gregory A. (2021): "About Three-in-Ten U.S. Adults Are Now Religiously Unaffiliated," Pew Research Center, December 14, 2021. https://www.pewresearch.org/religion/2021/12 /14/about-three-in-ten-u-s-adults-are-now-religiously-unaffiliated/.

Sosis, Richard (2000): "Religion and Intragroup Cooperation: Preliminary Results of a Comparative Analysis of Utopian Communities," *Cross Cultural Research*, 34: 70–88.

———— (2020): "Four Advantages of a Systemic Approach to the Study of Religion," *Archive for the Psychology of Religion*, 42(1): 3–17.

Sosis, Richard, and Alcorta, Candace (2003): "Signaling, Solidarity, and the Sacred: The Evolution of Religious Behavior," *Evolutionary Anthropology: Issues, News, and Reviews*, 12(6): 264–74.

Soullier, Lucie (2022): "Soupçons de maltraitance à la yeshiva de Bussières, en Seine-et-Marne," *Le Monde*, February 5, 2022, last modified February 6, 2022. https://www.lemonde.fr/societe /article/2022/02/05/soupcons-de-maltraitance-a-la-yeshiva-de-bussieres_6112444_3224 .html.

Special correspondent (2017): "Dera Chief Gurmeet Ram Rahim Singh Convicted for Rape," *The Hindu*, August 25, 2017. https://www.thehindu.com/news/national/other-states/dera -chief-gurmeet-ram-rahim-singh-convicted-for-rape/article19559885.ece.

Spelke, E., Breinlinger, K., Macomber, J., and Jacobson, K. (1992): "Origins of Knowledge," *Psychological Review*, 99: 605–32.

Spelke, E., Karz, G., Purcell, S., Ehrlich, S., and Breinlinger, K. (1994): "Early Knowledge of Object Motion: Continuity and Inertia," *Cognition*, 51(2): 131–76.

Spencer, Stephen J. (2019a): "Fear, Fortitude and Masculinity in William of Malmesbury's Retelling of the First Crusade and the Establishment of the Latin East," *Journal of Religious History, Literature and Culture*, 5(2): 35–50.

———— (2019b): *Emotions in a Crusading Context, 1095–1291*. Oxford: Oxford University Press.

Sperber, Dan (2018): "Cutting Culture at the Joints?," *Religion, Brain and Behavior*, 8(4): 447–49.

Sperber, Dan, Clément, Fabrice, Heintz, Christophe, Mascaro, Olivier, Mercier, Hugo, Origgi, Glori, and Wilson, Deirdre (2010): "Epistemic Vigilance," *Mind and Language*, 25(4): 359–93.

Spisak, B. R., Grabo, A. E., Arvey, R. D., and Van Vugt, M. (2014): "The Age of Exploration and Exploitation: Younger-Looking Leaders Endorsed for Change and Older-Looking Leaders Endorsed for Stability," *Leadership Quarterly*, 25(5): 805–16.

Squicciarini, Mara (2020): "Devotion and Development: Religiosity, Education and Economic Progress in 19th Century France," *American Economic Review*, 110(11): 3434–91.

Srinivas, M. N. (1956): "A Note on Sanskritization and Westernization," *Far Eastern Quarterly*, 15(4): 481–96.

Stacchini, Massimiliano, and Degasperi, Petra (2015): "Trust, Family Businesses and Financial Intermediation," *Journal of Corporate Finance*, 33: 293–316.

Stanley, Brian (2018): *Christianity in the Twentieth Century: A World History*. Princeton, NJ: Princeton University Press.

Stark, Rodney (1995): "Reconstructing the Rise of Christianity: The Role of Women," *Sociology of Religion*, 56(3): 229–44.

Stark, Rodney, and Bainbridge, William Sims (1985): *The Future of Religion: Secularization, Revival and Cult Formation*. Berkeley: University of California Press.

——— (1996): *A Theory of Religion*. New Brunswick, NJ: Rutgers University Press.

Statista (2017): "Restaurant Industry Food and Drink Sales in the United States from 1970 to 2017," Travel, Tourism and Hospitality, April 2017. https://www.statista.com/statistics /203358/food-and-drinks-sales-of-us-restaurants-since-1970/.

Steinfels, Peter (2013): "Andrew M. Greeley, Priest, Scholar and Scold, Is Dead at 85," *New York Times*, May 30, 2013. https://www.nytimes.com/2013/05/31/us/andrew-m-greeley -outspoken-priest-dies-at-85.html.

Sterelny, Kim (2003): *Thought in a Hostile World: The Evolution of Human Cognition*. Oxford: Blackwell.

——— (2007): "SNAFUs: An Evolutionary Perspective," *Biological Theory*, 2(3): 317–28.

——— (2018): "Religion Re-explained," *Religion, Brain and Behavior*, 8(4): 406–25.

Sterling P., and Platt, M. L. (2022): "Why Deaths of Despair Are Increasing in the US and Not Other Industrial Nations—Insights from Neuroscience and Anthropology," *JAMA Psychiatry*, 79(4): 368–74.

Stieglitz, J., Jaeggi, A., Blackwell, A., Trumble, B., Gurven, M., and Kaplan, H. (2014): "Work to Live and Live to Work: Productivity, Transfers, and Psychological Well-Being in Adulthood and Old Age," in M. Weinstein and M. Lane (eds.), *Sociality, Hierarchy, Health: Comparative Biodemography; A Collection of Papers*, pp. 197–221. Washington, DC: National Academies.

Stieglitz, J., Schniter, E., Von Rueden, C., Kaplan, H., and Gurven, M. (2015): "Functional Disability and Social Conflict Increase Risk of Depression in Older Adulthood among Bolivian Forager-Farmers," *Journals of Gerontology: Social Sciences*, 70: 948–56.

Stockemer, Daniel, and Sundstrom, Aksel (2021): "The Gender Gap in Voter Turnout: An Artefact of Men's Over-Reporting in Survey Research?," *British Journal of Politics and International Relations*, 25(1): 21–41.

Störkel, L., Karabatsiakis, A., Hepp, J., Kolassa, I.-T., Schmachl, C., and Niedtfeld, I. (2021): "Salivary Beta-Endorphin in Nonsuicidal Self-Injury: An Ambulatory Assessment Study," *Neuropsychopharmacology*, 46(7): 1357–63.

Strathern, A. (2019): *Unearthly Powers: Religious and Political Change in World History*. Cambridge: Cambridge University Press.

Stuart-Glennie, John S. (1873): *In the Morningland; or, The Law of the Origin and Transformation of Christianity*. London: Longmans, Green.

Sudam, Mohamed (2011): "Yemenis Turn Friday Prayers to Political Rallies," Reuters, July 1, 2011. https://www.reuters.com/article/columns-us-yemen/yemenis-turn-friday-prayers-to -political-rallies-idINTRE73L1PP20110701.

Sumption, Jonathan (2002): *Pilgrimage*. London: Faber and Faber.

Suzuki, D. T. (2010): *Zen and Japanese Culture*. Princeton, NJ: Princeton University Press.

Swatos, William, and Christiano, Kevin (1999): "Secularization Theory: The Course of a Concept," *Sociology of Religion*, 60(3): 209–28.

Szczerbiak, Aleks (2019): "Why Is Poland's Law and Justice Party Still So Popular?," *London School of Economics Blogs*, October 1, 2019. https://blogs.lse.ac.uk/europpblog/2019/10/01 /why-is-polands-law-and-justice-party-still-so-popular/.

Szeidl, A., and Szucs, F. (2021): "Media Capture through Favor Exchange," *Econometrica*, 89(1): 281–310.

Tasuji, T., Reese, E., Van Mulukom, V., and Whitehouse, H. (2021): "Band of Mothers: Childbirth as a Female Bonding Experience," *PLoS ONE*, 15(10): e0240175.

Temrin, H., Nordlund, J., Rying, M., and Tullberg, B. (2011): "Is the Higher Rate of Parental Child Homicide in Stepfamilies an Effect of Non-genetic Relatedness?," *Current Zoology*, 57(3): 253–59.

Tenenbaum, J. B., Kemp, C., Griffiths, T. L., and Goodman, N. D. (2011): "How to Grow a Mind: Statistics, Structure, and Abstraction," *Science*, 331(6022): 1279–85.

Tennie, Claudio, Call, Josep, and Tomasello, Michael (2009): "Ratcheting Up the Ratchet: On the Evolution of Cumulative Culture," *Philosophical Transactions of the Royal Society B*, 364(1528): 2405–15.

Tennie, Claudio, and Van Schaik, Carel P. (2020): "Spontaneous (Minimal) Ritual in Non-human Great Apes?," *Philosophical Transactions of the Royal Society B*, 375(1805): 20190423.

Terry, Karen, et al. (2004): *The Nature and Scope of the Problem of Sexual Abuse of Minors by Priests and Deacons, prepared by the John Jay College of Criminal Justice for the US Conference of Catholic Bishops*. Washington, DC: USCCB. Web version prepared by BishopAccountability.org. https://web.archive.org/web/20181012143358/http://www.bishop -accountability.org/reports/2004_02_27_JohnJay/index.html.

Thackeray, William Makepeace (1902): *"The Paris Sketch Book of Mr. M.A. Titmarsh" and "The Irish Sketch Book."* London: Macmillan. Digital edition available at https://www.gutenberg .org/files/42890/42890-h/42890-h.htm#.

Thomas, K. (1971): *Religion and the Decline of Magic: Studies in Popular Beliefs in 16th and 17th Century England*. London: Weidenfeld and Nicolson.

Thompson, Damian (2023): "Inside the Catholic Civil War," UnHerd, February 1, 2023. https:// unherd.com/2023/02/inside-the-catholic-civil-war/.

Thornton, Rebecca (2008): "The Demand for, and Impact of, Learning HIV Status," *American Economic Review*, 98(5): 1829–63.

Ticku, Rohit, Shrivastava, Anand, and Iyer, Sriya (2023): "Economic Shocks and Religious Conflict in Medieval India," Discussion Paper no. 17986, Centre for Economic Policy Research.

Tilakaratne (2006): "The Role of Buddhist Monks in Resolving the Conflict," in Mahinda Deegalle (ed.), *Buddhism, Conflict and Violence in Modern Sri Lanka*, pp. 210–25. London: Routledge.

TimesofIndia.com (2018): "Gurus in Trouble: Charges against Some of India's Self-Styled Godmen," *Times of India*, April 26, 2018. https://timesofindia.indiatimes.com/india/gurus-in-trouble-charges-against-some-of-indias-self-styled-godmen/articleshow/63921518.cms.

Tishelman, Amy, and Fontes, Lisa (2017): "Religion in Child Sexual Abuse Forensic Interviews," *Child Abuse and Neglect*, 63: 120–30.

Toelken, B. (1996): *Dynamics of Folklore*, Kindle. Logan: Utah State University Press.

TOI Staff (2019): "Smotrich Says He Wants to Be Justice Minister so Israel Can Follow Torah Law," *Times of Israel*, June 3, 2019. https://www.timesofisrael.com/smotrich-says-he-wants-justice-ministry-so-israel-can-follow-torah-law/.

Tomasello, Michael (1990): "Cultural Transmission in the Tool Use and Communicatory Signaling of Chimpanzees?," in S. Parker and K. Gibson (eds.), *Language and Intelligence in Monkeys and Apes: Comparative Developmental Perspectives*, pp. 274–311. Cambridge: Cambridge University Press.

——— (1999): *The Cultural Origins of Human Cognition*. Cambridge, MA: Harvard University Press.

——— (2019): *Becoming Human: A Theory of Ontogeny*. Cambridge, MA: Harvard University Press.

Toneatto, Valentina (2012): *Les banquiers du Seigneur: Evêques et moines face à la richesse (IVe–début IX siècle)*. Rennes: Presses Universitaires de Rennes.

Turchin, Peter (2023): Religion Is Different," *Cliodynamica* (blog), January 8, 2023. https://peterturchin.com/cliodynamica/religion-is-different/.

Turchin, Peter, Whitehouse, Harvey, Larson, Jennifer, Cioni, Enrico, Reddish, Jenny, Hoyer, Daniel, Savage, Patrick E., et al. (2022): "Explaining the Rise of Moralizing Religions: A Test of Competing Hypotheses Using the Seshat Databank," *Religion, Brain and Behavior*, 13(2): 167–94.

Turner, Victor (1969): *The Ritual Process: Structure and Anti-structure*. Chicago: Aldine.

Turpin, Hugh (2022): *Unholy Catholic Ireland: Religious Hypocrisy, Secular Morality, and Irish Irreligion*. Stanford, CA: Stanford University Press.

Turpin, Hugh, and Willard, Aiyana (2022): "Credibility Enhancing Displays, Religious Scandal and the Decline of Catholic Orthodoxy," *Evolutionary Human Sciences*, 4: e20.

Tversky, A., and Kahneman, D. (1974): "Judgment under Uncertainty: Heuristics and Biases; Biases in Judgments Reveal Some Heuristics of Thinking under Uncertainty," *Science*, 185(4157): 1124–31.

——— (1983): "Extensional versus Intuitive Reasoning: The Conjunction Fallacy in Probability Judgment," *Psychological Review*, 90(4): 293–315.

Ucerler, M., and Antoni, J. (2021): "The Story of the Jesuits: How the Society of Jesus Charted the World," Engelsberg Ideas, December 20, 2021. https://engelsbergideas.com/essays/jesuit/.

Ukiah, A. F. (2005): "Those Who Trade with God Never Lose: The Economics of Pentecostal Activism in Nigeria," in John David Yeadon Peel, *Christianity and Social Change in Africa: Essays in Honor of JDY Peel*, edited by Toyin Falola, pp. 253–74. Durham, NC: Carolina Academic.

United States Commission on International Religious Freedom (2020): *Violating Rights: Enforcing the World's Blasphemy Laws*. USCIRF. https://www.uscirf.gov/sites/default/files/2020%20Blasphemy%20Enforcement%20Report%20_final_0.pdf.

UN Women (2023): "Facts and Figures: Women's Leadership and Political Participation," Leadership and political participation, last updated March 7, 2023. https://www.unwomen.org/en/what-we-do/leadership-and-political-participation/facts-and-figures.

Urban, Hugh (2011): *The Church of Scientology: A History of a New Religion*. Princeton, NJ: Princeton University Press.

Valentino, R., and Van Bockstaele, E. (2015): "Endogenous Opioids: The Downside of Opposing Stress," *Neurobiology of Stress*, 1: 23–32.

Van Nuffelen, Peter (2020): "Religious Violence in Late Antiquity," in Garrett G. Fagan, Linda Fibiger, Mark Hudson, and Matthew Trundle (eds.), *The Cambridge World History of Violence*, vol. 1: *The Prehistoric and Ancient Worlds*, pp. 512–29. Cambridge: Cambridge University Press.

Van Rhijn, Carine (2022): *Leading the Way to Heaven: Pastoral Care and Salvation in the Carolingian Period*. Abingdon, UK: Routledge.

Vardy, T., Moya, C., Placek, C., Apicella, C., Bolyanatz, A., Cohen, E., Handley, C., et al. (2022): "The Religiosity Gender Gap in 14 Diverse Societies," *Religion, Brain and Behavior*, 12(1–2): 18–37.

VaticanNews.va (2021): "12-Year-Old Martyr Beatified in Guatemala," *Aleteia*, April 24, 2021. https://aleteia.org/2021/04/24/12-year-old-martyr-beatified-in-guatemala/.

Venkatesh, Sudhir Alladi (2009): *Off the Books: The Underground Economy of the Urban Poor*. Cambridge, MA, Harvard University Press.

Veyne, Paul (1983): *Les Grecs ont-ils cru à leurs mythes? Essai sur l'imagination constituante*. Paris: Editions du Seuil.

Volk, A. A., and Atkinson, J. A. (2013): "Infant and Child Death in the Human Environment of Evolutionary Adaptation," *Evolution and Human Behavior*, 34(3): 182–92.

Voltaire (1734): *Lettres philosophiques*. Rouen.

——— (1763): *Traité sur la tolérance*. Geneva: Cramer Brothers.

Von Rueden, C., Redhead, D., O'Gorman, R., Kaplan, H., and Gurven, M. (2019): "The Dynamics of Men's Cooperation and Social Status in a Small-Scale Society," *Proceedings of the Royal Society B*, 286: 20191367.

Wall Street Journal and NORC (National Opinion Research Center (2023): "WSJ/NORC Poll March 2023." https://s.wsj.net/public/resources/documents/WSJ_NORC_ToplineMarc_2023.pdf.

Walsh, J. (1972): "Methodism and the Mob in the Eighteenth Century," *Studies in Church History*, 8: 213–27.

Warner, S. (1993): "Work in Progress toward a New Paradigm for the Sociology of Religion," *American Journal of Sociology*, 98: 1044–93.

Watts, Alan (1957): *The Way of Zen*. London: Penguin Books.

Watts, Joseph, Bulbulia, Joseph, Gray, Russell D., and Atkinson, Quentin D. (2016a): "Clarity and Causality Needed in Claims about Big Gods," *Behavioral and Brain Sciences*, 39: e27.

Watts, Joseph, Greenhill, Simon J., Atkinson, Quentin D., Currie, Thomas E., Bulbulia, Joseph, and Gray, Russell D. (2015): "Broad Supernatural Punishment but Not Moralizing High Gods Precede the Evolution of Political Complexity in Austronesia," *Proceedings of the Royal Society B*, 282: 20142556.

Watts, Joseph, Sheehan, Oliver, Atkinson, Quentin D., Bulbulia, Joseph, and Gray, Russell D. (2016b): "Ritual Human Sacrifice Promoted and Sustained the Evolution of Stratified Societies," *Nature*, 532: 228–31.

Weber, Max ([1905] 1930): *The Protestant Ethic and the Spirit of Capitalism*, translated by Talcott Parsons. London: Allen and Unwin. Digital edition available at https://archive.org/stream /protestantethics00webe/protestantethics00webe_djvu.txt.

——— ([1922] 1947): *The Theory of Social and Economic Organization*, part 3: *Economy and Society*. New York: Free Press of Glencoe. Digital edition available at *German History Intersections*. https://germanhistory-intersections.org/en/knowledge-and-education /ghis:document-156.

——— (1958): *The Religion of India: The Sociology of Hinduism and Buddhism*. New Delhi: Munshiram Manoharlal.

——— ([2013] 2019): *Economy and Society: An Outline of Interpretive Sociology*, translated and edited by Keith Tribe. Cambridge, MA: Harvard University Press.

Weizenbaum, Joseph (1966): "ELIZA: A Computer Program for the Study of Natural Language Communication between Man and Machine," *Communications of the ACM*, 9(1): 36–45.

Werner, Dennis (1981): "Gerontocracy among the Mekranoti of Central Brazil," *Anthropological Quarterly*, 54(1): 15–27.

Whalen, Jeanne (2022): "Russian Orthodox Leader Backs War in Ukraine, Divides Faith," *Washington Post*, April 18, 2022. https://www.washingtonpost.com/world/2022/04/18/russian -orthodox-church-ukraine-war/.

Wheeler, Michael (1999): *Ruskin's God*. Cambridge: Cambridge University Press.

Whitehead, Deborah (2021): "Women Lead Religious Groups in Many Ways—besides the Growing Number Who Have Been Ordained," *Conversation*, December 8, 2021. https:// theconversation.com/women-lead-religious-groups-in-many-ways-besides-the-growing -number-who-have-been-ordained-170433.

Whitehouse, Harvey (1995): *Inside the Cult: Religious Innovation and Transmission in Papua New Guinea*. Oxford: Oxford University Press.

——— (2000): *Arguments and Icons*. Oxford: Oxford University Press.

——— (2004): *Modes of Religiosity: A Cognitive Theory of Religious Transmission*. Walnut Creek, CA, Altamira.

——— (2018): "Dying for the Group: Towards a General Theory of Extreme Self-Sacrifice," *Behavioral and Brain Sciences*, 41: e192.

——— (2021). *The Ritual Animal: Imitation and Social Cohesion in the Evolution of Social Complexity*. Oxford: Oxford University Press.

Whyte, Anne (2022): *The Whyte Review: An Independent Investigation Commission by Sport England and UK Sport following Allegations of Mistreatment within the Sport of Gymnastics.* Sport England, June 2022. https://www.whytereview.org.

Widom, C. S., Czaja, S. J., and DuMont, K. A. (2015): "Intergenerational Transmission of Child Abuse and Neglect: Real or Detection Bias?" *Science,* 347(6229): 1480–85.

Wilde, Oscar (1898): *The Importance of Being Earnest.* London: Leonard Smithers.

Willard, A. K., and McNamara, R. (2019): "The Minds of God(s) and Humans: Differences in Mind Perception in Fiji and North America," *Cognitive Science,* 43: 1–30.

Willard, A. K., and Norenzayan, A. (2013): "Cognitive Biases Explain Religious Belief, Paranormal Belief, and Belief in Life's Purpose," *Cognition,* 129: 379–91.

Wilson, Andrew (2009): "Large-Scale Manufacturing, Standardization, and Trade," in J. P. Oleson (ed.), *Handbook of Engineering and Technology in the Classical World,* pp. 393–417. Oxford: Oxford University Press.

——— (2022): "Introduction: The Economy of Roman Religion," in Wilson, N. Ray, and A. Trentacoste (eds.), *The Economy of Roman Religion,* pp. 1–29. Oxford: Oxford University Press.

Wilson, Bryan, and Cresswell, Jamie (1999): *New Religious Movements: Challenge and Response.* London: Routledge.

Wilson, David Sloan (1975): "A Theory of Group Selection," *Proceedings of the National Academy of Sciences of the USA,* 72(1): 143–46.

——— (2005): "Evolutionary Social Constructivism," in Gottschall and Wilson (2005), pp. 20–37.

Wilson, David Sloan, and Sober, Elliott (1994): "Reintroducing Group Selection to the Human Behavioral Sciences," *Behavioral and Brain Sciences,* 17: 585–654.

Wilson, Peter (2009): *The Thirty Years War: Europe's Tragedy.* Cambridge, MA: Harvard University Press.

Winfield, Nicole (2019): "Pope Denounces 'Rigidity' as He Warns of Christian Decline," AP News, December 21, 2019. https://apnews.com/article/pope-francis-europe-ap-top-news-religion-international-news-6acc18ccaa58f7629007fb9a70c43aef.

Wittgenstein, Ludwig ([1953] 1972): *Philosophical Investigations,* translated by G.E.M. Anscombe. Oxford: Basil Blackwell. Digital edition available at https://archive.org/stream/in.ernet.dli.2015.124286/2015.124286.Philosophical-Investigations_djvu.txt.

Wood, Ian (2022): *The Christian Economy in the Early Medieval West: Towards a Temple Society.* Binghamton, NY: Gracchi Books.

Wood, Robert (2014): "Invent a Church, Skip Taxes, Enrage IRS, Go to Jail," Forbes, September 28, 2014. https://www.forbes.com/sites/robertwood/2014/09/28/invent-a-church-skip-taxes-enrage-irs-go-to-jail/.

Woodberry, Robert D. (2012): "The Missionary Roots of Liberal Democracy," *American Political Science Review,* 106(2): 244–74.

Woodhead, Linda (2022): "Truth and Deceit in Institutions," *Studies in Christian Ethics,* 35(1): 87–103.

Woodhead, Linda, Partridge, Christopher, and Kawanami, Hiroko (2016): *Religions in the Modern World: Traditions and Transformations,* 3rd edition. London: Routledge.

Wrangham, Richard (2019): *The Goodness Paradox*. New York: Penguin Random House.

Wright, Lawrence (2013): *Going Clear: Scientology, Hollywood and the Prison of Belief*. New York: Vintage Books.

Wright, Robert (2009): *The Evolution of God*. New York: Little, Brown.

Xu, F., and Garcia, V. (2008): "Intuitive Statistics by 8-Month-Old Infants," *Proceedings of the National Academy of Sciences of the USA*, 105(13): 5012–15.

Xygalatas, Dimitris (2022): *Ritual: How Seemingly Senseless Acts Make Life Worth Living*. London: Profile Books.

Xygalatas, Dimitris, Khan, Sammyh, Lang, Martin, Kundt, Radek, Kundtova-Klocova, Eva, Kratky, Jan, and Shaver, John (2019): "Effects of Extreme Ritual Practices on Psychophysiological Well-Being," *Current Anthropology*, 60(5): 699–707.

Yeginsu, Ceylan (2017): Doubts Grow over Archbishop's Account of When He Knew of Abuse," *New York Times*, October 14, 2017. https://www.nytimes.com/2017/10/14/world/europe /justin-welby-archbishop-of-canterbury-iwerne-abuse.html.

Yost, Julia (2022): "New York's Hottest Club Is the Catholic Church," *New York Times*, August 9, 2022. https://www.nytimes.com/2022/08/09/opinion/nyc-catholicism-dimes-square -religion.html?searchResultPosition=1.

Zech, Charles (2001): "An Agency Analysis of Church-Pastor Relations," *Managerial and Decision Economics*, 22: 327–32.

Zhang, Chunni, and Lu, Yunfeng (2020): "The Measure of Chinese Religions: Denomination-Based or Deity-Based," *Chinese Journal of Sociology*, 6(3): 410–26.

Zhang, Daye (2013): *The World of a Tiny Insect: A Memoir of the Taiping Rebellion and Its Aftermath*. Seattle: University of Washington Press.

Zhu, L., and Gigerenzer, G. (2006): "Children Can Solve Bayesian Problems: The Role of Representation in Mental Computation," *Cognition*, 98(3): 287–308.

INDEX

Page numbers in italics indicate figures and tables.

José de Arrese, Pedro, *Baptism through Incision*, 130
Joseph Campbell Foundation, 382n21
Joseph of Arimathea, English Church by, 205
Judaism, 80; emergence of, 195; MacCulloch on Judea under Hasmonean dynasty, 81–82; members sharing supernatural beliefs, 33
Julius Caesar, 242
Jung, Carl, 155; notion of archetypes, 156; on religion in Christian West, 85
Jungian psychology, 156

Ka'ba in Mecca, 223
Kali (goddess): homage to, 264, 266–67; sacrifices to, 266–67
Kalinga, conquest of, 6
Kanter, Rosabeth Moss, study of utopian communes, 176
Karbala, festival of Ashura, *149*, 150
Karlan, Dean, evaluating a Protestant Christian education program, 230
karma, Hindu and Buddhist traditions, 292
Kenya, 12; Christian respondents, 49; importance of religion, 359; Pentecostal churches, 49; Turkana pastoralists of, 193
Keyes, Charles, converting villagers to Buddhism, 384n63
Khaire, Mukti, study of US magazine industry, 207
King Herod and Salomé, sculpture of, 279
Kirill, Patriarch: sermon by, 5, 365n1; supporting Russian invasion, 366n22
Kitiarsa, Pattana, on harmonious coexistence of deities in Thailand, 212–13
Knapp, Jeffrey, on people thinking religion brought worldly benefits, 69–70
Knox, John, *The First Blast of the Trumpet Against the Monstrous Regiment of Women*, 265
kolangal (sing. *kolam*): geometric design, 65, 66; homage to goddess Lakshmi, 65; Pongal harvest festival, 66; story of, 67

Koyama, Mark, on evolution of political power, 256–57
Krishna, stories of, 156
Kuchler, Theresa, study examining social network ties, 100
Kumbo: imams of, 50; as center of violent struggle, 369n1
Kuran, Timur, on stability in Ottoman Empire, 249

labor market: on identity markers for integrating, 74; platform, 96
Lagos, mosque, 31
Lakshmi: Hindu goddess of prosperity, 31; *kolangal* (sing. *kolam*) as homage to, 65, 66; offering to, 83; temple to, 31
large language models (LLMs), 326–30; chatbot program, 329; ChatGPT, 326; on difference between true and false religious messages, 329–30
Lassébie, Julie, on Pentecostalism in Ghana, 77
Latimer (Bishop), execution of, 135
Latin America, 46, 49; Catholics in, 48; importance of religion in lives, 51; Pentecostal presence, 12; religion in, 28; Roman Catholic Church in, 49; shares of Christian denominations in, 349, *350*
Law and Justice Party, Poland, 57–58
leadership, candidates for, 204, 390n13
"Lebensraum", Hitler's Germany, 173
legislation, controversial issues, 55, 371n44
Leppin, Hartmut: on election of bishops, 209–10; on Gnostics, 192
Leucippus, atomism, 313
Levy, Honor, conversion to Catholicism, 128
Lewis, C. S., on religion in Christian West, 85
Liberius (bishop of Rome), death of, 250
life expectancy of rulers, Christian and Muslim worlds, 249, 395n39
Lightner, Aaron, on simple explanations outperforming complex ones, 187–88
limerick, 326

A NOTE ON THE TYPE

This book has been composed in Arno, an Old-style serif typeface in the classic Venetian tradition, designed by Robert Slimbach at Adobe.